Reader Series
in Library and Information Science

Published *Readers* in the series are:

Reader in Library Administration. 1969.
Paul Wasserman and Mary Lee Bundy.

Reader in Research Methods for Librarianship. 1970.
Mary Lee Bundy and Paul Wasserman.

Reader in the Academic Library. 1970.
Michael M. Reynolds.

Reader in Library Services and the Computer. 1971.
Louis Kaplan.

Reader in American Library History, 1971.
Michael H. Harris.

Reader in Classification and Descriptive Cataloging. 1972.
Ann. F. Painter.

Reader in Technical Services. 1973.
Edmond L. Applebaum.

Reader
in
Technical Services

edited by

Edmond L. Applebaum

1973

NCR Microcard Editions

Published by NCR/Microcard Editions,
901 26th Street, N.W.
Washington, D.C. 20037

Printed in the United States of America

Foreword

Unlike many other academic disciplines, librarianship has not yet begun to exploit the contributions of the several disciplines toward the study of its own issues. Yet the literature abounds with material germane to its concerns. Too frequently the task of identifying, correlating, and bringing together material from innumerable sources is burdensome, time consuming or simply impossible. For a field whose stock in trade is organizing knowledge, it is clear that the job of synthesizing the most essential contributions from the elusive sources in which they are contained is overdue. This then is the rationale for the series, *Readers in Library and Information Science*.

The *Readers in Library and Information Science* will include books concerned with various broad aspects of the field's interests. Each volume will be prepared by a recognized student of the topic covered, and the content will embrace material from the many different sources from the traditional literature of librarianship as well as from outside the field in which the most salient contributions have appeared. The objectives of the series will be to bring together in convenient form the key elements required for a current and comprehensive view of the subject matter. In this way it is hoped that the core of knowledge, essential as the intellectual basis for study and understanding, will be drawn into focus and thereby contribute to the furtherance of professional education and professional practice in the field.

Paul Wasserman
Series Editor

Contents

V

THE FUTURE

Reader
in
Technical Services

Introduction

This collection attempts to bring together a readable and germane group of materials ranging from history, review papers, and practical exposition to reports on current research and development and conjecture about the future. It is expected that these selections will be of interest and use to the teacher and the student. It is also hoped that they will be of equal interest to the professional librarian and researcher. There has been a deliberate attempt to exclude materials that have appeared in recently published collections. It is for this reason that the names of Panizzi, Cutter, Martel, Hanson, Dewey, Rider, Bliss, Haykin, Shera, Lubetzky and others do not appear. A specific focus has been given to this book. It is in the direction of a rational sharing of local, national, and international efforts and the eventual coordination and standardization of practices in the technical services insofar as this is practical.

I

LIBRARIANSHIP AND THE TECHNICAL SERVICES—HISTORICAL PERSPECTIVE

We are prone to assume that certain problems are unique to each time, place, and condition. The first two items that follow show that a hundred years ago there already existed an awareness of what the era of high speed printing and public education for all would mean to librarians. Meaningful observations appear about cooperative and centralized cataloging, the desirability of cards with books or cataloging in publication, library standardization, the need for reform in the printing, distributing, and bibliographical control of public documents, the utility of the dictionary catalog as compared to the divided catalog, the desirability of the published shelflist, the need for "superior paper for catalogue work," and the triangle of disagreement between librarian, publisher, and bookseller. In addition, the two proceedings provide an opportunity to contrast the differences in outlook of American and British librarians as well as to measure the similarities and note the auguries for future cooperation.

Selections from the Proceedings of the First Conference of the American Library Association

FIRST SESSION.

[Wednesday Morning.]

The Conference of Librarians opened at the rooms of the Historical Society of Pennsylvania, Wednesday, October 4th, 1876. The meeting was called to order at 10:15 A.M. by the Chairman of the Committee of Arrangements, Mr. Justin Winsor, who said that the committee had made the necessary arrangements for the Conference which was there assembled, and that they now desired those present to assume control of the meeting, and appoint a Committee on Organization. On the call of the house, the Chairman appointed as such committee Hon. Horatio Gates Jones, Prof. O. H. Robinson, and Mr. Samuel S. Green. This committee having retired, Mr. John William Wallace, President of the Pennsylvania Historical Society, was introduced, and delivered the address of welcome.

Mr. Wallace's Address.

Librarians of the United States:

In behalf of the librarians of this city—seated in the circular recess behind me—I welcome you cordially to Philadelphia, and in behalf of the members of the Historical Society of our State, and for myself as well, I welcome you most cordially to this our hall: Philadelphia, in the course of her history, has been the seat of many conventions. Until this year, however—this great year, both of our city and our nation—she has never had the happiness, so far as I recollect, to see within her limits a convention of librarians. The centennial year cannot, I think, but lend some distinction to IT; and IT, perhaps, will not be the least worthy of the distinctions of the centennial year.

But I regard this great anniversary of the nation less as the cause of this new sort of congress than as the occasion of which it avails itself to assemble.

It has been somewhat obvious, I think, for several years past, and is now entirely plain, that, with the much-increased and still much-increasing issue of books from the printing-press, several matters up to this time little thought of by librarians—indeed, not requiring to be much thought of by them—now demand consideration and, so far as practicable, a provision for the time, not far distant, when they are likely to come upon us.

The increase of books to which I refer is to be attributed in some part, I suppose, to the facility with which of late times, in consequence of the application of chemical agencies, instead as formerly of mechanical ones alone, to the paper maker's art, paper itself is made; in greater part still to the power which steam has given to the printing-press, and in greatest part of all to the establishment of common-schools and colleges everywhere throughout this country, by which both the capacity to write and the disposition and the ability to read are vastly increased. And as I see nothing which is likely to arrest this progress of things, alike scientific and social, I see nothing which in coming years is to stand between the librarian and an issue upon him of books upon books, so vast and so uninterrupted that unless he brings the benefit of something like SCIENCE to his aid, he will be overwhelmed and buried in their very mass.

This vision of the future suggests a variety of thoughts.

In the first place, a problem arises—one which concerns more especially our opulent libraries, or such a library as that of Congress, where every book that secures a copyright is preserved—a problem as to what form of building is best suited for the library edifice. It is plain, if our larger libraries are to continue as most of them now are, libraries of a general sort—pantological collections, as we may call them—that before another century is over, immense edifices will be required, through the mere force of accumulation, to hold the volumes of which the libraries are composed. What form of such large edifice will best unite external effect with capacity of extension—indefinite extension, it must be, in some direction—with safety, with convenience, and with beauty of interior?

SOURCE: Reprinted from the *American Library Journal* I (1876), pp. 92-143.

And how far, if all these things cannot co-exist, must that characteristic which delights the eye give way to that which saves the feet and assists the hand; in other words, with that which promotes a capacity for getting volumes promptly from their places—often in the huge edifices which the mental eye already sees before it, far distant from the seat of the librarian—and, after they have been used, of getting the volumes promptly again to their places?

Next. In the much-increased and ever-increasing number of books coming into our libraries—those which have already entered being, we must remember, always to be preserved—how are all best to be disposed of locally; disposed of, I mean, upon the shelves of those vast buildings which the coming years present to our view? Are they to be disposed of by subjects, by size, by alphabetical arrangement; by order of publication to the world; by order of advent to the library, or by something different from each of these? If arrangement be by subjects, or alphabetically, then, in the progress and prospects of every sort of science and of every sort of human thing, and of treatises upon them all that are sure to follow, what extent of open space is to be left in each subject for probable additions of future works upon it? And in what way are these voids to be disguised so as best to obviate the appearance of a library ever incomplete? If a library has books divided according to subjects, and if all the space allotted to each subject is occupied by the books of the day when the library is formed, rearrangement, on the shelves, of the classes—nay, frequent rearrangement of the books *in* the classes—becomes requisite to accommodate in the best way future treatises in the same class. And the like thing is true of one arranged alphabetically. Rearrangement of a small library is a small matter, one which is easily accomplished, and which, for the sake of giving better order and system to the whole, it is always worth while to effect. But rearrangement of a large library is a different thing indeed. Rearrangement implies renumbering. Renumbering implies recataloguing. Recataloguing implies reprinting. And when the library counts its books by hundreds of thousands —and even by millions, as in the coming times our large libraries seem likely to do—when the books cover acres of shelves and weigh hundreds and thousands of tons, the rearrangement will become nigh to an impossibility. It would consume the lives of the learned and exhaust the fortunes of the beneficent. Vastly important it therefore is to any library which sets out with the prospect or even

with the possibility of being a large one, that a comprehensive, and a rightly comprehensive, scheme for the disposition of it externally be had in the very origin of things. But who is *now* to say—to say in advance of actual experience, and in advance of the reduction of that experience to a scientific and admitted truth, what is a *rightly* comprehensive scheme for libraries such as the century on which we are entering may witness? Finally, when the library edifice stands in broad extent erect, and its million books are arranged in order on its shelves—after this comes a problem greater than all. How most easily—how most economically—how to be most useful, and how to prevent the necessity of frequently rearranging, of frequently reprinting that which in its largest part has once or oftener, with great pains, been arranged, and once or oftener, with great cost, been printed—how best to secure all these ends, are these immense collections which stand up in more than imagination before us—to be classified and arranged in the printed *catalogue?* Supplements, of course, are easily to be made; but when we shall have looked painfully through some dozen volumes of catalogue, how are we to follow up the search still more painfully through some scores of pamphlet supplements? We shall abandon our search in despair.

To a certain extent all the questions of which I speak have been for some years serious questions, and for some years have occupied the minds of thoughtful librarians everywhere throughout our country. But even of the latest years they have been questions of no difficulty compared with that difficulty which the future is beginning to reveal to our view.

I have said, gentlemen, that there are several problems for us to resolve. But after these problems have been resolved in the abstract—resolved, I mean, in a general way—we have many matters also acting as forces of "perturbation," the exact value of which we must calculate and allow for. The conclusions as to local arrangement, or as to the form of catalogues which would be true ones for a library of consultation, for a library which is the resort of men of trained and disciplined minds, might prove false in a library destined for circulation chiefly; that is to say, for popular use; and the rule which would rightly prevail in a library seeking a universal character might not be found so good for collections that are content with more limited outlines. A hundred qualifications suggest themselves in every part of our subject to any conclusions which we might form on any general head.

In the midst of these questions, some of which seem nearly insoluble, and terrified as we are by the prospect of library edifices to which Versailles, the Escurial, or the Vatican shall be of humble size, comes a new question altogether—a question radical and revolutionary. Will it be practicable to continue through another century the formation of libraries which shall contain all books upon every subject? Will not such libraries, if continued and formed, tumble to pieces by their own weight, and when the subjects into which their infinite volumes are divided have all grown sufficiently large, break up and resolve themselves into their primordial elements? Our general libraries have already unloaded themselves of law, unloaded themselves of medicine, and unloaded themselves to a large degree of all books of mere physical science. Why shall they not throw off divinity and metaphysics, and a hundred other things; leaving each to establish itself as law has done, as medicine has done, as physical science in part has done, on its own special basis, and leaving itself, too, disintegrated into unity of subject? This would give us a hundred small libraries in the place of one immense one; and doubtless in some respects a small library devoted to a single subject has advantages over a large one, which is rarely perfectly complete in any.

Supposing pamphlets to come forth for another century as pamphlets are now coming forth, and for that other century to be preserved, the collection would fill a room larger than the Bodleian. No general library will or can ever preserve the half of them. Yet while in many cases most useless, in many cases they are most useful, and where not useful often most curious. A library of pamphlets —a library which should embrace every thing that bears a pamphlet's title, and which should exclude every thing which does not—would be a library often and to many of great utility.

Nay, why shall we not go further?

If railway companies, and coal companies, and hospitals, and colleges, and penitentiaries, and benevolent institutions of every sort—to say nothing of historical societies and library companies— keep publishing their annual reports for another century as they publish them now, may it not require the most active labor of the best librarian in America to collect, to preserve, to bind, to arrange, and catalogue them all? Yet few books are more instructive as to special matters; few more often wanted by a large class of readers.

But here the benignant Genius which ever presides over the labors of the learned interposes.

"Your thoughts are at variance with the ideas of the learned in every age and every clime. They are rebellious and irreverent. They savor of State rights. They look unkindly at the Union. All the sorts of knowledge dwell lovingly in one abode. All the forms of truth live ever in unity and love. Diplomacy and statesmanship here are met together. Science and revelation here have kissed each other. Build your edifices as large as you will. Let story rise above story, and wings spread for infinite distance the capacities of your main edifice. The very volumes which you fear will kindly show you how to use the largest of them all as easily as in earlier days you have used those which were among the smallest. Is not the 'elevator' to be seen in every large factory and in every large hotel? Does not the elastic tube afford means of transmitting messages through the largest buildings of our cities? Why may not the electric telegraph, itself the child of science, minister to her honored parent; and why may not the librarian, seated at his desk in the centre or on the circumference of his library-room, send his orders to the remotest part of the immensest building, to be obeyed, perhaps, through the pneumatic tube, returning, with a velocity only less than that of the telegraph itself, the volume which he asks for? Are ropes and pulleys, which the world has used these thousand years, and which are used in every large factory to carry parcels from floor to floor and from one extremity of the edifice to another, to be forgotten in the places where their history and uses are recorded in a hundred tomes, and at a time when they should be called on for their noblest work?

"Why, indeed, if locomotion in horizontal space is largely needed—why may not the railway itself—traversed perhaps by cars whose form shall be the library's cushioned chair—drawn by some graceful 'dummy' whose silence shall not disturb even 'the still air of delightful studies'—why shall not the railway itself, laid in bars of steel so polished that friction and noise no less than space are annihilated—why shall not even IT come in and complete the ministration which the mechanic arts, if rightly invoked, will ever be proud to give to the labors of the learned and the good? Books of municipal law; books of medicine and surgery; books of mere science; books for professional use alone—these you can segregate from others of more general interest; but beyond this you cannot go. The student is referred by one book to a hundred others, all unlike it, and perhaps unlike each other. Will you send him to a hundred libraries? A hundred persons would know that such and such a building contained a library, but not one in the number might know, until he had entered it and found that it was *not* the sort of library which he wanted, what sort of a library it really was. To say nothing of the fact that these special libraries might each consider that certain books belonged not to *it*, but to a sister 'special,' so that a book which might not unreasonably be looked for in any one would be found in none; ending thus in the result that with libraries everywhere, books were nowhere."

But, gentlemen, I will detain you no longer. With little practical experience in this matter, and with no reflection upon it at all, I see before me in the future many questions in regard to the subjects upon which I have spoken; and yet upon another subject which I have not touched, the conduct and management of these vast libraries themselves when every thing else has been adjusted. You, with your great experience and deep reflectiveness, I doubt not must have seen and now behold a hundred more. Before another century rolls by, they will be practical questions.

I know of no way in which these questions can be settled, but the way in which questions of science are always settled—that is to say, by careful observation and collation of facts, and, when facts sufficiently numerous are observed and collated, by the application of intelligent judgment, and the formation, through induction, of a sound result. The field is a large one. It is completely and purely a field of science. The same careful observation of phenomena which is necessary in astronomy, in chemistry, in medicine; the same right judgment to perceive what they teach, which gives to the world a Herschel, a Davy, or a Physick —these same are the qualities which are needed for any valuable conclusions about the work of which I speak. The time has arrived then for a new science—BIBLIOTHECAL SCIENCE, a wide science, a difficult science, a science of value.

Gentlemen, a good librarian has ever been a valuable minister to letters. He has always stood between the world of authors and the world of readers, introducing the habitants of one sphere to the habitants of the other; interpreting often obscurities where the fault is with authors, imparting often intelligence where the fault is with readers. This, his ancient title, he still possesses. But in this day and for the future he is called to new offices and to higher distinctions. His profession belongs to the SCIENCES. He requires some fine faculties of mind. He takes his rank with philosophers.

To promote this science, you, gentlemen, assemble to-day. Much to be considered, so far as it relates to the future, is new. The soundings upon the old charts have imperfect value. New soundings and new observations must be taken by yourselves. I hardly suppose that numerous conclusions of value will be reached at once. But it is a great thing to have met in corporate strength, with a united sense that much is needed, and with united experience and reflection and wisdom to consider by way of remedy what is wanted. I doubt not that this Congress will be the first of a series of bibliothecal conventions, or congresses of librarians; that your purposes, as yet unshaped in part, will here take form, and that future years will feel the beneficial influence of what is here accomplished.

Most cordially, therefore, and again do I welcome you to our city and to our hall, and pray for every blessing upon your consultations and your work.

At the close of the address, the Committee on Organization reported that it seemed desirable that those who had thus far had charge of the Conference should continue the work so well begun, and nominated the following officers, who were unanimously elected:

President.—Justin Winsor

Vice-Presidents.—A. R. Spofford, James Yates, William F. Poole, Lloyd P. Smith.

Secretaries.—Melvil Dewey, Charles Evans, Reuben A. Guild.

● ● ● ●

Co-operative Cataloguing.

MR. DEWEY proposed that the subject of "the preparation of printed titles for the common use of libraries" be taken up for discussion, as there was still some time remaining before adjournment. In introducing the subject he said, "This is another matter very like the Poole's index business. People on all sides are continually urging the great desirability of doing something. About once in so long articles appear in different countries rehearsing the follies of the present system of doing the same thing over a thousand times, as we librarians do in cataloguing books that reach so many libraries. But right here they all stop. There somehow seems to be an idea among certain leaders of our craft, that such a thing is wholly visionary, at least their failure to take any practical steps in the matter would seem to indicate such a belief. Now, I believe, after giving this question considerable attention, that it is perfectly practicable; and, further, I know of a competent cataloguer who shares this belief so thoroughly, that he recently informed me that he should attempt the supply of catalogue titles on his own responsibility, if nothing could be done by the librarians as a body. If we have sufficient faith to take the matter in hand, I have full confidence that we shall make a success of this co-operative cataloguing. I hope there will be free discussion, and that those who think it impracticable will give their reasons.

MR. WINSOR.—The method which the Boston Public Library now employs for the duplication of its catalogue cards has grown out of the heliotype process. It was found that the action of tannin upon a sheet of gelatine was similar to that of light coming through the unobscured parts of an ordinary glass negative. The work of the cataloguers is handed over to the transcribers, who, using an ink with tannin in it, copy in a very legible hand, which has been adopted as the library chirography, this work upon a sheet of paper, ruled so as to present the equivalent surface of twenty cards, arranged in four columns, of five cards each. This sheet is dampened and laid face down upon a sheet of gelatine, attached by atmospheric pressure to a plate of metal. The writing, wherever it touches the gelatine, renders it insoluble, the other portions remaining absorbent. The rest of the process is precisely like the ordinary lithographic one. The plate is put in the press; the soluble parts are kept damp with a brush, the insoluble parts, corresponding to the writing of the copy, repelling the water; the ink-roller is run over the surface, and the ink is attached to those portions only which remain dry; the cardboard is laid on; the press is screwed down, and when lifted you take from it the exact fac-simile of the transcriber's work. A cutting-machine at once converts the pile of sheets, which may be printed, into equivalent piles of cards, all ready, so far as the main entries go, for the assorters, who are to put them away in our double catalogue, for we keep up one for the public and one for official use. About seventy thousand of these cards were put away in these two catalogues last year. The same card is used for the cross-references, and the necessary headings are written at the top of the card, the cataloguers having indicated what such cross-references should be on the slips which contain their original work. Economy of card is secured by grouping, as far as is practicable, those titles on the same sheet which require about the same number of cards. The matter is sometimes further equal-

ized by the transcribers repeating in their work, two or three times as the case may be, such titles as may require many cross-references; as, for instance, a collection of plays, which require a record under the author and title of each. A few more than the present use requires are printed and kept as a reserve for contingent purposes.

MR. EDMANDS.—Are the plates from which these titles are printed, preserved?

MR. WINSOR.—I am not able to state whether they are or not.

We formerly printed our titles from type on sheets of thin paper, to be cut up and pasted upon cards, at about three times the expenditure of time and money. We pull some impressions on ordinary printing paper, and these are used for posting in our several libraries, and they are likewise given to such of the officers as require to be kept mentally posted on the accessions as they come in. Our assistant superintendent, Mr. Whitney, has the immediate charge of the cataloguing department and could tell us more about it.

MR. WHITNEY said that the new method was not only cheaper but more convenient and accurate, for there was no danger of type dropping out or of other accidents peculiar to printing.

PROF. ROBINSON.—This subject should be carefully considered, and some plan for cooperation devised. Nothing can be more annoying than to do work which one knows is done by others over and over in all our libraries, and which might be done once for all. Much of this work falls upon librarians who are burdened with other work, and have to do it in little intervals of time to their great discomfort. It is often done also by very inexperienced persons, and hence done very poorly.

It may not be improper to add that the subject of co-operation among college librarians, in the work of cataloguing and indexing, was presented in a paper read by myself at the University Convocation at Albany, in July last. The discussion which followed led to the appointment of a committee to report at the next annual meeting a plan for such co-operation, if any is found practicable. It was my fortune to be appointed chairman of that committee. On careful consideration since then, it has seemed to me that the movement thus made should be a more general one. It should not be confined to a single State nor to a single class of libraries; though I believe that even with such limitations, co-operation might be made exceedingly profitable. I shall therefore be very glad if such action is taken here as will lead to some simple, general, and permanent plan for combining our resources, so as to secure more perfect indexes and catalogues, and at a cheaper rate. I doubt not the other members of my committee will share with me in a feeling of relief if such action is taken by this body.

MR. WINSOR.—I got the idea of our previous printed card from the Library of the University of Leyden, but I found that, owing to the difference in cost of labor, etc., the cost to us was double per title that to them. If by the type and the gelatine process the cost was precisely the same, you see the great advantage in a completed card of even thickness over one of uneven thickness where titles are pasted on. The great use that comes upon our cards disclosed that cardboard, made up of various layers, will split, and so, at a little additional expense, we employ a bristol-board which has no layers.

MR. CUTTER'S experience was that cards do not split. Both Harvard College Library and the Athenaeum got their cards of Storrs, of Boston, and neither had had the slightest difficulty of this kind.

MR. WARD thought stiff ledger paper the best.

MR. POOLE used stiff paper and found that it did not split, and that it wore better than card board.

MR. EDMANDS.—In the Mercantile Library of Philadelphia we catalogue all of our books received since the date of the catalogue on slips of paper $5\frac{1}{2}$ inches long by $2\frac{3}{4}$ inches wide. We use the heaviest grade of blank-book paper, as being less expensive than cards and taking up much less room. These slips are very readily handled, are durable, and we are satisfied with their use.

MR. DEWEY.—It seems to be the general feeling that the work is feasible, and I therefore move that the Committee on Co-operative Indexing be instructed to report a plan for co-operative cataloguing.

MR. EDMANDS suggested that the assistance of the publishers might be obtained, since such a catalogue would be of great value as an advertisement.

MR. DEWEY.—I am confident that the great gain to the publishers of having their books kept on permanent record, as they would be kept in the

plan proposed, would induce them to incur the expense.

PROF. ROBINSON.—I do not believe in the plan for having the publishers prepare the cards. There would not be sufficient care in their preparation. It should be done by an expert. I think of no better way than that which I proposed for the preparation of an index—let the libraries combine to pay one man a salary for doing it. They might employ the same man and keep him at work—with assistance if necessary—all the time at these two things, keeping the general index and the printed titles up to date. But at all events let us have some plan devised. I think it would be well to refer this subject to the same committee which is to report a plan for indexing.

MR. DEWEY.—I regret that the gentleman has so misunderstood me. I would not for a moment think of trusting the publishers to prepare their own titles. I meant that they would be willing to pay for having it done by a competent person appointed by the librarians.

MR. WINSOR had two years ago approached the Osgood house on the subject, but had accomplished nothing.

MR. DEWEY thought that the publishers would co-operate if it was the unanimous request of the Conference, and described the method devised by Battezzati, of Milan, and employed by several Italian publishers.

MR. POOL suggested that the further discussion of the question be postponed till the arrival of Mr. Spofford, as he would be able to enlighten the Conference as to the practicability of having these titles printed at the Congressional Library.

MR. BARNWELL moved that Mr. Dewey's motion be deferred until to-morrow, when Mr. Spofford would be in attendance, and could perhaps afford assistance.

MR. DEWEY.—I think that it is impossible for some time at least for Mr. Spofford to give the help which has been suggested. I ask the Chair if he cannot give us information on this point?

MR. WINSOR believed that the Library of Congress was so crowded and limited in help that it could not give any assistance now.

MR. DEWEY.—I have been informed that Mr. Spofford is in favor of something of the kind, but does not think it possible to attempt the matter in the Congressional Library at present.

MR. CAPEN thought it very desirable for a library to have a catalogue not only of its own books, but of all that were published, and hoped that the plan would be found practicable. He would move that some action be taken by the Conference expressive of the value to other libraries of the catalogues of the Boston Public Library. (Applause.)

MR. WARD said he had thought a good deal about this proposition for a general or universal catalogue. He had imagined the great advantage to be derived from one grand catalogue of all known books, at least such as were extant and likely to be possessed by some library. But he had further thought that this general catalogue, to be effective and universally useful, must really be complete. And he had supposed the possibility of every important library being supplied with a copy of some such catalogue, in which each librarian, in some suitable manner, should simply mark for himself the titles of such of the books named therein as were contained in his own library. This would be a comparatively easy and thorough way of making a printed catalogue—serving the double purpose of showing a librarian not only what he had, but what he had not. The plan would further be perfected if by some temporary exchange of these volumes so marked each librarian should become possessed of the knowledge of what books were in the possession of all other libraries, and so correspondingly mark, on some simple system, *his* own catalogue. The result would be thoroughly and permanently advantageous. But fancy the labor consequent upon so stupendous an undertaking. The possibility of its accomplishment seemed utterly hopeless; but was not this at least one idea of a complete universal catalogue?

MR. VICKERS urged that the titles be made complete even to collation of plates and pagination, and thought when we could be supplied with full titles of all books published, we should have attained to the first stage of a librarian's heaven.

MR. WINSOR.—We keep our newspaper catalogue in a double form; first, in the natural alphabetical manner by titles; and, second by a chronological method, under which all papers of any given year are arranged under that year—a great convenience to historical students. I owe the idea of it to Prof. Abbot, of Harvard University, who prepared such a catalogue of those in the

College Library. There are from 10,000 to 12,000 bound volumes of newspapers accessible to the investigator in Boston and Cambridge; and the newspaper catalogue of the Public Library is made to include that of the Boston Athenaeum and the Massachusetts Historical Society, for the convenience of those who would search those collections for what they are not able to find with us.

MR. SMITH thought that the universal catalogue should come from Washington, in return for the copies of new books sent there.

MR. WINSOR.—I entertain a strong conviction that publishers will yet see their advantage in pursuing some scheme of this kind, by which the purchaser of their books will have their cataloguing ready made. I suggested a plan for this purpose to one of our prominent Boston publishers perhaps two years ago, but it has not yet been carried out, though the *Publishers' Weekly* has urged it. We offered to do the cataloguing for them from advance copies. The plan was this: A fly advertising sheet, of stiff paper or thin cardboard, was to be divided by printer's rules to a size of card determined upon—that of the Boston Athenaeum and of our branch libraries being probably the best suited. The sheet should be large enough to hold three of these spaces, for such books as may be required to be catalogued under author, title, and subject. The surplus surface of the sheet and the reverse side could be filled with any advertising matter the publisher may desire. If the book was a small one, and it was necessary to fold the sheet to keep it from protruding beyond the covers of the book, the card spaces could be arranged so as to bring the advertising part on the line of the fold. The cards when used are, of course, to be cut apart on the division lines. It would naturally be for the interest of the different publishers to follow the method and size of card of the first to employ the plan. In my judgment, the interests of the publishers and the public are the same in this matter, and will be sooner or later understood.

MR. CHRISTERN suggested that, as the Boston Public Library received nearly all the books as fast as published, the other libraries might contract with their printers for duplicates of the titles prepared by them.

MR. WINSOR.—I have had occasional applications for our broadsides of titles, and have referred applicants to our city printers, leaving them to make arrangements for such regular supply.

MR. WHITNEY explained that their old and new books were bulletined together, and so other libraries could not use their sheets to advantage.

MR. DEWEY called for the question on his motion to instruct the Committee on Indexing to report a plan for co-operative cataloguing. The motion being put, was carried by a unanimous vote.

• • • •

SIXTH SESSION.

[Thursday Evening.]

The Conference was called to order by the president at 7:30 P.M.

The Secretary read communications from several American libraries, one from West-Bromwich, England, and the following as bearing directly on the subject of the late discussion.

Boston, 18 Pemberton Sq.,
Oct. 2, 1876.

MY DEAR SIR: I send with this a volume in illustration of the system of preparing catalogues of libraries that was briefly mentioned to you at the Boston Library on Friday afternoon last. Its value will depend upon the *general adoption* of the plan, and I think it will be for the interest of publishers to introduce it. The idea is simply that of printing a duplicate title-page, a literal copy, upon one of the fly-leaves or the last page of the last signature of a book, this leaf to be taken out and pasted upon a card of the size now in use, as shown by the enclosed specimen; or it can be pasted to the blank pages of the books now in use for catalogues.

In the beginning this system will be of little advantage; but if generally adopted, it will become more and more valuable. Books not thus printed would be catalogued by *writing* upon the cards in the same manner as at present.

Publishers who are in the habit of sending notices to customers of books in the press would find detached copies of these slips convenient for sending by mail. The name of the publisher will appear on all catalogues.

The cost of printing (if on the first or the last signature) will be the same as at present, and the "composition" will be required but once for a whole edition.

I do not consider the specimen sent as perfect in form and arrangement as may be desirable, but I have endeavored to conform to the points mentioned by Mr. John Fiske in his recent article, in the *Atlantic Monthly*, in relation to this subject.

I have adopted the size of the cards used in Harvard College Library, supposing that it would be sufficiently large to embrace complete copies of nearly all title-pages, the size of a part of the type being varied to match the required space. The size when fixed should be uniform in all cases.

If convenient to you, please show this volume to other members of the Conference, and if you think it desirable to mention the matter at the regular sessions, I shall be glad to have you do so. I am yours very truly,

John M. Batchelder.

MR. JUSTIN WINSOR.

MR. EDMANDS.—There is great need of a reform in the printing and distribution of our public documents. There has apparently been no system in the matter. Sometimes the same matter has been printed twice, and so it is found in the documents ordered by the Senate and also by the House, and the volumes are made up so carelessly that it is impossible to ascertain what constitutes a full set of the documents of each Congress. Sometimes a report will be printed without any indication in it of belonging to the series, and yet it is included in the printed schedule of the documents.

There is need of a change in the manner of distributing the books. Hitherto it has been impossible to get information about the time of their issue so as to be able to apply for them, and the most of them are squandered instead of being judiciously placed where they will be of service to the country. They should be advertised as soon as issued, sold at about the cost of printing, and the number of copies printed fixed by an estimate of the probable demand.

On motion of Mr. Edmands, the following resolution was adopted:

"RESOLVED, That a memorial to Congress be prepared by this Convention, of which the subject-matter shall be the changes desirable in the present mode of distributing the public documents and other publications."

Library Journal.

MR. VICKERS asked whether any action was necessary in regard to printing the proceedings, to which MR. DEWEY replied that it was generally understood that the second number of the *Library Journal* would be given up to the proceedings, and that he should be glad to make that report as full and accurate as possible.

MR. SMITH moved that the *Library Journal* be the official organ of the Association, and that all reports and papers be printed therein, but thought his motion should go before the Committee on Resolutions.

MR. DEWEY.—That essence of perversity at my elbow—a reporter—suggests that in case this resolution prevails I shall be an organist. I suggest that *journal* be substituted for *organ*.

MR. GUILD urged that each member of the Conference should feel that he was an agent for the *Journal*, and to an extent responsible that it had sufficient support to be continued permanently.

On motion of MR. VICKERS, Mr. Smith's motion was referred to the Committee on Permanent Organization.

PROF. ROBINSON asked if abstracts of the remarks made were wanted for the proceedings.

MR. DEWEY said the Committee of Arrangement had not employed a short-hand reporter, because of the expense, but that they desired each speaker to furnish the secretary with their remarks, in writing, so that the report might be full and thoroughly accurate. He urged that this matter receive special attention, in order that from the report the Conference might be reproduced as nearly as possible.

DR. H. A. HOMES, of the New York State Library, was then introduced, and read a paper on "Subject Indexes."

Subject-Indexes for Popular Libraries

By H. A. Homes, New York State Library

In our eagerness for facilities in the acquisition of knowledge, amid increasing difficulties from the wideness of the field over which its treasures are spread, we would all welcome a universal catalogue of books, and a universal subject-index to point out all the books which contain information on any subject of research. The duty of authors to facilitate the use of their books to readers by copious indexes is of late frequently suggested to them by complaining minds.

There will occur to those present various instances in which this duty has not been neglected, and large and important works have had such indexes provided as to make them a hundred times more useful to the public than they had been before. Poole's "Index to Periodical Literature" was such a book to the student that the literary community is impatient for its continuation to the present time.

Librarians themselves, in a benevolent and apostolic spirit, are desirous that the books under their charge should not remain sealed treasures, but should be easily accessible to the demands of readers; and, not content with being merely perfunctory officials, are anxious to be to them like helping friends: much to the astonishment, frequently, of the reader himself, who anticipated nothing but cold civility. It is with these and similar thoughts passing through my mind that I have been led to present for your consideration the topic of *Subject-Indexes for popular libraries*.

The popular or free town libraries especially are recognized by their prominent supporters as educational institutions, and it is felt by the librarians that every exertion should be made by them to make the readers easily acquainted with the character of the topics of the volumes under their charge. Many catalogues which have appeared in the last fifteen years bear witness to their zealous and effectual efforts to respond to the necessity of readers, these catalogues surpassing in utility for the purpose any which had previously been printed. But it has been in noticing the comparatively great size and cost of these elegant volumes that the thought has suggested itself to me whether the wants of readers could not be responded to at much less expense, and, on the whole, with better results generally. All librarians recognize the great value of subject-indexes for the books of a library, but will not probably be equally ready to have them adopted so as to replace every other form of printed catalogue for the ordinary reader. Still I desire to suggest, as a fit topic for discussion among us, a proposition very similar in its character, though I limit its application to popular libraries. I would for convenience formulate the suggestion in these terms:

It is desirable that popular libraries of limited pecuniary means should print subject-indexes for public use as a substitute for all other catalogues.

The other forms of catalogues most in use are: 1. The alphabetical catalogue by authors, with a moderate subject-index at the end, arranged either as a dictionary or in a philosophical classification. 2. The same catalogue (by authors alphabetically), with the subjects or topics arranged in the same alphabet. 3. A catalogue on the same plan as the last, embracing under the same alphabet the books in the library by the first word of their titles, the name of the author following the title. There is thus created an exceedingly useful triplicate catalogue under a single alphabetical arrangement. It is the plan mainly inaugurated by the Boston Public Library, and since followed by many other institutions.

If a sole subject-index such as I am contemplating should be adopted by any library as its only printed catalogue, it would imply the omission, in print, both of its catalogue by names of authors, and its catalogue by the title of the books. The arrangement of topics would, in the main, accord with that of the Encyclopaedia Britannica, or of Appleton's Cyclopaedia, and there would be no attempt at philosophical or scientific classification further than to indicate by cross-references from some of the most comprehensive headings the special names under which the topics sought for would be found. Where a subject-index is made to serve as a substitute for a catalogue, it is obvious that there must be introduced headings for topics which are not so much in the nature of a subject as of a class of books. I should therefore expect that as the list of the fiction in a library is made frequently a separate catalogue, so would the class of juveniles, the drama, poetry, the newspapers, and the periodicals come under the initial letters of the alphabet of those words in the index. Under Bible there would be found the editions of it in various languages. The collected works of an author might be announced, if on the shelves of the library, by a single word in connection with his life, so frequently found associated with his works, and in connection all the other books referring to him would follow.

Now, if I am disposed to advocate for many, perhaps for the larger number, of our popular libraries the substitution of the subject-index catalogue for the full triplicate catalogue, it is not with the slightest disposition to undervalue the excellence and comparative perfection of those catalogues. The chief positive argument to be urged in favor of the proposition is on the score of economy; and negatively, that such subject-indexes will be very nearly as useful as the full catalogue.

In regard to economy, it is obvious that there would be a saving of two thirds of the cost in the matter of printing, besides the saving in the cost of salaries for the assistants who would be employed in editing the full catalogue. The saving would amount to considerably more than two thirds of the present rate of expense, if the catalogue by authors should be as full as those of the catalogues of the Congressional, New York State, and Boston Public Libraries.

The expense incurred for printing catalogues is an important consideration in the administration of a library. On our present system we are to look forward to the printing of thousands of such catalogues for town libraries, of from ten to fifty thousand volumes each, each catalogue including in great part the titles of the same works. The catalogue of a library of 30,000 volumes fills, when compactly printed on the triplicate plan, about seven hundred pages, and at the end of five years does not contain the titles of one quarter of the books most sought for—that is, the newest books.

Now, in view of this great expense of printing catalogues, and of the fact that in a few years they fail to give the information desired by the majority of readers, great libraries in Europe, possessed of ample means, have concluded not to print catalogues at all, or to defer doing so indefinitely. The same principle has its application to town libraries possessing relatively no greater means than the libraries of European States. Our taxpayers are liberal out of their great love for the town library; but though the tax is now cheerfully paid, it is well to proceed in such a manner as not ultimately to give rise to vexatious complaints that will diminish the sums to be voted for the purchase of books, which are more necessary than catalogues.

For the sake, therefore, of this saving of expense, the printing of a simple subject-index as a substitute for the present full catalogue is recommended as a not unwise concession on the part of the trustees or committees of libraries. It is true it may seem like a retrograde measure to adopt in any case, after so much thought has been expended in developing the present improved and perfected catalogues. Still, if the principal object of printing a catalogue at all can be gained for the great mass of readers by a subject-index only, I do not see that we ought exceedingly to regret that the printing of a full catalogue should come to be the exception rather than the rule. The more curious reader in our American libraries, wishing to become more intimately acquainted with the titles of books, would always be able to obtain from the library of his town the full catalogues of some of the larger libraries for his information.

Now, a subject-index does answer to the wants and necessities of ninety-nine in a hundred readers in town libraries. Any one of them, after looking over a catalogue by authors solely, is liable to come to a librarian and say that he wants a book on such a subject, but that he can not meet with any thing upon it in the catalogue. I think that the testimony of Mr. Abbot, regarding the comparative use of the two branches of his manuscript catalogue of the library of Harvard College, was that the subject-index was used at least twenty times as much as the catalogue by authors. It certainly corresponds with my own experience in the New York State Library.

I have not proposed to present any elaborate plan for a subject-index for a popular library. Librarians working in co-operation or independently would gradually perfect one. In my opinion, however, in each article of the index, printed in double-column pages, and for a majority of the titles in one line of the column, information can be given on from four to six points regarding each book—its subject, the author, a portion of the title, the date, place where printed, and perhaps the number of the pages and of the volumes. More than this is rarely needed by any reader. While accuracy is always necessary, minute bibliographical information is not sought for except by very few persons. For American books it can be obtained from the larger catalogues, and from Sabin's Dictionary; for other works it can be obtained from the dictionaries of the bibliographers.

It might be desired by some librarians that the subject-index should be made more full. Just in proportion as it should be done completely, it would render the catalogue by authors less necessary. With more labor on the index, the same work would naturally appear twice or three times, or more, under different headings, when the work treated of different subjects. Indeed, the perfecting of an index of subjects for a library can be indefinitely extended, in proportion to the time and attention the librarian and his assistants can devote to it. For example, it can be made to include just as many of the topics treated of in the current and past periodicals which belong to the library as opportunity is offered to the librarians to record. The indexes prepared for other libraries and for periodical literature can be freely used in the preparation of each new index without rendering the librarian liable to the charge of plagiarism.

The finding-list of the Public Library of Chicago illustrates the value of and demand for a subject-index. Hastily prepared for temporary use in the absence of any catalogue, it has already gone through three editions, and paid its own expenses by the sale.

● ● ● ●

Finding Lists.

MR. POOLE.—Our experience in Chicago, in furnishing our readers with simple and inexpensive printed finding lists, may be of service to some of the librarians present. January 2d, 1874, I entered upon my duties as librarian. There were collected about 7000 volumes, mostly English donations, but none of them had been catalogued, arranged, or prepared for the shelves. I immediately made plans for fitting up library-rooms, and prepared lists containing the titles of 30,000 volumes to be purchased. On the 1st of May we were ready to open the circulating and reference departments to the public, with about 17,000 volumes on the shelves. All these volumes had been catalogued on cards, classified, stamped, labelled, and numbered, and complete shelf lists of them had been prepared. There was no time to print the catalogue, and if there had been time, it was not desirable to print a catalogue when not one third of the books ordered had been received. We adopted, as a temporary substitute for the catalogue, printed finding lists, of which I have with me a specimen copy for your inspection. As our books were classified on the shelves with considerable minuteness, and the shelf lists followed this classification, the finding lists were made by simply printing our shelf lists, using only the surname of the author, the briefest title, and the shelf mark of the work. We used brevier type in two columns on a

common octavo page. The specimen I show you is
the second edition printed about nine months
later, after some 12,000 more volumes had been
added to the library. It is printed, you will see,
on a calendered manila paper, which can be
bought for nine cents a pound. The advantage of
the manila paper is not merely its cheapness, but
that it will outlast for library use ten copies
printed on the best book paper, and it has a tone
and finish which makes a presentable volume.
About ten thousand copies of the volume have
been sold, and we have been able to sell it for ten
cents a copy, from its desirableness as a means of
advertising. In consideration of our allowing the
printer to insert unexceptional business advertisements on flyleaves placed at the beginning and end
of the text, he has contracted to furnish the volume for ten cents, and to supply the library gratuitously with all the copies it needs for its own
use. The finding lists are therefore no expense to
the library. The third edition, the matter entirely
recomposed, and containing the titles of 50,000
volumes, was issued early in the present year, and
a supplement a few months later, all of which is
still sold for ten cents. The paper of this edition,
through the fault of the manufacturer, was inferior to that of the second edition, and hence I have
exhibited the edition which will show both the
paper and the style of the work. The use of fine
manila paper for catalogue work is well worth the
attention of librarians. Our card catalogue is complete and ready to print; but from want of the
necessary funds the printing has been delayed.
The only printed manual through which the public
have had access to the books has been the finding
lists which have been described; and our annual
circulation has been more than four hundred
thousand volumes.

MR. CAPEN.—Mr. President, the remarks of the
gentleman from Chicago have an especial interest
to me, from the fact that I was placed in a situation in Haverhill, where a similar plan could have
been adopted, greatly to the convenience, I doubt
not, of many of our patrons. We were called upon
to open the library at once, as the season for reading had come, or to postpone for months until a
catalogue should be completed. Delay would be
inconvenient, and might hazard the popularity of
the library, and thereby its welfare. We opened
without a catalogue, spreading our popular books
on our counters, as does the bookseller in his
store, making search specially for books asked for
by title, and allowing borrowers to go to the

shelves for a book on a special subject. The plan
succeeded, not, I confess, without misgivings, and
we disposed of about 250 volumes a day, on an
average. The plan adopted by the gentleman, I can
see, would have aided us.

MR. WALTER had used the manila paper and
found it admirable.

MR. WINSOR had used some 200,000 manila
paper covers, but as yet had not tried it for cataloguing.

Duplicates.

MR. BARTON called up the subject of duplicates, and how we can make the best use of them.
He suggested that libraries without large purchasing funds, but blessed with stores of early and late
historical matter in duplicate, are most anxious to
make good use of such material by sale or exchange. He offered the collection of the American
Antiquarian Society as one containing much not
easily found in the market or in younger libraries,
and stated that it is carefully classified for easy
examination and selection.

MR. WINSOR had a collection of 10,000 duplicate pamphlets, and would like an expression of
opinion from the Conference as to the best manner of effecting exchanges.

MR. BARNWELL also had about the same number of pamphlet duplicates, and was similarly
interested.

MR. VICKERS hoped that the *Library Journal*
would be able to furnish an opportunity for effecting exchanges hereafter, by giving lists of duplicates.

MR. BARNWELL thought that even if the *Journal* was made accessible for this purpose, the labor
of making the lists would prevent its being generally used.

MR. WINSOR said that he disposed of pamphlets in lots of a thousand each, without making
out lists, and while many duplicates were received,
believed it to be the best plan for both parties.

PROF. ROBINSON often disposed of duplicates
to students.

MR. DEWEY had also tried this method with
good results, having sold about a thousand vol-

umes to students, most of them at auction. He said, in regard to the *Library Journal*, that it was proposed as a regular department to announce valuable duplicates that were for exchange, charging only enough to keep out lists of worthless books. He thought the best method, if it were practicable, would be to turn all duplicates into a common depository, and then contributors could draw from that source, the manager of the depository giving credit for all books sent in, and charging all drawn out.

Card Catalogues.

MR. POOL.—I would like to ask a question relative to card catalogues.

About two years since, a gentleman in Paris, M. Bonnange, invented a new form of card to be used for catalogues; it consisted of two parts, connected by a cloth hinge—one part for the inscription, the other acting as a kind of lever. The lower part of the card was grooved out, and through it was passed an endless screw. When the cards were placed in a box, the screw compressed them together, and the cards were then turned like the leaves of a book. I would like to inquire as to the advantage and utility of this form, if the chairman or any one else can answer.

MR. WINSOR detailed the method of M. Bonnange, and showed how even a wire and notices failed to keep some self-sufficient people from taking the cards from the drawers.

MR. CUTTER read an extract from the Library Report (p. 559) showing the large amount of room occupied by the Bonnange cases, as compared with the cases used in this country.

PROF. ROBINSON explained his method of keeping the slips in order in his catalogue of periodical literature, illustrating his remarks from a volume shown the Conference, and referring those interested to the full description of his plan given in the Government Report.

MR. WINSOR said he should like to know the policy of other librarians in regard to the price charged for catalogues.

MR. EDMANDS.—The catalogue of the Mercantile Library of Philadelphia, roy. 8vo, pp. 700, issued in January, 1870, cost $5000—without including salary of those engaged in preparing it, or the binding for 2500 copies. We sold it bound in

cloth for $2.50. As few were sold, the price was afterwards reduced to $1. Altogether we have received less than $1100 from the sale of the catalogue. Doubtless this small sale is due in a great measure to our bookcases being open to all the members.

MR. WINSOR.—It seldom or never happens that a catalogue can be made to pay the cost of printing, making no account of the cost of preparation and the labor of seeing it through the press. We have pursued the policy at Boston of attaching only such a price to our catalogues as will prevent waste. The latest of our issues, that of the Roxbury Branch, cost a dollar and a quarter to print, per copy, and we sell it for thirty cents. The printing of a catalogue is a great expense to a library, but it is a necessary one for a popular library. A large library seldom prints more than one; and the Boston Public Library will probably hereafter confine the printed catalogues of its *main* collection to such as may cover special classes or collections. With its popular departments it cannot fail to make frequent reissues, corrected to date.

SEVENTH SESSION.

[Friday Morning.]

The Conference was called to order by the President at 10 A.M. The Secretary read a letter from Mr. Saunders, of the Astor Library, announcing the illness of Mr. Brevoort as the reason for his absence. A cordial letter from W. J. Hagerston, librarian of the Public Library of South Shields, England, explained that illness had prevented him from attending the Conference, as he had purposed, and expressed a desire to join any association of librarians that might be formed by those present.

MR. POOLE introduced the following resolution, which was unanimously adopted.

Resolved, That the thanks of this Conference be tendered to the Pennsylvania Historical Society for its hospitality in furnishing its beautiful rooms gratuitously to the Conference; to John Jordan, Jr., Esq., Chairman of the Library Committee of the Historical Society; to Floyd P. Smith, Librarian of the Philadelphia Library Co.; to James G. Barnwell, Vice-President, and John Edmands, Librarian of the Mercantile Library, for their unremitting attentions to the members of the Conference; to John Wm. Wallace, Esq., for his eloquent and appropriate address of welcome, and his presentation of the same in a printed form to the Conference.

MR. POOLE then offered the following resolution:

Resolved, That the discrimination against libraries in the rules of the American Booksellers' Association, which forbids the trade from supplying libraries with books at a greater discount than twenty per cent, is unjust and impolitic, and is a rule which no librarian is bound to respect.

In its support he said: In the summer of 1874, a convention of American booksellers at Put-in-Bay adopted the rule named in the resolution which I have read. Their right to adopt such a rule, as a regulation of their own trade, is unquestioned. They had no right to compel other booksellers who did not belong to their association, and who did not approve of their proceedings, to adopt their rule; and this injustice the association has attempted to enforce. It is right and becoming for the librarians, who have been forcibly invited to walk under this twenty-per-cent yoke, to express their opinion concerning the rule, at this their first meeting since its enactment. In the resolution I have offered, I have endeavored to state the case mildly—that the rule is "unjust and impolitic, and one which no librarian is bound to respect." My individual opinions would seek expression in more positive terms than these. I have not, however, the slightest personal or official interest in the rule. I have never observed it; it has been an annoyance, but never a restriction to my buying all the books I wanted, at prices that were entirely satisfactory.

When the rule went into effect, the two largest houses in Chicago were competing for the business of our library, and were supplying current American books at 35 per cent discount, which I candidly think is a larger discount than the trade, as a rule, can afford to give. Shrewd and intelligent booksellers, however, seek the trade of public libraries, for it leads to other business; and hence they give libraries, as they should, the largest discounts. They know, also, that the library is the best friend and ally of the bookseller, as it creates a taste for reading in the community, and a desire to possess books. The spirit which animated the booksellers assembled at Put-in-Bay, and of which the rule we are considering is an offspring, may

perhaps be best illustrated by an incident in my own experience. When the rule went into operation, our business relations with the leading houses of Chicago were at an end. A smaller house in that city, that did not belong to the association, and did not approve of its action or rules, stood ready to supply the library with books at reasonable prices, and I gave the house an order. Before the order was wholly filled, information came to one of the larger houses as to the manner in which the Public Library was supplying itself with books. A meeting of the partners of the larger houses was immediately called, and a committee, one from each house, was appointed to warn the parties who were supplying us. The committee called and threatened the house that if they did not stop furnishing us with books at a larger discount than 20 per cent, the book trade of the city would discontinue business relations with them, and would report them to the publishing-houses in New York, Philadelphia, and Boston, who hereafter would not supply them at the usual discounts. The smaller house was obliged to succumb to these threats, and sent me a note stating that they were unable to fulfil their agreement, and giving the reasons. The fact that the house did not belong to the association of booksellers, and had never subscribed to its rules, had no weight with the committee. They had then, but have not to-day, the power to enforce the rule in such instances, and in so doing they violated every principle of free trade and common justice. This interference was no inconvenience to us, as other parties were ready to do our business. Is it wise or politic to introduce "Molly Maguirism" into the ethics of the book trade?

The rule from its inception to the present time has been a farce; and yet we read about it in the *Publishers' Weekly*, under the euphuistic appellation of "reform." It has been a farce because it has has not been applied to the large libraries of the country, while it has been forced upon the smaller and feebler institutions. I hope we shall hear the experience of the librarians of Boston, New York, Philadelphia, and Cincinnati. If I have not been misinformed, none of these libraries have come under the rule, and some have been regularly supplied at the old rates by regular members of the Booksellers' Association. It is a farce for a fragment of any trade or profession to meet and enact rules which are to govern the whole trade or profession, and to attempt, by interference with the personal rights of parties who do not accept those rules, the enforcement of these enactments. It is a farce to set up the claim that the book trade is a guild endowed with superior intelligence, and hence entitled to special privileges, and authorized to enforce obedience to its demands. The book trade has the same rights and privileges as any other trade, neither more nor less. The rule is a farce because it cannot be put into general execution. It is not possible to make a rule of this kind which experienced book-buyers will not evade, and ought not to despise. My free-trade catechism is simple and concise: it is "free trade in books." When a ring is made on boots, hats, and groceries, it will admit of an additional clause. I have had scores of letters from librarians in the Northwest, asking how they could buy books at the old rates, and I have freely given them the information. Most of this trade has been lost to Chicago, as the orders have largely been filled in New York. The Chicago trade, about two weeks ago, in view of this state of affairs, held a meeting and resolved to discard the rule. The trade with us is again free, and our leading houses are now happy to supply libraries in any part of the country at the old rates, provided the orders amount to one hundred dollars. The rule, I understand, is still enforced in some parts of the country. It is for the encouragement of libraries in those regions, and for a warning to booksellers when they again meet in convention, that I ask the adoption of the resolution.

MR. CAPEN.—The element of opposition in my nature is sometimes pretty strong, and I should feel called upon to exhibit it on this occasion, even if I found myself in a minority of one. From the time of the formation of the Book Trade Association I have taken a deep interest in its objects, and have made myself more or less acquainted with them, through the pages of the *Publishers' Weekly*. I wish I were better able to state them. But, if I understand the matter, the book trade had reached a point where it became necessary to take action, and prompt action too, or the large majority of the booksellers in the country towns would inevitably be ruined. The action of the trade was intended to provide a remedy; and that remedy was, to fix the rate of discount. The price of the book was to be assigned by the publisher, and every member of the trade was to be able to buy at a certain discount, and to librarians was given a discount of twenty percent. Now, sir, for one, I cannot question the right of the trade to take this action, nor can I see that we are fairly constituted the judges of the necessity. It may be very pleas-

ant for me to buy books with a large margin of discount; but if, in doing this, I am going to injure the trade and contribute to the ruin of my neighbor, I am ready to forego the pleasure. "Live and let live" I believe to be a fair motto for this business.

Now, sir, if we feel aggrieved; if we feel that justice has not been done, and that a larger discount should be made to libraries, cannot the end be reached more satisfactorily to us, and more satisfactorily to the trade, by appointing a committee to confer with their association? For one, I hope the resolution will not be adopted by this Convention.

MR. BOWKER said that his connection with both the *Library Journal* and the *Publishers' Weekly* made him doubly interested in the question under discussion, and with the permission of the Conference he should like to state the case as it appeared to him. He then gave a brief but very clear statement of the factors involved, the reasons that led to the reform in discounts, and the present feeling among booksellers regarding the library clause. He thought that since special attention had been called to their claims, the trade were inclined to make a larger concession to the libraries.

MR. YATES.—I find the same errors which have prevailed in England prevail here, for there is no doubt a feeling that our influence is inimical to that of the trade of bookselling in our localities, as has been shown in this instance.

If all books were of equal value, this might be the case, but as this is not so, the best thing is to get the great mass of people informed of the merits of a work, to secure its extended sale. This position, I am glad to say, is being accepted by such publishers as Messrs. Grant & Co., publishers of the *Gentleman's Magazine*; Messrs. Cassell & Sons, and others, who present a copy of new works, knowing that where one reader appreciates it, fifty others are induced to do likewise, but not being able to get it at once from the library, some are led to buy a copy, and make it their own.

I have no doubt your publishers could save a vast expense incurred in advertisements, which never reach the bulk of readers, by adopting this method of seeing a copy on the shelves of all public libraries. I would not speak as to its success, if trashy books were tried to begin with.

MR. CAPEN thought that the libraries certainly did not detract from the sale of books.

MR. SMITH said it was his custom to support local booksellers without discriminating. He announced that he would buy of the dealer who first sent in the book for approval.

MR. GREEN.—Mr. President: I am glad to hear the remarks of Mr. Smith and Mr. Capen. We buy six or seven thousand dollars' worth of books and periodicals every year for the library at Worcester. We ought to have a larger discount from the booksellers than we receive.

I have been approached by persons who, while subscribers to the agreement to give only twenty per cent discount, were really ready, for the sake of getting our trade, to make us a larger discount. I have declined the proposition, however, because I did not like to contenance the treachery of the proposer. I felt that if I bought at these prices, it would be like buying smuggled tea or coffee.

It seems to me that the booksellers have aimed at a good thing in trying to make bookstores in the smaller cities and larger towns prosperous. It is an advantage to such a place as Worcester to have a good bookstore. It is a source of education to its citizens.

I would be conciliatory with the booksellers, and while acknowledging that there is good in the purposes for which they have been working, insist that a larger discount is due to libraries.

I am not at all sure that I shall not in future buy my books where I can buy them cheapest, since, from the statements made by librarians here to-day, the rule seems to be practically set aside, and booksellers are not able to enforce it. Still I would not have this Conference put itself in the position of antagonism towards the trade, and hope that Mr. Poole's resolution may be referred back to the Committee on Resolutions for modification in its tone. Let us have a resolution that will meet with the unanimous approval of the members of the Conference.

MR. GUILD.—It is very evident that there are two sides to this question. The appointment of a committee of conference, with Mr. Poole as chairman, can certainly do no harm. It may do good. I am in favor of such a committee.

MR. SPOFFORD.—The trouble lies in part behind any of the considerations yet adduced. It is the inordinately high retail price of books, which has gone up to double or more than double what it was before the war, that is depleting the funds of our libraries. And just at the time when the price of books to the general public had reached its maximum, the rate of discount to libraries was fixed at a minimum. This, too, in the face of a general and growing decline in the market price of nearly all commodities.

The librarians of the country are right in resenting this, and the confessed inability to maintain the high rates is proof enough that they are essentially wrong. I rejoice that an era of low prices has set in, that the inflated prices of books are coming down, and if the time is to return when we shall once more have in this country an honest dollar (and this time, it is to be hoped, is not far distant), we shall once more be able to buy with it (what we cannot latterly do) an honest dollar's worth of books.

MR. EDMANDS.—The following may be given as a fair illustration of the working of the present plan of discounts: The distinguished house of Brown, Jones & Robinson publish a book of which we want fifty copies. The publisher declines to allow a greater discount than twenty per cent. I tell Mr. B. I want fifty copies of the "Sweetbrier." He goes into Lippincott's (Laughter)—the house of Brown, Jones & Robinson, purchases them, and sells them to us at thirty per cent off, and still makes a profit.

MR. WARD.—Though I have many causes of prejudice against the publishers, I think they ought to have a hearing from their own point of view. The question is one in the consideration of which it is especially important to hear both sides, even though the arguments for the other side may not always be of the most persuasive sort. As in the case of one who replied, to my own appeal for a little better terms, that a public library, especially a free one, had no claims at all upon a publisher for even the moderate discount he was willing to allow it—since the library bought one copy of a book for fifty or one hundred readers, and so directly interfered with the publisher's general popular sales, making one book answer the purpose of a hundred, it was of more consequence to consider the unfairness and inequality of the existing state of affairs between the booksellers and the numerous libraries of the country. Mr. Poole has shown us how he is able to buy his books at as high a discount as 30 and even 35 per cent. But there are others, like myself, unable to avail themselves of such desirable facilities. We all want to buy as low as we can. But what are we to do who are away from the centres? [MR. POOLE.—Send out to Chicago. (Laughter.)]

There is Appleton's Cyclopaedia, a book which

is sold only by subscription. [MR. POOLE.—Except when it is sold some other way. (Laughter.)] We were offered a copy in cloth at the price of $75. I made an inquiry as to the cost of other parties, and while waiting the answer, there comes a finely bound copy for only $80.

MR. SPOFFORD.—I have lately bought the eighty-dollar "Appleton" for forty dollars. I don't know how it was done.

MR. VICKERS said that the trustees of a library held its funds in trust for the good of the public, and not specially for the purpose of fostering the book trade. The dealer contrives to get round his conscience in selling at low prices, and the librarian is not the keeper of that conscience, but of the public money. The libraries were not at all in the way of the book trade.

MR. GREEN, while in favor of the general tenor of the resolution, wished that it might be worded a little less harshly. He asked to have the resolution re-read.

MR. SMITH thought that the delay might prevent action, but still was in favor of a committee to confer with the booksellers. He himself did not follow the rule laid down by the publishers in his purchases.

MR. VICKERS said that he addressed to the Convention of Booksellers a letter explaining the position of the librarians, but in the proceedings printed in full in the *Publishers' Weekly* the letter was suppressed.

MR. BOWKER, having been familiar with all the facts in the case, and especially with the publication of the proceedings, explained that the letter was referred to a committee that failed to furnish a report for publication. The letter was thus lost from the proceedings, but there had been no design of suppressing it, and he regretted that such an impression existed.

There was present a bookseller whom every librarian respected, and who, familiar with the whole subject, was still disinterested personally, as he did not deal in American books. He asked Mr. Christern of New York to give his opinion on the subject.

MR. CHRISTERN.—I have no direct interest in the controversy, but having been present at the Convention in Niagara, think that I can give an impartial view of the matter. The general feeling of the retail trade is, that the retail prices are too high, and it is the desire of all booksellers to have them so reduced that they cease to be imaginary. No greater mistake has ever been made than giving discount to professional buyers, as—with the exception of general literature—no books, medical, theological, etc., are published for any other buyers than those belonging to the corresponding profession. If this abuse could be abolished, the libraries would be in a preferred position, as they and the schools would be the only parties to whom the discount of twenty per cent would be allowed. To allow more than twenty per cent will not only deprive the bookseller of his legitimate profit, but will involve a direct loss, as the expenses for handling books are uniformly found to be fifteen per cent in a well-paying business, and comparatively more in small establishments. The whole question seems to be, whether it will be desirable to break up the retail stores all over the country, rather than for librarians and booksellers to co-operate in abolishing abuses, of which both complain. Consequently, I think that it should not not be exclusively a matter of dollars and cents how libraries are provided with books, and that it is wrong to buy from unreliable sellers, who can be proven to sell for less than cost, and therefore *must* become dishonest. The comparison between a man who buys silver-ware for less than the acknowledged value and becomes liable to the law, and the buyer of books at less than cost price, when he has been informed of the fact, may be a little too strong, but certainly there is some justice in it.

MR. PEOPLES.—Since the organization of the American Book Trade Association, most all of my purchases have been made from some of its members. I have been able to obtain as good rates as I received before the association was established. In order to do this, I have not been compelled to go in back-doors or in out-of-the-way streets. Soon after its formation, I received from members of the association offers to furnish books at the old rates, and in some instances better terms have been offered than I was able to get when there was no association.

MR. CAPEN moved to strike out the clause, "No librarian is bound to respect," and DR. HOMES seconded the motion, while MR. POOLE wanted the resolution to stand just as it was.

MR. GREEN did not think that there ought to be any antagonism, such as was expressed in the clause, between the two associations, and would favor the amendment.

MR. CUTTER.—I don't see how we can be "bound to respect" a rule which "is both unjust and impolitic." If we vote for the first clause, we vote for the second.

MR. WALTER, having profited by MR. POOLE's skill, felt bound to stand by his resolution, and so was not in favor of the amendment.

The question on the motion to strike out the clause was lost, after which the original resolution was adopted.

• • • •

Amherst Catalogue System.

MR. SMITH said he had carried away from the Convention of 1853 but one idea of special value —that of Mr. Folsom's card catalogue. He felt that the most valuable idea which he should carry away from this Conference would be the system of cataloguing and classification devised by Mr. Dewey, Would Mr. Dewey favor the Conference with a description of his method?

MR. DEWEY.—While I acknowledge the compliment which has been paid to the Amherst method, I must beg to be excused from presenting its claims before this meeting—not that I lack faith in its merits, for the more we use it the more we are convinced of its great value; but the prominent part which I have had in calling this Conference makes me unwilling to use any of its time for a matter in which I have so much personal interest. I have therefore asked several friends who had proposed to call the matter up that they would not do so. Those interested will find explanations in the Government Report, and I shall gladly furnish any additional information at any time.

MR. CAPEN.—Mr. President: On several occasions, since the opening of this Convention, we have heard the plan of our Secretary alluded to as one of great value, as the discovery of the age, in face, in regard to library management. But every attempt, thus far, to draw it from him has resulted in postponement, as I have fondly hoped, only for a favorable opportunity to disclose it. It now seems that we may adjourn without having our curiosity gratified. For one, I must express myself in terms of great disappointment, and hope that our friend will suffer our many entreaties to prevail over his modesty.

MR. DEWEY said he was willing to answer any

questions or give any explanations that the Conference might require, and being again called upon, briefly described his method. In answer to inquiries he further said, We do not claim that our scheme solves all the difficulty of cataloguing and administering a library. We only claim that it helps very much in many respects, without any corresponding loss. I am often asked, "What would *you* do in such and such a case?" and I often answer, "What do *you* do in such a case?" and an answer being given, I say, "Well, do just the same in using our system, which neither removes nor increases the difficulty you mention." Our system won't make folios and sixteens fit the same shelf without undue waste of space; it won't secure a perfect regularity in the sequence of the different colored bindings at the same time that the books are minutely classed by subjects; it won't remedy leaky roofs nor entirely atone for defective ventilation. These things, and others that I might mention, are out of its province.

There is one objection to our system which does not apply to the common method of numbering shelves and books. In the common system this book which we find to-day at the end of this shelf nearest this window, will be found just there ten years from to-day, and knowing its place, we might in this special case come in here and get the book in the dark. In our system, new books on this subject coming in would probably make it necessary that this book should dress down the line and make room for the new recruits, so ten years after we should be unable to find the book in the dark.

MR. SMITH.—I should like to say that the number of people who visit our libraries in the dark is not large enough to make this objection very formidable.

MR. DEWEY.—This was the only point on which we had any doubt in adopting our plan some three years ago. After actual trial we found that the difficulties were mostly imaginary, and since I have been here I have been surprised and delighted to learn that a number of the largest and best managed of the Western libraries, as well as some in the East, and in England, use this same principle of which we had a fear, and which I term, in distinction from the absolute location on a given portion of a given shelf, the relative location. Among these libraries are Cincinnati, Chicago, St. Louis, and San Francisco, and I no longer doubt that the library of the future is to assign numbers to its books, which are permanent, and not to its shelves, which are liable to frequent changes. The librarian should be able to marshal, arrange, and manage his books as a commander does his troops. Each book in the relative location has its space relatively to its fellows, and the library can be arranged in any building, on shelves of any length, or on the floor if necessary, without confusion or disarrangement.

MR. SCHWARTZ.—I wish to ask Mr. Dewey what provision there is in his system for subdividing his classes. Suppose he has in a certain class a series of books numbered from one to one thousand; he wishes to subdivide this class; what is he going to do with these numbers?

MR. DEWEY.—Our system is not excelled for the facility with which the classes themselves may be subdivided; 4th, 5th, etc., figures may be added indefinitely, each new figure dividing the subject into ten sub-headings. This principle is of the greatest value in indexing and analyzing, especially periodicals and collected works. This subdivision may be applied to catalogues and shelves, or to either separately. If extended to the shelves, there are in our present plan two ways of over-coming the difficulty of which Mr. Schwartz asks. One is to erase the book numbers (written in pencil as most libraries write all their numbers) and assign new numbers. This involves no change in the class number, which is written in ink and is permanent, the subdivision being effected by simply adding the required figures to the end; *e. g.,* The History of England is 942. If the Reign of Elizabeth were the third sub-section of English history, it would bear the number 9423. A second method of meeting the difficulty is to write the book-numbers in ink, and, when a subdivision is made let the book-number accompany the book to its new sub-section, filling in the occurring vacancies with new books.

Either of these plans works perfectly in practice, still this subdivision of book-numbers is one of the points on which we claim no improvement on ordinary methods. We commenced an alphabetical arrangement, in which, of course, this difficulty would not arise. Because of the greater simplicity, and more because of the greater convenience in calling for and charging books, we afterwards adopted our present, the common, plan of giving in each class consecutive numbers to the books received. I have thought that the system of Mr. Schwartz might be used to advantage in our book numbers, but I have never given it actual trial. The use of the book number admits of shelf lists in book form, and the annual examination and daily circulation can be managed more easily than where the alphabetical arrangement is adopted. Still the rapidity with which Mr. Yates handles his alpha-

betically arranged books must convince us all that some of the objections to that arrangement are more imaginary than real.

The Secretary requested those desiring to become members of the new library organization to sign the articles of association which were on the table. He also requested all those who had copies of the Government Report to sign a receipt for the copy taken. The fact that the twenty-five copies of Mr. Cutter's rules (which were on no condition to be taken from the room) had lasted not quite as many minutes after being placed on the table, was mentioned as an illustration of Wednesday night's warning to beware of specialists who were prone to carry off the volumes which they most thoroughly appreciated.

He also specially requested the librarians present to remember practically the collection of library blanks, catalogues, and other appliances for illustrating in detail the management of libraries. All approved highly of the collection, but many would neglect to contribute their share. It was the property of the Association, and would be free to every member for consultation, and every member should feel bound to send the requested two copies of each catalogue, blank, card, slip, or any appliance used in his library, noting on each its ues, cost, and any improvement to be suggested after actual use. As foreign librarians would be specially invited to contribute to, and draw from, this collection, there would thus be gathered by the Association a Museum of Comparative Bibliography and Bibliothecal Appliances.

The session having extended an hour beyond the usual time for the noon recess, the president announced that there would be no meeting in the afternoon, and that in the evening the librarians of Philadelphia would entertain the members of the Conference socially, in accordance with the invitation which each delegate had received personally.

On motion, the Conference then adjourned, to meet again at the call of the board of officers.

During the afternoon a large number of the delegates accepted the invitation to visit the magnificent Masonic Temple, where the librarian, Mr. Meyer, showed them every attention.

In the evening the librarians, with other literary gentlemen and ladies of Philadelphia, received the visiting delegates at the rooms of the Historical Society. The evening was spent in informal social intercourse, during which an elegant collation was served. And thus ended, with pleasant words and good cheer, the Centennial CONFERENCE OF LIBRARIANS.

Selections from the Proceedings of the Conference of Librarians

London, October 2nd, 3rd, 4th, and 5th, 1877.

FIRST SITTING,

TUESDAY MORNING, OCTOBER 2nd, AT 10.

The members assembled in the lecture theatre of the London Institution, Finsbury Circus, which had been offered for their meetings by the Board of Management of the Institution.

• • • •

The officers having taken their places, the President proceeded to read the

Inaugural Address

By John Winter Jones, Librarian of the British Museum, and President of the Conference

Ladies and Gentlemen,

We live in an age of congresses and conferences—which means that we live in an age when the advantages of the interchange of thoughts, ideas, and experiences are fully appreciated, and the benefits to be derived from unity of action in the affairs of life are recognized. The idea of holding a Conference of Librarians originated in America—in that country of energy and activity which has set the world so many good examples, and of which a Conference of Librarians is not the least valuable, looking to the practical results which may be anticipated from it. The present meeting differs somewhat from that held last year at Philadelphia. At Philadelphia there was but one visitor from Europe, and the members were naturally and necessarily engaged in constructing plans, discussing questions, and arriving at conclusions with the object of perfecting their library system; but with little personal aid from the experience of other countries. The present Conference will have the advantage not only of the presence of many of the able and accomplished men who took a leading part in the Philadelphia Conference, but also of the representatives of many of the important libraries of the Continent, from whom we may also look for much assistance in our deliberations.

Prior to the year 1835 there had been little discussion, if any, about public libraries. In that and the following years a committee of the House of Commons held an inquiry into the condition of the British Museum, in the course of which much valuable information was collected bearing upon the questions which will form the subjects of our deliberations, and especially upon the nature and extent of libraries, home and foreign, and upon the degree in which they were made to promote study and learning. In the years 1848 and 1849 another inquiry by a Royal Commission took place into the constitution and management of the British Museum, and of this inquiry the question of catalogues and the principles upon which they should be compiled formed a prominent feature. These inquires, and the discussions to which they gave rise, brought prominently forward the importance of framing catalogues systematically, and, in fact, gave the first impetus to the study in this country of what the Germans call *Bibliothekswissenschaft*. The chief promoter of these questions in both inquires, and especially in the latter, was my predecessor, Sir Anthony Panizzi, who fought his battle against difficulties which would have been discouraging to many. But he was well supported by the sympathy of learned men, not only in England but on the

SOURCE: Reprinted from *The Library Journal* II, 5–6 (January–February 1878), pp. 245–246, 99–119, 259–265, 267–270.

Continent and in America. There is also another gentleman, whose early efforts for the extension of libraries ought not to be passed over without acknowledgment. I allude to Mr. Edward Edwards, whose works on libraries are well known, and who exerted himself to bring together information respecting the libraries of different countries under circumstances necessarily of considerable difficulty.

So far as the public libraries in America are concerned, the Bureau of Education issued last year a special report, showing their history, condition, and management, the first part of which fills an octavo volume of 1,187 pages. This is a remarkable document and stands alone. It brings into one view the results of the exertions made by the American Government for the education of the people, and contains ample evidence of the care and ability with which their national libraries are administered.

Unfortunately we do not possess the same ample details respecting the libraries of the British Colonies. In New South Wales there is the Free Public Library of Sydney and the Library of the University of Sydney. Melbourne is much better supplied. In addition to the Melbourne Public Library, there is the Library of the Parliament of Victoria, the Library of the Legislative Council, the Library of the Supreme Court of Victoria, the Library of the University of Melbourne, and the Melbourne Diocesan Library. In South Australia, Adelaide has its Library of the South Australian Institute, and Tasmania the Tasmanian Public Library established in Hobart Town.

The President of the Public Library of Victoria, Sir Redmond Barry, will probably communicate to the members of the Conference some details relating to these libraries, which cannot be otherwise than highly interesting.

The objects of the present Conference are simply practical. It would, therefore, be out of place to occupy many minutes with speculations about ancient libraries. It may be assumed that wherever writing has been practised libraries of some kind have been formed. The evidence of the existence of ancient libraries is very scanty, depending much on the nature of the material upon which the writing was inscribed. We know more of the collections of Assyria and Babylonia than of other countries, from the simple fact that their records were inscribed on clay and stone instead of on perishable materials.

Many early writers have referred in their works to libraries, but we have no precise account either of their nature or extent. According to Diodorus Siculus, a public library was founded in Egypt by King Osymandyas, who is supposed to have reigned about 600 years after the Deluge. Large collections of Manuscripts were formed at a later period, and especially that founded at Alexandria by Ptolemy Soter, which developed into the celebrated Alexandrian Library under the fostering care of subsequent kings. The number of volumes contained in it must have been very large, although it may be doubted whether it ever reached the enormous quantity of 700,000. The story of its destruction in the seventh century, as recorded by Abu-lfaragius, is too well known, and its accuracy too uncertain, to make repetition desirable.

Of the early libraries of Greece little is recorded, and still less positively known. The libraries formed in Rome appear to have been more numerous than those of Greece, dating from about the second century before the Christian era. Isidorus, Plutarch, Suetonius, and other writers, mention the libraries of Paulus Aemilius, of Sulla, of Lucullus, &c., but none of these collections have descended to us. As collections they have been dispersed or destroyed, and all that we now inherit of these treasures are copies, the oldest of which does not date farther back than about the fourth century.

Of many of the royal and monastic libraries formed during the Middle Ages we have more precise accounts, but any statements respecting them would extend this address far beyond its proper limits.

Let us turn now to the branch of our subject in which we are more immediately interested—printed books. The opposing claims of Germany and the Low Countries, of Mentz and of Haarlem, to the honour of having produced the first specimen of typography, have long been under discussion. For upwards of three hundred years learned and ingenious men have occupied themselves with this subject. The claims of Haarlem have, of course, been loudly advocated by Dutchmen, and Germans have been no less earnest in their advocacy of the claims of Mentz, leaving the question very much as they found it. A Dutchman named Hadrianus Junius commenced the discussion in favour of Haarlem about the year 1569. Another Dutchman, Dr. Van der Linde, has taken the opposite side. By his exhaustive work, "De Haarlemsche Costerlegende wetenschappelijk ondersocht," a second edition of which was published in 1870, he proves that Junius's statements are not founded on facts, that many of his documents are myths, that Haarlem has no claim at all, and that all the evidence is in favour of Mentz.

The first printing types were generally cut in close imitation of the writing used in manuscripts, and, as the caligraphers of each nation had their peculiar style of writing, the early printed books display a striking national character.

At the time when printing began to be exercised there was little intercourse between different countries—the human mind was not so cosmopolitan as it has become since the invention of printing. The earliest books, therefore, show especially the prevailing studies of a nation—jurisprudence and speculative philosophy in one, classical learning and poetry in another, history and romance in a third, and theology in all.

It is not known that any book was printed out of Germany up to the year 1462. No book is known bearing the date 1463 or 1464. This circumstance is attributed to the war between Adolph von Nassau and Diether von Isenburg, the two rival archbishops of Mentz. The former obtained possession of Mentz and sacked the city in 1462. The printers were dispersed, and printing slumbered for the next two years. But light soon sprang up from this darkness. The wandering printers settled in different places on the Continent, spreading a knowledge of their art wherever they went, and especially in Italy. In Rome there were more than twenty Germans who printed from the year 1465 to 1480. In Venice there were upwards of twenty Germans whose books are dated from 1469 to 1480. In Naples there were eight Germans and one Belgian, and in Padua eight Germans and one Dutchman, up to the year 1480. There were about 110 Germans exercising their craft prior to the year 1480 in twenty-seven different cities. About the year 1480 there were established in Italy alone not less than forty printing presses in as many different places, whilst in Germany there were only fifteen. Printing was introduced also into France and Spain by the Germans, who likewise came into England and worked at Oxford and in London, and possibly also at St. Alban's, soon after Caxton established his press at Westminster Abbey. The above statements will show how largely the world is indebted to the Germans not only for the introduction of printing, but for its diffusion throughout Europe during the fifteenth century. The wonderful activity of the printing press during that period is not generally known. Hain, in his "Repertorium Bibliographicum," published in the years 1826 to 1838, enumerates 16,299 works and editions which were issued prior to the year 1500. Considerable additions could now doubtless be made to this number.

A list of some leading subjects connected with library formation and management has been placed in the hands of the members of the Conference. This list is of a very comprehensive nature, embracing as it does a reference to all the details which demand the attention of the librarian, and upon the due appreciation of and mastery over which must depend the success of his administration. It is evident that in an address these subjects can only be very slightly touched upon, and that they must be left to be worked out by the papers submitted to the Conference and the discussions amongst its members.

The first subject proposed for discussion is the extension and first formation of libraries.

This is a large subject. It is at the same time a subject of the gravest importance, comprehending as it does the foundation of the library system, upon which rests the usefulness of these institutions.

Libraries are general or special.

Whether a library should be general or special must depend upon the locality in which it is placed, and the class of persons for whose use it is intended.

Of the importance of libraries for large communities there can be no question, and it is equally true that no community is so small as to render a library unnecessary or undesirable.

Forty years ago the subject of the formation of public libraries had hardly been mooted. London, Edinburgh, Dublin, and the two English Universities had their libraries—more or less accessible to readers; Manchester had its Chetham Library, and London had also Archbishop Tenison's Library. Sion College Library and the Library at Lambeth Palace were also accessible to scholars. There were also libraries in certain parts of Ireland and Scotland more or less available for the purposes of study and research. But it was not until the years 1849 and 1850 that the subject was brought prominently before the English public by the labours of the Select Committee of the House of Commons, appointed on the motion of Mr. William Ewart, the member for the Dumfries Burghs, on the best means of extending the establishment of libraries freely open to the public, especially in large towns in Great Britain and

Ireland. In their second report, issued in the year 1850, the Committee say: "Your Committee are of opinion that the evidence which they have received shows the expediency of establishing in this metropolis other public libraries of a popular character, by which the British Museum would be relieved from a numerous class of readers who might be equally well accommodated elsewhere." And again: "Your Committee see no reason to vary the general conclusion arrived at by your Committee in the last Session of Parliament respecting the main object and scope of their inquiry, that this country is still greatly in want of libraries freely accessible to the public."

These inquiries led to the passing of the Public Libraries Acts, the provisions of which were at once adopted by Manchester, Salford, and Liverpool, and subsequently by other great commercial and industrial centers, with a success which must have amply rewarded the earnest and intelligent men who saw with intuitive appreciation the advantages, moral and intellectual, which would result from placing within reach of their diversified populations the means of mental culture, special education, and innocent amusement.

Libraries for general readers are desirable in all localities, for, however each particular community may be constituted, there must always be many who desire general education, and many to be allured from idleness and dissipation. But the formation of such libraries is a serious charge, the weight of which increases in inverse proportion with the extent of the population. A librarian ought to be much more than an officer to take charge of a collection of books; he ought to be an educator; he has to consider the characters of those for whom the library is formed, and to make his selection of works accordingly. Where the population is large, and the library to be formed large in proportion, this is a comparatively easy task. But when the community is small, the greatest care is required to insure the formation of such a collection as shall be strictly adapted to its wants, and shall supply the most nutritious pabulum for the mind.

Early in the present century efforts were made in several districts to supply the means of self-culture by the formation of literary institutions, of which a library was a prominent feature. These were followed by mechanics' institutes; and for several years the movement was successful. But some of these establishments, so far as London is concerned, have not maintained their original vigour. Some are already dead—one at least may be considered to be dying, for it has recently changed its lecture room into a billiard and smoking room, which is certainly far from a literary or intellectual purpose. The London Institution stands out an honourable exception to these indications of decay. I do not here allude to the thirty or forty small associations established in the various suburban districts, or the Young Men's Christian Association with its 150 branches.

It may be asked, Why should there be this falling off amongst the older institutions if the necessity for the formation of libraries be so strongly felt? The reason may be looked for in the fact that mental inquiry has penetrated much deeper than it had when these institutions were first founded, and that the increase of knowledge has brought with it the natural subdivision of subjects, and the consequent concentration of thought upon the several distinct branches of investigation. Hence the multiplication of societies, each with its library devoted to the particular study which occupies the attention of its members.

The above remarks apply to libraries formed for general readers. Those collections which are brought together for the use of students of special branches of learning are certainly not of less importance; their practical utility may be indeed considered to exceed that of the general library.

In our manufacturing districts it is a matter of necessity that the managers of the various establishments and the workmen employed therein should have ready access to all such works as can assist them in their special faculties, either by suggesting new forms or constructive details, or by cultivating their taste and enabling them to appreciate the beautiful in art, and to distinguish between what is true and what is false. London has been recently visited by a deputation representing sixty of our principal cities and towns, whose object is to obtain for their districts assistance in the way of gifts and loans of books and works of art which may help the manufacturers and artisans in their respective productions.

The next subject for investigation is that of library buildings.

In selecting the site for a library care should be taken to make it as accessible as possible to those for whose use it is constructed. If a general library, that it should be central. If special, that should be placed as near as possible to the locality frequented by those who require its aid. This may appear to be a truism; but it is something more; for it touches the question of providing more libraries than one in wide-spreading districts, where the one library or one museum cannot be brought to the doors of all. Those who have experience in the management of a library will know how important it is to save the time, the labour, and the money of students, all of which must be expended overmuch if the visitor to the library find himself at a distance from the collection he desires to consult.

The material of which library buildings should be constructed is a most important subject for consideration. The great danger to be guarded against is, of course, fire. For this purpose iron is better than stone, and brick better than either. A great authority upon such subjects (Captain Shaw) has stated that he considers staircases constructed of stone to be more dangerous than those made of wood, because, although wooden staircases will ignite and burn, stone staircases when over-heated are liable to split and fall bodily, and thus the communication for which they have been erected to be lost. Iron and brick, therefore, appear to be the materials which should be used whenever it may be practicable to do so.

Iron is particularly applicable to the construction of presses for the books. Each press may be formed by iron standards placed at distances of, say, three feet apart. The shelves also may be made of iron set in wooden frames, with nosings, as they are technically called, so constructed as to allow of the insertion of the leathern or cloth fall intended to protect the tops of the books from dust. The shelves should be covered with leather for the purpose of protecting the books from injury. A depth of fifteen inches will take a large folio, and where still greater depth is required a second standard placed in front of the first will afford all the necessary additional space. It is most important that the distance between the standards, which regulates the length of the shelf, should be in all cases exactly the same. The reason for this will appear in a subsequent part of this address. It is also to be recommended that the presses should not be more than about eight feet high, so that books on the top shelf may be reached by means of light, dwarf hand-steps. Ladders or high steps in a library are very inconvenient and very dangerous.

The system here recommended is economical as well as safe. Each standard or shelf is a multiple of its fellow—one mould serves for all—and a library so constructed may almost defy fire. Books, we know, are not easy to burn, and in the event of a fire they would be more injured by the water used to extinguish the flames than by the fire itself.

As economy of space is of the utmost importance in arranging the contents of a library, it is very desirable to adopt such a plan for raising or depressing the shelves as shall leave no more space than may be required by the height of the books to be inserted. Supposing the shelves to be supported by pins let into the woodwork of the shelves, if the peg of the pin be cranked the shelf can be raised or lowered one-half of the distance between the holes in which the pegs are inserted by simply turning them half round. In a large library the amount of space saved by this arrangement will be very considerable.

The furniture of a library must very much depend on the nature of the library for which it is required. There is one point, however, to which it is desirable to draw attention. Every table on which a book is laid or used, and every barrow which is used to carry books from one place to another in the library, should be padded. The additional expense caused by the adoption of this precaution will be amply met by the protection from injury which it will secure for the books.

Where libraries are open in the evening the question of lighting becomes of the first importance. Gas, as commonly used, is bad. It is impossible to secure perfect combustion with the ordinary burner, and nothing can be more destructive to books—and especially to their bindings—than the unconsumed gas, which dries up and rots everything with which it comes in contact. The sunlight burner appears to be the safest form in which gas can be used, but a particular construction of building is necessary for the introduction of this mode of lighting.

There are three systems of warming buildings in general use where open stoves cannot be employed—warming by heated air, and by hot-water pipes, and by steam pipes. Of these three systems, the heating by hot-water pipes is preferable. The heated air is dry and exhausting; all the moisture is burnt out of it, and it is as bad for those who come within its influence as for the books. This objection does not apply to the heating by hot water where the temperature is kept at a moderate height. The air does not come in immediate contact with the fire, and retains its moisture.

Ventilation has always proved a difficult problem to solve: how to get foul air out of an apartment and fresh air in without creating draughts. Where open fires can be used the process is easy enough, but in large rooms without open fires it is otherwise. If the temperature of the air cannot be equalized, the cooler air must move to the place where the air is warmer and more rarefied, and draughts ensue, to the great annoyance of those who have to sit in them. This often leads to the adoption of the use of curtains, closed doors, increase of the temperature, and a consequent increase of mischief in the form of present discomforts and a greater susceptibility to atmospheric influences. This subject is one which deserves, and will amply repay, the most careful consideration of the Conference.

The building in which the library is to be deposited having been constructed, the next question to be considered is, by whom the library is to be governed, and by whom the books are to be selected.

There must be a controlling power, and experience has shown that this power may well be exercised by a committee. But having got so far the difficulties begin to manifest themselves. What is to be the constitution of the committee; what its numbers; what its powers? If the committee be numerous, there is the risk that members will attend irregularly, so that the business transacted at one meeting may at a subsequent meeting come under the consideration of members who know nothing about it. Some members may attend at rare intervals, in which case they may become responsible for orders which they have not given, and may be called upon to legislate upon subjects with the details of which they are unacquainted. The best form of committee would appear to be one composed of about five or seven members, who, by constant attention to the duties committed to their charge, would thoroughly understand the working of the institution, and would be prepared to appreciate the relative importance of the several questions submitted to them for consideration.

It is questionable whether the selection of books for a library should be undertaken by a committee. The formation of a library should be carried out on one uniform plan, an arrangement which is hardly possible where several persons have the right to interfere, each of whom will in all probability have views of his own. There is danger of undue prominence being given to one faculty to the sacrifice of others; or of some class or classes being neglected or prohibited from a want of due appreciation of their value or utility. This risk is greater in small than in large libraries.

The safest, and therefore the best, course is to be very careful in the choice of a librarian, and then to leave the selection of the books to him, subject, of course, to the control of the committee of management wherever the exercise of that control may be deemed to be advisable. However modest the library may be in extent and character, the librarian ought to be a man who has experience in his work. The necessity for this qualification of course increases with the extent and importance of the collection. A librarian cannot know too much, or be too catholic in his knowledge. Devotion to a particular branch of study is a rock which he ought to avoid; and this ought to be borne in mind by those who select him, for it is not given to many men to be able to resist the temptation to follow a favourite pursuit in order that they may devote themselves to the multifarious details of a librarian's office. The man who proposes himself to be a good librarian must be satisfied with knowing an infinite variety of things; he must be content with a general insight into the various faculties, but must not endeavour to be great in any.

The learned author of the life of Isaac Casaubon, Mr. Mark Pattison, says "the librarian who reads is lost;" and this is to a great extent true. It was certainly true in the case of Casaubon, who, in his love for the contents of the books placed under his charge, forgot his duties as a librarian. The licence which a librarian may be allowed to take while in the discharge of his duties was well indicated by the amiable Cary, the translator of Dante, who used to describe himself and his colleagues, while engaged in their task of cataloguing the books of the British Museum Library, as sheep travelling along a road and stopping occasionally to nibble a little grass by the wayside.

A librarian ought, above all things, to possess a knowledge of several languages. In making selections for his library, in cataloguing his books, in conducting his correspondence, this knowledge of languages is of great importance; but he would be wise always to write his letters in his own language, whatever that may be, and not in the language of the person to whom they may be addressed.

A librarian who does not understand several languages besides his own, will find himself constantly at a loss. Many of the most important bibliographies and biographies will be sealed books to him, and it will be impossible for him either to select foreign books for his library, or to catalogue them properly if they come under his charge. He will be dependent on others, which is an unsatisfactory position for a librarian.

Libraries in general obtain accessions through various channels—the first and most direct is by purchase from booksellers or at auctions. Gifts and bequests are the accidental sources through which libraries are also increased. In conducting his purchases each librarian will follow his own system, but it may be remarked that the employment of agents for the purchase of books is not always the most economical mode of procedure, excepting in the case of purchases at auctions, or in foreign countries where the transactions are large and extend over several countries. Agents must of course be paid for their time and trouble and skill, and it is very desirable that a careful balance should be struck between the commission paid to them and the saving otherwise effected by this mode of transacting business. It may be that the purchases abroad would involve so large a correspondence, and consequently occupy the time of so large a staff, that the employment of an agent might be the best economy. In this case the librarian will have to pay particular attention to the fluctuating exchanges of the several countries concerned. As regards purchases at sales by auction, it is always the most prudent course that these should be effected through the agency of booksellers, who keep their clients' names in the background, and occupy in every respect a neutral position.

There is no branch of the work of the librarian which has given rise to so much discussion within the last forty years as that of cataloguing. The battle of short titles or full and accurate titles has been fought with as much pertinacity as that of the broad or narrow gauge for railways. Whatever is worth doing is worth doing well, and this hackneyed truism applies as forcibly to the work of the cataloguer as to any other operation. When Dr. Cogswell was engaged on the formation of the Astor Library, he issued what he called a finding catalogue, with the title "Alphabetical Index to the Astor Library, or catalogue with short titles of the books now collected and of the proposed accessions, as submitted to the Trustees of the Library for their approval, January, 1851." This, no doubt, was well adapted for the purpose for which it was intended, viz., to give a general idea of the collection he had brought together, and an indication or list of books which he desired to

procure. But his list was not a catalogue in the true sense of the term—nor did he consider it to be so—and yet the same form has since been adopted in many instances. The first step in advance towards fulness of titles is the form more usually employed, comprising the prominent part of the title, with imprint and date and indication of the size of the volume, but this still falls far short of the full and accurate title.

A good title ought to give all that appears on the title-page of the book, with such further information as to authorship, or editorship, &c., or the nature of the contents, as may in addition be derived from the work itself. The catalogue ought to give the person who consults it all the information he can require as to the work described in it.

It is not proposed in this address to criticize existing catalogues, or to institute comparisons between one catalogue and another; but rather to endeavour to lay down a few general principles to be considered and developed by the Conference. It may be permitted, however, to refer to two or three catalogues, with the view of illustrating what is here meant by a full and accurate catalogue. The first to be mentioned is the catalogue of the Bodleian Library, prepared by Hyde, in two parts, and published in 1674. The next, that of the Library of Cardinal Casanate, compiled by Audiffredi, and published as far as the letter K, in the years 1761 to 1788. The last is that of the British Museum Library. These catalogues are mentioned only as examples which may be followed with advantage.

In addition to a careful description of the contents of a book, so far as this information can be derived from the title-pages and introductory matter, or from the volume itself where the title-page does not fully or properly describe the contents, there are cases in which further details would be both interesting and instructive. My attention was drawn to this point by reading an account of the recent Caxton Exhibition, in which it is stated that Caxton did not print the Bible, or any portion of it. This is a mistake. In his edition of Capgrave's "Golden Legend," printed in 1483, Caxton has translated very many passages from the Scriptures, and has thus been the first who printed any portion of the Bible in English. He also, by his translation of verse 7 of the 3rd chapter of Genesis, anticipated the peculiar version which has procured for the Geneva Bible, printed in 1560, the name of the Breeches Bible. He says: "And they toke figge levis and sewed them togyder in maner of brechis." The translation of those portions of the Bible which Caxton has printed is not the same as that by Wyclif, who preceded him by more than a hundred years.

There are other bibliographical details which may well be added as notes to the titles of the books to which they respectively relate.

Aldus, it is well known, introduced the italic type. His object was to print cheap books, and for this purpose to use the type which would allow the greatest quantity of matter to be brought within the smallest space. For the designing of this type he employed the celebrated painter and goldsmith, Francesco Raibolini, also called Francesco da Bologna, and commonly known as Francia. It is said that Francia took the handwriting of Petrarch as the model for his type. This type was first used in printing an edition of Virgil, which bears the date of April, 1501. Aldus also printed in the same year, but three months later, a beautiful edition of "Le Cose Volgari di Petrarcha."

Printing had been in existence several years before any system of punctuation was generally adopted. A straight stroke passing obliquely through the line generally indicated a pause, and a full point closed a paragraph. A colon was occasionally introduced, and the "Lactantius," printed at Subiaco in 1465 (the first book printed in Italy), has a full point, colon, and note of interrogation. But improvements by one printer were not followed by others, and it was not until about the year 1470 that we approach to the mode of punctuation adopted at the present day. The first book printed in France was the "Liber Epistolarum" of Gasparinus Barzizius, which was produced by three Germans, Crantz, Gering, and Freiburger, and contains the full point, semicolon, comma, parenthesis, note of interrogation, and note of admiration. But the semicolon appears to have more force than the full point, for while it is used reversed indiscriminately with the full point in the middle or at the end of a sentence, it is alone used at the end of a chapter or of a heading to a chapter, and then turned as we use it now. It will be observed that the colon is wanting in this book altogether.

The necessity of some guide for the proper arrangement of the leaves of a book was not met until the year 1470, when Arnoldus Terhoernen, of Cologne, introduced a modified pagination by numbering the leaves of his edition of the "Sermo ad Populum." In the following year he printed the "Liber de Remediis utriusque Fortunæ" of Adrianus Carthusiensis, in which he placed the numbering in the centre of the margin of the recto of each leaf.

The early printers neglected the use of signatures, although they had been used by the copyists of manuscripts long before the introduction of printing. The earliest instance we have of the use of signatures is in the "Præceptorium Divinæ Legis" of Johannes Nider, printed at Cologne, by Johann Koelhof, in 1472.

Catchwords were introduced before signatures, and were doubtless intended to answer the same purpose. They appear for the first time in the first edition of "Tacitus," printed by Johann de Spira, at Venice, about the year 1469.

The last step towards the completion of a printed book was not made until some years later—viz., in 1487—when the "Confessionale" of Antoninus, Archbishop of Florence, was printed with a regular title-page at Strassburg, probably by Martin Flach. An approach to a title-page had been made as early as the year 1476, at Venice, by Bernardus Pictor, Petrus Löslein, and Erhardus Ratdolt, who in that year printed an edition of the "Calendarium" of Monteregius.[1] To this calendar the printers prefixed a leaf containing, in ten lines of Latin hexameters, a laudatory description of the calendar, and the names of the printers, with the place of printing.

It would also be interesting to show that the "Etymologiæ" of Isidore of Seville, printed by Günther Zainer at Augsburg in 1472, was the first book printed in Germany in which the Roman character was used. Also, that this character was used for the first time in Italy by Sweynheim and Pannartz in 1467, when they printed at Rome the "Epistolæ ad Familiares" of Cicero. That the Roman character was introduced into England by Pynson in 1509, who printed in it some portions of his "Sermo Fratris Hieronymi de Ferraria," and that his edition of the "Oratio Ricardi Pacæi," printed in 1518, is said to be the first book wholly printed in this character in England.

These instances are only introduced *exempli gratia*, as a bibliographical dissertation would be out of place on the present occasion.

There is much diversity of opinion as to the best form of catalogue, that is, whether the titles should be arranged alphabetically under the author's names, or whether they should be classed according to the subjects. Each system has its advantages, and each its difficulties. Readiness of reference is one of the first objects to be considered. If the author's name be known, his works will be found more readily in an alphabetical than in a classed catalogue; if not, a classed catalogue may, perhaps, be the best guide. But difficulties again present themselves under both systems. It may be doubtful what is the real name of an author, or what form of name ought to be used. Melanchthon's name was Schwartzerd, but his uncle thought proper to give it a Greek form, and he himself adopted that form. Dante's surname was Alighieri, but his father's name was Frangipane. De Rossi sometimes translated his name into Greek, and called himself Erythræus, and sometimes into Latin, and called himself De Rubeis. Proctor had made the name of Barry Cornwall so completely his own that by some he was not known under his proper name; and, if we turn to the early painters, the rejection of the surname in favour of an appellation, as Tintoretto, or the Christian name, as Michael Angelo, is almost universal. It is hardly necessary to refer to the gifted ladies who have given a world-wide fame to the name of Bell, or to other modern writers of the same class. French names present considerable difficulties. In the catalogue of the British Museum these are met by adopting the first family name, as Arouet de Voltaire, and not Voltaire, and the article instead of the preposition, as La Grange, and not De la Grange. But the rule of adopting the article instead of the preposition ought to be confined to France and her dependencies. In Belgium there are many such names, but the preposition, article, and name are all combined in one, and therefore the name ought to be entered in the catalogue under "De," as it would be in England in such cases as De la Beche, De la Rue, &c.

It has been proposed by some to enter the book under the name which appears on the title-page; but this system would certainly scatter the works of some authors throughout the catalogue, and be no better than an excuse for idleness or a cover for ignorance.

The safe course is to adopt one form, and to make cross-references from all the others. If this course be strictly carried out, the particular form adopted for the general heading becomes a matter of secondary importance.

But there is a very large class of books which present greater difficulties than those which bear names of uncertain form—that is, anonymous works. These works have at all times presented a stumbling-block to cataloguers. When it was

determined to reduce to one system the several catalogues of the British Museum library which had been compiled at different times and on different plans, it was anticipated that about thirty rules would suffice for the purpose, and it was proposed, *inter alia*, that anonymous works should be catalogued under the first word, not being an article or a preposition, following in this suggestion the rule laid down by Barbier in his "Dictionnaire des Anonymes." It was ultimately determined that the leading word should be adopted, and then our troubles began; what was to be done when there were two or more leading words, and was the first always to be taken, or was the cataloguer to decide which was the most leading word? In the effort to meet all these cases, and others of equal difficulty, the thirty rules grew to be nearly one hundred.

In the construction of a classified catalogue doubts will frequently arise as to the class under which a particular work should be entered. The life of a distinguished individual may be more nearly allied to history than to biography; what is the exact class under which works on canals should be entered? Is it known to every unscientific reader that peat moss is a mineral? The remedy which has been suggested for these difficulties is to enter the doubtful title under each of the classes to which it may be supposed to belong; but this is a very unscientific mode of procedure, and in the case of a large catalogue (and every librarian hopes that his catalogue may become large) the addition of titles produced by such a process is a serious evil. It may be assumed that the books in all libraries will be classed on the shelves, and will have attached to each volume a mark indicating its particular place in the library. Where an alphabetical catalogue is adopted, if one copy of the title-slips be mounted on cardboard and arranged according to the press-marks, a classed catalogue will be secured. The reverse process could not be so well adopted with a classed catalogue, as this would involve the addition of authors' names, &c., to each of the titles. Many, if not all, of the difficulties above referred to would disappear if an index of subjects were added to the catalogue. Each thing would be entered under its name, and peat moss would find its name under letter P, without the cataloguer having to learn whether it belonged to botany or to mineralogy, neither would he have to enter into the question of the claims of botany for those remarkable and innumerable productions known as Diatomaceæ, which he would place at once under letter D. Indices of this nature are very elastic, and meet all the cases of works treating on several subjects, for each subject would have an entry to itself. The entries would be very short, not exceeding one line, and would be very rapidly made, provided they were made at the same time that the book was catalogued, when the subject of the book would be full in the mind of the cataloguer. When he had written the title for the catalogue, the index-slips could be prepared without effort, and certainly in less than half the time they would occupy if made subsequently; for it must be borne in mind that the index-slip ought to be made from the book and not from the catalogue title. The adoption of such an index would also enable the cataloguer to dispense with very many cross-references.

The rules for all catalogues ought to be as simple as possible, but for small libraries more simple than for large libraries. Not that the same amount of information ought not to be given in each title, but that a certain amount of classification which may be useful in the catalogue of a large library is not required in that of a small collection of books. It may be well that the catalogue of a large library should show under one heading what periodicals or transactions of societies it may possess, but such works may very well be catalogued separately in libraries of small dimensions.

Professor Jewett, the first librarian of the Smithsonian Institution, has said that the scholars of all nations demand of Great Britain that the catalogue of the library of the British Museum should be well done, and should be a work of bibliographical authority. What is here said of the catalogue of the British Museum ought to be said of all catalogues. Every librarian ought to compile his catalogue with these same results in view, and endeavour to make it as perfect as possible: not to be contented with producing a work which shall be merely generally satisfactory. Cataloguing against time is a mistake.

The subject of rules for catalogues will occupy the attention of the Conference, and can only be slightly touched upon in this address. There are, however, one or two points on which it may be well that I should say a few words. One of these points is the designation of the sizes of books. As regards modern books, the folding of the sheets of paper is generally received as the guide, but it is not a guide which speaks to the eye. Some duodecimos may be larger than some octavos, and some octavos may be larger than some folios, to

say nothing of the uncertainty of the quartos. When we come to ancient books, the matter is still worse. The early printers did not use large sheets of paper and fold them twice or more to form quartos, octavos, &c., but merely folded their paper once, thus making what is now understood by the terms folios or quartos according to the size of the sheet of paper. Three or more of these sheets were laid one within another, and formed gatherings or quires, each sheet after the first in each gathering being called an inlay. This printing by gatherings was adopted for the convenience of binding. The consequence of this practice would be that the printer would either print one page at a time or two, but no more. If two, he would have to divide the matter to be printed into portions sufficient for eight, twelve, sixteen, or twenty pages, according to the number of inlays in each gathering, and then print, say, the first and twelfth, then the second and the eleventh, and so on; and the result of this practice is occasionally seen in an inequality in the length of the pages, particularly in the centre inlay, which would be printed last, and would therefore have either too much or too little matter if the calculation of the quantity necessary for each page had not been exact. It has been suggested that the difficulty might be met by adopting the size of the printed page as the guide, but such a guide would certainly be fallacious. It would not indicate the size of the volume; it would not allow for the many cases of "oceans of margin and rivers of text;" it would not speak to the eye without opening the book. The better plan would appear to be to adopt, to a certain extent, the system used by book-binders. As they regulate their charges according to the size of the millboard required for binding their book, their scale is independent of the folding of the printed sheet. It contains twenty-nine divisions or designations of different sizes, of which twenty-six represent modifications of the five sizes of folio, 4to, 8vo, 12mo, and 18mo, a striking proof of the uncertainty of the sizes supposed to be indicated by these five terms. I speak, of course, of the measure used by English bookbinders. It would certainly be advisable that some rule should be laid down, which might apply to all countries, by which the general sizes of books might be designated and minute subdivisions be avoided. Why should we designate sizes by paper marks, and talk of pot quartos and foolscap octavos? The pot and the foolscap are things of the past. It would surely be better to adopt some such rule as the following: to designate as 12mo all books not exceeding 7 inches in height; as 8vo all those above 7 and not exceeding 10 inches in height; as 4to those above 10 and not exceeding 12 inches in height; and as folio all above 12 inches. The folios might be further described, according to the fact, as *large* or *super*, in order to avoid the various subdivisions of crown, copy, demy, medium, royal, imperial, elephant, and columbier folio.

Other designations applying to the bulk or substance of a publication are equally indefinite. A distinction ought to be drawn between a volume, a pamphlet, a single sheet, and a broadside; or rather one general agreement ought to be arrived at upon this branch of our subject. It may be urged, and with much reason, that every work which is bound should be treated as a volume. A work of an ephemeral nature may be called a pamphlet, but such a work may extend to more than a hundred pages. When is such a work to be raised to the dignity of a volume? It is assumed that the question of pamphlet or no pamphlet will be confined to works in prose. It would be the safest course to apply the term single sheet to a sheet of paper folded once, or printed on both sides without being folded, and the term broadside to a sheet printed only on one side.

But what is to be done with that large and important class, academical dissertations? It is to be assumed that these will not be considered to be pamphlets. And here—as the question of rules for cataloguing is at present being noticed—I may venture to draw attention to the necessity of care in assigning the authorship of these dissertations. In some countries—Germany, for example—the Respondens is, as a rule, the author; in others, as in Sweden, the Præses is the author.

Another point which is of much importance, but upon which there is not at present any agreement among librarians, is the system of literation to be adopted where it becomes necessary to represent in English characters, names or words from languages having special characters of their own. The guide ought to be the pronunciation, but this again may lead to a difficulty. The Russian language, for example, has not the sound which we represent by *th*, but *th* is pronounced like the English *f*; thus, the Russians say "Fedor," and not "Theodore," although they spell the name with a Greek theta. They have the same letter for the soft *v* and the hard *v*. The Germans represent this letter by a *w*, because they pronounce the *w* like an English *v*. Is the Russian letter which is in form like an English *y* to be represented by the vowel *u* or by two *oo?* This question of literation is well deserving the attention of the Conference.

I cannot quit this branch of the subject without alluding to the second part of the Special Report on Public Libraries in the United States, comprising Mr. Cutter's scheme for a Dictionary Catalogue. Mr Cutter has evidently thought out his subject with great care, and has produced a code of Rules of a very comprehensive and exhaustive character. The Dictionary Catalogue appears to comprise in one the alphabetical catalogue, the catalogue by titles, the catalogue by subjects, and the catalogue by classes. The bulk of such a catalogue would be a question demanding very serious consideration. Supposing the titles of a catalogue to be written on separate slips and multiplied, there can be no doubt but that the formation of such a set of catalogues would be of great advantage.

The books in all libraries ought to be carefully classed on the shelves, and the classification to be more minute in proportion as the library increases in extent. The books in the library of the British Museum are separated into nearly 700 divisions and subdivisions. This extent of classification has grown up with the increase of the collection of printed books, and is not found to be more minute than is necessary. The system of classification to be adopted is a question which demands the most careful consideration by the librarian. The decision will naturally be greatly influenced by the character of the library and its future prospects. Many different systems have been proposed from the time of Bacon, who classes human learning under History, Poesy, and Philosophy, down to the present period.

In classifying the library of the British Museum, five principal divisions have been adopted, namely, Theology, Jurisprudence, Philosophy, History, and Belles-Lettres. These are all comprehensive branches, and admit of subdivisions which will embrace every possible class of works.

It has been suggested by some that books should be arranged according to their languages; but this would be a very vicious system, and merely one of the curiosities of classification. It may be interesting to know how many languages are represented in a library, and their relative extent and proportion; but it is much more interesting to be able to see together all the works in the library upon any given subject. An arrangement by languages, moreover, would separate all the translations of a work from its original, and "Uncle Tom's Cabin," for example, would, be scattered all over the library. The same may be said of classifying books according to their place of printing, which would give very interesting and sometimes very useful information. But such objects are better attained by arranging copies of the catalogue upon such systems than the books.

It is necessary to indicate the particular place a book occupies in a library by a press-mark, and it is also necessary so to arrange the system of press-marks that it may be possible to make additions to the library and still keep the several classes together. In the Museum library this object has been secured by distinguishing the presses by numbers, allowing a certain number of presses to each division and subdivision, and then passing over consecutive numbers to be filled in as the accessions to the respective classes outgrow the space occupied by such classes in the first instance. Thus, if works on Danish history occupied one press, and it were calculated that they would ultimately require three, and the first press were numbered 500, the next press, to be occupied, we will say, by Swedish history, would be numbered 503, the numbers 501 and 502 being omitted until press 500 was full, when the Swedish history would be moved on, and the press it occupied would be numbered 501, and receive the continuation of the Danish history. For this system it is of course necessary that all the presses should be of the same width.

The scheme of omitting numbers, which is very simple in principle, is applicable to publications issued periodically, and also to maps. Maps should be placed in Solander cases, where their size does not necessitate their being kept in rolls. The Solander case takes the place of the press, and will be numbered on the same principle; so many numbers being allowed for each country or great division, and the contents of each case having also a subnumber.

But not only ought each press to be numbered, but each shelf ought to be distinguished—and for this purpose a letter of the alphabet is most convenient—and, in addition to this, the place of each book on a shelf ought to be marked by a number. Thus a book may be numbered 400. b. 25, which means that it is the 25th book on the b. or 2nd shelf of press 400.

It is very desirable, where practicable, that hand catalogues, or shelf lists, should be prepared. These are particularly necessary for those parts of a library to which the public may be admitted,

and the contents of the shelves ought to be examined by the shelf lists at short intervals. It secures the maintenance of the books in their proper places, and also indicates the absence of a book from the library. It is also a very useful check upon thieves. The books open to readers in the Museum reading-room are examined every morning—about one-third being passed under review every day—so that in three days the whole of the library of reference is examined, and then the inspection begins *de novo*.

The press-mark of every book ought to be marked upon it inside; it ought also to be clearly indicated on the outside, as this course avoids the necessity of opening the book to ascertain its place in the library, and saves in this way a great deal of time.

The proper mode of dealing with pamphlets is a question of some difficulty. In a large library which is used by many readers, and which possesses adequate funds, the most advisable course would appear to be to bind each pamphlet separately; in this way the person who is consulting one pamphlet will not interfere with others. But this course is much more expensive than binding them in volumes, and for libraries where the income is small the best course would be to arrange the pamphlets in Solander cases according to their subjects, marking on a sliding piece of cardboard the contents of each case, and binding them when enough have been accumulated to form a volume; taking care to bind in the volume only those which treat of the same subject, and which are of the same size.

Public documents and newspapers ought to be bound as soon as possible, as no class of papers are more liable to injury from use without the protection of binding.

Broadsides and single sheets may be conveniently pasted into guard books, as this course admits of their being protected from injury without delay, and renders the use of them more convenient.

With respect to manuscripts, too much care cannot be exercised as to their preservation. Their arrangement cannot be too simple. A strict classification may not always be possible with many collections so far as the manuscripts themselves are concerned, and therefore the best course would be to classify the entries in the catalogue, and adopt a simple plan for finding each manuscript. This may be done by assigning to each manuscript a consecutive number as it is acquired, and then referring from an index of these numbers to the place occupied by the manuscript in the

library. With respect to the preservation of manuscripts, it may be laid down, as a general rule, that
no ancient manuscript already bound ought to be
rebound. It is better that it should be placed,
ragged and dirty, in a case made for its reception
than that it should be exposed to the risks
attendant on cleaning, sizing, &c. The most careful and skilful binders may make mistakes, or, as
it is called, have accidents, and no amount of
regret will remedy an injury to a manuscript. I
have known irreparable mischief done even to
early printed books—the edges of vellum books
cut; vellum plunged into water and shrivelled up;
manuscript notes carefully obliterated, leaving
just enough to show that they were of great importance, and marginal notes cut in half by the
process of ploughing.

The only safe course is to rebind early manuscripts as seldom as possible, and never to allow
any writing, however worthless it may appear, to
be removed. Moreover, where binding is necessary, the process should be carefully watched by
the librarian at all stages of the work.

Drawings and prints may be arranged in various
ways, according to their nature—by schools or by
masters; if topographical, by countries, &c.; but I
would venture to make one suggestion, viz., that
all drawings, and also prints other than those of a
very common kind, should, as far as possible, be
preserved in sunk mounts, so as to protect the
surface from abrasion.

It is greatly to be regretted that the cost of
binding has increased so largely within the last
few years. Bookbinding ought to take its place
among the decorative arts. When the mechanical
operation of sewing the sheets of a book together,
and placing them in covers, is accomplished, the
finisher steps in and completes the work by ornamentation and gilding. The tooling of a book
admits of the greatest variety and elegance of
design, as is shown in the bindings of the sixteenth
century, especially in those for Grolier and Majoli,
and from that time to the present, not forgetting
those of Bauzonnet-Trautz and our own Roger
Payne. But, like all other works of art, fine binding is expensive, and can hardly be indulged in by
public libraries. The skill is not wanting at the
present day, for there are several bookbinders
quite equal to the task of giving to a binding all
the graceful finish that could be desired, but the
cultivation of bookbinding in its highest forms
must now be left for the most part to private
individuals.

In binding books for libraries used by the

public, the first point to be considered is solidity,
so that the book may resist injury from constant
use. To secure this advantage, every sheet ought
to be stitched round each of the bands, which is
not done with cheap binding; and the covers
ought to be fastened by joints. A book so put
together will bear a great deal of handling; and,
although such binding may be more costly in the
first instance, it is the most economical in the
end.

As a general rule, half-binding is sufficiently
strong, and morocco will wear better than any
other leather. It is not liable to split like russia,
which is often injuriously affected by heat. The
leather called imitation Levant morocco is a very
good substitute for morocco and very much
cheaper. But the question of the leather to be
used must depend upon the amount to be expended on this branch of the library service.

It will be found very useful to appropriate a
particular-coloured leather to each of the principal
divisions of the library. It enables the librarian to
see at a glance to what faculty a book belongs. It
will also economize time very much to make the
letterings on the back of a book as full as possible, particularly where a bound volume contains
more works than one.

Loose book-covers are sometimes used for the
purpose of protecting the richly-bound books, but
great care ought to be taken that such covers do
not fit the book tightly. If not large, they are apt
to strain the binding, and in this way do as much
mischief as they prevent, or even more.

Covers of a simple nature are of course necessary
for serials and periodical publications, but the best
course is to bind such works as soon as sufficient
numbers are issued to form a volume.

The library appliances which may be necessary
must depend much on the nature and extent of
the library for which they are required, and will be
naturally suggested by experience. Some indication must, however, be supplied of the books
demanded by readers, and some record kept of the
books which may be in hand. The first of these
objects will be attained by requiring a reader to fill
up the particulars of the book he requires in a
blank form, to be supplied to him for that purpose, which makes him responsible for the book
until he is properly relieved of his responsibility;
and the second either by retaining the form so
filled up, or by entering the particulars in a
register and thus securing a record of the number
and nature of the books used.

The facilities which should be afforded to the

public for admission to public libraries must be regulated by the nature, extent, and object of each particular library. The age at which persons should be admitted must also be regulated by the same conditions. Readers visit libraries for different purposes. The student and writer ought not to be mixed up with the mere reader of novels and periodical literature or newspapers. This consideration has led to the establishment of two reading-rooms, where such accommodation can be afforded, and this in foreign countries as well as in our own. Where there is not available space for two reading-rooms, and the visitor to the one room may ask to be furnished with rare and costly works, the only course is to limit the admission to persons of a certain age, and to require from each applicant a guarantee of his or her respectability. It is much more easy to do this than to say that a particular reader may have one kind of work and may not have another.

The days and hours of admission must again depend upon the character of the library and of the readers who frequent it. It is a mistake to suppose that it is not necessary to close a library occasionally; cleansing and rearrangement cannot be properly carried on while the library is in use; but the closing need not be for long or at frequent periods. Opening a library in the evening is a much more serious question, although in many localities it may be unavoidable. The risk from fire is always present, and the general supervision cannot be so perfect in the evening as during the day. It well deserves consideration, therefore, whether books or manuscripts of great rarity and value ought to be placed in the hands of readers in the evening.

It is a great advantage to a reader to be able to consult the catalogue of a library; it facilitates his work in every way; but it may be doubted whether it is convenient or safe to allow readers access to the title-slips. The slips themselves are records which should be most carefully protected from loss, or displacement, or injury. A catalogue comprised in bound volumes would appear to be the most convenient form for consultation, but it should be so arranged as to show the accessions to the library. And this leads to the question about which there has been so much discussion, whether a catalogue of a daily increasing library should be printed or preserved in manuscript. There is perhaps no detail of library management about which more mistaken opinions have been held and expressed than about the expediency of printing catalogues. One reader advocated the printing of

the catalogue of the British Museum library, because it would occupy less space in print than in manuscript, and it would be so much more convenient to have the catalogue on his table for consultation than to have to go to the presses of the reading-room for it. It never occurred to him that forty or fifty folio volumes would leave but little space on his table for other materials for literary work; and that, although a printed catalogue would show that certain works were in the library, the absence of the title of any particular work was no proof that it was not in the library. The best answer to the call for a printed catalogue is the fact that so few printed catalogues exist, and that some which have been commenced have been discontinued. In 1739 the first volume of a classed catalogue of the National Library of Paris was printed. The class Theology was completed in 1742. Belles-Lettres followed in 1750, and Jurisprudence in 1753, and the work was then discontinued. In 1852, M. Taschereau, who became Administrateur-en-chef of the library, submitted a scheme to the Minister of Public Instruction for the completion of the catalogue, which he undertook to have finished in twelve years. That is twenty-five years ago. Two classes only have been undertaken: the History of France, and Medicine. Of the History of France, ten volumes out of thirteen have been published; and of Medicine, two volumes out of three. We have reason to believe that the printing will cease with the completion of these two classes. The publication of the celebrated catalogue of the Casanate Library, undertaken by Audiffredi, was commenced in 1761. Vol. II. was published in 1768, Vol. III. in 1775, and Vol. IV., which brought the work down to letter K, was published in 1788, or twenty-seven years after the appearance of the first volume; and then the undertaking was given up.

The objection to printing a catalogue—apart from the question of expense, and the small probability that the outlay would ever be repaid— rests upon the impossibility of keeping the catalogue on a level with the actual state of the library. But this objection does not apply to printing catalogues of special classes of books where the collection in the library may be nearly complete, or the additions to which must be of necessity few and slow of acquisition. Acting upon this principle, the Trustees of the British Museum have printed catalogues of their Hebrew, Chinese, and Sanscrit books, and of some of their collections of manuscripts.

The system of building up a catalogue adopted at the British Museum is found to work well in practice. The original title-slips are copied on thin paper; these transcripts are laid down by the book-binder in volumes in such a manner as to allow of their being shifted and reinserted, so as to admit of the addition in proper alphabetical sequence of the daily accessions to the library. By this system the contents of the library can be made known to the readers without the costly and dilatory process of printing the catalogue and adding to it by supplements. The slips which are inserted in the catalogue volumes might be printed instead of written, and in this way a printed catalogue might be obtained, but not a printed catalogue for circulation. This course has been adopted to a limited extent in the University Library of Cambridge.

There are other questions which are suggested for consideration by the Organizing Committee, such as—

1. The qualifications of librarians. I have already had the honour to express my opinion that the qualifications of librarians cannot be too high or too catholic, and that librarians ought to be good linguists. They ought also to be good administrators, to be prepared to exercise a strict and personal superintendence over the library staff, and to give their attention to details, however ordinary or minute. This attention to details (which was one of the secrets of the Duke of Wellington's success in his military operations) will amply repay all librarians who exercise it.

2. Distribution of functions. This point must be regulated to some extent by the size of the staff, but I would desire to express my opinion that no one operation ought to be entrusted exclusively to one person, unless of absolute necessity. There ought always to be two at least who can do the same thing, in order that the particular branch of work may never be impeded or suspended by absence on vacation or illness of the person employed upon it. I believe it to be the practice in some continental libraries to place particular classes of books under the exclusive charge of one librarian. By practice the librarian becomes so well acquainted with the books committed to his care that he is independent of press-marks, and deposits the book after use in any part of the division to which it belongs. The consequence is that no one but himself can find it again without great loss of time. It is not, however, the principle which is here so much at fault as the application of it. The library of the British Museum is marked out into divisions for the purpose of supplying books to the readers. In each division certain attendants are placed whose duty it is to receive readers' tickets, to enter the book wanted in a register, and then to hand the book to another attendant, who carries it to the reading-room. By this division of labour a saving is effected of more than half the time which used to be occupied in procuring books for the readers. The attendants become more ready by having their attention confined to a small section of the library, but they are transferred from time to time to other divisions, in order that they may thus become familiarized with the contents of the entire library.

3. As to the hours of duty and vacation, each library will form its own regulations. Care should, however, be taken that the hours of duty be not so long as to produce exhaustion of body or mind, and that the term of vacation should be sufficiently long to restore the tone of the tired energies.

4. The question of salary is a delicate one, upon which, it may be assumed, librarians can do little more than express an opinion. It is well, however, that it should be understood that the life of a librarian is a hard one; that his work never relaxes; and looking to the importance of his functions, and the special nature of his qualifications, he ought to be well paid. He ought to be so remunerated as to be placed above the necessity of supplementing his income by literary work. I have heard it said that the work of a librarian is so agreeable, that the constant association with books and learned men and students is so delightful, that he ought to take these charms of his occupation into account in estimating the value of the salary which may be awarded to him. The agreeableness and the delightfulness may be doubted; but, admitting them for the sake of argument, the hard fact remains that they cannot be employed in satisfying the claims of the butcher, the baker, and the schoolmaster, and, therefore, have little influence on the stern realities of life.

It is purposed to submit to this Conference a scheme for the formation of a Library Association of the United Kingdom. Such an association would appear to be a natural and, indeed, a necessary result of our labours, in order to reduce to a permanent form the various opinions which will be elicited in the course of our discussions, and to secure the maintenance of the resolutions at which the Conference may arrive.

The joint and continuous action which will be obtained by such an association will render practicable the accomplishment of many works which would otherwise be impossible. As an instance, I would beg to refer to the very numerous parochial libraries which are scattered over the kingdom. We possess incidental notices of a few of these, but by far the greater number are totally unknown. They are for the most part unguarded and uncared for; exposed to pillage and decay. It would be a work well worthy the attention of such an association as is proposed, to obtain lists of these books—catalogues would not be necessary—and to publish them from time to time in a journal, with a separate pagination and register. These lists could then be separated from the journal and bound by themselves, and would ultimately form a most important and instructive bibliographical work. Many rare and valuable books would be found amongst them. If the plan were extended, and made to include school libraries and cathedral and chapter libraries, the results would be still more remarkable and valuable. Mr. Beriah Botfield's work on Cathedral and Chapter Libraries contains much useful information, but it is very insufficient as a guide to those important collections.

Ladies and Gentlemen,—I will not detain you longer. I have touched very slightly on some of the principal topics which have been proposed for discussion, and have merely ventured to indicate some of my own experiences, and to lay down a few principles which I believe to be sound. I do not expect, nor, indeed, is it desirable, that my opinions should pass unchallenged by the Conference. But I do earnestly desire to promote discussion, to promote that ventilation of thoughts and opinions on the subject of library science which may tend to further the objects of this Conference of Librarians of All Nations.

• • • •

The long-continued applause with which the address was received having subsided,

Professor JUSTIN WINSOR, V.P., said:—I accept with satisfaction, and as the representative of the youngest nation here, the duty of offering respects to the President of this Conference and the principal librarian of the greatest library of our hosts the British people. I move that the thanks of this Conference be presented to Mr. Winter Jones for his instructive and much welcome address as an opening to our proceedings.

The resolution was carried by acclamation.

• • • •

On Cataloguing.

MR. ROBERT B. SPEARS, librarian of Glasgow University Library, read his paper "On the Catalogues of Glasgow University Library."

MR. CORNELIUS WALFORD read his Notes on Cataloguing.

MR. C. A. CUTTER made some remarks in regard to card catalogues, and in explanation of an easy method of fastening the cards in the drawers so that the public could not disturb the order and yet that facility of consultation should not be in any way interfered with.

He went on to say:—Card catalogues are as characteristic of American libraries as pasted slip-catalogues are of English libraries. In the twenty-five or thirty English collections of books which we have visited I have seen no card catalogue, and, although I hear of some, they are in no case, I believe, accessible to the public, whereas in my own country I know of only one library which has a pasted catalogue, and that is to be given up as soon as possible. I find also another noteworthy difference between the two countries. My English friends seem to consider a subject-catalogue as something very excellent, to be sure, but utopian—impracticable. With us, on the contrary, a library that has no subject-catalogue is regarded as little better than one which has none at all. As to the difficulties of classification and the liability to mistakes in dealing with subjects with which one is unacquainted (which has been rather despairingly insisted upon), in all the works upon library economy you will find that the first qualification of the librarian is universal knowledge. Of course if this requirement is fulfilled, the objection is removed, and if it is not, Carlyle's dictum may profitably be applied here: "After all, the worst catalogue is none at all," or, as it is expressed in an old proverb, very worthy to be taken to heart by librarians, "Half a loaf is better than no bread." Even supposing the enormous amount of five per cent of the entries should be erroneous, which is utterly improbable, the subject-catalogue ought nevertheless to be made for the sake of the assistance which will be afforded to students by the ninety-five per cent of correct entries.

Professor JUSTIN WINSOR, V.P., said:—Adding as we do to the Boston Public Library from 15,000 to 30,000 volumes a year, and entering them in our catalogue with such a profusion of subject-references, in addition to the ordinary main and cross references, and keeping up that catalogue in duplicate for public and official uses, so that from 100,000 to 150,000 entries are now made yearly in it—you can conceive that we have been put to our wit's end to accomplish this work with an expedition that will satisfy the American notions of rapidity. We do it in this way. The work of the catalogue face goes to transcribers, who in a fixed library chirography—to which our people are drilled—copy the entries on sheets ruled to correspond to the faces of twenty cards, using an ink with tannin in it. Sheets thus written are dampened and laid on plates of prepared gelatine; the ink renders the gelatine horny, where it touches, the rest remaining porous. The plate is then put on a press, dampened, and, the ink-roller going over it, the ink adheres to the writing, and is repelled by the porous parts. Impressions are now taken to any number required, sometimes as many as hundreds, on Bristol board, and, being cut up according to gauges, the cards are at once ready for insertion for the main entires, and they only need a top inscription in the library hand for the other entires. We estimate that we save about one-half in time, and as much in money, as compared with an old system of printing from type.

Professor E. P. WRIGHT said that, had Mr. Cutter only happened to land on the first island to be met with on the way from America, he would have found card catalogues rather the rule in the libraries of Ireland than the exception. Some of the slips in the Trinity College public library are nearly half a century old, and are not yet worn out. In this library the card catalogue was under the charge of a special officer, and there was therefore little probability of slips getting astray. As to subject-catalogues, time would only permit him to say that while he thought that in our library catalogues every word on a title-page should appear, with all the needful cross references, these titles should not be added to, nor an attempt made to make a library catalogue an introduction to the classification of science and literature.

Mr. EDWIN WALLACE, while allowing that subject-catalogues were of considerable utility, quoted Professor Stanley Jevons's saying, "A classified catalogue is a logical absurdity," and doubted whether the work could be done, except roughly and by the use of some wide divisions, which in the case of libraries like that of the British Museum would themselves comprise so many works as to be of little service to most readers. He especially objected to such sub-clas-

sification as characterized Mr. Anderson's specimen catalogue of works in mental philosophy, and called attention to the difficulty a librarian would find with reference to the later German philosophy in distinguishing works on metaphysic from those on logic.

MR. G. BULLEN said that he could not conceive how any one should depreciate the importance of a subject-catalogue. However excellent might be the alphabetical catalogue of authors' names now available in the British Museum, it was only half perfect, as lacking an index of subjects. Let such an index be provided, and the full idea of a catalogue would be realized. When superintendent of the reading-room, he had continually felt the need of an index of subjects, and often found his brain harassed by the demands made upon it by readers to tell them what book or books they required to see on some particular subject. He trusted that the Conference would give such an expression of opinion in favour of a subject-index as would strengthen the hands of the officers of the Museum in procuring from the Government the finances necessary for its production.

MR. RICHARD GARNETT confirmed the experience of Mr. Bullen from his own, and added that a great step had already been taken towards the preparation of an index of subjects to the Museum catalogue. Titles written for books were transcribed quadruply, and one set of slips arranged, not in alphabetical order, but according to the place of the books on the shelves. Books in the Museum being arranged strictly according to subject, this was practically equivalent to a classed catalogue, which only needed more accurate subdivision to be ready for use in any form desired. Its final preparation and publication were, in fact, simply questions of money.

MR. W. LYALL said:—I am glad that Mr. Cutter has introduced the matter of subject-catalogues. It is my firm opinion that no librarian can have a proper grasp of his library without a subject-catalogue. Whether the catalogue be arranged this way or not, there ought to be a good subject-index. The best arranged alphabetical catalogue is that of the Public Library at Boston, U.S.

The REV. T. VICKERS, librarian of the Public Library, Cincinnati, said:—It is far more important to print classed catalogues of a library for the use of the public than the complete catalogue in one alphabet. For the mass of readers it is more important to be able to take in at a glance all that a library contains on a given subject than to know whether it contains all the works of a given author. Those who care to read all that an author has written are, for the most part, readers of novels. There should be a complete alphabetical index to every large collection of books; but, in order to keep it complete, it is necessary to refrain from printing it in book form. There are in reality no such difficulties of classification as were suggested by Mr. Wallace. Even the example he adduced proves this; for he must be a tyro indeed in the history of modern German philosophy who does not know that all the so-called "logics" written by Hegal and his followers ought to be classed under the head of metaphysics. In the Cincinnati library we have adopted the plan of making the complete printed catalogue consist of class-catalogues published in separate volumes. This plan has the great practical advantage of placing an index to any special department at the disposal of the man who wants it at very small cost. In a public library it hardly seems fair to compel the man whose chief interest is confined to a single branch of literature, to buy a catalogue of a dozen branches in which he has no interest at all, in order to control that which does interest him. The medical student will cheerfully buy the medical catalogue, but what sense is there in forcing him to buy the theological one also? The volumes of such a catalogue as we propose, and are now printing, are moderate in size, and, as fast as the edition of any of them is exhausted, it can be reprinted *de novo*, with all the additions down to the date of issue, without involving a great additional outlay of money. It seems to me that this plan should commend itself to all rapidly growing libraries. A library which is increasing at the rate of 10,000 volumes a year needs to reprint its catalogues at short intervals.

DR. ANDREA CRESTADORO said:—A catalogue without index is imperfect. If the index be both of authors and subjects, it does not matter what arrangement is given to titles. This removes the great printing difficulty. Thus we may have a continuous catalogue, without supplements, always in progress.

MR. W. LYALL said:—With respect to the printing of special parts of a subject catalogue, I might say, in the absence of Mr. Yates, that this is done in the Leeds Public Library, but I do not know to what extent.

MR. LLOYD P. SMITH, V.P., regretted that his friend Dr. Allibone, a person perhaps as familiar with the subject of printed catalogues as even any-one at that Conference, was not present. The fact that Dr. Allibone had repeatedly pronounced the catalogue of the Library Company of Philadelphia to be the best printed catalogue known to him might be an excuse for explaining the plan of that work. It is a classified catalogue with a copious alphabetical index of all the important words in each title. Coming down only to 1855, the printed catalogue is supplemented by an alphabetical catalogue as well of subjects as of authors, so that, by referring to two alphabets only, any book in the library can be found by the author's name, the title, or the subject.

SIR REDMOND BARRY, V.P., said:—As in this discussion reference has been made to the catalogues of several libraries, allow me to introduce that of the Melbourne Public Library of Victoria.

The classification is eclectic, including certain features recommended, others excluded by authors, and some perhaps original. It follows the arrangement of the books in the recesses, each of which contains about 2,000 volumes.

Down the west side the books run thus:—

Animal Physiology	Chemistry.
and Psychology.	Meteorology.
Botany.	Cosmical Science.
Agriculture.	Voyages and Travels.
Geology.	&c. &c.
Mineralogy.	

On the east side are books relating to history and literature in all its branches, and we adopt what has been condemned—namely, the grouping of books on all subjects written in dead or foreign languages in recesses by themselves, finding it more convenient for our readers of different nationalities—French, Italian, Spanish, German, Scandinavian, and others—that they should find assembled in one chamber the authors they wish to consult. No inconvenience is felt from a practice which obliges a reader to move from one recess to another where he may supply himself with what he may require.

The catalogue is twofold:—

1. Of authors arranged alphabetically, with name of work, size, number of volumes, place of publication, date (name of publisher is omitted), edition.

2. Index of subjects. Copies of this and the supplements lie on the tables accessible to readers, who can ascertain the resources of the library on any subject, and refer to the author at once.

In illustration of this, to meet objections of former speakers, take the subject.

Theology.

The index gives subdivisions:—

Buddhist.	Mahommedan.
Catholic.	Parsee.
——Sermons.	Patristic.
Eastern.	Protestant.
Hindu.	——Sermons.
Jewish.	

—all these in one volume.

If the author required be not found in that volume nor in any other issues, there is in addition in each recess a catalogue of its contents, alphabetical and *raisonné*: consequently, in some recesses there are three or four, according to the number of subjects included. These are partly printed, partly written. Cross references are numerous, and, where the works of a copious writer comprise various subjects, the volume containing the specific information required is expressly named.

The grand division of the recess is denoted as usual by a plate having on it in large gilt letters the subject. Smaller plates on the shelves indicate the subdivisions. These conspicuous aids to the eye almost supersede the necessity for a catalogue, as a reader may scan in a moment the names of the books.

Cards—ingeniously contrived and useful as they undoubtedly are—we consider to be expensive and superfluous.

MR. W. F. POOLE, V.P., said:—In the Chicago Public Library our books are catalogued on cards under authors and subjects, and the cards are placed in alphabetical arrangement; this catalogue has not been printed. We have, however, printed a "finding-list" of all the 52,000 books in the library, which we have been able to sell to the public at the actual cost of fivepence per copy. More than 12,000 copies of these lists have been sold, a specimen of which I hold in my hand. The work, it will be seen, is printed on Manila paper, which costs only half as much as good book paper, and in service lasts five times as long. The use of Manila paper for catalogues for public use in libraries is worth the consideration of librarians. The list is made from the shelf lists, and hence is classified by subjects: prefixed is a table of contents, and also an index to subjects. The volume is furnished at so low a price by the printer because he is allowed to insert advertisements in the fly-leaves, for which he receives compensation from the advertisers.

MR. PETER COWELL exhibited a somewhat ingeniously constructed book, much resembling a photographic album, which was to be placed in the students' room of the Liverpool Free Public Library, for showing the regular accessions of new books in strict alphabetic order. He also showed a model illustrating the plan used in the general reading-room of that library for effecting the same object, but differing in form and construction. He said that the system adopted there was to print the titles of all the new accessions to the library in good legible type immediately upon passing the committee at their weekly meetings. The titles were supplied in galley by the printer, several copies being struck off in stout cardboard. They were then cut up singly, those on cardboard arranged in the album-like book in the students' room, and those on paper pasted on small wooden strips of wood and arranged in frames supported against the wall in a convenient part of the public room. The album-like catalogue is a book capable of being increased or reduced in bulk at pleasure, as each leaf is separate from its fellows. They are united by being laced together through eyelet-holds let into a narrow strip of cardboard of equal length to the leaf itself, and joined to it by a hinge of stout calico so as to admit of easy working. Each leaf is $16\frac{1}{2}$ inches by $14\frac{1}{2}$, and has two openings in each side, measuring 12 inches by 5, as if for receiving photos of similar dimensions. The titles printed on cardboard are slipped into the openings crosswise, instead of at the foot as in an album. The leaves are separate in order to admit of the insertion of new ones, as the others get filled up and the titles require opening out to receive others in their proper alphabetic order. The cover is in three pieces—the two sides and the back. The back is flexible and has a number of eyelet-holes let into it, so as to allow of expansion in the lacing as leaves are inserted. The sides, back, and leaves are capable of being united into a firm, compact whole by strong laces passing through the eyelet-holes and being tied tightly together.

The frames in the general room are each 2 ft. 6 inches long, by 6 inches wide. A half inch beading of oak runs round each. At one side the beading is loose, except just at the top and bottom, so as to admit of the narrow wooden tablets being slipped in sidewise. The beading at the opposite side has a small groove to receive the tablets and prevent them falling out. The partly loose beading under which the tablets glide is made firm by a small brass hook and eye. The frame is always kept filled with tablets either bearing titles or blank, the blanks being withdrawn as the others take their place. The plan is simple and works exceedingly well. The clear printed titles of the new books, posted in a convenient part of the room, are found to be an attraction in themselves, and are believed to be a means of inducing many to read the books who would never have done so otherwise, or would perhaps never have known of their existence. The printed catalogue was on the plan of authors, titles, and subjects. Supplements were published every two or three years. A catalogue would be kept up in future on the card-system, and would include the valuable articles contained in the leading reviews, the scientific papers of various societies, and the numerous pamphlets which were only too frequently neglected.

● ● ● ●

FOURTH SITTING,
WEDNESDAY EVENING, OCTOBER 3rd, AT 7.

In the absence of the President, SIR REDMOND BARRY, V.P., was unanimously voted to the chair.

MR. H. B. WHEATLEY, assistant librarian of the Royal Society, London, read his paper

On the Alphabetical Arrangement of the Titles of Anonymous Books.

MR. ROBERT HARRISON suggested that leave should be given to enter anonymous books under some word other than the first or leading word, if by so doing its subject could be better indicated.

MR. E. B. NICHOLSON said that in that case it would be infinitely more difficult for the reader to find whether an anonymous book was in the library; indeed, if he were unacquainted with the subject-matter of the book it would be quite impossible for him to do so.

MR. JON A. HJALTALIN said:—Anonymous works should be entered under a name or title if they have one—e.g., "Mordaunt Hall." If there is no name, and a locality is treated of, it should be put under that locality; a historical account of Leeds, for instance, should be under LEEDS. My reason is that you remember a proper name or

title better than a common heading. 'First-word" headings would be impracticable on account of their length—e.g., such headings as would be necessary under "Sermon," "Account," &c.

DR. ANDREA CRESTADORO said:—Every title should have a heading, that is, a word taken from the title-page. This word should be the author's name, if given. If the author's name is wanting, then the word indicative of the subject-matter, or in the third instance the title if distinguished from the subject properly so called.

DR. RICHARD CAULFIELD had often found valuable memoranda written on the fly-leaves of books published anonymously, which had often given the author's name, and other information about a book. Binders often destroyed such leaves and inserted new ones, which owners of books should be careful to forbid when sending books to binders. He had also sometimes found the name by writing to those interested in the history of the locality where the book was printed; but this could only be done when the book appeared in some provincial town. For instance, about the last quarter of the last century some very curious pamphlets of a controversial nature were printed in Cork, under the pseudonym of "Michael Servetus"—they say, one Dr. Blair, about whose history there were some curious particulars which would never have come to light but for the hunt after his name. Again, it was the custom in Ireland, about a century or more ago, to write laudatory poems on the leading members of society, both male and female, giving only the first and last letter of the name. Such names might easily be identified by persons in the locality; he had seen the omitted letters filled in by a contemporary hand in such publications. Pamphlets of a political character were often of a personal nature, and often appeared after this fashion: he had often seen the name of the writer placed on the title-page under the initials, and not unfrequently scratched out or otherwise obliterated. In arranging such books in the catalogue he placed them under their subjects, but kept a register of the *initials* in a different book set apart for the purpose, having space beneath each for such conjectures as might be made by himself or the writers quoting the book, and always citing authorities.

MR. RALPH THOMAS said, in reply to a question which he had heard, that in his experience the British Museum did strictly adhere to their rules for cataloguing anonymous and pseudonymous works. He disagreed with Mr. Wheatley's view that an anonymous work should be catalogued under the author's name when found. He thought the rule of the Museum was the scientific rule—viz., to catalogue under the work or the pseudonym.

MR. G. W. PORTER was sorry that he had not had the advantage of being present when Mr. Wheatley's paper was read, but he had formed a very strong opinion that the best way of treating anonymous works in a large alphabetical catalogue was to enter them under the first word of the title which was not either an article or a preposition. This was Barbier's plan, and had been followed by Kayser, Melzi, and other bibliographers. No one who had consulted the "Dictionnaire des Ouvrages Anonymes" of Barbier could have failed to be struck by the ease and precision of his method. The great object was to have a fixed and certain rule which every one could apply without hesitation or doubt; so that a librarian or reader might be able to say with respect to anonymous works, just as confidently as in other cases, whether any particular book was or was not in the library. This could not be the case where the subject or leading word was adopted as the heading: people were apt to take different views as to which was the leading word, and in the titles of many anonymous books it was really very difficult to decide. All the advantages to be derived from taking the subject or leading work could be much better attained by cross references or entries in an index of subjects. Sir Anthony Panizzi, at the commencement of the Museum catalogue, had recommended that the plan of Barbier should be adopted for anonymous books, but he was unfortunately overruled, and a system of taking the proper names of person persons, of parties, sects, or denominations, and of places according to a settled order of preference, was adopted. This had been an unfortunate decision, and had materially contributed to delay the progress of the work, and to lessen the utility of the catalogue.

MR. B. R. WHEATLEY said that he considered that cross references could be quite as readily and much more appropriately made from the anonymous or pseudonymous entry to the real author, as in the opposite mode adopted by the British Museum and in Mr. Cutter's "Rules." The doubtful cases as to real authorship would be comparatively few and would only be the exception necessary to prove the rule. It was an object of such great importance to get the entire works of an author together under his name (the anonymous ones being distinguished from the others by brackets) that in debating the question it ought to out-weight most other considerations. The opposite rule, in instances where an author had successively adopted several pseudonyms, might scatter his works in a dozen different places over the catalogue. Cross references must always be considered in the light of helps, and should therefore be from the unknown to the known, from ignorance to knowledge, and not from knowledge to ignorance. The cataloguer should make his catalogue up to his knowledge, as perfect as he can, adding helpful cross references for the consulter to follow him in his track, not backwards from his own knowledge to the consulter's ignorance.

One of the Secretaries then read the note by M. GUILLAUME DEPPING

On Co-operative Cataloguing,

and after it the following letter from PROFESSOR F. MAX MÜLLER, late assistant-librarian of the Bodleian Library, Oxford, was read:—

7, Norham Gardens, Oxford,
Sept. 17, 1877.

"DEAR MR. NICHOLSON,—I am sorry I shall not be able to join your Conference of Librarians. I hope it will be a great success. Though an ex-librarian only, I take a great interest in the reform of libraries, and I tried to point out some years ago how much the work of cataloguing might be simplified, and the expense lessened by means of co-operation. I forget whether I sent my letter to the 'Times' or the 'Academy,'[2] but I have no doubt that the subject will now be taken up and settled by the Conference. If each publisher of a book printed a slip, according to rules to be fixed by the Conference, and if one such slip was attached to every book, and more could be bought by libraries, the work and expense of libraries would be considerably reduced. To the publisher the expense would be very small, and fully covered by sale of extra copies of slips.

Yours very truly,
F. MAX MÜLLER.

Professor JUSTIN WINSOR, V.P., said:—We in America look to the publishers doing much, as far as current books go, in helping our co-operative cataloguing. We hope to induce publishers to put into every copy of every new book issued a stiff paper sheet. This sheet shall be the size, say, of a commercial note-paper, divided into two horizontal spaces above and below a vacant centrespace, which can be filled with the publisher's notices, and along which the sheet can be folded for small books. The title is to be repeated in these four spaces, as needed, for main and other entries. The sheet, when cut up, on the printed rules, gives four cards, while the surplus vacant space can be discarded. The cards are thus ready made for a card catalogue, and, all publishers working on a uniform plan, any purchaser of books, and any small library buying only current books, will have in ten years a more perfect card catalogue, with no trouble of making it, than most such purchasers or libraries can possibly otherwise have. We look for co-operation in this direction producing most important results.

MR. B. R. WHEATLEY said:—I am afraid the scheme could hardly be carried out beneficially to all. A librarian requires the growth of experience —it is simply by his coping with the difficulties that surround him in his work that he grows to be a good cataloguer, and, though he should imbibe knowledge and good ideas wherever he can from the experience of others (as exemplified, for instance, in the experiences to be gained from the detailed accounts of these Conferences), he should still do the work himself for his own library. If it is to be done by central committees, or by booksellers and publishers when publishing their book, and he is merely to be a recipient of the slips, good librarians, instead of increasing, will soon become an extinct race; for we know that in all knowledge it is by that which we teach ourselves, or learn by thought from the works of others—and not by what we receive parrot-like without thought from them—that we become true men in the vocation we are following.

MR. C. A. CUTTER reminded Mr. Wheatley that he would still have the old books to catalogue.

The REV. W. H. MILMAN, librarian of Sion College, London, said:—With respect to the proposal to have catalogue-slips printed of every book to be hereafter published—such slips to be furnished with all copies of the books sold, and also to be purchasable separately—I quite agree with Professor Winsor that if it could be carried out it would infinitely and agreeably lighten the labours of a librarian. But I venture to remind the Conference that the recommendations of M. Depping went much further. He recommends that arrangements shall, if possible, be made for printing slip-titles of all works already published, and that a beginning should be made by providing slips of

all bibliographical works. This proposal also has my full approval in spite of the objection advanced by a preceding speaker, that, if such slips could be purchased, the librarian's occupation or chance of distinction as a good cataloguer would be gone. To this I reply that the object in view is not to give librarians an opportunity of earning distinction, but to provide a good and satisfactory catalogue; that this obviously would be much facilitated by putting printed slips in the reach of every librarian, and so diminishing his mechanical labour and the cost of the catalogue; and that plenty of opportunities of distinction, would remain to librarians in the intelligent use, and even corrections of these slips. Whilst, on the other hand, when once a title of any book has been prepared as perfectly as it can be prepared, there is little distinction to be earned in reproducing, whether with or without a questionable variation from the form already in print.

PROFESSOR E. P. WRIGHT said that no more important subject than that of co-operative cataloguing could be brought before the Conference, and it appeared to him that, if, through the influence of the Library Association, a system of registering the titles of all works of every kind could be carried out after a certain date, an immense step would be taken towards a universal catalogue. Thus, taking this country as a type, if it were enacted that so many copies of every title-page of any work published in Great Britain, printed on paper of a certain size, should be sent to Stationers' Hall, the arranging of these once a year in alphabetical order would constitute so many complete catalogues of all the works for that year, and if the same were done in each publishing country, a complete catalogue of all published works would be year by year attained, which could be bought by all the larger libraries of the world. The details of press-reference to such works as each such library contained, and cross references thereto, were matters of detail that could easily be left to the librarians. And, if thus from a certain date a universal catalogue could be made, there might be some chance of printing a complete catalogue of all works published before that date.

MR. CORNELIUS WALFORD then read his paper on "A New General Catalogue of English Literature."

This was followed by the paper of MR. J. ASHTON CROSS, late librarian of the Oxford Union Society, on "A Universal Index of Subjects."

MR. E. B. NICHOLSON heartily approved Mr.

Cross's project; but, as its author had so emphatically laid down the principle that every library ought to have a speciality, and had made somewhat sarcastic reference to the abandonment of this principle in the library of the London Institution, he must take leave to say that he regarded the principle as entirely false in theory, and that he knew it to be most mischievous in its results. There was no security whatever that the importance of the speciality selected would justify the unusual expenditure it involved; and to this he would add that there was a strong temptation to buy every new book relating to it, good, bad, or indifferent, in order to keep up the reputation of the library in the literature of that particular branch. There were plenty of libraries already founded for specialities, and a library for general readers, instead of stinting all sections of its constituents except one for the purpose of surfeiting that one, should be fair to all, allowing no disproportionate addition of any class of works, except those connected with the history or interests of the locality in which it was situated.

Professor B. S. MONDINO, V.P., suggested that the catalogue of the British Museum might be printed in slips, so that every sheet of paper contained a certain number of titles which could be cut out and arranged either alphabetically or by subjects. Every librarian might buy copies and make for himself an alphabetical or subject-catalogue of the Museum. The expense of printing would be covered by selling the slips, which not only many librarians, but many private gentlemen would be glad to buy. He suggested that, if these slip-sheets were sent to other librarians throughout the world, they would gladly insert the titles of any books in their possession which the Museum might lack, and that by such co-operation a general catalogue of printed books might very easily be made. He felt also that a general catalogue of MSS. was wanted, the very existence of some MSS., and the locality of others, being unknown, while of those supposed to be unique it was not known whether there might not be duplicates. Such a catalogue might be compiled under the direction of a special committee, who would lay down rules for uniform cataloguing of MSS., and arrange the printed slips sent in to it by each library. In such a catalogue the MSS. in private libraries should of course be included. General catalogues of books and MSS. would be of such obvious value to all students that if the Conference resolved on their preparation the world would at once applaud so thoroughly practical a resolution.

FIFTH SITTING,
THURSDAY MORNING, OCTOBER 4th,
AT 10.

In the absence of the President, PROFESSOR B. S. MONDINO, V.P., was unanimously voted to the Chair.

MR. RICHARD GARNETT read his paper "On the System of Classifying Books on the Shelves followed at the British Museum."

PROFESSOR B. S. MONDINO, V.P., said that in the Biblioteca Nazionale of Palermo, as in many Italian libraries, the place of each book was expressed in such a way as to avoid several numbers coming one after the other, and consequently a stated number of shelves was indicated by Roman numbers, each shelf by a letter, and each book by an Arabic number—V. C. 16, IX. D. 56, would tell at once the place of a book, the letters also showing the size of the book.

PROFESSOR JUSTIN WINSOR, V.P., said:—
We have planned a system for reclassifying the University Library at Harvard, in the new building now just completed, which I venture to name the *mnemonic system*, the object being, by a numerical correspondence of sections, to let certain parts of great divisions, bearing fixed relations to the whole in equivalent treatments, be distinguished by the same digits, in the same position of the sequence that constitutes a book number. For instance: "Travels in England," would have the same range-number with "History and Biography of England," &c., though the other figures changed.[3] The classification is carried throughout all departments of knowledge as a system intelligent rather than philosophical, regard being had to the mnemonic principle, as the essential one to facilitate use, which is in fact the prime element in all practice.

MR. MELVIL DEWEY described briefly the Amherst College scheme of classification, according to which the library was divided into nine "classes," each of which was split up into nine "divisions," each of them in turn subdivided into nine "sections." There was an alphabetical subject-index, and, if you looked for SYNONYMS, you would find after it the number 444, which showed you that you would find all books on synonyms in section 4 of division 4 of class 4. For a detailed account of this scheme he referred to the American Library Report, chapter xxviii.

MR. LLOYD P. SMITH, V. P., desired to express his cordial adhesion to Mr. Dewey's plan, and said that, in his opinion, if no other benefit grew out of the present Conference, the knowledge of this ingenious method of arranging books on the shelves must repay the gentlemen present for the trouble of coming together. He was pleased to find that the classification of his own library at Philadelphia was essentially that so ably described by Mr. Garnett. He ventured to think, however, that in some few points the classification of the Philadelphia library was preferable.

MR. EIRÍKER MAGNÚSSON said that the local classification of a library by the contents of its shelves was the most important subject on which the Conference was called upon to express its opinion. It resolved itself into the four propositions—1. Was it possible? 2. If possible, at what cost then? 3. Were the results commensurate with the expenditure? 4. Was it the cheapest and most practical way of putting the contents of a library within the reach of the reader? In deciding the question of possibility, a clear line must be drawn between an old-established and a new library. The old library had grown in an irregular and unsystematical way into its present shape. To reorganize it he maintained that the methodical removal of each single volume would take ten minutes at the lowest estimate. The enormous expense of the process was therefore obvious, and that in itself was a sufficient answer to the second proposition. But, after all, the classification was far from perfect; all periodical and academical publications, and in fact all social works of miscellaneous contents, had to be left out of this system, more or less completely. A writer's collected works, however miscellaneous, would have to occupy one place. And, after all, books would consume space, and buildings would not expand with the increase of their contents. Consequently there was a periodical break-up of the systematized classification, and multifarious was the inconvenience to which it would lead. By the immense growth of the large libraries there would be required in time a special staff to take the readers to the classes they wanted to examine, and when there the real trouble began, the reader had to go through the class more or less completely before he had satisfied himself of having got what he wanted. The whole scheme presupposed open libraries. But as libraries grow the impossibility of keeping their shelves open to the general public would enforce itself upon every librarian. Libraries were not meant for readers only, but also and especially for men of research; they had as large claims to be accommodated as the general reader. They came to libraries to consult them, with the least loss of time: they had a definite object, and wanted it effected in the least possible space of time. Their method of consulting a library was to verify the whereabouts of the books they wanted from the catalogue, and to go straight to them, or to have them fetched. If they wanted to find out what the library had on such and such a subject, they must go to the class and examine the books on it, from the folios down to the infinitesimos, which all stood on different shelves. This took such time that it destroyed the object in view. These were some of the results of this shelf-classification system. A cheaper and certainly a more practicable way of making a library useful to readers and scholars was to keep a classified subject-catalogue of it side by side with the alphabetical catalogue of authors. That solved all the difficulties, broadly speaking, which shelf-classification could never solve.

MR. E. B. NICHOLSON was amazed at the views taken by Mr. Magnússon, and, as the best answer to them, would state his own practical experience. In the library which he represented, and which contained 60,000 volumes, if not more, there had been formerly only a very rudimentary classification, and even that had completely broken down through fresh accumulations. He had determined on re-classifying the entire library, and subdividing as minutely as might be done without causing perplexity. In doing this he had the help of a single assistant librarian (the other assistant librarian being otherwise occupied) for roughly sorting books in the first instance, and for arranging rows of periodicals and parliamentary papers; he had also the carpenter to alter shelves and remove large piles of books. The pressure of other duties had prevented him from arranging a book for months together, while the construction of the library had compelled him to arrange some classes of books half-a-dozen times over, and almost every everything twice; yet with no more help than he had stated he had got within 4,000 volumes of the end of his task in less than four years. That was his answer to the questions whether a classified arrangement was possible, and, if so, what it cost. To Mr. Magnússon's inquiries whether it was *worth* the cost, and whether it was the cheapest and most practical way of putting the contents of a library within the reader's reach, he would reply emphatically, Yes. No one set a higher value than himself upon subject-catalogues and subject-indexes. But neither for readers nor for librarians did the best subject-catalogue in the world render a thorough shelf-classification the less desirable.

Reading the titles of books on any given subject was never the same as being able to see them standing side by side, and to take them down and examine them one by one. The librarian, too, gained a far more thorough knowledge of the contents of his library in any particular department, if, whenever he turned his eye towards a shelf, he saw books on the same subject grouped together. Even in fetching and replacing books, shelf-classification yielded an immense saving of time; for not only were most of the books a reader required sure to be close to each other, but in nearly every case the librarian was able to walk to the exact place of each book, without looking out its press-mark; while readers became familiar with the classification, and in libraries, such as that of the London Institution, where free shelf-access was allowed, saved the time of librarians by fetching their books for themselves. It was undoubtedly true that a work relating to one subject, if it were inseparable from its writer's collected works, might have to be placed among the works relating to another; but such cases were comparatively rare, and, as regarded these, the library was no worse off than it would have been without classification; while, as regarded the arrangement of the vast majority of books it was very much better off. As to the argument that libraries were apt to outgrow their space, and classification to break up in consequence, a library would not hold more books unclassified than classified; new shelves must be provided in any case, and to these entire classes might be removed without any break up whatever of the principles of subdivision. It was true that, if the books on a given subject had to be divided, for want of room, into many sizes, the convenience of a classed arrangement was less; but it was only less, and he had found it practicable in almost every instance to keep the largest and the smallest sizes so close together that a reader might consult them all without moving two yards to right or left.

In classifying the books on the shelves he had separated two classes on the same shelf by an upright partition of wood, which stood firm but might be shifted in a moment by slightly lifting the shelf above. Every subdivision had or would have on the shelf beneath it, its title, lettered in gilt on a label made of black buckram; at each end of the label was an eyelet-hole, through which a brass-beaded nail was run into the shelf, firmly enough to hold, but with the head standing out a little, so that it might be twisted out in a moment and the label shifted. Much larger labels of the same kind were affixed to each recess, giving a complete index to its contents. When the arrangement was completed, the shelves would be numbered on a decimal system, every book would have its exact place numbered inside (and perhaps outside) as well as in the catalogue, and shelf-lists would be compiled. As every shelf was made deep enough for two rows of octavos, the even numbers of any series of octavo volumes were put at the back when a division outgrew the shelf-frontage assigned to it, while space had been left for any probable additions in larger sizes.

He did not wish for a moment to say that shelf-classification was an easy task: it was very far from easy. The librarian who undertook it was bound to get a clear idea of the subdivision of many branches of knowledge with which, unless he were a walking encyclopaedia, he had no previous acquaintance: but the educational advantage to himself in so doing far outbalanced the trouble. Again, when weary with classing books for hours together, he was apt to take the frequently deceptive title of a book as a guide to its subject-matter, to place it wrongly, and to prepare for himself much self-humiliation when he found out his mistake on the thorough revision to which he ought to subject his arrangement. But both this and the former difficulty were equally applicable to the formation of a classed catalogue, and he was sure the Conference would agree with him that the only question to be considered was, whether shelf-classification was desirable and practicable: if so, no amount of mere trouble ought to be let stand in the way of it.

MR. J. ASHTON CROSS urged that the question could not be discussed in such an abstract form. In large libraries the great thing was to find the books readily. For them, therefore, Mr. Melvil Dewey's system was the best; and really more logical than the professedly logical scheme still followed in the British Museum. But small libraries ought to be educational: to see the books grouped on the shelves was infinitely more impressive than to scan the names in a subject-index. For all but the largest libraries therefore a shelf-arrangement according to the most natural classification of subjects was essential.

DR. RICHARD CAULFIELD considered the shelf-arrangement in the British Museum as near perfection as possible under the circumstances, making due allowance for the magnitude of the library. After nearly twenty years' practical experience of the Museum, periodically, he might say that he had never been allowed to want a book, and had never met with anything but the greatest courtesy. He had often recommended young friends making their first acquaintance with the Museum to spend a few days in ascertaining the details of the plan, and to study the card of reference to the contents of the reading-room—by doing which they would save much trouble. The conduct of some persons, he well knew, was most unreasonable: they expected to get everything without the slightest trouble on their own part.

With respect to special collections of books, such as might be left by bequest and so would never be added to, he had always found that by *lettering* each case and *numbering* each shelf and book (as Case B, Shelf 3-14), a book could be got in a moment, provided the catalogue was correct. He had lately arranged on this principle an old cathedral-library of about 6,000 or 7,000 books, chiefly patristic and mediæval, the bequests of former generations of ecclesiastics, and it had succeeded admirably.

MR. G. BULLEN was surprised that Mr. Magnússon, with his large experience of public libraries, should say anything against the desirability of shelf-classification. We were not called upon to decide as to the preference to be given to a classified catalogue or a classified arrangement on the shelves. Both were desirable if they could be obtained, but, if the latter only, then let us have it by all means. Such classification exists at the British Museum, originated by the late Mr. Watts and notably carried out by Mr. Garnett. For himself he found the greatest advantage in being able to go at once to the press containing books on any particular subject, especially if one not ordinarily asked for. He had sometimes permitted a reader to go under the charge of an attendant into the inner library and look for himself at those particular books, and take notes of the names and titles of such as he might desire to see in the reading-room. Sometimes also he had given a seat in the inner library to a reader engaged upon some particular out-of-the-way subject, and had shelves of books conveyed to him there, which had proved to be of the greatest advantage to him, besides sparing the attendants much additional labour.

MR. W. E. A. AXON said that he wished to correct the impression that he had suggested a classified catalogue at the British Museum. He was perfectly indifferent to the form; all that he wanted was the titles in any manner, provided there was an index that would take them to the authors and subjects. The simplest and most philosophical system of classification was that of Mr Dewey, which was equally applicable to large and small libraries. He had himself classified his own private library of about 5,000 titles by it, and the process had occupied little more than a week. This facility was due to the excellent index of subjects. He strongly recommended the decimal classification as easy to be worked by the librarian, convenient for the reader, and thoroughly philosophical in principle.

MR. C. A. CUTTER said:—Let me bring forward one instance in support of Mr. Bullen's advocacy of shelf-classification. I have for a dozen years had in hand a bibliography of works relating to the Devil. I am encouraged by what Mr. Bullen has said, to hope that he will allow me to visit, under the supervision of an attendant, that portion of the British Museum which is devoted to Demonology. There, in an hour or two, I can make valuable notes of many works hitherto unseen; whereas, if there were no shelf-arrangement, I should not even attempt to look through the million and a half volumes. And even a classified catalogue would not answer the purpose so well, for then I should be obliged to write two or three hundred slips, and send two or three hundred attendants running all about the library, instead of sitting down quietly with all the desired works almost within reach of my table.

MR. G. BULLEN said that, if Mr. Cutter wished to extend his acquaintance with the Devil, he should be happy to hand him over to Mr. Garnett, who would doubtless assist him to the utmost in his diabolical researches.

NOTES

[1] Otherwise Johann Müller, who, being a native of Königsberg, was called Johann von Königsberg, which he latinized into Johannes Regiomontanus, or Montereguis.

[2] "Academy," March 18, 1876, copied by "Times" of the same day, quoted in American Library Report, p. 513.

[3] The speaker made the plan more apparent by a diagram on the blackboard.

II

ACQUISITIONS

There is a misleading simplicity about the standard statement that "library materials are generally acquired by purchase, gift, exchange, or legal deposit." The acquisitions librarian ideally should be a knowledgeable bookman, a practical businessman, a diplomat, a fiscal expert. He should know something about tax laws and other laws, about the evaluation of publications and manuscripts, he should know his geography and history well, be adept at languages; he should know the collections of his library and be alert to incipient trends that may affect future acquisition policy. He should be skillful in relationships with all of the library's constituency—students, faculty, other library staff, potential donors and others. In character he should be polite, aggressive, convivial, persistent, energetic, curious, and alert. If in addition he is expert in several subject fields and knows something about automation he is on his way to becoming a good acquisitions librarian. . . . Of course several years of experience will also be necessary before he attains that ranking.

The Essentials of an Acquisition Program

Keyes D. Metcalf

At the Harvard College Library we have a discussion group made up of the junior professional members of the staff, but to which under sufferance I am invited. Ordinarily we are pretty matter of fact in our discussions and deal with concrete not abstract problems, but one evening we had a hot argument on the topic, "Is Librarianship a Science?" The controversy took a philosophical turn and was soon so far over my head that I had to give up even trying to follow it. It was recalled to my mind, however, when the topic of this paper, "The Essentials of an Acquisition Program," was assigned to me. It would seem as if essentials should have something exact or scientific about them, but your speaker, who under ordinary circumstances deals in the concrete not the abstract, fears that this will not be the case as he presents the subject. My comments, you will find, will be chiefly suggestions rather than definite statements, and I should be the last to claim that there is anything authoritative about them.

The topic has been divided into four main divisions. To these four have been added, as a kind of supplement, a few notes on two other matters—matters of importance but of which my knowledge is even less than in the case of the first four. In order that you may know where we are going, or at least where I am trying to lead you, I shall name these divisions at this time:

1. The administration of a book-selection program and a method of book selection for a university library
2. The organization and administration of an acquisition department
3. The staff of an acquisition department and its training
4. The types of records and accounts kept in an acquisition department

And then the two subjects that will receive less detailed consideration:

1. Co-operative buying
2. The essentials of an acquisition program in a small library

When I was first consulted about this paper, nothing was said about a book-selection program. It was rather indicated that the administrative side of the acquisition department should be my chief consideration. But it seemed to me, after reading the volume that was the result of last summer's Institute, which you will remember dealt with *The Practice of Book Selection,* that the whole question of book selection for a university or research library had been omitted; that in many ways book selection was an administrative problem and that that phase of it might well be brought up this year. So I have included in my talk a statement in regard to administrative methods that might be pursued by university and research libraries in selecting material. I am glad to do so because, in spite of the great interest that I have in other library problems such as personnel, cataloging, and microphotography, I have always believed that, if we have the future in mind rather than the immediate present, the most important single task that any librarian can perform is to build up the collections in his library. I feel that too many of us have been inclined to take a passive attitude in this regard and that the methods of book selection and the directions in which the book selection turns are too often determined more or less haphazardly rather than with what might be called "malice aforethought." If I am correct in thinking that the administration of the book selection is in the long run the most important single task for which a librarian is responsible, I am sure that we cannot

SOURCE: Reprinted from William M. Randall, ed., *The Acquisition and Cataloging of Books* (Chicago: University of Chicago Press, 1940), pp. 76–94, by permission of the author and the publisher. Copyright © 1940 by the University of Chicago Press.

overemphasize the importance of dealing with it systematically. That means that we must decide, to start with, where we are going and what we are trying to accomplish. Let me hasten to repeat that I am considering now the university and research library, not the college library and not the public library. The public library has done well in its book-selection program. Public libraries as a whole know where they are going. The same holds true, though perhaps to a lesser degree, with the college library where, with the aid of the Shaw and Mohrhardt lists, many of them have been decidedly successful, or at least are doing well now. But when it comes to the university library I have no great confidence in the results of our book-selection programs. We must admit, of course, that a number of university libraries have built up fine research collections, but most of them have left much to be desired, and I have wondered if the chief cause for the relative failure was not the more or less passive attitude already referred to, added to too great reliance on faculty initiative. This is a dangerous statement for me to make, since I have been in university library work for only three years, and I must admit immediately that my own library is not at present on a satisfactory basis in this regard and that it is probably not typical of university libraries in the United States.

The problem divides itself in two: (1) What is it that we want to do? and (2) How are we to go about it?

We shall take the points up in that order. What is it that we want to do? We want, of course, to acquire the best all-round library for research purposes that we can with the funds that are available. Just saying that, however, does not settle the question. We must decide whether our first duty is to acquire as large a percentage as possible of the current new books that we feel reasonably sure will be wanted sooner or later or whether we should put the emphasis on rounding-out the older material and buy new books and pamphlets only when there are special requests for them. You cannot spend the same money for two different things. My own opinion is that in a large library with a reasonably adequate book fund, it is better to try to clear up the new material as it comes along, not buying everything, of course, but acquiring the important new things that are sure to be wanted. There will be others that will be called for later, but it is not an impossible task for a large library at least to consider all the regular trade publications for this country and the more important

foreign countries currently as they come out. It seems to me that this should be done; and, if this policy is carried out consistently, it should in time simplify very much the gathering-in of older books, as most of the essential ones will have been acquired when they were first published. It is only fair to add that many librarians disagree with me on this point and say that even a well-to-do library should not ordinarily buy a new book until there is a demand for it.

In this day and generation it must be remembered that the regular trade books that are listed in the weekly or monthly trade catalogs for the various countries do not represent by any means all the current publications. Unlisted ephemeral material of interest comes out in tremendous quantities, as do government documents. Many serials, old and new, are not recorded. Each of these groups requires special attention, but there is not time here to discuss them in detail. But, to go back to my question, I believe it should be decided whether or not a reasonably clean sweep of new publications in the regular book trade is to be made and how clean a sweep it is to be, and then proceed on that basis. The cleanness of the sweep may well depend on the funds available. It will also depend on the type of collections that we are trying to build up in the various fields. Let us say that most large university or research libraries will want to acquire all or practically all the important new reference and bibliographical tools; in addition, they will in many cases want to acquire good working collections of the more important books—how good depending again on the funds available. In addition to the reference and bibliographical books and the more important titles required to provide a good working collection, there may be for certain subjects special funds available or there may be conditions that make it wise to try to build up special research collections in limited fields. Here the technique will need to be somewhat different than in the other cases. Here the interest will be especially great in the ephemeral material, the documents, the serials, the continuations, particularly the out-of-the-way publications in all these categories.

Another question that must be decided is what should be done about manuscripts. Some libraries have more or less consistently said that they were not interested in manuscripts unless they came by gift, this largely because worthwhile manuscripts cost so much that it is deemed unwise to undertake obligations in that field. There should be,

I am sure, a more or less definite decision as to just what a library will undertake to do in the way of manuscripts. In this connection it must be remembered that there is not only the cost of acquiring the manuscripts to be considered but also the cost of putting them into shape for use and of servicing them later. Added to this is the question of their use. Who should be permitted to use unpublished material, and under what conditions may it be quoted and printed?

Another ticklish problem that must be decided is the attitude of a library toward the expenditure of money for what we are accustomed to call rare books. Many librarians are personally so interested in books and book-collecting that they are often tempted to buy collector's items. On the other hand, there are some of us who feel that we are being extravagant when we spend more than a very limited amount for any one volume. I shall not attempt to advise you as to what should be done in this connection except by saying that, unless a library has special funds given with the understanding that they are to be used for rare books of one type or another, the purchase of a book should be determined solely on the basis of its value to the library for research and not on whether it is a bargain or a nice museum piece. If we have $100 to spend, how can it be used to the best advantage for the university? Occasionally it may be wise to buy a museum piece when it can be obtained at a bargain because we believe it will encourage gifts of similar material. Occasionally a library will have all the books by a certain author but one, and that a rare one. If $50 will round out the collection, it may seem desirable to be what at other times would be called extravagant. The question immediately and very properly comes up as to the possibility and desirability of using photographic reproductions when the originals are expensive. We cannot take time for a long discussion on this point, but we should remember that inexpensive photographic methods have made possible the acquisition of materials that could not in other ways be obtained and that their value is not likely to be overestimated. On the other hand, we should remember the limitations imposed on scholars by photographic reproductions. We must realize, as some of us have not seemed to do, that there are many things that photographic reproductions cannot do that the originals can.

Before going on to a discussion of methods of obtaining material from the fields it is decided to cultivate, there is one other problem to be faced. That is the duplication of effort by libraries located in the same region. This is a matter of such great importance that it should be discussed on every possible occasion. I say this in spite of the fact that I realize that millions of words have been applied to it in the past generation with little to show as a result. Put briefly, the problem may be stated as follows.

If one library in an area already has an expensive volume or set, and there is little demand for it, is there any excuse for a second library in the same area buying it? My answer is emphatically "No!" In almost all cases, duplication of expensive material within an area should depend on the demand. The more expensive the material, the more hesitancy there should be in duplication; the smaller the demand, the slower we should be in buying second copies. In the case of very expensive and very little-used material, the region in which duplication is unnecessary may be greatly widened. The most satisfactory way to avoid duplication in the same fields by two libraries is the definite division of fields between them. Unfortunately, because of what has gone on in the past, this is always difficult and often impossible. However, with the aid of the new edition of the *Union List of Serials*, which will be out, we hope, next year, and with the use of the telephone or letter in the case of books costing, let us say, $25 or more, it should be possible to avoid much unnecessary duplication without the expenditure of too much effort. At any rate, this problem should be before us continually.

When we have decided what the acquisition program should be, and the type of material that we want to acquire in each field, we must then decide how to go about it to consummate the desired result. In the average large library—university or research—it seems to me self-evident that the librarian does not have time and probably does not have the knowledge or ability to do the selection himself, or even to guide it in any detail. In comparatively few cases will the man in charge of the order department or his assistants be able to take responsibility for book selection.

I have already stated my belief that too much reliance on faculty initiative has been unfortunate —I might almost say disastrous. What then can be done? It seems to me evident that the solution should be twofold.

1. While we should not expect the faculty to do the work without aid or compulsion, full benefit

of the special knowledge residing with its members should be taken advantage of, and every effort made to persuade its members to suggest freely titles for purchase and also to cover systematically the fields in which they work.

2. I believe that at least in a large institution the subjects which the library tries to cover should be divided between members of the library staff. In these libraries it should be possible to find men and women who have a fair, even if somewhat superficial, knowledge of most of the broad fields. These assistants may do very little of the book selection themselves, but they should have the responsibility of seeing that there are called to the attention of the faculty members who are specialists the various lists of new books and old books that are available and that these specialists shall be almost forced to make recommendations. The staff members should then try to cover material that falls between the different lines cared for by the faculty and thus round out the work.

I believe that a plan of this kind, carried out systematically, would result in better book selection than is now possible in any university library in the country.

So much for a book-selection program for a university library. I have taken too much time with it perhaps, but it is a basic problem. We come now to our second main point: the organization and administration of an acquisition department. Obviously a department should not be organized until we know what work it is to do. It must first be determined whether it should be the book-selection department as well as the order department. In my opinion the two do not necessarily go together and probably should not go together in most libraries. It happens rarely that a good book-buyer is also a first-class book-selector, and certainly the main and final responsibility for the book selection should lie not in the order department but in other hands: those of the librarian, the faculty, or the library assistants referred to in the earlier part of this talk. The order department, however, is not without duties in connection with book selection. It is the department to which information about books comes—trade lists, catalogs, etc.—and it is certainly its duty (1) to call to the attention of the proper officials of the institution material both new and old that is available for purchase and (2) to see that the selection is done and the fields in which the library is interested are covered. Later, when the material has been selected by others, the department must first learn whether it is yet in the library in a satis-

factory form and, if not, to see that it is acquired promptly and inexpensively. (3) In this connection and closely related to it is the responsiblility of the chief of the division who places the order for books to avoid ordering beyond the ability of the library to pay. When orders come in too thick and fast, he must be the brake—sometimes a four-wheel one—and prevent overordering or be sure that the responsibility for running into debt is thrown back on the librarian.

The organization of an acquisition department will naturally divide itself according to the types of material and the methods by which they are acquired. The bulk of the acquisitions fall into large groups: books and pamphlets and serials and documents. They are acquired ordinarily in one of three ways: (1) by purchase, (2) by gift, either as a result of begging or without begging, directly from those who publish it or from friends of the institution, and (3) by exchange.

But there is other work that is generally done by an acquisition department. This includes the handling of duplicates, the checking-up of books that have been requested for purchase to see if they are already in the library, the large amount of clerical work in connection with the various tasks assigned to the department, and the outside contacts with the book trade. It is unwise certainly to be dogmatic and say that an acquisition department of a library of 500,000 volumes with a book budget of $50,000 a year should be organized in two, three, four, five, or six sections covering the different points that have been suggested. The organization will depend on the size of the work and the size of the staff and also on the physical arrangements of the space it occupies, the acquisition policies, etc. In most large libraries it has been found advisable to place the straight purchasing in one group. As the department becomes larger, the ordering of documents and serials may well be divided from the book and pamphlet section, or at least the responsibility for this may be placed in the hands of a subsection. The handling of begging, the acknowledgment of gifts, can very well be put in a separate group when it becomes a large enough task to take the time of one or more persons, as this work needs to be handled very carefully in order to avoid unpleasant and disastrous complications. The exchange work may well be attached to the gift section, except in the very largest institutions. The handling of duplicates can sometimes be grouped with the exchanges. "Searching" may perhaps best be turned over to the catalog department rather than the acquisition department. In a very large institution a typists' pool should in some cases be established. Outside contacts that have been spoken of are ordinarily concentrated in the hands of the chief of the department so as to prevent difficulties that result when work of this kind is done by too many different people.

But before the department can be properly organized, decision should probably be reached as to its relationship with other departments of the library; for instance, should it be combined with the catalog department; with the accession department if there is one; what is its relationship to the various reading-rooms; to the business offices; to the faculty; to the chief librarian? Again it would be unwise to attempt to make a dogmatic statement. Circumstances alter cases. Personalities involved should be considered; fiscal arrangements and policies cannot be ignored. At any rate here are some suggestions: The acquisition department, other things being equal, may well be a department by itself instead of being combined with the catalog department and the other parts of the library that deal with the processing of books before they are available. However, if a library is large enough and complicated enough so that the chief librarian cannot pay direct attention to the work, and so that there are enough departments to make it unwise for him to attempt to deal directly with the chiefs of both the acquisition and the catalog departments, then there should be an assistant librarian who is in charge of all the processing groups. If this is the case, the assistant librarian will naturally be the administrator, not primarily a book-buyer or a cataloger himself, and will simply represent the librarian for this large section of the library's work. It would be difficult to find a man who was a first-class administrator and who was also a first-class book-buyer. The two do not usually go together; indeed it often happens that a good buyer is not enough of an administrator to handle a complicated acquisition department satisfactorily since that department often involves a tremendous amount of routine work. If this is the case, there should be a first assistant in the division who can take the responsibility for that part of the task.

The relationship between the acquisition department and the other parts of the library must always be close and on a cordial basis, not only in order to keep the wheels going smoothly but because, with any tendency in the other direction, records of various kinds will soon be built up to protect one department against the other, and

records made for no other use than protection against another department of the library are, in my opinion, pure waste and completely inexcusable.

The relationship with the business office brings up another problem. In many libraries the acquisition department simply turns over the bills to the business office of the institution and lets that office pay them. In others, work of this kind is actually done by a finance section of the acquisition department. I have no brief to hold for either method. Again the decision should be made according to the local setup.

The relationship with the faculty has already been spoken of in connection with the book selection. The faculty should be encouraged to keep in close touch with the order department. Otherwise full advantage cannot be taken of expert advice that might be obtained.

Satisfactory relations with the parts of the library that serve the public are also of importance in order to insure good service by the acquisition group to the readers. Books are acquired not for show or to preserve them but because someone is sometime going to use them.

One other point that may well affect the whole organization of an acquisition department and which might have been considered under the administration of the book-selection-program part of this paper is the need for an organization that will learn about and call to the attention of the proper authorities and then, if possible, acquire (1) new materials of all types published outside the regular trade (much of this can be obtained free of charge) and (2) special bargains of material that has been collected by others and has come on the market.

To do these things requires a wide-awake organization, and while, as I have said, it is part of the administration of a book-selection program, it is also a matter of the organization of the acquisition department itself and one for which the department must take most of the responsibility.

We have discussed a book-selection program particularly for a university library have said something about the organization of an acquisition department from an administrative point of view, taking up briefly in general terms the various sections into which the department might be divided. We are now ready to talk about the staff that will do the work considered earlier.

I shall not attempt to go into detail about the types of individuals required but will discuss the education and training that are of importance. I do want, however, to state that in my opinion no library has laid too much stress on the selection of personnel and that in the long run, if there are proper training facilities in a library, the selection of people with the right personal qualifications and natural ability means more than the selection of those who happen to have had the proper background and training. I say this in spite of my great interest in library schools. Poor people with good experience and training in the long run are generally less useful than good people with poor backgrounds. We want good people. Given them, what kind of training is required in an acquisition department? Should we have a large section of the staff with library-school training?

I would say without hesitation that the chief of the department *or* his first assistant should have library-school training in order to make sure that the point of view and the background so gained is available. It may well be, however, that the chief who often should be primarily a book-buyer will not have the training and that a knowledge of the book trade may be more important than a library-school education. If this is the case, the first assistant should be a library-school graduate. In a large library it is probably desirable that the heads of the various sections that have been discussed have training, but after we have gone that far I am heretic enough to feel that most of the other work in an acquisition department, even in a large one, can be done as well and often better by people without training in a library school.

This brings me to a point where I am glad to have an opportunity to express my opinion. It is extravagant and unwise to have work done by a library-school graduate that can be done just as well by a good clerical assistant. It is unwise and extravagant from the point of view of the library, the profession as a whole, and the individuals involved. It helps no one in the long run. Let me now go on and say that I think most clerical work can be done better by a well-trained clerical assistant than by a library-school graduate. This is not necessarily so if you are thinking of work for a day or a week or a month only. But taken year in and year out, the trained assistant will tend to go stale on a clerical job. A person should not be admitted to library school unless he is capable of doing something more than clerical work, and if he is capable of doing more than clerical work, he probably will not stay happy doing it. If I am correct in the statements just made, and if most of the routine work in an acquisition department is to be done by clerical assistants, it does not neces-

sarily mean that no special training is required. Typing, of course, should be done by typists who are well trained and experienced. Few of us realize how much more work a first-class typist will turn out than a second-rate one. In this connection I might mention the large and particularly well-trained typing staff in a university library that I know, the individual members of which turn out approximately twice as much work as the average typist doing similar tasks in other libraries. What has been said about typing applies equally well to stenographic work, to filing, and other clerical tasks. Having gone this far and having emphasized the desirability, first, of not having people with special library training doing routine clerical work, and having emphasized the importance of having the clerical work done by people who have the proper training for it, let me go on and say that I do not believe it is wise in any routine task to employ people regularly who are too good for the work they are doing. If you have people who have too much ability, too much training for the jobs that they hold, sooner or later they will become dissatisfied. With this in mind, it is of real importance to have a possibility of promotion for the capable and adaptable people who happen to come onto the staff. If an assistant with unusual ability has a good chance for promotion within the library, the danger that comes from having superior people in an inferior job may be avoided.

We are now ready for the fourth section of our subject—types of records and accounts to be kept in an acquisition department. Within the time allowed me it would be impossible to discuss even briefly all the records that can properly be kept in even a small acquisition department. It may be worth while to present a little general advice to start with. At best the records must be complicated and detailed. At best they must be numerous. In every organization that I know anything about which has routine records, these records tend to multiply as time goes on. It is always easy to find an excuse for installing a new record. Everything that is added takes time. We may think it will take only a little time and will be useful, but it must be remembered that it will take time this week, next week, and next year, and every effort should be made to keep the records simple, to keep them as few as possible in number. Notwithstanding all efforts that may be made in this direction, the records will accumulate, and in my experience I have found that it is necessary to go over them at regular intervals and find those that can be eliminated. I was once connected with an acquisition department where the records became so complicated that it took a year to break in a new assistant satisfactorily. The records were studied carefully and simplified, and it became possible to break in a new assistant in two weeks, and the discarded records were never missed. So my first suggestion is: keep the records simple.

One more piece of general advice. That is to watch for records that are partially or completely duplicated in other departments of the library. Each department naturally wants its own. It is often found, however, that one record will do for two. If an acquisition and catalog department are side by side, is there any reason why the acquisition department should have an outstanding order file and the catalog department have an "in process" file recording books for which the cataloging has not yet been completed? Why should not these two files be combined and between them give a record of all books that the library expects to have available in the near future but which are not yet cataloged? Only one file need then be referred to when new books are under consideration for purchase. If book bills can give the information required in connection with accession records, why should they not be used in place of such records? If there are now three records for the serial publications in the library, cannot one of them be given up?

Each record should be examined critically. Just because, by the use of carbons, six copies of an order slip can be made almost as easily as one, does not mean that six can be used as cheaply. Each must be filed, checked, and finally discarded. These processes take time and cost money. A record should not be kept unless in the long run it saves more time or money than it takes to make and use. If you will keep this in mind, you can go ahead and do as you like about records and still not come to grief.

We should not leave the question of records and accounts that are kept in an acquisition department without mentioning at least a few more specific points. In most libraries there should be a desiderata list—material that is wanted but that has not been available when wanted, or available only at a cost that seemed too high. There should be records kept in connection with the begging and the exchange work. There should probably be a special record in a large library for the part of the work that deals with languages not using the Latin alphabet. When it comes to serial as well as to other types of records, full advantage should be

taken of modern business methods and gadgets. For instance, visible indexes may save considerable time. There are various types and new varieties now available. Some of them are placed on wheels and at least one is electrically controlled through a keyboard. Do not install a record of this kind just because it is an interesting new gadget, but do acquire it if it will pay for itself within a short period. Look into the question of punched cards. They are used in some libraries in acquisition departments, although in my opinion not always to advantage. In other libraries they do save time and effort.

I am a great believer in co-operation and a great believer in any plan that will cut overhead and administrative costs. When it comes to the co-operative purchase of books, some basic principles are involved. Co-operation brings one more process between the producer and the consumer. That step means records and costs money. Does it save in some way more than enough to make up for the extra cost? To be sound, a co-operative plan must save more money than it costs. Now let us go one step further. How does it save? It saves through quantity purchases which make possible a larger discount. Quantity purchases may be many copies of the same book, or copies of many books from the same publisher. If libraries that buy the same book can combine and will take their time so that orders can accumulate, surely there are advantages in buying through the same place, but this holds true in our libraries in the United States only for new American and perhaps English books, and in the case of large research libraries these represent only a small part of the purchases. If it is agreed that there are savings, how should co-operative buying be organized? Jobbers such as Baker and Taylor and Putnam, who are now available, are co-operative buying organizations working commercially. They must make a profit. The crux of the matter is whether they are good enough business organizations so that they can make a profit and still do as well by the libraries as a non-profit-making co-operative plan. I cannot answer that question. Circumstances alter cases. At one time one plan is likely to be better; at another, the other way round. Just remember that few of us succeed for any length of time in getting something for nothing in this world.

Before leaving the question of co-operative buying, one other point of importance should be made. It might appear from what has already been said that co-operative buying in many cases is a questionable procedure. In my opinion one of its most favorable arguments lies in the fact that, through it, it is possible to avoid unnecessary duplication of purchases by the co-operating libraries. This may be of two kinds: unnecessary duplication of fields and within fields, as was indicated earlier in this paper. It is unfortunate when two libraries in the same region specialize in the same fields, as there are sure to be others that no one cultivates. Sometimes, however, because of developments that have occurred in the past and that cannot be changed, this is necessary. Even in these cases, it may be possible to avoid much duplication, particularly in the case of rare books and long, expensive sets.

Our final problem deals with the essentials of an acquisition program in a small library. As my direct contacts for many years have been altogether with the three largest libraries in the country, I know very little about small libraries and their programs, and anything that I have to say about them should certainly be taken with many grains of salt, and anything I can contribute must be superficial and general in character. The book-selection program in a small library is in some ways simple since it does not involve as much money and as many fields and because of the satisfactory aids which are available, such as the A.L.A. *Book List* and the *Book Review Digest*. It is complicated, however, by the fact that the governing board of the small library is more prone to interfere and because, with small funds and with many books available for purchase, selection must really be made more carefully and a smaller percentage of the available titles chosen. The large library with ample funds buys books not just because they are good books but because they illustrate some point of view on a subject in which the library is interested. A small library cannot afford, for reasons of space and money, to buy any book unless it fills a specific need and is a first-class book of its kind.

When it comes to the organization and administration of an acquisition department in a small library, the problem is comparatively simple. The staff will consist generally of only one person, or perhaps the part time of one person, and no division of labor between individuals is necessary. No comments seem needed in this connection except the general warning that I have emphasized all

through my paper that simplicity is desirable. As far as the selection of the staff is concerned, if the work is done by the librarian or the assistant librarian, who have other duties which may take more time, it may depend on the training and ability needed for the other work rather than for acquisition work. At any rate, the advice already given that personnel is a matter of first importance should be kept in mind.

The records needed may be very similar to those in a large library but should of course be on a smaller scale and again should be kept as few and simple as possible.

This talk, as I warned you at the beginning, is general in character. One cannot be specific on many things in fifty minutes, and there has been a wide field to cover. I fear I have been dogmatic and trite; I am sure that most of what I have had to say has been obvious, but I hope that most of the essentials have been covered.

I might summarize as follows: We do need to have a definite book-selection program and, when we have it, to administer it well. In a university library at least this involves a real problem. We must know where we are going, and someone must be responsible for seeing to it that we go there to the best of our ability, financial and otherwise. We must get all the help we can from the faculty, readers, and from the staff, but with the librarian lies the final responsibility.

In speaking of the organization and administration of the acquisition department, I have emphasized just as strongly as I could that there is no one arrangement that is right. The best arrangements in any library depend altogether on the local situation, and it is foolish to try to be arbitrary.

As far as staff is concerned, the need for the best possible personnel was emphasized, but I tried to make it clear that that does not necessarily mean, and probably should not mean, library training for a large part of the work. Clerical work should be done by people trained for that work, not by professional assistants.

The records kept in an acquisition department should be as simple as possible, the fewer the better. Each record should justify itself and each record should be considered from time to time to see if it cannot be given up.

The Administration of Acquisition and Exchange

Allen B. Veaner

SCOPE

Within the time allotted for this paper, I shall concentrate on those problems relevant to the procurement of current materials and retrospective materials still in print. I exclude from consideration the purchase of out of print books and micropublications, mainly because both are highly specialized topics which deserve separate papers.

THE UNIQUENESS OF BOOK PURCHASING

Of all the materials purchased on a continuing basis by universities and research centers, books are by far the oddest. They are bought by the tens of hundreds of thousands, yet any two hardly ever resemble each other. They are obtained from thousands of vendors in nearly every country of the world. Their physical characteristics vary widely: weight, size, paper, type font, shape, color, etc. Their languages, their intellectual qualities, and their bibliographic descriptions vary widely, and the latter two items are often the subjects of controversy. No other commodity, essential for the existence of a research center approaches the uniqueness of the book. This uniqueness is responsible for the charm they hold for bibliophiles, but this same individuality accounts for most of the difficulties in acquiring books.

INTERACTION OF FORCES IN THE BOOK TRADE

The acquisition of library materials brings about the interaction of many parties whose interests definitely conflict. They are the selectors—curators, faculty, students, staff—the acquisition staff, the cataloging and reference staff, the controller or agency carrying fiscal responsibility, the vendor, the international monetary system, the transportation system, and in a few instances, the political jurisdiction.

In terms of the above interests, let us define some qualitative and quantitative differences in products and services in a typical acquisition system.

This matrix is a highly simplified and abstract picture of a complex communication process between many parties, something that in modern parlance might be called a communication network. In practical terms, this reduces to people talking or writing to other people about the books they want, creating and maintaining records and files, updating messages from time to time, and recording the transactions.

FILE MANAGEMENT

The control center for all this activity is a set of files, usually consisting of an outstanding order file, a file of invoices, and historical records of expenditures, such as budget statements. Some systems will contain additional files which in effect index the master file by date, vendor, purchase order number, or local account number. Maintaining and searching a large multilingual file is an extremely difficult task and requires a high order of management skill. It is in the area of file management where some computer assistance may be helpful, though at this time there is very little experience in handling large computerized files of bibliographic data. Little is known about the psy-

SOURCE: Reprinted from a paper presented at the Japan-U.S. Conference on Libraries and Information Science, Tokyo, May, 1969, by permission of the author.

chological aspects of file searching, but it is apparent that the proficient searcher is the key to an efficient manual acquisition system which must necessarily provide a limited number of access points to each record.

In connection with file organization, it is useful to record a new and recent trend. For a long time, acquisition files were maintained in a primary sequence by author and secondarily by title, following the pattern of the conventional card catalog. Today, more libraries are adopting a straight title sequence, partly to combat filing difficulties and partly out of the realization that there is no reason why a temporary control file should slavishly imitate the dictionary catalog.

PROBLEMS OF FISCAL CONTROL SYSTEMS

Wide price variation is one of the factors which distinguishes book purchasing from any other buying in research centers, and it complicates fiscal control. Now some faculty members and book selection experts behave as if there were an infinite supply of money, but in this age of expensive reprints and keen competition for out-of-print titles, tight fiscal control is essential. In some libraries this means hiring a bookkeeper to maintain an independent, separate accounting system, in which each commitment or payment transaction is logged. The manager of the acquisition system must take care not to delegate book purchasing authority to the bookkeeper; a non-librarian should not be accorded the power to halt an outgoing purchase order.

In most large organizations, there is a substantial time lag in processing invoices because of the great number of documents and the batch processing method. Even if a computer is available, invoice documents must still be keyboarded before they can be handled by computer. It is doubtful that we will soon see the development of internationally standardized invoice documents printed in both human and machine-readable form. The handwritten or typed invoice is going to be with us for a long time.

Another problem with the invoice turns on the processing unit—for the buyer, the preferred processing unit is the title, but for the seller it is the invoice. To process a consolidated invoice for payment, the buyer has to determine what portion of that invoice is assignable to his several bibliographic and fiscal records. In particular, the buyer may have to apply portions of various book funds to one invoice, a process that is time consuming and cumbersome. The internal transfer of monies from various budgets to write a single check in payment of one invoice adds to the controller's overhead. One solution is to permit the library to commingle funds into a few large budgets and then make quarterly reconciliations to the multiplicity of funds supplying these budgets. It is a generous and understanding controller who will permit this. A few vendors provide individual invoices for each title purchased; this eliminates the problem, but such a service is only available from very large vendors. Therefore, the combined invoice is also going to be with us for a long time.

Selection and purchasing, then, are ideally one-for-one processes; as soon as fiscal and invoice processing enter the data stream, the processing mode shifts, to many-for-one: many books and many book budgets, one invoice, when these same invoices enter the controller's shop, processing is reversed and becomes one-for-many, i.e., one consolidated check is written to pay many vendor invoices. The blank check plan is an attempt to maintain a one-for-one processing mode throughout the acquisition cycle. A blank check valid for some upper limit—usually $100—is sent to the vendor as an integral part of the purchase order form. The vendor fills in the exact amount of payment and the cancelled check is used to post the budget statement. An advantage is the vendor is paid promptly and accurately; a disadvantage is that the vendor has to handle a large number of checks. The checks are usually valid for a limited time and there could be problems with books that are out of stock or awaiting reprinting—they might be ready for delivery after the blank check is no longer valid. Also in some institutions the controller is reluctant to delegate his check writing authority, or he may worry about the security of negotiable checks not under his direct control.

Librarians should be wary of permitting establishment of excessively restricted gift or endowment funds, regardless of their size. In some fields, the income might greatly exceed the cost of all the material published in a decade; in other cases, the restricted field may be so highly specialized that it becomes difficult to find material to buy. So in the end, the donor is unhappy, the librarian is unhappy, and the controller must maintain a fund that is not very active.

Despite advances in electronic data communication, there is little likelihood that the book trade

INTERACTION OF FORCES IN ACQUISITION OF LIBRARY MATERIALS

Product Service, or System Characteristics	Book Selector	Staff of Acq. Dept.	Reference Librarians	Catalogers	Controller	Vendor	Monetary System	Transportation	Political Jurisdiction	Faculty, Students Researchers	Serial Department
Required quality of bibliographic data	Low to medium	Medium to high	High	High	Low	Medium to High	–	–	Variable	Variable	High
Required quantity of bibliographic data	Low to medium	Medium	High	High	Low	Low to medium	–	–	Variable	Medium	High
Required delivery speed of books	Variable	High	High	–	High	High	–	Variable	–	High	High
Physical Unit of Processing	Vol.	Vol.; Packages	Vol., set, indiv. page	Vol.	{ Invoice; accts. payable; budget statements; payment vouchers; Checks	Vol. Checks	Checks	Packages	Vol.	Title; Vol.	Vol.
Information Unit of Processing	Bibl. record	Bibl. record; invoice	Bibl. record	Bibl. record	}	accts. receivable; invoices	–	letters; purchase orders; invoices	Bibl. record	Bibl. record	Bibl. record
Mode of Processing physical items	Unit; batch (rare)	Unit & batch	Unit	Unit	–	Unit & batch	–	Unit (rare) & batch	Variable	Unit	Unit
Mode of Processing information & data	Unit	Unit & batch	Unit	Unit	Batch	Unit & batch	Batch (many for one)	Unit & batch	–	Unit	Unit & batch
Degree of interest in fiscal control	Variable	High	Low	Low	High	High	–	–	High	Low	High
Interest in Intellectual quality of materials	High	–	High	–	–	Variable	–	–	–	High	–

Interacting Agency, Department

will soon be free of paper handling. There are too many different legal and managerial requirements among institutions, and developing countries will probably be dependent on manual data processing for some time.

PATTERNS OF BOOK PURCHASING

The classical pattern of book procurement has turned upon individual selection and ordering from announcements, advertisements, and national and trade bibliographies. Where budgets are severely limited (as in small public libraries) this method is practically obligatory, but for current materials, college, university, and research libraries are turning more and more to the approval order system, sometimes designated the "blanket order plan." In this scheme, the selectors draw up a profile which characterizes the desired acquisition plan within a given discipline or language. Actual selection of titles is then turned over to the vendor. Of course, to support this system the vendor must employ broadly educated selectors who know something about the academic program in a given institution. Periodically, he ships to the library his selection of newly published titles and the local selectors winnow the material by actual examination—no doubt the best way to pick books. The approval system has a built-in 100% return privilege for any title not desired by the customer. In effect, the vendor is gambling that returns will not exceed some maximum percentage beyond which his handling costs would make the arrangement uprofitable. The approval plan has two great advantages for the buyer: (1) he is assured of delivery immediately after publication of one copy of each new title of interest to him, thus practically eliminating the risk that a book may go out of print before an order can be placed, and (2) the book never enters the buyer's fiscal or bibliographical control system unless it is accepted. The buyer pays only for those books which he keeps; no refunds or credits need to be negotiated. Some vendors even prepare multiple copy control slips for a library's retention to assist in file maintenance and technical processing.

A major reason for this shift is the recent very great expansion of publishing and acquisition. Colleges and universities are growing at seemingly alarming rates; the federal government in the U.S. has been greatly assisting the purchase of library

materials under the Higher Education Act of 1965. The Acquisition rate in American academic libraries doubled in the six years between 1960 and 1966. Library schools have been unable to supply enough professionals to man acquisition services and there has been no easing of the recruitment problem with clerical support staff. These forces have combined to overwhelm the library's conventional ordering and receiving procedures, some of which may not have been rationally planned. There is much evidence that many traditional acquisition procedures lack rationality; were it not for the establishment of approval plans, the whole acquisition process in many libraries might have collapsed entirely.

The approval plan is not without some risks. One obvious problem is the quality of the vendor's selection. There is a risk that one may miss desired books or receive titles not really wanted. The only remedy is constant monitoring by local selectors and proper feedback to the vendor; without this an approval plan is likely to fail. A second risk to be weighted is the probability of inferior books getting into one's collection. However, elimination of the labor of selecting current items, searching them in the files, and typing purchase orders more than compensates for a few bad books.

A third problem with the approval plan is the possibility of conflict with long established standing orders, especially if standing orders have been scattered among many vendors. The ideal arrangement is to take the approval plan and the standing orders from the same vendor, but if this isn't possible an exclusion list can be helpful to the chosen vendor. The adoption of an approval plan may require some departures from traditional practises. I have heard of one library which wants to maintain a file of all the approval titles it has returned "just in case the vendor claims payment for a returned volume." This defeats a prime advantage of the system, whereby one's files need control only the items actually accepted. In those rare cases where the vendor submits an invalid claim, it is usually cheaper to just pay the invoice rather than keep superfluous records.

A variant blanket order plan is Stechert-Hafner's Latin American Cooperation Acquisition Program (LACAP). This plan is dependent upon travelling agents who try to cover the principal publishers and bookstores in each country. These itinerant agents also need to know the authors because in Latin America authors often negotiate directly with printers and distribute books from their own homes or offices.

In the United States certain libraries are required by law to work within a jurisdictional purchasing department or are compelled to purchase library materials by bidding. The expertise of the purchasing agent is invaluable for economizing on the commercial products essential for running a research center—he buys the blackboards, the consumable supplies, the furniture, etc. But his staff almost never has the linguistic competence and the bibliographic tools to provide a book purchasing service to the library. He also may lack motivation, since his customary purchasing is much farther from an academic program than is the library's work.

The bidding system usually goes hand in hand with the requirements that libraries obtain their books through a centralized purchasing department. Except for large quantities of the same title, we know, of course, that it is unrealistic to ask for bids on single copies of library materials. There are two powerful reasons for staying away from the bid system: first, it almost forces the buyer to do business with a single vendor; second, it is simply inefficient to bid for single, unique items which are relatively low in unit cost.

There is yet another hazard to the bid system, a danger that has been particularly troublesome in the United States. This is the problem of the unqualified vendor. The unqualified vendor needs only a typewriter, a telephone, a small office, and a few clerks. By bidding low, he tries to obtain an exclusive contract. From then on, he acts only as a clearinghouse, consolidating book orders from various sources and forwarding them to the publisher, usually with instructions that the ordered items be shipped directly to the destination. There are several advantages to this scheme and all accrue to the benefit of the vendor: since he stocks no books, he needs no warehouse; he can easily avoid hunting for an out of stock book by simply reporting to the library that the book is not available and cancelling the order. The problem became so acute that several years ago the American Library Association and the National League of Cities jointly sponsored a study of book purchasing in the United States. A principal recommendation of the report, which will be published shortly, is that libraries supported by jurisdictions be exempt from bidding requirements and allowed to use their experience and judgment in choosing vendors.

EXCHANGES

There are whole categories of material available only by exchange, either because certain publications are not distributed in the book trade or because the book trade in a given nation is not well developed. In countries like the U.S. where labor costs are high, exchange is one of the less efficient methods of obtaining materials, owing to the great amount of correspondence needed to negotiate each exchange. It is also laborious to post records of exchanges and such records must be kept for a long time to resolve controversies. Determining the economic value of a given exchange can sometimes take on the character of a delicate diplomatic negotiation. The "scorekeeping" aspects of exchange can be troublesome and irritating. It is hard to balance an exchange of goods where the traders differ substantially in prosperity. My own feeling is that if national currency policies permit, the advanced countries should give first preference to regular purchase routines, falling back on exchange only if the partner suffers hardship through lack of hard currency.

Various methods are employed to balance accounts between partners: page for page, volume for volume, or the "priced" exchange. In the last named method, each partner agrees beforehand to the equivalent cash value for certain publications, and a fictitious ledger is posted to keep account of the "money," although no cash ever changes hands.

Procurement by exchange is necessarily slower than direct purchasing, if only because of the normal time lag in correspondence. Additionally, communication and postal services in developing countries may be slow. Sometimes when the person in charge of exchange leaves, he takes his correspondence with him, and his successor has no record of your prior negotiations. Political instability contributes to the difficulty of maintaining continuity of exchanges.

Press runs in developing countries may be small, and current material may go out of print before it can be obtained by exchange. One effective countermeasure is to secure the services of a resident or regional agent who is well informed on the needs of your library. Owing to the vastness of its international exchange operations the Library of Congress is able to employ such persons who can see to the selection, wrapping, addressing and shipping of desired materials.

Some materials are not well suited for exchange. Irregular serials are among them. Even regular, dependable serials are difficult because in most cases the subscription supplied from the advanced country will be obtained through a subscription agency, while the periodical itself will be sent direct from the publisher. This multipath flow makes it hard to maintain continuity. Nevertheless, subscriptions are much in demand by partners exactly because they tend to be expensive and can easily drain off scarce hard currency.

The use of exchange for domestic procurement is declining and is considered an archaic practise by many. Commonly, a library obtained a quantity of its own institutions publications at a favorable price and exchanged them with other libraries which did essentially the same thing. Because of the aforementioned high overhead costs of correspondence, both lost in the process.

REPRINT PROCUREMENT

Reprints present two special problems, on bibliographic and one financial. Some reprinters persist in issuing reprints with titles differing significantly from those assigned to the original works. In my opinion, this constitutes a malpractise, because one can find oneself buying an expensive reprint of a title already in the library. The buyer should be wary of reprints advertised with scant bibliographic information and, if expensive, the titles should be searched with redoubled persistence until their identity, or lack thereof, is definitely established. Besides the risk of wasting resources on titles already in the library, the financial problem is additionally irritated by the high price of reprints and by the widespread practise known as "fishing." "Fishing" is the issuance of prospectuses and announcements without bona fide intention of publishing the reprint unless enough market is indicated by responses from purchasers. Often a special, prepublication price, which is difficult to turn down, is offered. There is a risk of tying down sorely needed funds in anticipation of needing them for the reprints when they arrive; if the reprints are never issued or are issued many years later, the library's purchasing power for other materials has been impaired. The bold solution to the problem is to call the reprinter's bluff, and order the material without encumbering funds. The other solution is to

learn from the experience of others and get to know who are the dependable reprinters.

Rapid expansion of educational institutions is making reprinting a very attractive business. Because reprinters concentrate mainly on material no longer protected by copyright, their capital investment is minimal: a good, clean copy of the original, suitable for photomechanical reproduction, a plate-making camera, offset printing facilities, and bindery. Hence, one can find the same title reprinted two or three times by different reprinters working from different copies of the original document. When this happens, prices may vary widely, and the buyer may benefit from the competition.

In the past, many libraries willingly lent books to reprinters without compensation, only to find the reissued works offered at prices judged exploitative. Also, in a few cases, to meet the needs of photomechanical reproduction processes, books have been damaged by reprinters. As an aid to libraries and reprinters, the American Library Association has adopted a set of guidelines, "Lending to Reprinters," in which are set forth basic principles of good practise for both the library and the reprinter. This statement has been published in the Spring 1967 issue of *Library Resources & Technical Services*, vol. 11, pages 229-231.

CENTRALIZED TECHNICAL PROCESSING SERVICES

In the U.S. the introduction of systems analysis and computer applications is furthering an already popular pattern of organizing acquisition and cataloging work, namely the formation of unified technical processing departments. Here the aim is to minimize doing the same job twice or more— mainly in searching for authoritative bibliographic data and in transcribing found data. This centripetal tendency is particularly beneficial for larger systems which need to supply purchasing and bibliographic services for outlying units which lack the staff or bibliographic tools for processing.

Essentially, the establishment of any centralized service by definition creates a large batch operation. The larger the batch, the less the unit processing cost, but the greater the turnaround time. It is the "large batch" characteristic which is responsible for the generally slow response time of centralized services. This phenomenon partly explains the performance difference between a library acquisition department and a bookstore. Popular titles, whether from trade or scholarly presses, often appear very early in bookstores. But compared with the university or research library, the bookstore's procurement efforts are spread over a much narrower range of titles—hence, it sometimes appears to students and faculty that the campus bookstore is more efficient than the library. However, bookstores buy titles in quantity, often directly from the publisher; therefore they often skip the middleman who caters to the library market. The college or university bookstore may show spectacular success with a relatively small number of titles, but very few of them have the talent or bibliographic tools to dig out the more obscure and difficult to obtain publications. Here is where the service facilities of the jobber outweigh a few extra points of discount.

An important new development is the growing popularity of commercial services which not only supplies books but also complete bibliographic data and processing services—even complete catalogs. In the U.S. it is possible to obtain from a single source book, plastic book cover, spine label, book pocket, charge card, and catalog cards for many in print titles likely to be purchased by school and public libraries. For books which sell in large quantities, such services are obtainable far more cheaply than any library could provide with its own resources.

When one adds the rapidly growing tendency to ship books by air freight to the possibility of utilizing the computer to process bibliographic data, one comes up with a powerful combination which could challenge the economic liability of local technical processing in the academic library. In the U.S. it appears a likely trend that the large vendors may become not only retailers of books but also retailers of complete bibliographic services, based upon a quickly obtainable machine readable record distributed by the nation's wholesaler—the Library of Congress.

PERSONNEL SELECTION IN ACQUISITIONS

Searchers are the heart of any acquisition system. Their recruitment and training are a challenging task for several reasons. A wide range of language and subject competence is needed—a combination not easy to obtain. Many of the personnel requirements are contradictory: constant alertness combined with the ability to withstand monotony. There are certain intangible characteristics of the good searcher; he is a persistent, dogged sleuth, perhaps resembling somewhat the dedicated police inspector. But searchers must not be *too* perfectionistic. Good supervisory practise calls for a chief bibliographer or head of the searching unit to sort incoming book requisitions into batches, which are then distributed to the searchers in accordance with their language facility and experience. A searcher should not receive a new batch of requisitions until all of the previously assigned searching work has been completed. This will serve to prevent searchers from burying the hard searches in their desk drawers and doing only the easy ones.

Searchers require a good deal of physical stamina—a searcher may walk greater distances each day than an airline stewardess. Finally, he must be willing to work for a relatively low salary. This last factor constitutes a real personnel problem for the manager and for the library profession. In some institutions, the nature of the searcher's responsibilities is not well understood by non-librarians; hence, searchers are sometimes treated as low grade clerks. If this happens, turnover will be high, costly duplication of orders will result, and important titles will not be obtained by the Library. To forestall such possibilities, the work of the searcher should be carefully documented and thoroughly explained. Good searchers are not easy to recruit and the good ones need to be nursed carefully. If searchers' salaries can be improved, then the manager must also strike some balance with the professional staff, few of whom will be willing to consider full-time careers as searchers.

Student wives seem to make good searchers—perhaps because they have already searched and found husbands! At any rate, they are often recent college graduates, well trained, alert, fast learners, energetic, and economically motivated. Such a candidate is well worth the risk of short-term employment. The worst risk is someone who is emotionally unstable or a misfit who imagines that the library is a convenient refuge from stress. In a large organization, it is well to consider cautiously anyone who requests a transfer to the library from some other part of the institution.

What is true for searchers applies equally to

filers. In order to fix responsibility in filing work, it is convenient to assign a specific part of the file to one individual for maintenance. This will motivate employees to care about the job they do.

TOWARDS WORLD BIBLIOGRAPHIC CONTROL

Global bibliographic control, which would be of immeasurable value to acquisition work, appears to be well on the way to reality with establishment of the Shared Cataloging Program, administered by the Library of Congress. Shared Cataloging brings under early bibliographic control several hundred thousand new publications each year. Within the past few years, it has enabled American academic libraries to increase their utilization of central bibliographic records from about 50% to nearly 75%. This program has further enabled accurate bibliographic data to enter the processing stream at a much earlier date, in some cases even before the books arrive in the library, which is naturally of great assistance to all technical processing operations.

Effectiveness of the Shared Cataloging Program is due entirely to the magnificent spirit of harmony shown by the national bibliographic centers throughout the world—a tribute to international cooperation.

A Symposium on Approval Order Plans and the Book Selection Responsibilities of Librarians

Perry D. Morrison

With reactions by LeRoy C. Merritt
Joseph P. Browne
Stanley A. Shepard

Of the numerous and pressing issues affecting the lives of acquisitions librarians in colleges and universities, this paper will deal with only two. Many and complex though the ramifications may be, the burden of the discourse may be stated simply: the "who" and the "how" of book selection and acquisition in academic libraries are both changing rapidly. The trend is away from exclusive dependence upon faculty-selection and title-by-title ordering of books to (1) a situation delegating a much larger role in book selection to librarians and (2) a growing reliance on blanket approval orders for acquiring books.

Evidence of these two rather profound changes is visible everywhere. These developments have not as yet received wide discussion in the professional literature. Robert P. Haro recently conducted a survey of 67 libraries. Of these, 62 reported that librarians were engaged in book selection beyond the traditional level of "reference materials and occasional general items." Haro found that larger libraries were tending to employ subject specialists in technical processes departments for selection work rather than depending exclusively upon reference librarians to perform selection in addition to their other duties.[1]

No overall assessment of blanket-order approval plans has yet appeared in the literature. However, the amount of effort dealers, and to some extent,

publishers, are devoting to these plans certainly indicates that they believe a market exists. One dealer based in the Pacific Northwest, for example, states that approximately 90 academic libraries are currently participating in one or more of his approval plans.

The reasons for the trend toward book selection from approval copies supplied automatically by publishers or dealers are not difficult to discern. First, the rapid rate of increase in academic library acquisitions programs is taxing the capacity of existing procedures. According to the statistics published by ALA and the University of Wisconsin at Milwaukee, academic libraries in the United States acquired twice as many books (and other library materials) in 1966 as they had in 1960. Furthermore, the rate of increase is rising: preliminary estimates place the increase in acquisitions between 1965 and 1966 at 29%.[2] Moreover, this reflects only the beginning of the influence of federal programs.

According to Theodore Samore, lately of the U.S. Office of Education but now with Wisconsin-Milwaukee:

With the assistance of Federal funds it appears that academic libraries are in a "take off" stage. Very likely, library resources 10 years from now will bear little or no resemblance to the here and now. For ex-

SOURCE: Reprinted from *Library Resources and Technical Services* XII, 12 (Spring 1968), pp. 133-145. Revised text of material presented to a workshop sponsored by the College Division of the Pacific Northwest Library Association at its Conference in Coeur d'Alene, Idaho, August 23, 1967, under the chairmanship of Mrs. Claire A. Marston, University of Washington Library.

ample, new academic institutions are being established at an average rate of 50 per year. This means at least 500 new institutions by the fall of 1975. . . . College and university libraries will be spending almost 900 million dollars by 1975, and some 300 million of this sum will go toward the buying of library materials. Academic library resources will . . . nearly double the number of volumes reported in 1963-64.[3]

Second, there is a greater need to acquire materials from areas for which there is no adequately organized bibliographic apparatus. The bibliographies and reviews on which our traditional selection system operates are simply not available from some countries. The Farmington Plan was the first major attempt to cope with this problem by using the blanket order approach. The schemes developed by the Seminars on Acquisition of Latin American Materials represent another program.[4] The most recent and most ambitious is LC's National Program for Acquisitions and Cataloging, established under the Higher Education Act of 1965.[5]

Third, large doses of federal funds are available. This factor includes not only quantitative, but also qualitative, implications. The federal government works in strange ways and an acquisitions program must be flexible enough to act quickly when the waters rise.[6]

Fourth is a potpourri labeled "rapid rate of educational change." Not only is this seen in the case of new "instant colleges," but also in older institutions that suddenly decide to stop being normal schools and blossom into full universities.[7] Also, the trend in education toward more independent study, which was forecast by Johnson and Branscomb in the 1930's, is finally becoming a reality. The result is increased demands for more "research" materials in libraries for use by undergraduates.[8]

Fifth is the increasing rate of obsolescence of knowledge in many fields. Like atomic particles, books have half-lives. The exact half-life of the average monograph, in for example chemistry, has not been measured but it is short and probably getting shorter. True, few books ever become entirely useless. Conceivably a historian of a subject may covet the old, the obsolete and the discredited book for those very reasons. However, the period of maximum use—if not of usefulness—is very brief in the natural and behavioral sciences. Allied to this tendency is the growing trend toward publication of materials in ephemeral formats of which the research report is the prime example. Reports are often produced in small quan-

tities and quite outside the usual book-reviewing system on which traditional selection methods are based. (One must hasten to add that, so far, the typical approval order scheme does not deal with report literature.)

All of these complexities are reflected in the cost of doing business in libraries, the sixth factor. The rise in the cost of materials as well as the salaries of librarians has exceeded the rate of inflation in the economy generally. The controversies over what it really costs—or should cost—to add a book to a library have become acrimonious—particularly since the publication of a particularly controversial piece in the *Bulletin* of the American Association of University Professors.[9] More sober analysis of the costs of acquisitions and cataloging have shown that these are very high indeed. Paul J. Fasana and James E. Fall found that the total processing cost for adding science monographs to the Columbia University Libraries is $10.26 per title, not including the cost of the book itself.[10] Anything that promises to reduce that figure should have great appeal to administrators with budgetary problems.

Finally, in the wings is the spectre of automation. We hope that the computer's tail will not wag the intellectual dog in colleges and universities, but suffice to say that the traditional book selection system is not as amenable to the punched-card as programmers might like.

Even the most radical thinkers in the field will probably admit that the traditional system of having most of the books in college and university libraries selected by the faculty has borne the strain of change remarkably well. However, the present selection process is often slow and occasionally desultory. Something is needed to speed up the selection cycle.

Publishers and dealers (jobbers) seem quite willing to offer plans for more nearly automatic selection and acquisition of books than the present "one shot" order systems provide. The prospect of saving clerical time and money benefits them as well as the library. Furthermore, once a library has selected a particular jobber's plan, that dealer has a rather desirable portion of the library's business well in hand. Thus, some very elaborate and attractive plans with intriguing fringe benefits are being devised. We shall discuss a few of these as examples, knowing full well that there are other plans that we have not investigated.

Before discussing specific plans, we must stress the essentialness of librarian participation in selection to the success of the approval order plans.

Once books are obtained on approval it is essential that someone with authority to accept or reject them within a reasonable period of time be available. Some faculty members may be able to arrange their schedules to take care of approvals in their areas. However, in areas in which faculty members are not able or motivated to screen titles, librarians must be able to act in their stead or much of the time-saving advantage of the approval system is lost.

Approval order plans have two types of sponsors—publishers (or publishers' associations) and dealers. The Association of American University Presses' blanket order plan was a pioneer effort. It simply ships to the library on approval all books published by the member presses in the subjects selected by the library. The Collier-Macmillan "Service Order Program" offers a similar service for Collier, Macmillan and Free Press imprints. Collier-Macmillan offers a variety of plans. There is a general plan for colleges and universities and one for schools and smaller academic libraries. The general plan provides for choice among eight very general categories and provides for special instructions. Library of Congress cards are furnished at no extra cost.[11]

Approval order plans from publishers have advantages and disadvantages similar to those of ordinary direct orders to publishers. They may offer some speed and, often, some discount advantages, but they entail the tedium and expense of dealing with each individual publisher. The dealer, on the other hand, offers the convenience of block shipments of books from many publishers with only one billing operation as far as the library is concerned. Dealers' plans may be arbitrarily divided into three categories: (1) specialized (usually in science and technology), (2) general academic, and (3) international or foreign languages.

The elaborate plans offered by Stacy's Scientific and Professional Book Center typify the offerings of jobbers in specialized areas.[12] A library may specify the subjects (broad or specific), publishers, series, and level of study it desires. One might wish to see, for example, "all biological and physical science titles at the junior college level." Library of Congress cards are furnished with the books without additional charge. Full return privileges are offered without a stated time limit. As if this were not enough, Stacy's also offers, at an additional charge, MARC format cataloging information on punched cards or tape. Stacy's claims that this record will conform to "present or future Library of Congress cataloging standards."

(However, the cataloging is not directly derived from LC's MARC project.) Whether Stacy's will be successful in persuading libraries to start collecting machine-readable tapes now in preparation for future automation remains to be seen, but it is an ambitious program. Sci-Tech Book Service Inc. of New York offers a less elaborate plan than Stacy's but claims to offer large discounts. The service-versus-discount dichotomy will continue to be with us in the approval order field just as in traditional systems.

Richard Abel and Company, which originated in Portland but is now international in scope, offers approval plans in the remaining two categories: general academic publishing (1) in English and (2) in foreign languages. Abel describes his service in these terms:

> Simply stated, our approval program is designed to get all new significant books to our library customers who then review the books to determine which ones they will keep. With that, simplicity ends. Specifically tailored parameters have been mutually agreed upon by us and approximately ninety libraries currently participating on the basis of subject fields, academic level, country of original imprint, publisher, reprint vs. original status, paperback vs. cloth, series, and price. There is also, of course, the general exclusion relating to our specialization in scholarly titles.[13]

Abel's English Language Approval Plan, referred to as ELAP, provides books from the United States, the United Kingdom, and Continental publishers in English. His FLAP scheme (Foreign Language Approval Plan) will be administered from a new office in Amsterdam after about January 1, 1968. It includes foreign language titles from Continental publishers only. Abel also has an approval plan for smaller libraries, called Academic Library Approval Plan (ALAP). The firm is also working on a plan for vocational and community colleges which it has dubbed VOLAP. Apparently all Abel selections are made in accordance with a "profile" developed for each customer specifically. The firm will provide catalog cards or Flexowriter tape data which can also be used as computer input, but both of these services are supplied at additional cost. Discount policy is not stated in the material at hand. The Abel service includes provision of "all forms needed by the library for its internal operations connected with handling the book"[14] should these be desired.

Another example in the international field perhaps should be classified strictly as a blanket plan rather than an approval one. We are referring to the Stechert-SALALM scheme. (SALALM is the initialism for Seminar on Acquisition of Latin American Library Materials.) Whereas the other plans deal largely with publishers whose materials appear in the regular book trade, the Stechert-SALALM plan [Latin American Cooperative Acquisitions Plan or LACAP—Ed.], like the Farmington plan, attempts to secure blanket coverage of Latin American countries where much publishing is quasi-private and the book trade not well organized. Dominick Coppola describes the advantages of this service in these words:

> A library interested in fairly complete coverage might find it advantageous to purchase the publications from an area like Latin America, for instance, on a comprehensive basis instead of assigning a person in acquisitions to check bibliographies, announcements, etc., and to select therefrom. As a result it would receive practically all of the material that it would ordinarily have selected. A few receipts might be superfluous, but this should be a negligible consideration.[15]

Having outlined a few of the approval plans being offered, we shall close by suggesting a few advantages and difficulties associated with this mode of acquisitions, leaving more detailed technical, moral and philosophical considerations to the panel reactors.

The advantages of approval plans may be simply stated: They are faster, books are shipped to the library on or near the publication date. They save money not only in terms of personnel engaged in ordering books title-by-title but also, it is claimed, in the selection process and in cataloging. One dealer estimated that his approval-order-with-cards service can produce savings of up to $10.05 per title.[16] Another estimate of between $3.00 and $4.00 seems more typical.[17] The further contention is that since selection is done with the book in hand, evaluation can be sharper (if one has the courage to return marginal items). To the present writer, the speed factor is paramount since information is so perishable in many fields (to a medievalist this may or may not be important; but to a physicist it almost always is).

A few objections to heavy dependence upon approval plans come readily to mind: In the first place, the whole psychology of selection is changed and, in many cases, uncritical collection of what the dealer selects may be substituted for on-campus selection in terms of the needs of faculty and students. Furthermore, in most cases, the books must be selected without the aid of reviews in scholarly journals or reviewing media such as *Choice* or *Booklist*. (Of course, these must be read—post mortem, so to speak—to fill in gaps in the approval selections[18] and to sharpen one's critical faculties.) For the large university which collects most regular publications in well-defined fields, the ultimate results under approval plans may be the same as those under traditional methods, but in the smaller college, approval plans may tend to provide a "standard" collection rather than one tailored to the needs of the institution.

Nor are the plans invulnerable on the economic front. Although the costs of selection may be less if the time of all concerned is counted, the costs to the library may be higher since work formerly accomplished by the faculty must now be done by librarians who are supported by the library's budget. Also, it may be doubted that enough subject specialists with suitable training are available to libraries at a price they can afford to pay, or for that matter at any price.

Another subtle objection is that if faculty members tend to withdraw from the selection procedure, a valuable communication link between instructors and the library will be lost. For this reason alone some areas of selection should be left to the faculty; furthermore, some instructors should be involved in reviewing approval shipments to the extent that they can be persuaded to participate. Actually, this danger may be more apparent than real since there are many areas of specialized and nontrade publishing, not amenable to blanket order procedures, on which faculty selectors can concentrate. To take an extreme example, few libraries would be interested in receiving on blanket approval all the publications of the so-called "vanity" presses—yet many valuable books are published in this way. The out-of-print and scarce-book areas may employ limited approval-order plans, but in most libraries these books will continue to be selected by traditional methods.

A final objection revolves around the danger of becoming too dependent upon a single supplier and subject to the tyranny of his computer, so to speak. Fiscal authorities, who deep down in their hearts still believe that libraries should put each and every title out to bid, may become unhappy if the library decides to give the bulk of its business to one dealer on the basis of service rather than price; but this is a problem to be solved, perhaps, rather than a basic objection. The real concern, if any, is that with dependence on a single supplier one must accede to whatever he demands or face the task of reworking the entire automated order program. This can be avoided but it is a danger.

In summary, it would seem that these new acquisition methods have rather "sneaked up" on many libraries and need to be studied further, both in their immediate and long range effects.

This writer feels that they are basically beneficial and here to stay if our acquisition rates continue to climb and our costs to mount. However, there is still lots of life in the traditional faculty-selection, ad-hoc ordering system; and, as a faculty member himself, the present writer would not feel that his interests were being served if it were all to become automatic—and superficial.

REFERENCES

1. Robert P. Haro, "Book Selection in Academic Libraries," *College and Research Libraries,* 28 (March, 1967), 104-106.

2. American Library Association, Administrative Division, *Library Statistics of Colleges and Universites 1965-66* (Chicago: ALA, 1967), pp. 6-7; Theodore Samore. "College and University Library Statistics and Legislation: Review and Report," *Bowker Annual*, 1967, pp. 20-31.

3. Samore, *op. cit.*, p. 21.

4. Report on the Twelfth Seminar on the Acquisition of Latin American Library Materials, University of California at Los Angeles, June 22-24, 1967, *Library of Congress Information Bulletin*, 26 (July 6, 1967), 423-25.

5. J. W. Cronin, "Library of Congress National Program for Acquisitions and Cataloging," *Libri*, 16, no. 2 (1966), 113-17.

6. For a discussion of expected implications for academic libraries see "The Higher Education Act of 1965: A Symposium," *College and Research Libraries*, 27 (September, 1966), 335-53.

7. Jerome Cushman, "Instant College Libraries: The University of California's New Campuses at Santa Cruz and Irvine," *Library Journal*, 92 (February 1, 1967), 540-43.

8. Arthur T. Hamlin, "Impact of College Enrollments on Library Acquisitions Policy," *Liberal Education*, 52 (May, 1966), 204-10, deals primarily with the need for duplication of titles for undergraduate use.

9. Daniel Gore, "Mismanagement of College Libraries: A View from the Inside," *AAUP Bulletin*, 52 (March, 1966), 46-51.

10. Paul J. Fasana and James E. Fall, "Processing Costs for Science Monographs in the Columbia University Libraries," *Library Resources & Technical Services*, 11 (Winter, 1967), 97-114.

11. Brochure issued by Collier-Macmillan, 1967.

12. Extensive pamphlets describing the plans are available from Stacy's.

13. Letter from Richard Abel, dated July 6, 1967.

14. *Ibid.*

15. Dominick Coppola, "The International Bookseller Looks at Acquisitions," *Library Resources & Technical Services*, 11 (Spring, 1967), 205-06.

16. Stacy's.

17. Abel, *loc. cit.*

18. Alice T. Copeland, "Philosophy Journals as Current Book Selection Guides," *College and Research Libraries*, 27 (November, 1966), 455-60.

Are We Selecting or Collecting?

Reaction by *Le Roy Charles Merritt*

Since I understood my assignment to be one of tempering the opinions of an uncritical proponent of approval order schemes, I was somewhat disappointed as I read Morrison's article to find that I am in substantial agreement with the main burden of his discourse. It is quite true that traditional selection methods have not produced ideal college libraries. Harry Bauer, writing in the *Anti-*

quarian Bookman (AB, 24, July 1967), states the point with his typical clarity:

During the forty-seven years I have been in the bibliographic borrow pits, I have never worked in or visited a library of 500,000 or even 50,000 carefully selected volumes; faithfully selected, yes: carefully selected, no. Libraries acquire books mostly on faith or on hearsay evidence. When a library acquires a new book, it purchases a pig in a poke. Most of the pigs in a poke prove to be good pigs because reputable publishers are reliable manuscript rejecters. The publishers do the book selection; all the librarians do is the book collecting.

Whether approval order plans will contribute to better selection is a moot point. My contention is that the quality of the collection produced, not the promised increase in efficiency of ordering procedures, is the true issue.

Approval ordering if honestly, diligently, and conscientiously done is one thing. Abrogating the selection function to dealers or publishers is another. If communication between librarian and dealer is not consistent and rational, some very lop-sided collections can result. For example, if the only means of communications is through the books returned to the dealer by the librarian, the latter will tend to send fewer and different things next time. As this process continues, coverage of desired areas is lost. A whole subject area may be blocked because of the return of one or two books for reasons not properly understood by the dealer.

Blanket orders without return privileges are suitable only to the large library which is committed to collecting indiscriminately in a subject or geographic area. They are virtually never suitable to the average college library. The point is that either approval ordering or simple blanket plans turn over to the publisher or bookseller the basic, initial selection function. The task of the faculty member or librarian is, then, to reject rather than to select, quite a different process, as Morrison points out.

I would like to comment on some of the details in Morrison's arguments: He says that few books ever become entirely useless. My contention is that far too many volumes retained by college libraries are never used—even though they may conceivably have some possibly useful information in them. The tragedy is that academic libraries store these unused—and for all practical purposes, useless—books forever. It takes only one librarian or faculty member to get a book into a library but takes the agreement of practically the whole faculty to get it out. Under these conditions, weeding is just not done! This puts a burden of prophecy on the initial book selection system that it ought not to be required to bear.

Similarly, I am not quite happy with Morrison's reference to the perishability of information as a justification for approval ordering on the basis of speed in getting the book on the shelf. If the information in a book is *that* perishable, I would argue that it should not be selected at all. I say this at least in the case of the typical college library, and I am not sure the principle should not apply to the university library as well.

Some of Morrison's arguments against approval plans do not really bother me very much. It seems to me that selection by librarians is not nearly so essential to blanket order plans as he thinks. Nor is selection by librarians incompatible with traditional ordering systems. I contend that, in either case, most selecting is better done by staff than by faculty. The question of whose budget is charged with the work is not material.

It seems to me that Morrison's fears that approval plans will alienate the faculty from the library are unfounded. Seeing the book itself is much superior to merely reading a review of it— both to the librarian and the faculty member. Better relations with the faculty should result from the librarian's showing him the book itself, rather than an excerpt from a review. I agree with Morrison that faculty members will still have much to contribute to the selection process under approval plans. It has been my observation that professors are happiest when working on retrospective and out-of-print buying anyway!

Lest I, too, seem to be going overboard for approval plans, I must reiterate my fear of turning too much responsibility over to the dealer. For example, in one quotation from Richard Abel's letter, he refers to the firm's specialization in "scholarly titles." I would point out that Abel must necessarily work from *his* definition of the word "scholarly," rather than the library's, if for no other reason than that no two librarians ever agree on a definition. And any given faculty member would have a third view. Books which Abel *includes* are no problem, but the books Abel considers are not scholarly and does not send can create difficulties because the "leftouts" may never be brought to the library's attention.

In summary, I wish to emphasize that blanket or approval plans, on the one hand, and selection by staff rather than faculty, on the other, are not necessarily dependent upon each other. Selection by staff can be done well without approval plans and selection by faculty can be done with them. But I think Morrison and I are in essential agreement that either a professor or a librarian can do a better job of selection with the book in hand than from, say a *PW* annotation, a blurb, or a review. Approval plans do have great potential—but only as long as the power to reject remains firm and arrangements with dealers are placed under continuous review.

Can Blanket Orders Help the Small College Library?

Reaction by the Reverend *Joseph P. Browne*, C.S.C.

We might begin by saying that the obvious answer to this question is an unequivocal affirmative. But I would immediately contradict that affirmative by saying that I am theoretically, professionally, and philosophically opposed in principle to such blanket orders.

To place some bounds on this discussion, I would like arbitrarily to define a small college as one with an enrollment of less than 5,000. Yet even such a limitation gives us a wide variety of institutions. Just in the PNLA area, the latest statistics from the Office of Education show more than 60 colleges of this size. Most of these are four-year, degree-granting institutions; but a great number are two-year "junior" or "community" colleges, and a few have highly developed graduate programs. In size, the libraries range from a few thousand volumes to over 360,000. Annual book and periodical budgets range from less than $5,000 to $88,000. The average seems to be about 70,000 volumes, with an annual expenditure of approximately $30,000.

There are almost as many varieties of blanket order plans as there are publishers, jobbers, or agents offering them. Essentially, however, they all involve the reception, without prior ordering, of a great many newly published works. Most schemes operate on an approval arrangement so that items not desired for the collection can be returned. If this approval feature does not exist, then all items must be accepted and paid for, the presumption being that very little undesirable material will be received. Blanket orders may involve specific subject areas or may cover the whole gamut of the library's collection, depending upon the arrangement that has been worked out between the library and the publisher, jobber, or agent.

The basis for my personal opposition to blanket order plans, particularly in the small college library, is my belief that the one really professional *library* activity which we, as librarians, perform is that of book selection. A library-oriented subject specialist can do much better at reference work; a person skilled in personnel and fiscal management makes a much better administrator; even cataloging can be efficiently performed by someone with an orderly and analytic mind who can cope with the intricacies of the cataloging schedules. But the selection of books for addition to our holdings is

a task that cannot be adequately and properly performed by one who is not a thoroughly professional librarian. The use of blanket orders allocates even this activity to others.

The choices of books received—though hopefully tailored to the library's individual needs—nevertheless are made not by the librarian but by an outsider. Also hopefully, the librarian examines carefully the materials sent to him, yet this remains a sort of "negative" selection—the librarian chooses those things which he does *not* want rather than those he wants. (And I say "hopefully" for I fear that many librarians do not have time to do an adequate job of reviewing such material.)

The fact that the selections are made by the publisher or jobber also means that book selection is not tooled to the needs of *this* library and the program of *this* institution, despite the best efforts of all concerned. College instructional programs are expanding rapidly and developing in all sorts of directions. It is a difficult enough task for the librarian, on the spot, to keep in touch with such developments; and a publisher's representative or a jobber is even further removed from the scene.

This in turn leads to a certain standardization of collections. Perhaps this is not a great problem on the lower academic levels where core collections are quite useful, but for the four-year college and especially for the graduate school such standardization can be crippling, if not down right disastrous.

Another difficulty is the cost of such programs. One which has come to my attention involves approximately 4,000 books per year at a cost of $28,000. (Of course one need not accept everything, but jobbers will tell you that a return of more than 5% indicates that the blanket order plan is not operating successfully.) This represents practically the whole of the average small college's book budget—and leaves nothing over for periodicals, binding, reference works, etc. Another plan (from the same agent) involves approximately half as much in books and money. Even this very basic collection would leave very little money for other recommendations from faculty and professional library staff.

Finally, I would point out the ethical problem that may be involved in concentrating too much of one's business in the hands of a single publisher or dealer.

On the positive side, it is fairly obvious that permanent order plans have several rather significant advantages, not the least of which is the saving of the time of already over-burdened library staffs. (But of course this saving will be minimized if the professional library staff does a reasonable job of reviewing the titles received and returning those which do not fit into the scope of the library.)

There is also a very definite financial advantage in the special discounts offered to those covered by such blanket order plans. But where budgets are already limited, the highest discount rate will rarely be obtained.

There is a very definite advantage to a library in which one or another section of the collection has been neglected in the past. A rapid strengthening of certain sections is easily possible by subscribing to a subject-area blanket plan. The same can be said of the whole collection in the case of what Dr. Morrison has called "instant colleges," if library budgets will permit. The precisely opposite sort of situation—in which a particular section is extremely strong (perhaps supporting a Ph.D. program)—can also benefit from a subject-area blanket plan. In such sections the librarian may want to purchase almost everything which is being published. A blanket order plan will assure that he will receive such titles.

Perhaps the solution to the dilemma raised here might be to make judicious use of such limited approval plans as might fit into the specific needs of the college involved, while retaining a rigid control over the selection process by returning *without fail* those items which do not appreciably strengthen the collection.

Approval Books on a Small Budget?

Reaction by *Stanley A. Shepard*

My part of the discussion today has been phrased as a question, "Is it possible to have an approval selection program on a small budget?" One is tempted to ask "how small is small." On the other hand, while the size of the budget is certainly an important factor, it is not the only one. Personally, I think the key question is whether the amount you have allocated, or might normally spend on a certain subject area, approaches the estimated cost of books published during the year in that subject.

I believe that some form of approval selection can make a worthwhile contribution to any acquisitions program, if a library can fit it into its budget. This depends largely on the total budget allocation for books, and the curricular program. In a full-fledged university, with a large number of courses and a substantial graduate program, it would be doubtful that in the face of other commitments, the library could consider a subject approval plan with a book budget of less than $100,000-$125,000. On the other hand, for a smaller institution with a less varied curriculum and limited graduate program, perhaps $50,000 to $75,000 would be sufficient. The best way to decide for your library, is to study the amount you are spending in certain subject fields in relation to the estimated cost of books published in that field in any one year. *Publishers' Weekly*, in its annual statistical summary of publishing which normally appears in late January, or early February, prints a table of subject categories and cost statistics. These must be used with some judgment as applied to your situation, as these tables include most books designed for various reading publics, many of which would not necessarily be useful to an academic program, but the tables will still provide a rough guide to costs. A somewhat more reliable breakdown for academic use is issued by Richard Abel & Company, a West Coast dealer.

In order to judge whether you are now spending an amount which would cover certain subject areas, consider "agriculture." The figure I have for the 1966 cost of books in this field, or more specifically for the S classification in the Library of Congress scheme, is $1,600. This also includes some "forestry and fisheries," but would not necessarily include the economic aspects of the subject. In any case, if a library is spending this much or more in agriculture, perhaps it should consider the possibility of receiving these on approval standing order. In the field of education, general education books covering school management, teaching techniques, educational psychology, etc. (LC class L) are estimated to cost $1,600-1,700; physical education, sports, games and dance (LC class GV), another $1,000. Thus about $2,600 would cover most of the education materials which a library would normally purchase anyway. If general psychology is included, then $1,500 must be added. Admittedly, these are small areas, but they are possible starting places for an experimental program. I have some estimated figures on some of the larger subject areas. Engineering, about $8,000; physical sciences, $13,000; and literature (all Western languages and including criticism), $11,000. Some of these figures may sound high; but remember that a library may return what it does not want to retain, and also bear in mind that a library probably already acquires many series in these subject areas on standing order.

I would recommend that a particular library give serious consideration as to whether the benefits of an approval program could be integrated into its operation. To do this a library should study its present system of allocations in relation to estimated costs. If some subject areas look as though they may feasibly be handled this way, it will then be time to secure the cooperation of the library staff, the faculty, and, if appropriate, the institution's purchasing agent. Faculty are often apprehensive of new schemes, and in many schools the Library Committee allocates funds, so it may be necessary to secure their agreement for a trial program. The proof is in the pudding; and it must be successful, as more than 80 libraries are using the selection approval plan. It has been shown that once the faculty get used to it, they have given their full support. The old ways are changing and we must progress, even as the primitive tribes of Africa. Recently a missionary deep in the jungles there stumbled across a native beating a large drum, and asked him what was the occasion. The native replied that they had no water. "Are you praying for rain?" asked the missionary. "No," the native replied, "I'm calling the plumber."

Acquisition Policy for University Libraries: Selection or Collection

Betty J. Meyer and John T. Demos

While the distinction between collecting and selecting library materials is real, its relevancy for major research libraries becomes tenuous as library book budgets approach the million dollar figure. In order to develop collections when given such large budgets, libraries must consider the merits of approval plans. This paper argues these merits and points out the importance of getting faculty support before engaging in approval plans.

To develop a policy for current acquisitions for a university library requires facing and resolving many problems, not all of which will be dealt with here. If Merritt's distinction[1] between selection and collection is the sole basis for a book selection policy and a policy is built solely on this, it is easy to become involved with semantic quarrels as to what is good, true, and beautiful, or what is permanent and of lasting value. If there is a distinction, and supposing there is, between selection and collection, that distinction often blurs as book budgets become large enough to satisfy most needs.

Unfortunately, book budgets tend to reach that state when most materials needed are out-of-print. Unrestricted current acquisitions combined with an unlimited budget are anathema if it is believed as Merritt believes that the acquisitions function is to select carefully. While selection may be proper for the college library serving twenty disciplines, it appears to be too restrictive for a university with, for example, sixteen colleges, ninety departments, and 40,000 students. The cost to collect everything would be beyond most budgets and to do so would mean a university library might be collecting much poor material. Indeed, it is because there is so much poor material that Merritt argues for a selective policy. And yet, it is precisely this poor material which one carefully avoided selecting in the past that happens to be out-of-print when it is badly needed.

In short, there is no argument with Merritt that much of what is published is ephemeral, trash, and without scholarly value—at this point in time.

Many librarians have had some subject background or develop some on the job—the form if not the content of their field—and given one hundred titles to reject or select, a librarian's selections of important titles would be similar to those made by a university professor in a discipline. Selection becomes difficult for both librarian and professor when titles appear to be a bit off center.

An acquisitions policy for current materials must recognize that:

1. Titles not selected now may be unobtainable later.

2. Much of what is acquired may have little immediate value.

3. Materials may be selected precisely because they are ephemeral or are illustrative of some passing sociological condition, e.g., comic books, pornographic novels, confession magazines—and yet scholars fifty or a hundred years from now may be grateful that a library had the foresight to collect so-called ephemerae that delineate one aspect of our culture.

4. The pattern of spending between current and retrospective materials will tend to shift as less and less of the budget need be allotted to filling lacunae. If a current imprints program provides coverage for 75 percent of the total titles in a given field, then in the following year only enough funds need be set aside for selecting from the 25 percent not previously covered. Over a long period of time, this suggests that funds for current imprints will remain major (and probably increase as the price of books and the quantity of books

SOURCE: Reprinted from *Library Resources and Technical Services* XIV, 3 (Summer 1970), pp. 395-399.

continue to rise) while funds set aside for retrospective buying will be less.

5. A fairly comprehensive current imprints acquisitions program is better handled through contracts with one or more dealers than through individual library effort. To this last point, the remainder of this paper addresses itself, with particular reference to the conduct of such a program at the Ohio State University Libraries.

Traditionally the faculty of Ohio State University selected the majority of materials to be purchased for the University Libraries collections on a title-by-title basis. There are sixteen colleges on campus, and each college is assigned a specific amount of money annually from the University Libraries state-allotted book budget. Each dean is notified of the amount of money which he may reassign to departments, subject areas, institutes or department libraries from his segment of the University Libraries book budget. Notification of such amounts assigned by the dean is sent to the Head, Acquisition Department, who is responsible for acquiring materials and handling the various funds. Both current imprints and retrospective materials are purchased from the various funds with a General Fund and a Serial Fund handled by the Library Faculty. In 1966/67 the state-allotted book budget was increased from $460,000 to $710,000 with little or no additional library faculty or staff being provided or anticipated. When a research library annually spends $710,000 for books and serials, the precentage of acquisition of the total current U.S. imprints of university research and instructional quality becomes exceedingly high. Due to a more comprehensive acquisition program and the accompanying rise in personnel costs, it becomes incumbent upon the library to use, if possible, some means of acquisition appropriate to the magnitude of the task. It seemed necessary to relieve the faculty of the responsibility of selecting some quantity of library materials, and the obvious solution centered around current materials. Under an approval plan the library could acquire most of the titles in a desired subject area as they were published and with no added responsibility on the part of the faculty member. In addition, it seemed likely that a more equitable and comprehensive coverage of the subject would develop than if the coverage depended solely upon the interest, aggressiveness, and influence of a limited number of faculty members.

Prior to January 1967, an approval plan in the humanities field was adopted with the cooperation of the faculty. In January 1967, an extended approval plan was instituted based on selection of subject areas by the faculty and library faculty. The approval plan in general was for English language materials of titles published during the current year. Exclusions were made and a profile was drawn up for the dealer concerning the needs of our campus and faculty. There were subjects which were deleted in the general plan due to the nature of some specialized fields such as music, and where the University Libraries already had a blanket order or approval plan in existence. Serial publications and numbered monographic series were excluded from the plan, as it was not considered advisable to change our existing subscription plans and policy. However, the first issue of a newly published numbered monographic series may be sent on approval. It was anticipated that current material would be received in the Libraries more rapidly than by conventional title-by-title ordering. The dealer or jobber would be able to order in advance or set up standing orders with publishers for review before supplying to the Libraries.

A factor which cannot be overlooked in any such plan is the economy of staff time. The major approval plan includes in the specifications the requirement that multiple order forms, designed to meet local needs and the approval of the University Office of Business and Finance, be supplied with each book. This makes it unnecessary to type a record for the department for the first copy, and the amount of bibliographic searching and verification by the Acquisition Department is reduced. However, it is necessary to check the order file and public catalog for titles already received or for added editions.

The blanket order program for current imprints is based on receiving *one* copy of every title published in certain specific fields. The titles are displayed in the Acquisition Department for one week to allow all faculty (including library faculty in subject areas) to select titles for purchase and to designate by streamers the location. If more than one copy is desired, the streamer is marked to indicate duplicate copies are being requested. The first copy goes to the location that has primary responsibility for the discipline under which the title falls, and additional copies up to four may be requested to be acquired out of the current imprints fund.

At the Ohio State University Libraries, the problem of duplicates is exacerbated by having twenty-three department libraries as well as the main library. Two undergraduate libraries plus a separate two-year college on the west campus are also planned. So long as faculty continue to use the old method of assigning specific reserve reading, the problem of how many duplicate copies to purchase will remain. In some cases photographic reproduction of journal articles suffices; in others, and these may be the majority of cases, it is necessary to purchase multiple copies. A current imprints program must recognize the difference between materials purchased for undergraduate collections and materials purchased to build a long-term research collection. Additional copies are purchased and the requests are reviewed by a member of the library faculty of the Acquisition Department. With this procedure there have been no major problems. Frequently a faculty member or librarian is satisfied to note that a book has been received somewhere in the system. With an enrollment of over 40,000 students, duplication of certain titles is inevitable and, on occasion, to be encouraged.

What are the advantages of approval plans?

1. Responsibility for selection of materials is not abrogated or assigned to the vendor. Instead, selection may more intelligently be pursued with the book in hand.

2. Materials not received on the current imprints plan can be acquired through routine acquisition procedures.

3. Bibliographers and bibliographic clerks can spend more of their time on retrospective buying orders. There is little likelihood that a large university library will reduce staff because of an approval plan.

4. Properly made, the statement submitted to the vendor as to the categories of materials the library will or will not accept should serve as a measuring instrument to determine the success or failure of the program. A book return rate above 7 percent to 10 percent might indicate that the statement to the vendor is either too loosely worded as to restrictions or that some area has been misinterpreted, e.g., receiving astrology books because the library has indicated that it will accept books on the occult. A book return rate approaching zero is not necessarily a measure of success because such a rate might indicate that the library was too undiscriminating in setting up its restrictions or undiscriminating in accepting anything that the vendor sends.

5. The library which promotes any approval plan must face the important task of winning over the faculty members who can be notoriously conservative about "their" libraries. Any program which appears to take money out of their hands and place it in a common pool for purchase of current materials is seen as a threat to the faculty's traditional control. It does not help, either, when a faculty member in a fairly conservative field sees some of the "frivolous" titles other departments are spending money to purchase. At least in the past each department worried about its own expenditures and made its own mistakes in book selection.

To win over the faculty is not easy. In any institution a middle group will go along no matter what the library does. This group is amenable, indifferent, approving, or unconcerned. It is the smaller, vociferous, discontented minority that the library must convince. By working closely with the department librarians so they understand what the plans are trying to accomplish and then having them serve as liaison with library committee chairmen and other faculty from their departments, the library hopes to have the program supported at the grass roots level.

NOTE

[1] LeRoy Charles Merritt, "Are We Selecting or Collecting?" *Library Resources & Technical Services*, 12 (Spring 1968), 140–42.

The Long-Term Effects of Approval Plans

Marion Wilden-Hart

Using approval plans, professional selection can start where the work of the jobber leaves off. Librarians should evaluate service received and the long-term effects on collection development. The cost should be weighed; selecting from more books may mean selection is improved. Cost is not only in budgetary terms but also in terms of the nation's resources. Approval plans do not build up special collections, but they gradually change the bibliographer's work. This is now a critical stage in the development of approval plans. Pertinent research is urgent.

The volume of publication and the rise in staff costs has forced us to seek methods of selecting the most books in the quickest way. This does not necessarily mean that by doing this the standard of selection must be lowered, for, indeed, something like 60 percent of the books that we add to our libraries "buy themselves." That is to say, 60 percent of the books we add are those that come to our notice that we cannot do without. To have these ordered for us, with minimum clerical and routine work, and if required, catalog cards provided, is time saving for other things. The time saved can, in fact, be used for professional selection. By using approval plans, we can use *all* our time on professional selection, starting the work where the approval plan leaves off.

If we are to use approval plans to our bibliographical, as well as our technical, advantage, it is necessary to select the method of approval plan that is:

(a) most compatible to the selection program designed to start where the approval plan leaves off;

(b) most readily adaptable to the exact needs of each institution and which is able to follow most nearly the acquisition policy as shown in the "subject profile," drawn up specifically for an approval plan; and

(c) adequate to meet individual requirements such as rush orders, series, and memberships if necessary.

TYPES OF APPROVAL PLANS

Clearly, with the number of publications on the market today, we need all the help we can get in processing, in cataloging, and in purchasing. Co-operative schemes or commercial services have been available for many years for processing and cataloging; it was in the order of things that purchasing systems should be developed, and as they improved with experience, gain favor. Types of approval plans available now are:

1. *Publisher Standing Order*. A list of publishers from whom *all* publications are required is drawn up and contracts arranged individually with each.

2. *Publisher Standing Order for Selected Subjects*. The same as above, but limited to certain specified subjects only. As publishers are not organized to handle complicated procedures for the sale of their publications, this standing order is limited usually to publisher's series in particular subjects.

3. *Jobber's Standing Order for Publishers*. Instead of the library doing #1 or #2 direct, the jobber does it, thus eliminating scores of small invoices and individual contracts.

4. *Jobber Notification Plan*. The jobber notifies the library by slips or catalog or lists, which books he has available for sale, inviting the library to make selection from the information he provides.

5. *Jobber Approval Plan, with Slips, Catalog, or*

SOURCE: Reprinted from *Library Resources and Technical Services* XIV, 3 (Summer 1970), pp. 400-406

List. The jobber sends books on approval, with some form of listing in addition to invoicing, to enable the library still to do full selection itself. Sometimes the notifications are sent ahead of the books and those slips sent back are those which the library rejects.

6. *Jobber Approval Plan.* Jobber sends books he thinks the library might be interested to buy. This is a reviewing service and may or may not be based on a policy collection statement drawn up by the library.

7. *Jobber Approval Plan by Subject.* The library prepares an acquisition policy statement in the form of a detailed list of subjects required. This is usually called a "subject profile." Levels of presentation, types of material, and format can be specified for inclusion or exclusion. The subject approval plan can cover one subject comprehensively, or the whole field of knowledge, or anything specified in between these extremes. Of all the approval plans it is the most professional, yet with all its advantages, it is the one that should cause most concern. It is the approval plan by subject that may be affecting the total national resources.

The purchasing system or approval plan chosen by each library was presumably, at the time of decision, the method most suitable then to it. It is almost too soon to do a thorough evaluation of any of these schemes, for all are relatively new; but it is not too soon for libraries to evaluate the service they receive from such plans, and the long-term effects they will have on collection development. To evaluate the adequacy, each institution needs to review its purchasing system in relation to its research and scholarly needs. It needs to weigh not only the amount of time taken to do selection, but how much of that time is spent on selecting the obvious. If a jobber now can take off the librarian's hands the routine buying, it should leave the librarian time to develop the collection as a whole, to build up strengths, and strengthen weaknesses. This is the value of approval plans. They are at least efficient purchasing systems. If based on a carefully compiled subject profile of requirements and developed through close cooperation with the jobber, controlled at the input end by at least sample checks by professional bibliographers, the purchasing system, through jobbers, can become the basic book selection process of the library. For the truth is that, today, we have to select how we will use our time, as much as how we will select our books. If we do not select how to use our time, we will in fact be se-

lecting from only a fringe of what is available. We can persuade ourselves that our selection is then what we choose, but if we pause to think, and are honest with ourselves, we know that we select from a selection—and that that selection is not governed by our needs and acquisition policy, but by what is most readily available, or what is put before us most blatantly. Retrieving material for a librarian is not a commercial process; it is a systematic search and a rational decision. If a pamphlet costs more to obtain and catalog than it does to buy, and if the total cost exceeds that for a fine art book or technical dictionary, then we must still buy it and make it accessible (and it may be of more useful value than the costly book we prize so readily).

In forming a selection policy, an order of priorities policy is formulated too. This will show that in every library there is a basic core required without which the institution the library serves cannot do its work. Previously, and in many cases even now, this basic core has taken up most of the time available for selection by faculty, or bibliographers. By using approval plans it is now possible to obtain the basic core, at relatively little extra cost and least cost in staff, leaving for faculty and library staff the time and energy to use their specializations and skills to develop the collection as a whole.

What is the cost of this? From the point of view of budgets, it is difficult to estimate in comparable terms; that is to say, how much it costs to obtain books through an approval plan system, versus the cost to a library of ordering and selecting everything on its own. Inevitably the first year at least will be costly, until problems are ironed out, duplication is avoided, the subject profile is edited from experience, and the librarian learns where to install control systems. By the time the problems are ironed out, it is difficult to assess how much more is spent on the *system* than is saved by professional staff no longer being expensively used as efficient clerks. Moreover, it is impossible to judge the value of books which would otherwise have been missed; for hindrances to scholarship and research have never been evaluated. In any case, selection from more books does not necessarily mean acquiring more. It may mean only that the selection process is improved. Approval plans, after all, involve books being sent on approval.

There is a need, however, for an economic survey to be made on behalf of all libraries using approval plans. There is the cost to a library in terms of discount. Ordering direct from publishers gives

a larger discount to the library. Is this counter-
acted by the amount of work? There is inevitably
a certain wastage in duplication and in the acceptance of books that would normally not have been
ordered. Approval plans sometimes focus too
much emphasis on current buying and not enough
on retrospective, too much emphasis on monographs with the danger of neglecting periodicals.
Jobbers are in this as a business, and pass on their
costs to their clients. We do not know how prices
are inflated due to lack of standardization in ordering and invoicing procedures. If it were possible for libraries to operate with more conformity, would jobber prices be reduced? Research
has yet to be done on the allocation of budgets by
libraries using approval plans. Does the proportion
for monographs, periodicals, serials, desiderata, or
binding remain the same, or does it change? And
if so, in what way? What is the saving in terms of
clerical costs to a library? Is selecting from books
sent, quicker and more efficient than selecting
from a list and then ordering? These are questions
not yet answered, but these are questions that
must be posed. A few thousand dollars unwisely
spent by each library cumulatively becomes a million dollars which should never have been wasted.
Is it the new method, the approval plan method,
that is wasting the money—or the old, the "individual selection of each title" method? The facts
should be established, for though each library
must be free to do as it chooses, the choice should
be an informed one.

The cost, however, is not only in budgetary
terms. The cost is also in terms of the nation's
resources. If a substantial number of the larger
libraries in the United States are using approval
plans from a limited number of jobbers, are they
all building up similar collections? Are all these
libraries missing the same publications? Since the
jobbers aim to be as comprehensive as possible for
United States publications, does feedback for requests not supplied by the approval plan from
individual libraries reach the Library of Congress
in case it, too, has missed the item and would like
it? (Cooperation with jobbers could give us this
information.) We have not done enough research
into which items are missed by jobbers. We know
for a fact that some are missed and not offered to
libraries; the jobbers themselves are aware of it.
Sometimes it is because publishers will only sell
direct to individual libraries—a shortsighted policy,
for it means to them not only individual invoicing
and accounting but also loss in sales that would
arise from the publicity inspired by the jobbers

when they send the publication on approval to
those libraries most likely to want it. If it is a
question of discount, most libraries would be prepared to pay extra for a handling fee rather than
have the annoyance of delay while it is reported
by the jobber not obtainable, and the library after
all forced into making personal application. The
type of publication that is not available through a
jobber is often the very type of material that specialization requires.

There are, however, other publications missed,
which emanate from diverse bodies but mainly
private research institutes or private membership
organizations: social surveys, public opinion statistics, etc. It would be interesting, for instance, for
a library having an approval plan for the last two
years, to check the holdings of conferences and
meetings in the field of computers and information science, against the official list of conferences
held during the same period in the same field. So
many varied organizations are concerned with the
subject that it would be impossible for acquisition
of such material to be obtained through selection.
But a librarian, trained in retrieval methods, is able
to systematically check that no wanted publication
is missed. It probably would not be commercially
possible for a jobber to do this, even if he had the
qualified staff to do it. But the point there is not
that the jobber misses these publications but that
those libraries depending on approval plans for
selection all miss them too. Cumulatively, this is
dangerous.

And if one library is assiduous in checking what
it does not receive through approval plans, is then
all the work involved for the benefit of one library and for one copy? The point is that here
there is room for cooperation. By notifying the
jobber that individual requests from libraries on
approval plans may be significant items for other
libraries, methods could be established to see that
others benefit from the individual checking done.
This could even be extended to sharing the bibliographical work in highly specialized fields, making
one library responsible for work in a field where a
bibliographer has particular subject competence
and giving another library the responsibility of
retrieval research in another field. The results
could either be published or offered to the jobber
firms to send the publications out on approval to
those libraries having each subject listed in their
subject profile.

Approval plans do not build up special collections. They do, however, take the great mass of
work of ordering the books that select themselves

off the hands of the professional bibliographer, leaving him free to do retrieval research and professional selection. The problem here, if using approval plans, is where to begin. Or, to put it another way, where do the approval plans leave off? This is possible to gauge sometimes. For instance, if a library has a standing order through a jobber for all publications issued from university presses, this is a clear definition of what is to be supplied. And it is known that it does *not* include any other publication issuing from a university, except from the university press. Thus it is possible to begin checking the special institutes and research bodies by subject, in all universities, and select further coverage. It should be possible, for instance, to pick up all publications put out by schools of journalism or communication research institutes from universities specializing in this field and place these on standing order. Some universities may have exchange programs with other universities in fields of interest. Exchanges are costly in materials supplied (the "exchange") and in staff time. It might well be cheaper to use a jobber firm to set up standing orders with the institutes chosen by the library, and cease altogether to rely on exchange systems.

The *Encyclopedia of Associations* is a magnum opus and indispensable to bibliographers. It is a pity that jobbers could not be persuaded to obtain publications emanating from associations (which are grouped by subject in the encyclopedia) on a regular basis, even if a handling fee has to be superimposed. Jobbers are so conditioned to the commercial publishers who offer large discounts from which the jobbers subtract a service fee and small profit before offering the rest of the discount to the library, that they have not had the perspicacity to see that the libraries are not in business to make a profit but to get those things they want. The publication price in relation to the cost of production is irrelevant to a library. A library values a publication according to its potential use, and according to the need it will fill. If, then, special organizations do not give adequate discounts on certain publications (or any at all) because they, too, are not commercial but are offering a service in the form of publication at cost price, then libraries will value the publications not for their remarkably low price but for their exceptional contribution to a subject. In other words, a library will pay for what it needs. Many of these special associations put out results of research which only they have been able to do; indeed, many of them are in existence just to do

that. At the present time, these publications are largely being missed by approval plans. So libraries are obtaining these individually on standing order, or writing individually for each one. By the time it is put into stock, it is a costly commercial publication being added to the collection. For this reason, the technical processing staff would try to eliminate them, or reduce them in number. Selection is forced onto a bibliographer by a criterion not acceptable to a subject expert. Ease of handling jousts with need and potential use, and might win. The dangers ensuing to scholars of such a possibility are disturbing, no less because by paying only a little extra, library staff time would be cut and handling would become easy. If jobbers could be persuaded to undertake this important work at a realistic price to them, dissemination of research would not be jeopardized by the technical processes of our library systems, and techniques would not come between the bibliographer and the user he serves.

It may be too soon to evaluate the long-term effects of approval plans. It is not too early, and hopefully not too late, to do research into what approval plans actually achieve, and how they are slowly changing the work of a subject bibliographer. As each library is able to assess the potential worth and danger areas of approval plans, and learns to use the first to the full and to control the latter, so cumulatively this becomes relevant information to the nation as a whole. Only with cooperation of the nation's resources can the enormous task of providing for the needs of academic and research scholars be achieved. Cooperation means shared responsibility, pooling of experience, and joint effort in a common cause. Some results of approval plans may already be felt by the interlibrary networks. To whom are they reporting, and what is the nature of their experience? It is possible that without monitoring the effects, the results will only be known when it is too late, when it is found that no library has a copy and that it is now out of print. Or it may be found that less interlibrary loan work is being done for recent items. This may be the success that approval plans can bring; it may also mean too much duplication of highly specialized items. Until we know, we are operating large budgets on a speculative hypothesis. The great collections in America have in the past faced their greater responsibilities, which they cannot jeopardize now.

I believe in approval plans. I believe this is the beginning of a new bibliographical experience. I believe it can achieve results not possible in any other way. I believe it will open up new network systems, some international, and certainly regional. I believe that the jobbers will work closer with libraries than they have ever done before; and in doing so, it will be good business for them but will yield extraordinary advantage for us as librarians. If jobbers have on their computers the subject profiles of libraries of different types, on different strata, in different regions, these can be linked by level of service, by subject coverage, and by region. Jobbers are able to offer a selection program never previously possible by even the largest bookshop; and on more remote campuses, librarians and faculty are able to select from books for the first time. I believe publishers will see the advantage of this and adapt themselves to it, thus helping the jobber in his work, which will aid us, too, indirectly. I believe that approval plans can lead to the development of the total resources of the country, but I also believe we have reached a critical stage in their development, and the time is now ripe for research to be undertaken into: (1) which approval plan method is most suitable to special types of libraries; (2) what methods are used to follow up approval plans by bibliographers; (3) the economics of approval plans; and (4) the long-term effects of approval plans on the nation's resources.

Future Prospects of Library Acquisitions

Robert B. Downs

Pioneer American University and research librarians were strongly addicted to rugged individualism in their methods of book procurement. Funds were limited and collections grew at a snail's pace, relatively speaking. Nevertheless, each library was regarded as a completely independent entity, its development proceeding with little or no consideration of its neighbors, and it was reliant upon its own resources except for an occasional interlibrary loan.

Establishment of the National Union Catalog in 1900, and publication of the *Union List of Serials in Libraries of the United States and Canada* in 1927, were the first major evidences of a change of direction. Thenceforth, librarians began to think of their holdings within a larger frame of reference, as segments of a national resource, the sharing of which could be of immense mutual benefit. Perhaps the coming of the Great Depression in the nineteen thirties expedited the process, when such cooperative enterprises were born as the regional bibliographic centers in Denver, Philadelphia, and Seattle, along with numerous local and state union catalogs.

Not until after World War II was there any major effort undertaken toward joint or coordinated acquisition. The first was the Cooperative Acquisitions Project for Wartime Publications, sponsored by the Library of Congress, which demonstrated several facts: American libraries could look to their national library for leadership in large cooperative activities; research libraries were able and willing to support a broad program for the improvement of library resources; the idea of libraries combining for the acquisition of research materials was feasible and desirable; and the research resources of American libraries were a matter of national concern.

Following close on the heels of the Library of Congress Project for Wartime Publications, and profiting from the experience gained in that program, came the Association of Research Libraries' Farmington Plan. The beginning, in 1948, was modest, comprising only publications issued in three Western European nations: France, Sweden, and Switzerland. Within five years, however, the Farmington Plan's scope was worldwide.

A natural outgrowth of the Farmington Plan was the Public Law 480 program administered by the Library of Congress. In 1961, the Congress authorized the expenditure of counterpart funds or blocked currencies for the acquisition of multiple copies of publications in certain countries where surplus funds had accumulated. The program presently includes Ceylon, India, Indonesia, Israel, Nepal, Pakistan, the United Arab Republic, and Yugoslavia. Millions of copies of books, pamphlets, periodicals, newspapers, and government publications have been procured and distributed to several hundred American libraries since inception of the project.

Another area of the world was covered, starting in 1959, by the Latin American Cooperative Acquisition Project (LACAP) in which some forty libraries are currently participating, utilizing commercial channels.

Also productive have been cooperative acquisition undertakings by smaller groups of institutions. An example is the Midwest Universities Consortium for International Activities—the University of Illinois, Indiana University, Michigan State University, and University of Wisconsin—which has provided funds for sending library staff members on collecting expeditions to the Far East, Southeast Asia, Africa, and Latin America. The representatives not only procured substantial

SOURCE: Reprinted from *Library Trends*, XVIII, 3 (January 1970), pp. 412–421, by permission of the publisher, the University of Illinois Graduate School of Library Science. Robert B. Downs is Dean of Library Administration, University of Illinois Library, Urbana.

quantities of material that in all likelihood would otherwise have been unavailable, but also established useful contacts with book dealers, publishers, and librarians abroad.

Sending its agents abroad is an old story, of course, to the Library of Congress with its global collecting activities, and scarcely less so to a number of other individual institutions, such as Stanford University's Hoover Institution Library, Northwestern University Library (chiefly to Africa), and the University of California (especially to the Far East).

Thus, with the rich background of experience gained from the Cooperative Acquisitions Project for Wartime Publications, the Farmington Plan, the Latin American Cooperative Acquisition Project, the Public Law 480 program, and its long-time procurement activities abroad, the Library of Congress was fully prepared to take advantage of special provisions in the Higher Education Act of 1965. This was the enabling legislation for the immensely important National Program for Acquisitions and Cataloging.

The specific provision is contained in Title II, Part C, entitled "Strengthening College and Research Library Resources," of the Higher Education Act of 1965, reading as follows:

> There are hereby authorized to be appropriated $5,000,000 for the fiscal year ending June 30, 1966, $6,315,000 for the fiscal year ending June 30, 1967, and $7,770,000 for the fiscal year ending June 30, 1968, to enable the Commissioner of Education to transfer funds to the Librarian of Congress for the purpose of (1) acquiring, as far as possible, all library materials currently published throughout the world which are of value to scholarship; and (2) providing catalog information for these materials promptly after receipt, and distributing bibliographic information by printing catalog cards and by other means, and enabling the Library of Congress to use for exchange and other purposes such of these materials as are not needed for its own collections.[1]

The program as it developed has had the dual purpose of building up the collections of the Library of Congress, as the national library, thereby benefiting libraries in general, and of providing catalog information to meet the needs of other libraries. It was agreed that all titles with an imprint date of 1966 or later and all titles listed in current foreign national bibliographies, regardless of imprint date, would be eligible for acquisition and cataloging under the program. Further, the program would cover all monographic publications, trade and non-trade; annuals, including reports, yearbooks, proceedings, and transactions;

selected foreign dissertations; atlases; and government publications, if they met the criteria. Periodicals and non-book materials, however, were not to be included at the outset.

Other significant aspects of the program as it related to acquisitions included the use of air mail to expedite deliveries; continuation of the Library of Congress' existing acquisition policy as it dealt with the purchase of books; blanket order arrangements with certain foreign book dealers; orders for all Farmington Plan titles; and the establishment of acquisition centers in areas where the book trade is not well-organized and where there is no national bibliography. To provide reasonable assurance of complete coverage, the Library of Congress supplied to each of a group of libraries for control purposes copies of catalog cards printed for current imprints; the cooperating libraries, in turn, were expected to send to the Library of Congress copies of their orders for current foreign acquisitions for which no catalog card could be found in the control file or in the published National Union Catalog.

Until congressional appropriations make possible full implementation of the National Program for Acquisitions and Cataloging (NPAC), the complete coverage visualized by the originators of the plan will be delayed, but it is apparent that in the foreseeable future the world's publishing output, promptly after it comes off the press, will be coming to the United States cataloged at home or abroad and ready for use. Within their respective spheres, the National Agricultural Library and the National Library of Medicine are active participants in the over-all program.

The question may properly be asked: Will the NPAC eventually supersede the Farmington Plan, LACAP, and similar efforts at co-operative acquisition? The answer is definitely in the negative. For insurance purposes alone, it will continue to be desirable to acquire more than one copy of every worthwhile book issued abroad and to decentralize locations. In a nation with a population in excess of 200,000,000, spread over a huge geographical area, among whom are tens of thousands of scholars, scientists, and research workers and millions of students, there is a clear and present need for multiple copies of materials of value to scholarship. Also, ready availability is an important factor. As Fremont Rider pointed out years ago, in *The Scholar and the Future of the Research Library*, "On one point they [scholars] all seem to be amazingly unanimous: they all seem to have a desire . . . to have their research materials available, not in New York or California, but under their own finger tips wherever they may happen to be working."[2]

The concept of collecting in the national interest is being furthered, too, by a relatively new type of institution, best exemplified by the Center for Research Libraries (CRL) in Chicago. The CRL was founded twenty years ago as the Midwest Inter-Library Center, to serve two main functions: to house and service little-used research materials for member libraries, and to purchase selected materials for cooperative use. After reorganization in 1965, the Center changed from a regional to a national, indeed to an international, institution, since there are several Canadian members, and adopted its present name. As of 1969, the institutional membership numbered thirty-eight, spread from coast to coast. Over the past four years, the Center's acquisition funds have grown from $43,000 to $404,000, based chiefly on current membership assessments and federal government grants.

By definition, the Center for Research Libraries concentrates its collecting activities on highly-specialized, little-used materials. Thus, it has assembled, for example, the most complete collection of foreign dissertations in the United States and maintains extensive holdings of foreign and domestic newspapers on film, foreign government publications, college catalogs, state documents, Russian Academy of Sciences documents, and textbooks. For about the past fifteen years, that is starting in 1956, supported by grants from the National Science Foundation, the Center has subscribed to several thousand rarely held serials included in *Chemical Abstracts* and *Biological Abstracts*.

From the point of view of the acquisition policies and programs of the individual member libraries, the principal value of such an organization as the Center for Research Libraries is to relieve them of responsibility for collecting a variety of fringe materials, expensive to acquire, seldom needed, and filling valuable space, but perhaps important when wanted.

Effective July 1, 1969, the CRL Board of Directors specified that regular and continued use of the Center's materials could be made only by members of the Center, effectively restricting loans, with occasional exceptions, to institutions providing financial support.

On a much smaller scale, the Hampshire Inter-Library Center in Amherst, Massachusetts, established in 1961, serves purposes similar to those of the CRL. The participating institutions are Amherst, Mount Holyoke, and Smith Colleges, the University of Massachusetts, and the Forbes Library in Northampton. The Hampshire Center was set up to purchase and store jointly-owned research materials. Its primary collecting interests are current and retrospective serial files and monumental sets.

For decades, university and research librarians have been pursuing a type of cooperation which has often turned out to be a will-of-the-wisp, i.e., specialization of fields. Acquisition agreements among libraries appear, theoretically at least, to be a logical alternative to the impossible goal of trying to collect everything. Skeptics who question the feasibility of dividing fields have frequently had their doubts justified by problems of distance and communication and by institutional intransigence. One can, of course, point to notable exceptions: Duke University and the University of North Carolina, Columbia University and the New York Public Library, Newberry and the John Crerar Libraries, etc., and the Farmington Plan is a successful example of specialization of collecting interests among the sixty or more participating libraries. It is realistic to expect, however, that university libraries will have to duplicate extensively the holdings of other libraries; otherwise, they will seriously inconvenience their faculties and students.

The success of programs of library cooperation in universities, it ought to be recognized, must depend principally upon over-all institutional attitudes, especially in the willingness to rationalize graduate and research activities. Librarians can hardly move farther or faster in inter-institutional agreements than their parent universities are willing to go. Universities must specify in detail, therefore, their fields of primary interest prior to having their libraries reach understandings for specialization.

Virtually every state in the union has seen the mushrooming of its institutions of higher education during recent years. Former agricultural and mechanical colleges and teachers colleges have been transformed, almost overnight, to the status of general universities. The financial implications for the states are staggering, if these expanded institutions are to become universities in fact as well as in name. A major item of cost is library expansion, including the building of university-level collections. Can the states afford to permit each library to grow separately and independently? Is it realistic to expect that state legislatures will provide the high-level support required for building strong university libraries? Is it feasible for state-supported university libraries to work together to bring maximum library service to their users at costs somewhere within reason?

It is in response to such questions as these that an intriguing proposal was made and is under consideration in the state of North Carolina. The plan, in brief, would be to centralize highly-specialized collections, rather than dispersing them over the fifteen state university and senior college libraries. The logical location for such a central facility, to be shared by all institutions, would be the Chapel Hill-Durham-Raleigh area, since the state's principal library resources are already to be found there. There would be established, separate from any existing library, a state-wide depository collection, which in addition to containing specialized holdings beyond the ordinary needs of the participating libraries would provide bibliographic services in the form of a revision and expansion of the North Carolina Union Catalog, through teletype connections among the libraries, and through rapid delivery service from the central facility and from campus to campus.

According to the proposal as visualized, the entire library research resources of the state would eventually be united to serve all students, scholars, and general researchers. There would continue, of course, to be special subject-oriented collections developed in individual institutions, complementing and supplementing the central depository. Bibliographic access to such collections would be provided through the North Carolina Union Catalog. The primary aim would be the creation of a cooperative service with a communications and transportation network assuring the availability of all resources to all legitimate users.

The sharing of library collections could be greatly expedited if telefacsimile systems were perfected, both to make the equipment more economical and more efficient. Even now, at least one library system, that of Pennsylvania State University, finds it advantageous to operate a telefacsimile service on a state-wide basis. That system's most recent annual report notes that telefacsimile equipment connects the University Park Library and eighteen scattered commonwealth campus libraries. When the telefacsimile network was first established, the decision was made to use the equipment only for the transmission of urgently needed material. That policy was found to be too restrictive, however, and commonwealth campus librarians are now permitted individual discretion—

a change in procedure which it is believed will result in considerably more frequent and effective use of the telefacsimile equipment.

Inter-institutional agreements for sharing resources have been influenced to some degree by huge micro-reproduction projects, which continue to proliferate. Few libraries can afford or would desire to subscribe to all such undertakings. In some instances neighboring libraries have divided responsibility for particular projects, an economy move which still gives their clientele access to large bodies of specialized material. A new dimension has been added, however, with the Rand Corporation's proposal entitled *A Billion Books for Education in America and the World*[3] and the Encyclopaedia Britannica's announcement of a series of "Resource and Research Libraries" in ultramicrofiche. A library that subscribes to all the series which the Britannica plans to produce would possess a million volumes in ultramicrofiche form at a price which would not appear to be astronomical. Will this development make less attractive, or will it promote, the idea of interlibrary cooperation, especially the division of fields? The incentive for collecting agreements may be lessened by the possibility of having virtually every book needed near at hand, even though in greatly reduced format.

Reproduction of material in full size is having a dramatic effect on library acquisition activities (i. e., publication in near-print form, by Xerox and photo-offset). Since the coming of Xerox, it has been stated that no book should be considered out of print, assuming that somewhere a copy is available for reproduction. The importance of this fact is accentuated by the requirements of the many new "instant" university libraries. In the past, it would have been virtually impossible for such libraries to have acquired the numerous basic periodical files, collections of primary sources, and reference works needed for a research library. The material had gone out of print and was simply unprocurable at any price. Within the past few years, reprinting has become big business. The 1969 edition of *Guide to Reprints* lists 183 firms which are engaged to a greater or lesser extent in reprint publishing, in the United States and abroad. Their productions include complete runs of general and special journals; society publications; bibliographical and other reference works; series dealing with special subjects, such as the Negro, law, theatre, American studies, criminology, and history of science; and innumerable individual book titles. Among the giants in the field are the AMS Press,

Johnson Reprint Corporation, Kraus Reprint Company, Gregg International Publishers, Burt Franklin, Gale Research Company, and Slatkine Reprints.

A parallel development has been to make any items desired available on an individual basis, in microform or by Xerox "copy-flo" techniques. A leader in the field is the Xerox Corporation's University Microfilms, which is building up an immense stock of microfilms of titles in all fields, from which reproductions in microform or full scale can be supplied. This is not a publishing venture, but a service tailored to meet a particular need for single copies of out-of-print titles. In many instances, the reprints are on better paper and produced in better formats than the originals.

By way of summary, it should be noted that the world output of published materials is increasing at a geometric rate, presenting research libraries with a dilemma of great dimensions in attempting to keep abreast of the flood. Beginning with World War II, the collecting concerns of American libraries, formerly largely restricted to the United States and Western Europe, have become worldwide. The expanding library holdings are a direct response to the increased scholarly preoccupation with area studies. The outpouring of print in all its forms points toward an increased necessity for carefully defined acquisition policies, specialization of fields among libraries, and co-operative acquisition plans.

The solutions being found for the problems created by the information and publication explosion are imaginative and practical. Among the highlights are the Library of Congress' global acquisitions program, the Farmington Plan, the Public Law 480 program, the Latin American Co-operative Acquisitions Project, the establishment of joint central facilities, such as the Center for Research Libraries, and agreements among individual libraries for divisions of fields of collecting.

The impact of technology on research libraries is accelerating. It is quite conceivable that libraries will eventually be linked together in an international network, drawing freely upon each others others' resources and sharing in great central reservoirs. But even before such a day of wonders dawns, libraries are using technical progress and mechanisms to improve communications, e.g., by teletype; to speed transmission of materials between libraries, e.g., by telefacsimile (a device that is obviously in its infancy); and to reproduce in microfilm, microprint, microcard, microfiche, and ultramicrofiche and in standard reprint format vast quantities of research materials. The influence of such developments upon individual libraries is almost incalculable. One result, undoubtedly, will be that every piece of literature or bit of information in any library can be made readily available to the seeker after knowledge. The laissez faire philosophy which university librarians, in particular, have been inclined to follow, attempting to achieve virtual autonomy in wide areas of knowledge and to serve all the needs of their clientele without reference to other institutions, will call for drastic revision.

The richness and variety of American library resources are unsurpassed by those of any other nation. In an article for the *Encyclopedia Americana* on "One Hundred Notable Libraries of the World," the present writer concluded that thirty of the 100 are in the United States. The college and university libraries of the nation alone hold in excess of 300,000,000 volumes, and are growing at the rate of 25,000,000 volumes annually. To these impressive figures can be added the holdings of great reference libraries, hundreds of special libraries, and thousands of public libraries, providing users of American libraries with bibliographical resources beyond compare. The users, however, will never be completely satisfied. They will constantly demand more.

REFERENCES

1. *U.S. Statutes at Large.* Vol. 79, p. 1228.
2. Rider, Fremont. *The Scholar and the Future of the Research Library.* New York, Hadham Press, 1944, p. 82.
3. Hays, David G. *A Billion Books for Education in America and the World: A Proposal.* Santa Monica, Calif., Rand Corp., 1968.

III

BIBLIOGRAPHIC CONTROL

Writings of general interest are provided here rather than works on a detailed technical level. The articles are broad in scope and may encourage discussion, reflection, and further research. For example, filing problems, thorny enough in the dictionary catalog, will pose different questions for the computer age. The debate over the card catalog and the printed book catalog is reviewed. Informed but informal and entertaining looks are taken at subject cataloging work and at the complexities of bibliographic control of serials. A project aimed at eventual total bibliographic control of serials is discussed.

The Crisis in the Voluminous Authors

David C. Weber

Finding a specific book by a 'voluminous author' whose name heads hundreds or thousands of cards is among the most difficult problems faced by the professor or student who uses a·university library catalogue. Satisfactory arrangements of cards cannot be worked out by the library staff unless the complexities of large files are clearly understood. This note is meant to discuss the more common difficulties which arise in filing personal authors, and to present some possible solutions as proposed in the eleven working papers on certain authors submitted to a special planning committee of the Widener Library staff early in 1952.[1]

During the year 1951-52 the Widener staff did the spade work on a new filing code for use in Widener's public catalogue of four and one-half million cards and union catalogue of over three million cards. As the various filing rules were discussed, it became increasingly evident that, while much of the filing presented no particular problem, certain entries were unusually troublesome. Among the most complex of these were the 'voluminous author' entries comprising several hundred cards at least and with production by the author in several forms of writing (or genres).

Where does this trouble arise? A group of subject cards, filed by author, has a clear arrangement. But where a work appeared under several titles, where a book may be approached by editor as well as date, where an author produced speeches and letters and novels and poetry which are important as separate genres, or where titles for portions of a work clutter a file, here a student can waste many minutes thumbing through several hundred cards when the arrangement is not obvious and distinct. As libraries add collected works, issues, selections, and miscellanies of prolific authors, the problems become urgent to a degree which has now affected Widener's catalogues in three or four hundred important places.

Cards under a personal author have generally been divided into 'Collected works,' 'Selected works,' 'Single works,' 'Translations,' and subject cards. Is this a satisfactory division? Or what refinements should be made for voluminous files? Alphabetical arrangement was favored by the planning committee as a working principle; but as specialists worked over particular authors, they proposed to the committee more rather than fewer special divisions. Definitions of the two terms 'collected' and 'selected' are necessary keys to the cards filed under these two exceptions from alphabetical order. 'Collected' is now given a broad interpretation so that it contains many partial collections, including any works which happen to begin with 'complete,' 'works,' or 'collected.' Titles such as *The skunk and other stories*, beginning as they do with distinctive titles, have generally been treated in the Widener catalogues as single works, though in content some of them are as broadly 'collected' as works so filed. *Two stories* would be treated as a single work, but would *Five stories* or *Ten novels*? Again, representative library catalogues and philosophical bibliographies differ about which of Immanuel Kant's works are to be considered as 'collected'; the printed Library of Congress catalogue segregates a minimum of items by this author as 'collected works.' The difficulty of making clear-cut decisions on such questions has prompted some people to consider a single alphabetical file for each author, even the most voluminous; but it should be evident that a point does come when a large and complex file presents problems that must be tackled. The recommendation might be that, for any voluminous author, only complete or

SOURCE: Reprinted from the *Harvard Library Bulletin* VII, 1 (Winter 1953), pp. 113-119, by permission of the author and the publisher.

nearly complete sets of works be filed as 'collected works.'

The term 'selected' is as troublesome as 'collected.' *Extracts from Areopagitica, The fly and other poems*, or *Three boys* may be found among the 'selected' file. Widener's planning committee agreed that a strict interpretation was more suitable. Where there is any doubt, only those works which begin with the words 'Complete,' 'Collected,' 'Works,' 'Novels,' 'Poems,' 'Poetical works,' etc., and 'Selected,' 'Chosen,' 'Representative,' etc., are to be filed as 'collected' and 'selected.' Problems will still remain, however, with titles such as *Stories, Collected prefaces,* and *Works of whimsy*. Distinctive titles should usually go with the individual works (*The cat and other tales* should be filed there) and vague titles (such as *Some collected items*) should also be placed there. The remaining problem-titles can be solved to some extent by observing the user of the catalogue. A student or scholar looks for a particular title or a complete edition, rarely for a selection. The library order department checks only a single title. Hence the 'selected' file, for the trouble it causes the library staff and the user, is perhaps not worth its salt. There are times when it is convenient; but in general it may be more satisfactory to have only the two files: 'collected works' and 'single and selected works.' The breakdown of an accumulation of cards depends on size *and* complexity, but exceptions from the straight alphabetical file must be made very carefully.

If special arrangements seem advisable for the arrangement of voluminous authors, can any standard plans be adopted, or must individual solutions be worked out? Standardization may be possible to a certain degree; and if it is, then the cataloguers can give direct aid to the clerical employees who do the filing. The degree of breakdown required in a large file of cards depends to a certain extent on the size of the file, to a small extent on the number of languages in which the author first writes his works, and to a great extent on the complexity of genre. For instance, artists and instrumental composers of any country may fit into a rather simple arrangement which might be:

Collected artistic works
  arranged by
    1. editor or titled edition
    2. untitled edition
Single and selected artistic works
Literary works
Cards for works about the author

Vocal composers, poets, and playwrights may fit into a second and somewhat more complex scheme, with a variation for those writing in a language other than English. Novelists may need a third special yet similar plan. And persons working outside the arts (speakers, essayists, historians, philosophers, and so forth) would need a fourth special scheme. The breakdown of files into two sections—novels, poems, plays, music, paintings, etc., versus letters, speeches, autobiography, travel, etc.—might be helpful if the division can be kept distinct. For instance, Disraeli's fourteen or more novels are distinct from his correspondence and political writings. Wherever the division is not perfectly clear it is certainly best *not* to divide.

The division into form of production (or genre) is worth investigation, but it must be done carefully. Standardization may be impossible here. Letters are an important form for many a person, and segregation would be of great help where titles vary, such as:

Benjamin Franklin and . . . , their
  correspondence
A collection of the familiar letters . . .
Curious and facetious letters of . . .
  Franklin
The ingenious Dr. Franklin; selected
  . . . letters
My dear girl; the correspondence of . . .
Private correspondence . . . of Franklin

Troubles arise, however, when Goldsmith's works are divided into 'Works (collected and selected),' 'Dramatic works,' 'Poetical works,' etc. There is a variety of Goldsmith's literary forms—poetry, fiction, essays, plays, history—which have been collected in various combinations. Inconsistencies have resulted from uncertainty as to whether such titles as *Poems and plays* and *Poems, plays and essays* should be filed behind the guide card 'Poetical works' or behind 'Works (collected and selected).' Also, titles like *Essays, poems, letters and plays* have been found under both 'Single works' and 'Works (collected and selected).' Not a few authors have turned out a work as a novel and then in a play form; or a novel may be largely autobiographical or a travel book largely fictional. Any arbitrary divisions are obviously dangerous. And it is evident that, when a person works in more than one of the four groups suggested in the paragraph above, there probably must be individual solutions. There are too many borderline cases for any one or even four standard plans to be indiscriminately applied.

Although straight alphabetical order is favored as the basic arrangement, divisions within an author may be made so long as the clarity of arrangement is not sacrificed. Divisions enable a person who has vague information or only general knowledge of a book to locate the title, yet they do not hinder the person who has an accurate title in hand. Perhaps a fourth of the people who look for a specific book in the catalogue do so without full author and title information. The catalogue should help these people if it can do so without penalizing those who do have the information. Various card divisions within an author file may be considered. Segregation of all subject cards and division by language are two common exceptions to straight alphabetical order. Segregation of various degrees of collection (i.e., collected and selected groups) is useful but should be done with caution. Division by genre is only one of other possibilities.

Arrangement within the 'collected' and 'single work' groups is a different and important problem. The planning committee unanimously favored inverse chronological filing throughout the catalogues. There are a few places, however, where other arrangements of editions may be preferred. An important proposal for classical authors argued for an arrangement by editor or translator instead of publication date; and the Widener solution may be to file in both catalogues by titles, and subarrange by date in the official catalogue and by editor or translator in the public catalogue. For recent authors the edition (or editor) is just as important, particularly for collected works. Over nine tenths of Dickens' collected works (and certainly every important one) have edition names such as: Authentic, Biographical, Booklovers, Boston, Cambridge, Carleton's, or Centenary edition. There are over a hundred of these names. In practically no cases are there more than one or two editions with the same name—and then not in the same period. It may be thought at first that an arrangement by edition would be disadvantageous to the acquisition department when it checks a bookdealer's catalogue. It is true that bookdealers cannot be relied upon to give the name of the edition, but it is certain that for a voluminous author only an edition which is fully described in the dealer's catalogue, or a new edition which is just appearing, would be ordered. Arrangement by edition would facilitate the searching and cataloguing of a work which has no date or merely the usual copyright date, or where the volumes have appeared over a number of years and only the late volumes are in hand. A professor looks for, or the student is sent to, a certain edition of a writer's works, and a date arrangement does not serve the purpose. There will be some trouble for the undergraduate when he wants a recent edition; but this student is usually looking for a special edition which the professor has listed, or he is reading on his own and will be more interested in a single work. (Havard has the additional advantage of its Lamont Library to serve the probing neophyte.) The alternative to the above arrangement is the use of index cards, filed in front of the date file, listing editions by name or editor and referring to the date of publication in the cards which follow. (It may be noted that in several places in its catalogue Yale has indexed all editors of works in the original language, as Harvard has for Shakespeare.) Yet an index card should be complete, and one hundred editions form a lengthy list, expensive to keep up to date. And in either arrangement there would be a troublesome residue of collected editions which have no name or editor. The problem of the collected works of recent authors might best be solved, as with classical authors, by filing one catalogue by date and the other by edition.

There are two peculiarities of book titles which cause major filing difficulties. The first is a title which begins with the author's name. When a work has such a title as: *Charles Dickens, Esq., on the late execution; Charles Dickens' birthday book; Charles Dickens, the writer and his work;* or *Dickens digest*, should the filing be by the first word or the first after all parts of the author's full name? The only consistent and permanent solution is to file under the first word after 'Charles' and/or 'Dickens,' and this practice may be supported by placing general cross-reference cards under these two names. This rule would supply a suitable title for filing even in the case of adjectives or prepositions; and a reference from the *full* name (including such modifiers as 'Jr,' 'the Third,' and 'Esq.') should take care of such cases as the first example above. Any other practice will result in inconsistent application, and unforeseen titles will continually be bringing trouble.

The second problem is a work which has appeared under variant titles. Here the question is whether to retain the title-page integrity of the variants or to bring all editions together under a chosen form. If the titles are retained as they appeared, Wordsworth's *A description of the scenery of the lakes . . . , Guide to the lakes,* and *A guide through the district of the lakes . . .* would appear in three places; and 'see also' references to the other titles make for clumsy use of the file. Yet if the alternative procedure is followed, with all variants gathered under a preferred title (and with 'see from' references for the variants) then the chosen form of the title must be inserted on the main card (presumably in brackets, beneath the author's name), or the order of cards will not be immediately evident and the user will have difficulty.

A refinement of the above problem occurs when two works usually appear together, but under varying titles. The following titles have been used for two of Daniel Webster's orations which nearly always have appeared together:

An address delivered at the completion of
   the . . .
An address delivered at the laying of the . . .
Bunker Hill address
Bunker Hill declaration
The Bunker Hill monument
The Bunker Hill monument orations
Daniel Webster's first Bunker Hill oration
The orations on Bunker Hill monument
Webster's 1st Bunker Hill oration

It seems best to collect the two orations under 'Bunker,' to disregard the separate publication of a single oration, and to arrange all editions by the date of publication. A by-product of this choice is that the file of 'Addresses' would be much shortened and easier to use. Variant titles may appear for parts of one work just as they may for one or two whole works. Wordsworth offers a good example of this separate publication of parts of a whole. *The recluse* has appeared in three major forms: part one appeared separately only once and then under the title of the whole work; part two, *The excursion*, is nine tenths of the extant work, and has so far always appeared under its own name in Harvard's holdings; part three was never written; the entire extant work, consisting of parts one and two, has appeared so far only under the title of part two! The curator of the catalogue or a member of the catalogue department obviously must integrate variant titles if the user is not to be confused, or even misled.

Finding a small single work in a file dominated by multi-card titles is a problem which deserves more attention than it has had. The Dickens file contains a dozen individual works which have over one hundred cards each. Could the major single works be arranged after 'Collected works' and before the minor works, or would the definition of

'major' and 'minor' present a problem? There is one easy solution. A guide card with the tab at the far right could be placed at the end of the major work to read 'End of *Dombey*' or 'End of *Pickwick*,' or a standardized 'End of title,' which would be less expensive. This termination tab would be inserted in every case where there was one half inch or more of cards and where the end of one major work was not adjacent to the beginning of the next major work. Such a guide would not give undue importance to a minor work, and it would indicate at a glance the strength of holdings of the major work. The reader might thus jump immediately to the last cards in a group, or quickly jump ahead to find a minor title which was buried between the bulky titles. In cases where cards are not filed in inverse chronological order, this small termination tab would also greatly aid in locating the latest edition of a multi-card title.

It is apparent from all the foregoing that the user needs special help to find his way quickly in a voluminous file. A card catalogue has certain inherent shortcomings which a printed volume corrects. For instead of a whole page, the eye can see only one card in a card file; and the catalogue user must thus be told at a glance what special arrangements have been made for a particular author. Guide cards and arrangement cards with protruding tabs are the solution. Concerning guide cards, there are two procedures to be reconciled. One uses guides to divide trays of cards alphabetically by placing guides at major alphabetical breaks. The second procedure uses guides only when files have been subarranged by degree of collection (i.e., selections and collected works), genre, language, subject cards, or in other ways. Alphabetized cards have a natural order and guides then are an amenity, but each subarrangement must unquestionably have a guide. It therefore seems advisable to follow the first procedure only when there is a considerable number of cards, or where a title with a great many cards exists within the alphabetical file. Color of guide, size of lettering, and length of tab are all devices to be utilized in distinguishing the two kinds of guiding.

'Arrangement cards' are also a means of setting forth the sub-divisions clearly. Several members of the planning committee urged the use of outline cards in voluminous author files which would explain the breakdown so that the user might choose the particular division to look through—such an outline as is found in most printed catalogues or bibliographies. During part of 1952, 'warning' cards for a temporary peculiarity were placed in the official catalogue; and it was reported that they caused trouble to many people who assumed that the warning applied only to the cards following or who thought that the warning card marked the end of a special heading. The wording on the tab is thus of the greatest importance. Further, one arrangement card presumably is not enough, and even two or three might not catch every user's eye. It might not be a waste of space if major information were printed on the top surface of a one- or two-inch block of wood to be inserted right in the middle of a tray of cards. The end here justifies the means, and any method that informs the user quickly and explicitly of the subdivisions deserves attention.

Harvard has left only a selection of editions of Thomas à Kempis' *De imitatione Christi* in the card file, with a card referring the user to the shelf list for a complete listing. This practice has been seriously considered for several other authors. Certainly the ideal solution for complicated arrangements, complex divisions, and large holdings is a printed bibliography which could be referred to in the card catalogue and which would supplement a working selection left in the card file. However, the problems of such a printed catalogue need more extended treatment than can be attempted here. This and such special problems as arise in translations, manuscripts, attributed works, music, and so forth, must be left for later discussion.

Voluminous authors are more important and troublesome than any other part of card catalogues in large research libraries. They need the particular attention of the librarian in order to make the catalogue of greatest use to the student and scholar.

NOTES

[1] The sixty-odd working papers on all aspects of filing were summarized by Edwin E. Williams, 'Alphabetical Dilemmas of Widener's Catalogues,' *Harvard Library Bulletin*, VI (1952), 322–335. These working papers are not available for general circulation.

Introduction to the Anglo-American Cataloging Rules, North American Text

C. Sumner Spalding

ORIENTATION OF THE RULES

A coherent code of cataloging rules requires a fundamental orientation in respect to the type of library, the type of collection, and the type of catalog for which it is designed. Thus an explanation of the orientation of the present rules is a natural starting point for an introduction to their nature, content, and structure.

These rules have been drawn up primarily to respond to the needs of general research libraries. This represents a continuation of the orientation that has characterized the rules of the American Library Association since the 1908 edition.[1] This orientation applies equally to the rules for entry and heading, which have been completely rewritten, and to the rules for description, which are essentially the *Rules for Descriptive Cataloging in the Library of Congress* (Washington, 1949), revised as to text and reorganized to fit the present structure. These Library of Congress rules were also the rules officially adopted by the American Library Association. Within the framework of this research-library orientation, however, an effort has been made to respond as much as possible to the needs of public libraries in which research considerations are not paramount. When the needs of research libraries and those of other libraries are irreconcilable, alternative rules have been provided for the use of the latter. Furthermore, considerable emphasis has been placed on providing more direct headings, reducing the complexity of certain headings, and substituting headings that correspond more closely to the normal usage of educated persons for certain former headings that emphasized technical correctness to the point of pedantry. All of these efforts tend to make the prescribed headings more practical for non-research libraries and for research libraries as well. It is assumed, so far as rules of description are concerned, that libraries preferring less detail will modify the rules as required to suit their needs.

The rules are as comprehensive as they could be made in their coverage of types of materials that are acquired in research libraries; monographs and serials, macroforms and microforms, published works and manuscripts, book-like materials and non-book materials. In addition to rules for maps, motion pictures and filmstrips, music, phonorecords, and individual pictorial works, rules are provided for cataloging collections of independent manuscripts and collections of independent pictures etc. that have been assembled into units either by a collector or by the owning library. The rules for these various types of library materials have been drawn up in such a way that the entries are compatible, thus permitting inclusion of all, or as many as may be desired, in the same catalog.

Finally, the rules have been designed to meet the requirements of multiple-entry alphabetical catalogs in which all entries for particular persons or corporate bodies appear under a uniform heading or are related by references. Sufficient entries for each cataloged item and sufficient references for each established heading have been prescribed to permit access under the approaches that may be reasonably anticipated on the part of readers who are not especially conversant with cataloging rules. When such a multiple-entry catalog is not a dictionary catalog, it has been assumed in a few instances that there will be a separate catalog in which collocation of entries under certain category headings will be provided.

SOURCE: Reprinted from C. Sumner Spalding, ed., *Anglo-American Cataloging Rules* (Chicago: American Library Association, 1967), pp. 1–6, by permission of the American Library Association.

Although the rules are oriented to multiple-entry catalogs, it has still been regarded as necessary to distinguish main entries from added entries. Since this distinction can be one of the most difficult operations in cataloging, it may be asked why it is necessary if all requisite entries are provided in the catalog and, when the unit-card system is used, the descriptive information on each entry is the same. The necessity persists because, for one thing, even in multiple-entry catalogs it sometimes happens that a work, other than the work being cataloged, must be identified by a single entry—e.g. a work about which the work in hand has been written or a work on which the work in hand has been based. Beyond this requirement in the multiple-entry catalog itself is the manifest general need, permeating all library, bibliographical, and book-trade activities, for a standard mode of identifying bibliographical entities. Such standard identification is of great importance in single-entry bibliographies, book lists, order lists, bibliographical citations, and everyday communications referring to bibliographical entities. By prescribing what shall be the main entry, the rules respond to this necessity for a standard mode of identifying a work. They follow the principle, firmly established in modern cataloging and bibliography, that a work should be specified by its author and title or, if it lacks an author, by its title.

UNDERLYING PRINCIPLES

The present rules are based on the "Statement of Principles" adopted by the International Conference on Cataloguing Principles in 1961 (hereinafter referred to as the Paris Principles).[2] These Principles, in turn, derive in great part from the rationalization of cataloging rules that was made by Seymour Lubetzky, first editor of these rules, in his *Cataloging Rules and Principles; a Critique of the A.L.A. Rules for Entry and a Proposed Design for their Revision* (Washington, Processing Dept., Library of Congress, 1953) and in his *Code of Cataloging Rules: Author and Title Entry* (American Library Association, 1960) and its *Additions, Revisions, and Changes* (1961). The Catalog Code Revision Committee adopted the Paris Principles, with certain limited qualifications, early in 1962. Shortly thereafter the Library of Congress made an intensive study of the theoretical merits of the Paris Principles and of the extent to which changes would be required in its card

catalogs if the Principles were to be applied retrospectively. The Association of Research Libraries supported the findings of this study and recommended to the Catalog Code Revision Committee that certain provisions of the Paris Principles be reconsidered and that one, 9.4, be modified in view of the heavy cost that would be entailed in applying its provisions retrospectively to the great numbers of catalog entries that would be involved in any research library catalog. These recommendations were accepted by the Catalog Code Revision Committee in June 1962.

The rules that have been finally worked out, after much careful study and deliberation, meet the requirements of the Association of Research Libraries' recommendation and depart very little from the Paris Principles. A brief summary of the noteworthy departures from these Principles is given below. The numerical rubrics are those used in the Principles.

9.12 (footnote 7) and 11.14.[3] In its rule for serials (rule 6) the Committee held that the inclusion in the title of a serial of the name or part of the name of the issuing corporate body is too powerful a criterion to be nullified when, in unusual cases, no account of the activities of the body is included in the publication. It also held that "known primarily or conventionally by title" is too vague a criterion.

9.4.[4] The most significant departure of the rules from the Paris Principles lies in the special exceptions (98–99) for certain bodies of an institutional nature. These exceptions exempt the specified bodies from the principle of entry under name (*9.4*) and substitute the rule of entry under the name of a place. They were made in response to the Association of Research Libraries' recommendation and they have the effect of greatly reducing the impact of the Paris Principle on existing catalogs which are heavily infused with entries for corporate bodies under place names in accordance with all preceding cataloging rules.

9.5.[5] The Committee interpreted the words "formal or conventional titles indicating the nature of the material," as applied to constitutions, laws, treaties, etc., as meaning titles that include a categorizing word or phrase followed by an individualizing element. It sanctioned the continued use of such categorizing words or phrases in the form of subheadings, rather than in the form of uniform titles. It further sanctioned the continuation of a categorizing subheading for liturgical works in consideration of long-established practice and the recommendation of special libraries.

10.3.[6] The footnoted alternative text (rejected by a majority of the conference), providing for the entry of collections under the compiler when one is named on the title page, was accepted by the Committee in preference to the principle of entry under title.

12.[7] Usage of the language in which an author writes was preferred to usage of the country of which he is a citizen as the criterion for determining the entry word in cases of multiple-word surnames.

GENERAL CHARACTER

In many respects the character of the rules for entry and heading is markedly different from that of the 1908 or the 1949 rules because of a basic difference in approach to the general problem of cataloging. Earlier codes emphasized specific rules for various types of publications and various classes of persons and corporate bodies. This approach often had the practical advantage of providing answers in one place to the questions involved in determining the entry for certain publications or the heading for certain persons or corporate bodies. Attendant disadvantages were apparent, however, whenever the work, or the person or corporate body, was not clearly of one type rather than another, or when it was of some type for which there was no provision in the rules. In such cases cataloging had to be by analogy. The best analogy in a given situation would not always be clear and quite different solutions to the problem might be reached depending on which of the analogies was chosen. Problems such as these often led to the growth of a body of glosses or ad hoc decisions varying from one library to another. Apart from such operational difficulties, this case-by-case approach to the development of rules tended to obscure underlying principles and basic system while opening the way to the inclusion of many exceptions and inconsistencies. The result was necessarily detrimental to the effectiveness of the catalog as a finding tool.

The difference in the character of the present rules lies first in the fact that they are based on a set of principles[8] that have been followed as consistently as possible, allowing for the necessity of reaching common agreement and, in certain cases, of coming to terms with economic imperatives.

Second, choice of entry and construction of heading have been treated as separate problems, except when form subheadings are involved.

Third, choice of entry has been treated as a problem of determination of authorship responsibility. Hence the general rules of entry are framed around an analysis of the various patterns in which this responsibility may be distributed between persons, between corporate bodies, and between persons *and* corporate bodies, in the publications that must be cataloged.

Finally, construction of heading has been treated as a problem of name. This problem of name is reduced to its own sub-problems: first, the choice of a particular name and a particular form of that name; second, the conformation in which the name should be presented as a catalog heading. In general, rules for determining this conformation are based on considerations of morphology, language, and custom that determine the entry element of the name, considerations of the possible dependence of the name on another name, and considerations of the relationship of the name to other headings in the catalog.

Rules for types of publications and classes of persons and corporate bodies have normally been included only when such types involve special problems in authorship responsibility or require special headings that could not be dealt with satisfactorily in the general rules.

This different approach to rules for entry and heading has resulted in a substantial reduction in the amount of text required to state them. They are only about four-fifths as extensive as the corresponding rules in the 1949 edition, yet they give substantially more guidance to the cataloger.

The rules for description are likewise based on principles which, for the sake of convenience, are stated at the beginning of Part II, immediately preceding Chapter 6. These principles also provide general guidance to the cataloger when specific rules are lacking.

STRUCTURE

A clear understanding of the principle underlying the structural plan of these rules is essential to their use. It is especially important to catalogers who are used to the case method of the 1908 or 1949 rules. This principle is that each rule dealing with a specific problem is to be understood in the context of the more general rules. This does not mean that there are no specific rules that completely cover specific problems, nor does it mean that aspects of more general rules are never repeated in specific rules. It does mean, however, that the relevant general rules apply to any aspects of a specific problem that are not dealt with in a specific rule.

The rules are divided into three main parts, the first two dealing with books and book-like materials. Part I is concerned with entry and heading; Part II with description. The chapters of Part III are devoted to specific types of non-book materials and the rules in each chapter are normally grouped into rules of entry and rules of description. The rules in each group are primarily those that are either additional to or different from those for book-like materials. In no case is a chapter of Part III completely self-contained.

In many chapters of Parts I and II the rules are grouped into general rules and special rules. This distinction between general and special is pervasive throughout the rules. Sometimes it is explicit (as when rules are captioned "General rule" or "Basic rule"); sometimes it is implicit as when a rule has subrules covering special instances of the topic with which it deals. The cataloger must always bear in mind the principle that specific rules are to be understood in the context of the more general rules.

SOURCES

Three basic works and three special works were indispensible in the drafting of rules for entry and

heading, namely the Paris Principles; the Lubetzky *Code of Cataloging Rules*; the *A.L.A. Cataloging Rules* (1949); *National Usages for the Entry of Names of Persons*,[9] parepared by A. H. Chaplin for the International Conference on Cataloguing Principles; *Revision of the A.L.A. Cataloging Rules of Entry for Legal Materials and Related Rules*,[10] a report drafted by Werner B. Ellinger for the Committee on Cataloging of the American Association of Law Libraries, Ervin H. Pollack, Chairman; and several special studies of problems involved in the cataloging of religious publications, with recommended rules, prepared by Theodore A. Mueller for the Catalog Code Revision Committee.

As indicated earlier, the rules for description are a revision of the *Rules for Descriptive Cataloging in the Library of Congress* (1949), including its separately issued supplementary rules: *Manuscripts* (Draft for a prelim. ed., 1954 and Preprint of the rules for collections of manuscripts, 1954), *Motion Pictures and Filmstrips* (1st ed., 1965), *Phonorecords* (2d prelim. ed., 1964), and *Pictures, Designs, and Other Two-Dimensional Representations* (Prelim. ed., 1959). Time limitations did not permit restating these rules in the active voice to conform with the rules for entry and heading in Part I.

C. Sumner Spalding, *Editor,*
Rules for Entry and Heading, and General Editor

NOTES

[1] American Library Association. *Catalog rules; author and title entries*. (American edition. Chicago, 1908)

[2] Contained in the Conference's *Report* (London, International Federation of Library Associations, 1963) p. 91–96; also in *Library resources and technical services*, v. 6 (1962) p. 162–167.

[3] "*9.1* The main entry for a work should be made under the name of a *corporate body* (i.e. any institution, organized body or assembly of persons known by a corporate or collective name) . . . *9.12* when the wording of the title or title-page, taken in conjunction with the nature of the work, clearly implies that the corporate body is collectively responsible for the content of the work."[7] *Footnote 7*: "e.g. serials whose titles consist of a generic term (Bulletin, Transactions, etc.) preceded or followed by the name of a corporate body, and which include some account of the activities of the body."

"*11.1* Works having their *main entry* under the title are . . . *11.14* works (including serials and periodicals) known primarily or conventionally by title rather than by the name of the author."

[4] *9.4*, in its essence: "The *uniform heading* for works entered under the name of a corporate body should be the name by which the body is . . . identified."

[5] "*9.5* Constitutions, laws and treaties, and certain other works having similar characteristics, should be entered under the name of the appropriate state or other territorial authority, with formal or conventional titles indicating the nature of the material. Added entries for the actual titles should be made as needed."

[6] "*10.3* The *main entry* for a collection consisting of independent works or parts of works by different authors should be made

    10.31 when the collection has a collective title

        10.311 under the name of the *compiler* (i.e. the person responsible for assembling from various sources the material in the collection) if he is named on the title-page;

        10.312 under the title of the collection, if the compiler is not named on the title-page;

10.32 when the collection has no collective title, under the *name of the author*, or under the *title, of the first work in the collection*.

10.33 An added entry should always be made under the *name of the compiler* (if known), when not chosen as heading for the main entry; and under the *title*, if the main entry is under the compiler."

7"*12* When the name of a personal author consists of several words, the choice of entry is determined so far as possible by agreed usage in the country of which the author is a citizen, or, if this is not possible, by agreed usage in the language which he generally uses."

8 See "Underlying principles" above.

9 Provisional ed. London, Organizing Committee, I.C.C.P., 1963.

10 In *Law library journal*, v. 48 (1955) p. [3]-39.

Book Catalogs: Pros and Cons

Scott Allison

The card catalog was originally developed in the late nineteenth century because of a great weakness in the book catalog and not because of any inherent value in the card catalog. This weakness was the notable difficulty of cumulating lists of new accessions into the basic list. One may note that the British Museum catalog, by way of a modern-day example, in its second edition was published irregularly for over thirty years (1931 to late sixties), and, by the time of completion, the first letters of the alphabet were already thirty years behind. The design of the present card catalog was determined by the technology available when it was first created—for example, titles are in roman type (not italics) because of the use of the typewriter; and, the idea of the unit card derives from the technology of printing available when the Library of Congress began card distribution. The greatest advantage of the card form is considered by almost all librarians to be the ease of cumulation. At least five other advantages, however, have been cited in the literature: the card catalog is flexible—new entries can be inserted at any time, in any place, in any number; it wears well and resists mutilation, although some large libraries such as the New York Public are now finding the need to replace theirs; changes are said to be easy to make, mistakes easy to correct, although the fact that, in practise, so few changes are made at so great a cost would seem to belie this; a person using one tray removes less of the alphabet from circulation than a person using one volume of a comparable book catalog—this argument is no doubt specious as we shall see later on; and, finally, tradition favors the card catalog, primarily, perhaps, because until recently nothing else was known (20). On the other hand, the card catalog has numerous disadvantages (18, 20). Only a limited amount of information can be placed on a card. If more information is needed, second or third cards are necessary, most of whose capacity will be used up by repeating essential information from card to card. (In the book catalog, this is not a problem.) Since only one title is visible at a time, individual entries tend to become lost among thousands of cards in a large catalog (whereas in the book catalog, the display potentialities of an entire page of entries are an enormous advantage to the user in finding specific items among the maze.) Misfiled cards are more difficult to locate in the card catalog for similar reasons. Bulk is a problem, and bulk is synonymous with cost: the cost of cabinets, the cost of floor space occupied, the cost of the labor involved in maintenance. The single copy of the card catalog—and very few libraries have more than one—is inadequate in colleges and universities with departmental collections and in public libraries with numerous branches; indeed, the staff itself almost needs its own catalog, since it often monopolizes the public catalog to the detriment of users. The card catalog, furthermore, is characterized by immobility and manipulative cumbersomeness. And finally, it is awkward for many persons to use the card catalog at the same time, unless drawers are carried away to be consulted at adjoining desks and tables. Despite all the disadvantages of the card catalog, the opponent—the book catalog—has far from replaced it. A 1966 report (30) revealed that there were fewer than fifty book catalogs in existence in the United States. We certainly cannot speak of a landslide movement, since these fifty catalogs had been developed over a period of fifteen years. We shall now examine in detail the book catalog, beginning with a look at the various techniques used in producing it, and continuing with a study of all the pros and cons which have been advanced in the literature concerning its utility and cost. In ex-

SOURCE: This previously unpublished paper (1968) is printed here by permission of the author.

amining techniques, we shall mention all pros and cons which are specific to the particular TYPE of book catalog, whereas in the succeeding sections we shall limit outself to a study of general factors, applicable to all types.

THE TECHNIQUES OF THE BOOK CATALOG, WITH THEIR PROS AND CONS.

The most primitive type of book catalog is exemplified by the LC *Author Catalog* of the 1940's (18, 26). This significant departure, extremely influential on succeeding book catalogs, was made possible by the development of photolithographic offset printing. Cards were mounted on huge sheets and reproduced by photography on lithographic plates. The publishing of supplements was greatly simplified by the development of listing cameras whereby cards are automatically fed through a camera and photographed. But such catalogs are still essentially *card catalogs in book form*. Each entry repeats information necessary because of the original card format, and thus the main entry is repeated each time for numerous works by a same author. All tracings are shown. Notations such as "see next card" appear. "Continued cards" show needless repetition of author-title information. Such a technique is very wasteful of space and, in the case of LC's first printed catalog, photographic reduction made many details illegible.

Another primitive, but reportedly very useful, technique has been used in a system of ninety public libraries in Western Australia, where all cataloging is centralized (24). Here a book catalog is a necessity since most of the ninety libraries are very small and have no professional staff to handle card catalog details. Furthermore, a central Request and Information service supplies any available non-fiction book to any requesting library, and so all the branches must be linked by a common catalog. In 1954, when the central stock was only 5,000 volumes, a loose-leaf-type book catalog was maintained, in classified sequence, with the replacement of pages as needed. In 1963, with a stock of 600,000 volumes (100,000 titles), the loose-leaf method became cumbersome, but punched card and computer-printout catalogs were rejected outright because of their unsightly appearance, as were photographed book cards. The authorities finally decided on the Kalamazoo Copystrip method. The methodology is rather simple. Short cataloging information is typed on a one-line strip if possible—sometimes two are necessary. These strips are then filed on "dividers" (bases on which pages of the catalog are built with interlocking strips). At the end of the process some pages are longer than others and the whole thing has to be refiled so that pages are all of a standard length. The Kalamazoo strips are sent to the printer. When returned they serve as a master catalog to which new titles are added and from which withdrawals are deleted. At the end of the next year, the whole thing is refiled again so that pages become of equal length and it is sent once again to the printer. The result is reported to be a very pleasant-looking catalog—and this was the aim—much easier to read than computer printout. The drawbacks, however, are only too evident. A tremendous amount of "juggling" has to be done—and this requires a large supply of very cheap clerical labor, which may be available in Western Australia, but is not available here. Such a method would be unmanageable for large collections.

Around 1950, a few county-metropolitan libraries, in particular, Los Angeles County, developed true book catalogs, using punched card equipment to prepare mimeographed catalogs of holdings. Entries were restricted to a single line, data was greatly abbreviated, and printing was in all-caps. The number of subjects assigned was arbitrarily limited to one or two. In the 1960's, a more advanced punched-card-printout book catalog was produced in the Monsanto Chemical Company library system (35) where duplicate catalogs were a necessity. A preliminary cost study had shown that it would cost Monsanto no more to prepare multiple book catalogs than to prepare one card catalog. Wilkinson gives us a how-to-do-it report for IBM equipment without a computer. The IBM 1403 high-speed printer is used for the main volume, and the Document Writer (slower) for supplements. Much of the filing is done manually since this is noticeably faster than machine sorting. The chief advantage claimed for such catalogs is the by-products, including book labels for spines, check-out cards, monthly library bulletins, overdue notices, and special bibliographies. Another advantage claimed is that this semi-automated method is particularly suited for a small library. Small-volume daily, weekly, or monthly needs can be filled right in the library by the Document Writer although large-volume processing, such as the yearly up-dating of the catalog, must be turned over to outside equipment for maximum efficiency. Numerous disadvantages of such catalogs have, however, been noted by at least seven different writers. The Los Angeles County Library System (3, 16) found that IBM print is unpleasant and difficult to read (all-caps) and lacks punctuation and diacritical marks. It is difficult to distinguish where the author entry ends and the title begins, where the title ends and the annotation begins. Patrons frequently miscopy information. The file word does not stand out (i.e., the author's name does not catch the eye). Subject headings do not stand out either though Los Angeles County centered them and allowed space above and below. Even when new IBM equipment came along with upper and lower case letters, the results were not good enough to warrant the extra expense of buying the machines. In connection with the poor appearance of IBM printouts we may register the claim made by Brown (6) that the typeface is not attractive enough to encourage public library patrons to use the catalog unassisted. The punched card technique was rejected in such far-apart places as Baltimore County (22) and Western Australia (24) for similar reasons. Another disadvantage, experienced in Montgomery County (17), is that underlining of subject headings has to be done by hand—and with IBM printout being so uniform, this extra step seems a necessity if headings are to be visible on the printed page. Furthermore, filing for each supplement has to be done manually, since most systems have learned that hand filing takes considerably less time than sorting by machine. (17, Montgomery Co.; 26, New York State Library; etc.). Catalogs of any size produced with this system experience increasing bulkiness and unwieldiness. They take up less space than the card catalog, but, in absolute terms, they still take up too much space. In Los Angeles County (16), volumes were $9'' \times 13''$, and $\frac{3}{4}''$ thick—too heavy and awkward to handle. Along with this unwieldiness goes a marked tendency to fall apart. An old edition, if used at all frequently, will be in tatters before replacement time (3). Another marked disadvantage of the technique is that keypunching of all titles in the collection is necessary. In Los Angeles County, it is reported (3) to have taken "several years" to convert the card catalog of 225,000 titles to punched cards. We have already mentioned that, in the name of economy, such catalogs generally drastically reduce the amount of bibliographic data given. This great abbreviation of data has been seen as a distinct disadvantage (3, 18), but the contrary claim has been made. In the New York State Library's *Checklist of Books*

and Pamphlets in the Social Sciences (1956), prepared from punched cards, the title-a-line approach was *deliberately chosen* (26). The stated aim was to make it as easy to find out what books the library has as it is to find telephone numbers in a directory. Abbreviation of data was thus in this case seen as an advantage. A final disadvantage of using IBM key-punched cards is that such a system is not easily (if at all) later incorporated into computerized systems (22).

A fourth technique of preparing book catalogs is to use a combination of the punched card and the listing camera. Catalog entries are typed by a Varityper on blank tabulating cards with the information to be reproduced recorded in traditional cataloging formats. Outside of the printing field, however, the cards are punched for sorting and interfiling by author, title, and subject-heading codes. Supplements can be collated into the basic file by means of these codes and the entire content photographed by listing cameras (card-actuated). After the card sets have been photographed in one arrangement, e.g. author, they can be sorted into another sequence, e.g. title, and rephotographed. The great advantage of this technique over the preceding one is the much higher printing quality. Since the process is photographic, the original data can be reduced or enlarged before printing. In Los Angeles County, for example, where this method was adopted after the preceding one was abandoned, in the juvenile catalogs, all printing was enlarged. Another advantage is that the book catalog now becomes more than a mere finding list: in Los Angeles County, annotations were even provided (26). Disadvantages linked to this technique are the high cost, and the fact that filing is still essentially manual in all systems where the coding is not extremely sophisticated (22).

A fifth technique involves the use of sequential card cameras, some of which are more expensive than others. Early cameras such as Foto-List (VariTyper Corporation) and List-O-Matic (Kodak) did not accept 3×5 cards, and thus cataloging records had to be retyped—an exorbitant expense for large libraries (6). Compos-O-List, however, does accept 3×5 cards. This means in effect that in libraries where such book catalogs are produced, such as the Free Library of Philadelphia, the central *card* catalog still must be maintained to provide copies of the cards to be photographed. Compos-O-List is a variable aperture camera which can photograph cards individually and automatically at speeds exceeding 7,000 per hour. Cards are sense-marked to indicate how much information is to be photographed; the camera then adjusts its bite to fit the card. From the negatives plates are made. The result is claimed to be an easy-to-read book catalog (6, 11, 16). The specific advantages attributed to this method over punched cards are numerous: there is no need for proof-reading beyond that of the initial catalog card; there is no need for page composition, which greatly increases printing costs; the master file can be easily consulted by catalogers or typists knowing nothing about punched cards; the typeface is better than IBM printout—a clear distinction can be made between the body of the card, the annotations, and the entry words; and in one particular case (16) it was found that the number of volumes was cut almost in half, and the bulk of each volume reduced too, after switching from IBM. This helped alleviate the size problem in a system whose "old-fashioned" book catalog was becoming too bulky. It is to be noted that such catalogs do not need to resemble the 1942 LC set where the process involved the mere photographing of catalog cards. In Los Angeles County, for example, the master file was completely remade, with the format designed primarily for public library users. (Entries were set well off to the left in very bold all-caps; no repetition of the main entry was made for various titles by the same author.) Variations on the scheme are, of course, possible. Jones (11), for example, recommends that for small runs it is cheaper to use the Multilith Photo-Direct camera. This requires the laying out of cards by hand in a jig ("shingling") and photographing the entire page instead of card by card. It must be mentioned that in such a creation of page masters it is much more economical to use the "shingling" approach than the "side-by-side" method, often used by G. K. Hall. This latter is very wasteful of space and thus very costly (10). Another system, developed by Alanar Book Processing Center, Williamsport, Pennsylvania, consists of photographing the shelf-list as the basic referral book: full information will be available since the whole card is photographed. Short author, title and classification entries can then be key-punched for sorting and run-off by IBM. Disadvantages associated with the Compos-O-List method are the following: cards still have to be filed manually in the desired order, although, of course, this is an operation that would have to be performed anyway if the card catalog were used; sense-marking of cards is a laborious process; it is still necessary to maintain a master card file. This file may prove to be more inefficient to maintain than an ordinary card

catalog, since in the latter case filing into the main catalog can be scheduled as part of each day's routine, whereas in the case of cards to be photographed, each year's accumulation of new cards must be maintained separately from the main file for the purpose of producing supplements, and then the whole mountain of cards interfiled at one time into the main file. The seasonal nature of this chore could well be disruptive of regular library routines.

The newest type of book catalog is computer-produced. Although the details are complicated, the basic steps can be very simply outlined. The contents of the basic catalog are stored on one magnetic tape; the contents of the supplement are stored on another magnetic tape. The tapes can be merged at very high speeds and, if more advanced techniques are not necessary, the catalog can be made up directly from the output: 600 lines per minute and up, with six readable carbons for a total of six copies. Bromberg (5) has provided an excellent how-to-do-it report for a small library of less than 5,000 titles having the use of a computer system and IBM card-punch equipment.[1] This consists of pulling all the author cards and preparing punched cards with shortened information. (Subject headings are reduced to a code, previously determined by going through the whole catalog and picking out all separate subject headings and all see and see-also references.) Punched cards are transferred to magnetic tape, tapes are run through the computer to produce a master printout, and the printout is reproduced by offset printing in reduced size and bound. This is the computer-produced catalog in its most elementary form. More sophisticated approaches immediately raise new problems. One of the chief of these is the question of filing.

A computer can handle readily only straight alphabetical filing. Thus the ALA filing rules are not easily reduced to a machine program. If the ALA rules are to be used, a complex coding system is necessary, and a librarian must assign a code from the system *manually*. Note, however, that the code only needs to be assigned if the heading is new to the catalog. The computer will assign filing codes automatically if the heading is already listed in the master authority file tape. If not, it will produce a printout of all new headings to be coded manually by catalogers. Some writers feel that this difficulty may call into question the necessity for maintaining the "over-subtlety" of many ALA rules, largely misunderstood by both patrons and librarians. This view is expressed most strongly by Simonton (27). The length of the filing medium also creates practical problems. Up till now there have been no constraints on the length of subject headings or of other entries with the result that some entries run to well over one hundred characters. Computer sorting of this magnitude is very costly. Kieffer (12) provides a fairly detailed discussion of the ALA filing rules and of the numerous concessions which the Baltimore County Public Library had to make to computer filing, both through lack of money and lack of skill necessary to program the rules adequately for machine sorting. One of the most interesting points is that very often the librarians were forced to spell entries exactly as they wanted them to be filed: for example: Gt. Brit. spelled Great Britain, De la Roche spelled Delaroche, "&" spelled and, etc. Initial articles had to be omitted entirely. (These concessions may be blessings in disguise!) The computer also imposed several *undesirable* filing orders: earlier editions were filed before later editions; Mc and Mac were filed in separate sections; certain pertinent items such as "ed." or "comp." in the entry had to be omitted entirely since the computer was using them as filing words. The problem of filing is still far from solved, with some librarians wishing to accept, without worry, any filing absurdities generated by the computer, and other librarians determined to impose ALA rules at any cost. Since much of the discussion is heated but meaningless, it is interesting to note here the recent well-reasoned stand taken by the authors of a California study (7). They show how the present ALA rules were designed to lend the catalog a structural pattern—

"not merely as a list of individual entries that might be arranged in one alphabetical order, but rather as an organized record that would include also groups and subgroups of related entries requiring a complex arrangement of alphabets within alphabets. . . . The rules were thus designed to provide an arrangement which would facilitate the location of an entry that could appear in different forms, and display related entries in a manner that would help the catalog user select the materials most appropriate. . . . But the underlying pattern of arrangement of entries was not readily apparent in the dictionary card catalog" (7, p. 21–22).

Many libraries thus adopted straight-alphabetical "simplification," not realizing that the "simplification" was only simpler for a user in search of a specific citation—but more complicated for the user who has to determine what the library has before he can decide which specific items he wants.

In the card catalog, with only one card visible at a time, the pattern of arrangements cannot easily be determined by the user but, in the book catalog, with two full pages of entries visible at a glance, the pattern of arrangement is much more easily spotted in all but the most mammoth catalogs. Thus the very fact of using the catalog in book form could re-establish the often-questioned validity of the complicated nature of present filing rules. The authors of the California study advise as close an adherence to existing filing codes as computer technology will allow. However, since present evidence seems to indicate that the ALA filing rules may never be programmable as they stand, it would be hoped that new national filing standards could be drawn up with machine applications in mind. In the meantime, filing is a real problem. One stopgap solution, already mentioned, is to retain the intellectual part of filing by having librarians assign a sequence designator to each entry heading to be used in the catalog. The computer would then file by number. This solution is *very expensive*. Another solution is to let the computer do the filing, but have librarians revise the format of headings so that the text of the heading is filable by simple sorting rules. For example, the present "U.S.–Hist.–Civil War" would be changed to "U.S.–Hist.–1861–1865." Extensive "file as" devices can also be used, for example, "356 jours," file as "trois cent cinquante six jours."

The computer-produced book catalog brings with it the possibilities for what many librarians have considered to be a new philosophy of cataloging. More primitive forms of book catalogs, of course, have already brought about changes in cataloging policy: due to the opportunity to scan a whole page of entries, title entries need no longer be made when subjects and titles file next to or very near one another (6). Furthermore, the author entry need no longer be printed for every title, but only when there is a change of author or the start of a new page (18). The computer, however, offers us a much wider range of possible formats, leading us to ask the question: is information now formated in the most effective way (27)? Might not, for example, some title-page information be best placed in notes instead of in the body of the entry? Do we need the same amount of information at each entry? Is the author statement as necessary as we have assumed? Might it sometimes be better presented in note form? For, in the computerized catalog, we can take advantage of the computer's ability to rearrange, add, and subtract data. We might decide, for example, that author entries should be brief for ease of scanning. (A work by two authors could be given two entries —neither as MAIN entries). Or we might decide that subject entries are best arranged in the order of cataloging on the assumption that subject entries are created for browsing, not for locating specific works. Full information could be given under subject entries to aid the user in selecting the book he feels most useful. The author statement could be relegated to a note at the end, thus eliminating the main entry—or appearing to eliminate it.[2] All tracings could easily be removed from the printed catalog, and this possibility has been seen as an advantage by writers such as Parker (18). Brown (6) on the other hand points out that reference librarians and users have often found these useful and regret their disappearance. Nevertheless, the true theoretical beauty of computer-produced book catalogs is that they can be printed using only that portion of data judged appropriate to the purpose of the particular catalog. Computerized techniques are thus invaluable for printing dictionary catalogs of complete holdings, divided catalogs, catalogs of special collections, lists of special series, special recurring bibliographies, etc. If expense were no object, we could have catalogs by publishers, place, date, language, literary form, prepared fairly easily. And, if present formats are proven by time to be inadequate, the data can be readily manipulated to print later catalogs in revised formats.

The philosophy of cataloging can also be greatly influenced by the computer's ability to print out all stored information on each entry, or only a fraction thereof. Some librarians have struggled with the question "Is the book catalog to be a finding list or a bibliographic tool?," and have decided that the use of the computer fortunately necessitates the finding-list approach. Baltimore County decided in this manner: "Taking an educated guess,[3] we estimated that only 50% of the people who came into our libraries use the catalog at all, and 98% of those use it as a finding list" (22, p. 264). Shera (25) likewise finds that the book catalog is an admirable means of achieving bibliographic simplicity. Although his arguments apply equally well to non-computerized book catalogs, they are mentioned here because most writers associate simplified listings with computer outputs, even though there is no necessary connection. Shera believes that scholars do not want an excess of bibliographic detail such as is found on most present 3 × 5 cards. The book catalog, where all this excess baggage can be trimmed away, is much more to his liking. It is ironic to note that some of the very persons who lauded the finding-list approach are now having second thoughts. A recent publication of the Baltimore County Public Library reveals that librarians serving the public often regret the abbreviated nature of the book catalog entries (once regarded as highly desirable) but agree that the costs of including more information would have been exorbitant (2, p. 43). (This double-take would seem to indicate that the mere thought of "computers and machines" brings on irrational thoughts in the minds of many!)

Just as pleas for minimum bibliographic information have been made, so have there been pleas for *complete* information *only* in the computerized book catalog. Since one of the aims of the book catalog is distribution widely, this means that it will often be located in offices and branches where no professional librarians are present to assist in its use. Thus the book catalog should provide for extensive assistance to users by including ALL the usual types of main, added, and series entries, and by including careful and extensive cross-referencing (7). Nevertheless, printing cost is a simple function of the total number of printed characters, or the number of pages. Therefore, one must question the necessity of repeating all bibliographic information for a title at EACH entry point. The sacrifice of data not only reduces costs but adds to ease of consultability, "a virtue unique to the printed book catalog" (34, pp. 186). Thus, in the California book catalog (7) complete information on a work is given only under the main entry and under the subject-heading. All title and added entries are extremely abbreviated and almost always refer the user to the main entry for complete information. It is maintained that such abbreviated statements with reference to main entries are economically essential. Two other authors suggest that such an idea is motivated by the "specter of the book catalog as a room-filling mammoth of paper, and subsequent baskets of money to pay the printer. . . if the medium [the book catalog] is to find application outside of small or special libraries" (34, p. 189). Perhaps one of the chief problems has not been adequately thought out. It is known that the format of a computer-produced book catalog can be identical to that of present card-catalog entries, or substantially different. Yet if changes are to be made, do we not need at least NATIONAL UNIFORMITY in the changes?

Stevens has commented on this problem. He feels that there are many "librarians who fashion. . . book catalogs purely in terms of local needs or in terms of the requirements of punched card or tape driven machines which may not as yet have sufficient capacity to meet the requirements of librarianship" (28, p. 130). He feels that in prostituting themselves to these local or machine constraints, these librarians are doing a disservice to the idea of standardization brought about by Dewey and Cutter. "The compilation of book catalogs on every level must be such as to permit eventual integration of the parts produced in different places and situations into a larger whole on either a regional or national level" (28, p. 130). One can thus only advocate the outright rejection of such abridged horrors as the title-a-line catalog, and urge all libraries to follow closely standards already existing for entry, description, transliteration, subject headings, cross references, added entries, and filing order. Without adherence to existing standards, cooperatively compiled book catalogs of the future will be difficult or impossible to produce. In particular, because of abbreviated entries used in many present book catalogs, it seems doubtful whether such entries will be sufficiently complete and consistent for use in libraries other than the original when statewide systems of interconnected computers are set up (19). It seems therefore that libraries are taking too narrow a view in thinking in terms only of their own particular system.

It has often been claimed that computer-produced book catalogs will free us from the "tyranny" of main entries. This is seen as a distinct advantage by Parker (18), by Weinstein and Spry (32), by Simonton (27), and by Weinstein and George (33). It is interesting to note, however, that it is much easier to wish oneself rid of something than to see it disappear. In the California Union Catalog (7), already discussed, the idea of main entry, far from disappearing, is reinforced by the fact that all title and added entries are extremely abbreviated and refer to the main entry. In the Boeing SLIP system (32), the authors claim to have no concept of main entry even though input is derived from LC cards. Instead of one main entry, there is supposed to be an array of equally weighted entries. Entry tracings are found only on the shelf-list card which is a mirror image of the paper tape prepared as system input. However, no matter how the authors seek to deny it, the idea of main entry is still there

tacitly: Cutter numbers reflect the choice of one "principal author"; likewise, although main and added author entries are not labelled as such, an examination of the "author listing" shows that there is a main entry lurking somewhere. Under the "added entry" (not so called) for an editor's name, for example, filing is still by old-fashioned main entry and not by title. It must be remembered that the typography is much changed from the LC format, and this helps to hide the fact. A more recent article by Weinstein and George (33) is less rigid on the main-entry question. Here it is intimated, although not so stated, that we could conceivably have two or more MAIN entries for one title. For example, in the proceedings of a symposium, ALL bibliographic details could be listed under each of the following: editor's name, symposium title, name of sponsoring body. Thus we would have, in effect, several main entries if so desired, with the specific details shifted around under each entry to hide the fact that one just might happen to be predominant. And so the computer-produced catalog continues to inspire debate on cataloging philosophy. Although some of the arguments are quite infantile, the end result of such discussion could well be salutary.

Many advantages have been claimed for computerized book catalogs over all other varieties. Foremost among these is the fact that the computer's capacity to change and add to a basic record can be put to good advantage in coordination of acquisition and cataloging procedures. Even though we can't always catalog a book when we order it, we can, by using LC proofsheets, often produce both acquisition and cataloging records from a single typing. When necessary, changes, additions, and subtractions can be made after the book actually reaches the cataloging department (10, 27). Baltimore County decided to use the computerized technique on the understanding that, although the book catalog would not be initially part of an integrated system including other library functions, it would be adaptable to such use in the future (2). Mention is made in the literature of possible future uses, not only in acquisitions, but in circulation and information retrieval as well (7). Some of the other particular advantages claimed for the computerized catalog are listed in point form below:

(1) Various varieties of input are possible. Input can be paper tape or punched cards prepared by Friden Flexowriter or key punch. The Flexowriter can produce machine-readable codes for

both upper and lower-case letters (3, 22). When using the Flexowriter to prepare paper tape input, the advantage is that it is easier to proofread through the secondary typed copy it produces than through the use of punched cards (32).

(2) Multiple copies can be created directly on the computer by using carbon paper forms. If still extra copies are required, the normal printout can be converted to printing masters easily by Xerography or other photographic methods (20).

(3) Input costs are nonrecurring for each item. Once the information is recorded, it can be manipulated in almost any fashion without further input expense. Furthermore, the higher initial cost of readying the data for computer processing is repaid in savings in the publications of subsequent cumulations (7, 20).

(4) The possibility of producing multiple publications is best realized if catalogs are put into machine-readable form (7). Some of the publications generally envisaged are catalogs of special collections, special lists, recurring bibliographies, and statistical surveys (20).

(5) Various output devices are possible, and the variety is likely to increase in the future. Linotype can be driven automatically from computer output and this can operate in several type fonts and sizes. The Photon is even more versatile than linotype and is also computer-operable (3).

(6) The computerized technique alone allows for truly efficient machine sorting. This is felt to be of very great importance for librarians not concerned with following ALA filing rules to the letter (22).

(7) Certain systems directly avoid the main burden of any card system, either printed or punched: deck maintenance (32). "Analysis shows that it is fully possible to dispense with the card catalog even within the library itself. This allows the possibility of a significant reorganization of physical work spaces of the library, since location of various work areas close to the various card catalogs is not a factor to be taken into consideration" (7, p. 2-3).

(8) Updating is much easier than with any other book-catalog method (7, 20, 22). This is particularly important in such matters as revising outdated entries, both author and subject (10).

(9) In a well-designed system, all data put into machinable form can be made compatible with MARC records. Thus MARC data as well as local data can be used in production of later catalogs. The California State Library plans to make its pool of retrospective data in a different format from that of MARC but plans for its own data to be "readily translatable into MARC format." (7, p. 7)

On the other hand, peculiar disadvantages also accrue to the computer method of producing book catalogs. Magnetic tape is more susceptible to destruction than either cards or finished book products (20). Secondly, unless very expensive printing mechanisms are used, the quality of the printout may be most undesirable (20, 24). This was found to be a particular problem in Baltimore County where certain aspects of the printout, for example the lack of diacritical marks, made the results highly undesirable for titles in languages such as French where diacritical marks are essential, not only for formal spelling but also for meaning (12). In the same library system, catalog searches were made on an experimental basis by the library staff in the old card catalog and in the book catalog. Author searches, and subject searches in particular, were found to take significantly LONGER in the book catalog. Although no satisfactory explanation has been given as to why, it must be assumed that the very poor typographical layout was at least, in part, responsible (2). The most important disadvantage of all is, of course, the extremely high costs. If only the actual use of the computer installation is allocated against the library budget, the computer is a very efficient approach to standard technical operations. However, the actual amount of use of the computer for producing a book catalog is very low and cannot justify a computer installation by itself. Only the largest libraries can justify a computer of their own (10, 20).

Having now examined all the techniques in use for preparing a book catalog and the particular advantages and disadvantages pertaining to each, we shall now look at those aspects of the book catalog itself which may make it desirable or undesirable in its own right, regardless of the technique used.

CON

By far the greatest disadvantage of a book catalog over a card catalog is that the former is doomed to be *always* out of date, even before issue. The problem of the supplement remains ever present. In a typical proposed schedule (18), a library would prepare a list of new titles each week. Each month, these weekly lists would be

cumulated and a complete monthly catalog prepared. In each succeeding month, the month's input would be merged with the input of the previous month or months, and so on until the end of
the year when the cumulative supplement would
be merged into the basic catalog and the whole
reprinted. Although this may be an ideal schedule,
it is totally impractical for libraries of any size.
Weber (31) calculates that in a large library, even
if printing costs fall considerably, it will probably
not be possible to cumulate book catalogs more
than every twenty or even fifty years. Furthermore, in many types of systems, a card catalog of
all titles in the book catalog may have to be maintained for purposes of updating and cumulating
(and thus, incidentally, the space problem will be
magnified, not alleviated). From the point of
view of the library patron, the necessity of consulting two alphabets in an ideal system is already
an annoyance which many will not tolerate. It remains to be seen what limits of toleration users
will have to muster up if ten, fifteen, twenty or
even more supplements have to be consulted in a
truly large library. Library staff who are required
at the present time to consult numerous alphabets
of the LC printed catalog are known to complain
bitterly—but at least they are paid for what they
are doing!

Although the data stored on magnetic tape may
be infinitely flexible, the book catalog itself is as
inflexible an instrument as it is possible to invent.
Changes or deletions can only be made by defacing
the printed work (20, 29). If new master sets appear yearly, this inflexibility might well be tolerated, but in systems which cumulate only every
twenty to fifty years, one can easily imagine a
catalog with almost all of its contents out-of-date.
Printed catalogs also present particular problems
of binding and handling. Binding and paper need
to be exceptionally strong to withstand constant
use, even if there are numerous multiple copies
(29). One can witness the state of advanced decay
from which LC printed catalogs are now suffering
in many large libraries—and yet these are still not
used by the vast majority of library patrons. The
Los Angeles County Library found that its book
catalogs were always in tatters before replacement
time (3). (It may be noted, however, that if libraries do not follow the British Museum pattern
of giant, unusable tomes, but limit themselves to
the ALA criterion of $5\frac{1}{2}$ pounds (1), some of these
present problems might not exist.) Nonetheless,
wear and tear on the pages is bound to remain a
major, and perhaps unsolvable, problem.

Numerous other disadvantages can be listed
briefly:

(1) Although the book catalog has been
heralded as the instrument which will put an end
to library space problems, it is not at all certain
that this is a valid expectation. We have already
mentioned Weinstein and George's fear of the
"specter of the book catalog as a room-filling
mammoth of paper" (34, p. 189), and this fear is
doubly valid if one remembers that many libraries
retain their card catalogs even after the book catalog is published.

(2) It has been argued that a reader using one
volume of the book catalog is monopolizing a large
part of the alphabet (6). (It appears, however, that
this argument is not particularly sound since book
catalogs are usually printed in multiple copies, and
since, in the case of the card catalog, a reader consulting one drawer of a catalog is cutting off all
those drawers above, beneath, and beside the one
he is concerned with.)

(3) Some librarians have feared that book catalogs would be easy victims for vandals and thieves
(20). The Philadelphia Free Library has found,
however, that threats of mutilation, theft, and
misshelving have not proved significant (6). In
the light of the modern-day trend of students to
destroy university-library card catalogs, it would
seem, in effect, that any catalog is vulnerable if
someone wishes to destroy it. And, at least if a
volume of the book catalog is stolen and destroyed, the library can readily determine what is
missing: this may not be the case when cards in
drawers are systematically destroyed in a deliberately random pattern.

(4) The mobility which is claimed as an advantage for the book catalog might easily become a
disadvantage. Needed volumes might often be
missing when wanted if someone has carted them
off to the stacks (29). This drawback could be
minimized by printing an exceptionally large number of copies of each volume, so that the user
would always be sure of finding at least one copy
when he needed it. But—printing expenses are
high!

(5) If both a book catalog and a card catalog
are maintained, anyone making a definitive search
and beginning with the book catalog will always
have to check all information in the card catalog
afterwards to see if reclassification or recataloging
haven't been done in the time since the book catalog was published (29). If no card catalog is
maintained for such purposes, then no definitive
searches can be made. One can readily imagine

the distinct possibility of several unofficial card files springing up in various parts of the library, particularly in the reference department, so that questions can be answered about available materials not yet listed in the book catalog or about materials from the basic stock which have been recatalogued but whose entry will not be changed in the basic volume for another twenty or fifty years.

(6) Any large library publishing and distributing a book catalog takes on several responsibilities which it might not be able to honor (13). It becomes a "library of record" and thus no longer has the right to rid itself of any of the volumes in its collection. Furthermore it must answer requests for reproductions in all cases where the original is not likely to be damaged in the reproduction process. Although these responsibilities may very well be advantageous to the general library world, they can easily inflict severe economic burdens on the particular library concerned.

PRO

The advantages of the book catalog have been loudly and longly vaunted. As a means of summarizing all these comments, we shall follow the outline suggested, but not exploited, by Harris (9):

(1) Ways in which catalog use is facilitated by having it in book form. The ability to display an entire page of entries in the book catalog is an important advantage to the user. Numerous entries can be scanned rapidly, thus making for easier browsing. It is, for example, easier to compare various works and editions of an individual author when all the entries are visible at the same time. This ease of consultability is perhaps the greatest advantage of all those attributed to the book catalog (18, 20, 29, 34). Catalog use is also facilitated by the book form due to the very simple fact that scholars not able to visit distant libraries merely to search the card catalog can now use the resource tool of the printed catalog in their local university library: catalog use is facilitated in such cases by its mere presence in a place where formerly it was absent (29).

(2) Changes the book catalog may encourage in terms of library service. It has been claimed that the switch to a book catalog will free time and labor: extra staff with more free time will now be available to devote attention to user services. This claim has proved to be true in practise in many public library branch systems, of which the Free Library of Philadelphia is a good example. When eighty separate card catalogs were replaced by two book catalogs, adult and juvenile, the branch staff involved in filing and revising the seventy-eight obsolete catalogs were completely freed from catalog maintenance work (6). It is not stated exactly WHAT chores these staff members were given in place of their old duties, but one must assume that at least some of their new free time was devoted to user services. Similar advantages were found in Montgomery County, Baltimore County, and Western Australia (17, 12, 23). It is interesting to note, however, that in Baltimore County, the branch staff *alone* profited from the shift to the book catalog: at the central office, clerical time spent typing headings on LC cards was merely transferred to the routine of filing input cards (12). The book catalog also has been found to profit library service to patrons in that transfer of resources between library branches is now much easier. It is possible to keep shifting resources to various parts of the community in which they will be most useful without the terrible headache of revising the card catalog in each branch after each transfer (6). (Such a free shift of resources means, however, that local holdings cannot be identified adequately—if at all—in the book catalog.) Patrons are also supposed to have profited from the fact that reference work is now much easier since the reference librarian can keep a complete catalog of the library on her desk (11). From a logical point of view, the ability of a reference librarian to consult the catalog much more quickly than it was formerly possible should give her extra time to devote to more clients or to more detailed service to the same number of clients. It is not known, however, whether these logical results really happen in practise: a report from the Baltimore County Library merely states that reference personnel make fewer steps in a day than they used to (2). It is not stated whether anyone but the fatigued reference staff profited from this. The same library system reports that catalogers also have fewer cases of swollen feet since they stopped walking back and forth to the card catalog (12), but we are not told whether the cataloging output soared because of this. One would imagine that a Parkinson effect no doubt set in.

(3) What the book catalog does that is different from the card catalog in terms of patron use.

First and foremost, the book catalog allows for multiple access. Book catalogs can be made accessible in all areas where they are needed in the library, and thus service and work areas no longer have to be built around the card catalog. Similarly, patrons can find copies wherever they happen to be in the library (within limitations, of course!), and staff members can always have a copy close at hand. The potential uses are very great: for the staff in private offices (particularly in book selection offices), and for the public in such widely scattered places as faculty offices, bookstores, schools, reading rooms, stacks, other rival or cooperating libraries, etc. All these suggestions, and more, are to be found in the literature (6, 10, 11, 17, 20, 29). The greatest single advantage to patrons already in the library building is no doubt having book catalogs accessible in stack areas, particularly in libraries with several stories.

Patrons also benefit greatly from having the resources of the entire system available to them in catalog form, no matter how small the branch library they may happen to be in. Such union lists are particularly needed in all branch public library systems, in "multi-versities" and in wide-open areas where libraries are few and far between. This is the case in the 80-branch Philadelphia Free Library system (6) and in the thirteen branches of Montgomery County (17), to name but two public libraries whose book catalogs have been much discussed. In universities it is becoming more and more important for departmental libraries to have records of total system holdings due to the growth of interdisciplinary studies (10). Although the book catalog is best known in highly populated areas of the United States, a case could be made for its being even more valuable in underdeveloped and sparsely populated regions (23). Indeed the ninety libraries stretched out over the huge expanse of Western Australia could not have functioned at all without a book catalog (24), and right here in the United States, the Department of the Interior Library, Portland, Oregon, can only serve its 5,000 employees scattered from Alaska to California through the use of a book catalog (5).

The union-list concept has had significant effects on patron use of library resources, particularly through the greatly increased possibilities of interlibrary loan and/or centralized loan services. In Philadelphia, copies of the Free Library catalog are distributed to other local libraries for interlibrary loan purposes; furthermore, as a side benefit, small libraries can use the book catalog of the larger library as a tool in acquisitions and cataloging (6). In Baltimore County, patrons have had their eyes opened to the real resources of their

system: during the first year of the book catalog, interlibrary loan requests within the system itself increased 63% (12); in the same period, the number of reserves increased 51%, and most of these had to be obtained on interlibrary loan (2). In backwater areas where no professional staff is available, the book catalog "both opens readers' eyes to wider book resources and mitigates the lack of book knowledge on the part of inexperienced staff" (23, p. 25).

The book catalog has still other significant advantages in terms of patron use. Users can now readily Xerox any section of the book catalog for personal use—a physical impossibility in card catalogs where cards are not to be removed except by authorized staff members (20). Patrons can thus compile bibliographies in much less time than formerly, since Xeroxing a page or two is noticeably less time-consuming than copying out by hand numerous individual cards (29). Indeed, patrons and staff alike are spared the burden of copying down any call numbers at all, since the book catalog can be transported directly to the shelves (2). And, as one final direct advantage to patrons, we could mention the opinion, voiced by Shera (25), that only with the book catalog can scholarly patrons and research workers feel "confidently secure"—since, according to him, "a book catalog 'looks good like a bibliography should'."

(4) Internal questions of cost and efficiency.

The greatest number of advantages claimed for the book catalog relate to questions of administrative efficiency which may or may not have any noticeable benefits for the patron. Quite obviously, in large branch systems, the book catalog can cut down appreciably on the number of separate card catalogs to be maintained. In turn this elimination of branch catalogs eliminates many of the numerous nightmares which formerly centered around long-distance editing of card files—endless telephone calls from and to branches requesting information on cards missing or arriving in surplus, endless correspondence relating to revisions to be made in subject headings or in call numbers. Such work can now be done all in one central office (6). The book catalog also provides the possibility of eliminating the card catalog completely, although the reports of libraries which have done this are not outstanding in their clarity of detail as to results (11, 32). Libraries dealing mainly with current materials cannot keep up to the task of interfiling new cards and withdrawing older records: mechanically produced catalogs alleviate some, BUT NOT ALL, of this problem (10).

It has been stated, too, that if errors are to be corrected, this only needs to be done in one place rather than in a host of card catalogs (17). The fallacy of the argument is, of course, that if a mistake is worth correcting, it is worth correcting in all copies of the book catalog, by hand, before the next whole reprinting in one, twenty, or fifty years. The ability to make multiple copies presents undeniable internal advantages: we can note that, after typesetting, little additional cost is involved in printing one hundred copies rather than twenty-five (20). The same cannot be said for producing even one extra copy of the card catalog. The book catalog of any collection must necessarily occupy less floor space than the card catalog of the same collection—and this is a true advantage if, as mentioned above, it is truly possible to scrap the card file completely. The switch to a book catalog can also be very beneficial to the library inasmuch as it is often seen as the opportunity for revising or reforming the old cataloging information. This revision is costly, but it seems to be less costly to do at a time when the whole catalog is being changed anyway. Bromberg states that to "produce a precisely accurate book catalog, a thorough, painstaking revision of the card catalog should be the first order of business" (5, p. 614). In this way, at the very least, previous typing errors are spotted, and blind references are eliminated. The changeover also provides an excellent opportunity for weeding out useless titles. Baltimore County, for example, did not include any titles more than five years old in its book catalog until it had been decided whether they were worth keeping (22). In "going book," librarians find themselves forced to re-examine their philosophy of cataloging: details of such re-examination have been given in the above section on computerized techniques.

By far the greatest advantage offered by the book catalog may not lie in its ability to replace the card catalog, but rather in its very real assets as a *supplement* to the basic card file. The University of Rochester Science Libraries, for example, use both types of catalog to do the things that each is best suited for (21). One-line, short-title printed catalogs are distributed to each faculty member and to each science librarian: these serve, as do telephone books, to give information as to whether a known work can or cannot be located locally—and if so, where. All other information is searched in the card catalog. Although this procedure is useful for small departmental libraries, it also has great possibilities for use in conjunction with very large catalogs. Related categories in the classification system can be chosen and supplementary book catalogs produced from the shelf-list. Or, for those scholars, who, like Shera, want their book catalogs short and sweet, the CARD catalog could be used to supplement the BOOK catalog by recording substantial amounts of bibliographic detail in which the librarian is interested but to which the scholar doesn't wish to be exposed (25)! The printing of special subject catalogs might make available valuable reference tools for reference librarians, while, at the same time, permitting a cut-down in the size of the card catalog. In large libraries where cumulations are economically infeasible, the "divide-and-conquer" technique recommended by MacDonald (14) might be more approachable. One could decide at a specified date to freeze the present card catalog by reproducing it in book form for all time-and-eternity and then start anew with an entirely new card catalog. This new card catalog would retain the virtue of flexibility and, at the same time, would not be tied down to the tyranny of out-dated practises in subject headings and in pre-1966 cataloguing rules. In 1962, Weber predicted that in the future, the card catalog and the book catalog would come to supplement each other: card catalogs for recent accessions, and book catalogs for older materials (31). In 1967, five years later, he reinforced his statement by pointing out that the continuously-cumulating book catalog is simply not practical for large libraries (30). He documented his stand by a survey of several libraries which are attempting to cumulate in book form with great difficulties, and by a statement by Ritvars Bregzis of the University of Toronto who believes that the book form is NOT a suitable medium for displaying large bibliographic files requiring frequent updating. If the cataloging is to be full, Bregzis would limit the size of the library to 50,000 titles. Beyond this it seems necessary to freeze the past once and for all, as in a permanent book catalog of old titles, and to carry on with a card catalog which still has at least the remote possibility of being kept up to date. The book catalog may thus come more and more to be seen as an adjunct to the card catalog, but not a replacement.

As a final advantage of the book catalog we may note that the book catalog fits in very well with interlibrary cooperation by encouraging closer ties in the loaning of books, in book selection, and in the formation of a last-copy depository. An excellent example of this is the cooperation which the book catalog engendered in the Santa Barbara area when six libraries in the Black Gold Cooperative Library System joined forces (8). A joint book catalog there was only possible because each of the six libraries agreed to follow LC cataloging practise to the letter—already a big step forward in standardization. It has since been found that the common catalog has emphasized and strengthened the trend toward selective acquisitions: each library now collects in specialized areas and loans to the other five. Book catalogs, if published and circulated in line with the general criteria proposed by the ALA (1), will also lead to each library being more responsive to its responsibilities for photocopying material for other libraries. Book catalogs and centralized processing may go hand in hand as stated by Weber (30, p. 152): "The book catalog published by a county or state may influence a small library to enter a cataloging center or cooperative plan so it can use the book catalog with its own collections. This would also encourage uniform cataloging, classification, and subject headings. All present evidence lends support to the belief that book catalogs and cooperative processing centers lend a hand one to another."

COSTS OF THE BOOK CATALOG

There are few really good cost studies in the literature of the book catalog. Nevertheless, it is possible to list several factors which will inevitably enter into the cost of any book catalog, and to mention certain expenses which will definitely NOT be lower if book form is adopted. Costs depend on the extent to which retyping or keypunching is necessary, the number of cumulations required per year, the number of copies printed, the kind of binding used, and the buying pattern of the individual library (6). In particular, the cost of a copy of a book catalog is nearly linear with respect to the number of pages it contains, and is therefore a direct function of the density of entries per page. Density of entries is in turn a direct function of the number of characters or lines per entry and the character size (or reduction ratio) used (10). The greater the typographical quality, the more expensive the creation of the page master. However, better typography does permit a higher density of entry, thus somewhat helping to counterbalance the higher costs involved (10). Any of the above-mentioned factors could conceivably result in a book catalog MORE expensive than a traditional card catalog, so that it is seen, right from the outset, that programs to convert to a book catalog should not be undertaken with the thoughts of making monetary savings. Furthermore, it is well known that certain costs cannot possibly go down: for example, it is evident that the actual number of professional catalogers employed will not be reduced just because of the physical form of the catalog chosen. Classification and cataloging take the same amount of time no matter which form is used, that is, unless catalogers are given extra duties such as assigning codes, in which case the book catalog will require an *increase* in professional staff. It is possible, although unlikely, that some savings in personnel might occur at clerical levels (6). Perhaps the best statement of all regarding cost advantages was made in 1964, a year or more before the major existing cost studies were published in the library literature. Brown claims that it is meaningless to compare costs of book and card catalogs because one is not really comparing like things. "How do we evaluate [in dollars and cents] the convenience of having a book catalog in a private office or in a District library or in another part of the state" (6, p. 356). One might also wonder how it would be possible to measure in dollar terms the disconvenience of having to search several alphabets or of consulting an ancient book catalog which no longer reflects the true holdings of the library. A decision to switch or not to switch to a book catalog must be done primarily in terms of convenience, not of cost.

Despite the relative invalidity of most cost studies (for reasons mentioned above), it is still interesting to look at a few figures quoted in the literature. Montgomery County found that in 1962, cataloging costs with a card catalog amounted to 80 cents per book processed, whereas in 1963, with a book catalog, costs fell one cent per title. The slightly cheaper cost of the book catalog was attributed to the fact that the library does not have to rent its own IBM 407; this reduces costs considerably (17). A rather superficial cost study at Monsanto Chemical Company led to the following estimates: (costs include ordering, cataloging, and processing costs per volume):

$2.80 with one conventional card catalog
$6.20 with six conventional card catalogs
$2.55 with six IBM-produced book catalogs (35)

It will be noted in this example that the real advantage of the book catalog for Monsanto centers around the number "six": the book catalog would be best justified in terms of user convenience. In Baltimore County processing costs were studied in both the central cataloging department and in the branches, before and after the advent of the book catalog. A cost study in the central department showed an increase in cataloging costs per title when using the book catalog, but these extra costs were offset by a beneficial change in cataloging department routines. As far as the branches were concerned, a definite saving occurred because of the book catalog: this saving can be attributed almost solely to the cessation of all filing duties in all the branches. Despite increased costs in some areas and decreased costs in others, the conclusion of the Baltimore County study was that the book catalog had caused a total increased expense of 1% of the total library budget (2). On the whole, despite the frightening mass of figures, diagrams, equations, and charts found in such studies as the one by Hayes and associates (10), no one appears to have justified either type of catalog on economic criteria alone.

CONCLUSION

Much of the writing in the literature on the book versus the card catalog is totally irrational. The card catalog is shown to be a hideous monster and its faults are enumerated: it lacks uniformity in entries; it has inadequate cross-reference structure; it has subject-heading problems; it is full of misfilings (15). Then the book catalog is held up as the solution to all these problems. Few writers, however, stop to ponder whether all such problems as those just mentioned might not be equally as serious in the book catalog. It is especially ironic that the author of the most virulent attack on the uselessness of the card catalog (15) is the same author who recommends a joint book catalog for all large research libraries in the United States (14). One can readily envisage this giant book catalog suffering from all the internal inadequacies of our present card catalogs to an extent as yet undreamed of! Other writers have been swept away by the book catalog trend to such a degree that they are no longer capable of comprehending the facts which they themselves present. A perfect example of this is the Stanford case, which is worthy of presentation here since it illustrates to an outrageous extent the type of trap into which

even the most statistics-minded costs analysts can fall (10). The idea at Stanford was to issue each student with a subject catalog of the brand new Undergraduate Library collection (40,000 titles initially, increasing by 10,000 a year to the 100,000 limit). This was supposed to simplify access to the collection and thus make of the library "a more efficient instrument of teaching". The clash between theory and practise soon saw practise winning out, for the final outcome was that only fifty copies were made, only sixteen of which actually went into the Undergraduate Library. (Four of these sat on librarians' desks or in their offices!) The cost of preparing these fifty was compared with the costs of maintaining three card catalogs—one per floor. The study showed that the initial cost for the book catalog would be $13,000 less, but when the collection was seven years old, the book catalog would cost $9,000 per year *more*. To cut down on this cost differential, probable procedure will be to print the complete catalog only every two or three years instead of annually as originally planned. The authors' analysis of the Stanford case ends here, but we can make the following points ourself: use of the book catalog at Stanford will not fulfil the original objective of aiding teaching, since students will have no easier access to it than to a traditional card catalog; the book catalog will always be a minimum of two years out-of-date and thus would not be a very "efficient instrument of teaching" even if every student DID own a copy; the twelve book catalogs to which students will have actual access will cost the university considerably more in the long run than the three card catalogs considered as a substitute. There are no advantages at all left to the user, except perhaps ease of scanning—and the cost is higher. One wonders why Stanford even bothered to do a cost study at all!

Baltimore County decided on a book catalog not because it was known to be cheaper, but because it was "known" to give better service to users (22). As a matter of fact, no such thing is *known* at all. Most of the literature states OPINIONS pro or con, but much of the enthusiasm for and against needs to be tempered by a great deal more factual study. It is commonplace, for example, to read in the literature of the early 60's that library patrons appreciate the "comfort" of a book catalog (6, 25), but it is certain that this "comfort" has not been measured very adequately in terms of actual improved service. Now perhaps the pendulum has swung the other way: a 1968 article by two special librarians at the School of Medicine, Washington University, St. Louis (4), suggests that twentieth-century readers have greeted the re-naissance of the book catalog with the same indifference that nineteenth-century readers greeted the book catalog of the nineteenth century. Nineteenth-century librarians had trouble *giving* book catalogs away to readers; in the 1960's, users don't want copies in their homes and offices (or even in their libraries) when it is so much easier to use the telephone instead. Like the early laudatory comments, these recent denigrations are supported by no factual evidence, but merely on "experience." Are there no FACTS to be marshaled anywhere? We only know that many libraries are satisfied with their book catalogs and that various others are not (in particular, the University of California, Santa Cruz, and the New York State Library, which has terminated its book catalog.) (30)

The book catalog, as now produced, would seem to be more useful to some types of libraries than to others. The case for a book catalog in branch public library systems and in special libraries has been well made in the literature, although, in some of the latter cases, it has been suggested that book catalogs have been produced simply because IBM equipment is available and cries out to be used (11). In public libraries it is essential to be able to draw on the resources of the whole system through a local union catalog. In universities, on the other hand, numerous departmental libraries are likely to be located close together on the same campus or even in the same library building. Here it would seem that small, separate catalogs of specialized departmental holdings represent one of the raisons d'être of the separate department. Book catalogs listing complete university holdings are likely to be of far less use than would be accurate up-to-date catalogs of holdings in one particular subject field. (Exceptions to this in interdisciplinary studies have been pointed out above.) Likewise it should be noted that, at the present time, book catalogs find much greater favor in small libraries than in large libraries where

the problems of conversion of records for a basic stock of millions and the cumulating of supplements into the basic volume stagger the imagination. In all the literature examined, only one example can be found of libraries of over 500,000 titles adopting the book catalog: in California, the State Library Catalog contains 550,000 titles, and the California Union Catalog contains 1,005,000 titles (7). However, due to the size of the collection (still small in comparison to research library standards), it is not expected to ever cumulate the whole file. Instead, if and when a new basic catalog is printed, it may only include works published in the last twenty years. All the other libraries adopting book catalogs have been very small: Baltimore County has a mere 56,000 titles (22) fewer than the number added by many libraries in a single year–, Los Angeles County has only 225,000 titles (3), and Montgomery County apparently falls somewhere in between. For a truly large research library, the book catalog has simply not proved itself feasible. David L. Weisbrod of Yale University reports: "The cost figures on just the computer time were high enough that we temporarily decided to put off a book catalog and go to card production as our first effort" (30).

It may be indeed that book catalogs are merely a temporary measure until all libraries can be linked up to an electronic computer memory holding the contents of the National Union Catalog, with connections provided by high-speed data transmission links (3). Both card and book catalogs may become equally obsolete when it becomes possible to replace them by querying an UNPRINTED computer store of bibliographic data. In the meantime, however, the use of machine-readable data puts the library in an excellent position to profit from technological advances that will occur in the future. Since new matured "on-line" technologies will allow routine consultation of machine-readable files in all those situations in which one now consults the catalog, a library having prepared a book catalog with computerized methods stands ready to profit from advanced technology (7).

NOTES

[1] Kieffer (12) has also described the trials and tribulations of preparing a computerized book catalog when you don't know what you're doing. Weinstein and Spry (32) have given a lot of "how-to" information on various input devices and computer programs.

[2] The above few suggestions are given by (27)–presumably without too much thought to the implications. The question of "main entry" will be raised again shortly in this paper.

[3] There is no supporting data in the article.

SOURCES

1. American Library Association. Book Catalogs Committee, "Preferred practices in the publication of book catalogs," *ALA Bulletin*, vol. 56, no. 9, October 1962, p. 836-837.

2. Baltimore County, Md. Public Library, *Book catalog and card catalog: a cost and service study*, Towson, Md., 1967.

3. Becker, Joseph, "Automatic preparation of book catalogs," *ALA Bulletin*, vol. 58, no. 8, September 1964, p. 714-718.

4. Brodman, Estelle, and Bolef, Doris, "Printed catalogs: retrospect and prospect," *Special Libraries*, vol. 59, no. 10, December, 1968, p. 783-788.

5. Bromberg, Erik, et al., "Preparation of a book catalog," *Special Libraries*, vol. 55, no. 9, November, 1964, p. 611-614.

6. Brown, Margaret Cornelia, "A book catalog at work," *L.R.T.S.*, vol. 8, no. 4, Fall, 1964, p. 349-358.

7. Cartwright, Kelley L., and Shoffner, Ralph M., *Catalogs in book form: a research study of their implications for the California State Library and the California Union Catalog, with a design for their implementation*, [Berkeley?], Institute of Library Research, University of California, 1967.

8. Chadwick, Catherine Strahorn, "The book catalog—new hope for cooperative programs," *L.R.T.S.*, vol. 10, no. 2, Spring, 1966, p. 160-163.

9. Harris, Ira, "Reader services aspects of book catalogs," *L.R.T.S.*, vol. 8, no. 4, Fall, 1964, p. 391-398.

10. Hayes, Robert Mayo, et al., "The economics of book catalog production," *L.R.T.S.*, vol. 10, no. 1, Winter, 1966, p. 57-90.

11. Jones, Bob, "The compact book catalog—by photographic process," *L.R.T.S.*, vol. 8, no. 4., Fall, 1964, p. 366-369.

12. Kieffer, Paula, "The Baltimore County Public Library book catalog," *L.R.T.S.*, vol. 10, no. 2, Spring, 1966, p. 133-140.

13. Kingery, Robert E., "Building card catalogs for eventual migration into book form," *In*: Kingery, Robert Ernest, and Tauber, Maurice F., eds., *Book catalogs*, New York, Scarecrow, 1963, p. 55-68.

14. MacDonald, Margaret Ruth, "Book catalogs and card catalogs," *L.R.T.S.*, vol. 6, no. 3, Summer, 1962, p. 217-222.

15. MacDonald, Margaret Ruth, "Recataloging," *Medical Library Association Bulletin*, vol. 49, no. 3, July, 1961, p. 426-433.

16. MacQuarrie, Catherine, "The metamorphosis of the book catalogs," *L.R.T.S.*, vol. 8, no. 4, Fall, 1964, p. 370-378.

17. Moreland, George Boulton, "Montgomery County Book Catalog," *L.R.T.S.*, vol. 8, no. 4, Fall, 1964, p. 379-389.

18. Parker, Ralph Halstead, "Book catalogs," *L.R.T.S.*, vol 8, no. 4, Fall, 1964, p. 344-348.

19. Pastan, Herbert M.E., "Book catalogs and automation," *Maryland Libraries*, vol. 33, no. 1, Winter, 1964, p. 12-13.

20. Pizer, Irwin H., "Book catalogs versus card catalogs," *Medical Library Association Bulletin*, vol. 53, no. 2, April, 1965, p. 225-238.

21. Richmond, Phyllis Allen, "Book catalogs as supplements to card catalogs," *L.R.T.S.*, vol. 8, no. 4, Fall, 1964, p. 359-365.

22. Robinson, Charles Weld, "The book catalog: diving in," *Wilson Library Bulletin*, vol. 40, no. 3., November, 1965, p. 262-268.

23. Sharr, F.A., "Book-type catalogues for developing countries," *UNESCO Bulletin for Libraries*, vol. 20, no. 1, January, 1966, p. 24-26.

24. Sharr, F.A., et al., "The production of a new book-type catalogue in Australia," *L.R.T.S.*, vol. 10, no. 2, Spring, 1966, p. 143-154.

25. Shera, Jesse H., "The book catalog and the scholar—a reexamination of an old partnership," *L.R.T.S.*, vol. 6, no. 3., Summer 1962, p. 210-216.

26. Shoemaker, Richard Heston, "Some American twentieth century book catalogs: their purposes, format, and production techniques," *L.R.T.S.*, vol. 4, no. 3, Summer, 1960, p. 195-207.

27. Simonton, Wesley, "The computerized catalog: possible, feasible, desirable?," *L.R.T.S.*, vol. 8, no. 4, Fall, 1964, p. 399-407.

28. Stevens, Robert D., "Bibliography and cataloging standards for book catalogs," *In*: Kingery, Robert Ernest, and Tauber, Maurice F., eds., *Book catalogs*, New York, Scarecrow, 1963, p. 129-143.

29. Tysse, Agnes N., "Card catalogs versus printed book catalogs and the library user," *In*: Kingery, Robert Ernest, and Tauber, Maurice F., eds., *Book catalogs*, New York, Scarecrow, 1963, p. 55-68.

30. Weber, David Carter, "Book catalog trends in 1966," *Library Trends*, vol 16, no. 1, July, 1967, p. 149-164.

31. Weber, David Carter, "Book catalogs: prospects in the decade ahead," *College and Research Libraries*, vol. 23, no. 4, July, 1962, p. 302-310.

32. Weinstein, Edward Allen, and Spry, Joan, "Boeing SLIP: computer produced and maintained printed book catalogs," *American Documentation*, vol. 15, no. 3., July, 1964, p. 185-190.

33. Weinstein, Edward Allen, and George, Virginia, "Notes toward a code for computer-produced printed book catalogs," *L.R.T.S.*, vol. 9, no. 3, Summer, 1965, p. 319-324.

34. Weinstein, Edward Allen, and George, Virginia, "Computer-produced book catalogs: entry form and content," *L.R.T.S.*, vol. 11, no. 2., Spring 1967, p. 185-191.

35. Wilkinson, William Archer, "A machine-produced book catalog: why, how and what next?" *Special Libraries*, vol. 54, no. 3., March 1963, p. 137-143.

Subject Heading in Dictionary Catalogs

William Warner Bishop

No library worthy of the name fails to give its readers some sort of clue or guide to the contents of its collections. Its first purpose is, generally speaking, to provide an inventory of its books as they stand on the shelves (the shelf-list), then to give an inventory by authors (the author catalog), and last, perhaps because most difficult, comes the index, or guide, or key to the subject matter of the books. Most librarians are fairly well satisfied with their shelf-lists and author catalogs if they are reasonably up to date and accurate. But few librarians and fewer scholars who use libraries are thoroughly well satisfied with their subject catalogs. The principles of author entry are indeed not all determined. Few matters engage our interest more keenly than the long-expected agreement between our association and the British association in this particular. But the comparative simplicity of the rules now in force, and the substantial progress already made toward uniform and sane entries encourage us to think that we are pretty well off on the side of author cataloging. Our methods of indicating to readers what the library possesses on the subjects of interest to them are by no means so simple or so uniform. It may not be out of place, then, to discuss some of the important problems of subject cataloging.

It must be laid down as the prime essential of all subject catalog work that the end in view is the rapid and easy consultation of the catalog by the student who uses it. I say "student," because no one spends much time on a subject catalog who is not interested in some subject to the extent of wanting to see what books the library has on that topic. Now he must not be discouraged at the outset by any formidable and intricate machine which only an expert can use. The catalog must be so constructed that he can discover easily and quickly what he wants to know. This seems a simple requisite. Yet practice shows that it is one of the most difficult ends to secure. No amount of ingenuity can make a subject catalog which shall be absolutely without flaw in the matter of uniformity; no one can always consult it without effort. The student who knows at least a little of his subject and related subjects must then be the normal "public" of a subject catalog. But his road must be made straight and the rough places must be made plain for him. Ease of consultation, then, may be laid down as a fundamental basis for work.

Rapidity and ease of consultation will be secured only by most careful planning. There are certain decisions which must be made by every librarian beginning or revising a catalog of subjects. Once taken, these decisions must be adhered to, while a change once decided on must be carried out root and branch. Too many of our subject catalogs of all sorts are medleys of opposing decisions of different catalogers, all made in good faith and with the best of motives. As compared with an author catalog there are few means of checking divergences. Careful planning, then, is half the battle. It matters little, from one point of view, what the decision is. The important thing is to have a conscious policy and to stick to it.

The larger the library the greater is the need for uniformity in the matter of subject headings. The small library need not bother itself greatly about principles of subject entry. When its books are all easily accessible, its readers and the library staff alike will rely on classification and current bibliography rather than on catalogs. When you can go straight to the shelves and pull down in a few minutes all the books in the library having any possible bearing on the thing your want to know, you don't care much for a set of cards in a tray. But the library which confidently expects to be-

SOURCE: Reprinted from the *Library Journal* XXXI, 8 (1906), pp. 113–123, originally presented at the ALA Naragansett Pier Conference, 1906.

come large must needs beware. The day when the librarian or reference librarian with his ordinary tools can answer all ordinary questions will pass suddenly, and then, if the subject catalog work has been badly or inadequately done, comes confusion and trouble. Particularly is this true of the college libraries. Their catalogs are likely to get out of hand easily, and they are liable to periods of sudden inflation by gift, and the most careful attention is needed lest the entries under subjects become the butt of students and faculty, the despair of the reference librarian, and the torment of the cataloger.

One of the greatest obstacles to successful work in the field we are considering is the unfortunate fact that fashions in nomenclature change rapidly. Such headings as Mental Philosophy, Natural Philosophy, Fluxions, and scores of others current not so long since would hardly help the student of to-day. But more puzzling to him than these odd and old-fashioned forms will be the vague sort of "catch-all" headings that so frequently get into catalogs which do not have to be subjected to the test of cold print. "Practical Piety" in one card catalog I have seen was made to cover all modern sociological and economic works. The one essential for securing continuity and correctness in subject work is definition of the subject heading combined with sharp directions as to its use in the library's practice. It is not enough to determine on a heading. It must in all doubtful cases be defined most carefully and the definition preserved. The manner of interpreting the definition in practice must also be indicated. In other words, a (card) list of subject headings in use with all needed notes should be kept in every cataloging room. The extent to which these notes should appear in the public catalog is a matter for individual judgment.

In this paper there will be no discussion of the relative merits of classed, partially classed and dictionary catalogs of subjects. These matters have been long before us, and their respective claims are well understood. The dictionary catalog has—for good or ill—been generally chosen in our American libraries. Hence our study will be directed toward certain typical difficulties which are met with in actual work.

Before taking these matters up in detail, let me call attention to one source of assistance and guidance which we too often overlook. Since the seventeenth century the makers of encyclopædias have been working at this problem. Scores of excellent encyclopædias have been in constant use in our reference rooms—and even in our cataloging rooms—but have they been studied diligently as models for headings? We may be very sure that they have been studied by their makers with exactly our chief problem in mind; and that is how to choose a caption which shall in a single easily understood word or phrase express the topic to be treated so clearly and definitely that it may be found and comprehended at once. The good encyclopædias do not show the fatuous entries and references found in even our good catalogs. There is doubtless a reason. I suspect it lies partly in the excellence of the editorial supervision for which publishers can afford to pay, and partly in the undoubted fact that each encyclopædia is based on half a dozen, or perhaps half a hundred, predecessors, and thus the headings as well as the articles are in a continual state of revision. The fact that the headings are all in print in convenient form, and are easily seen and found, is also a great aid in producing uniformity of editorial treatment. Still the fact remains for us to ponder. Encyclopædias seem to present fewer difficulties in consultation than subject catalogs, and are familiarly and easily used by many people to whom a card catalog is a bugbear.

Everybody is agreed on the fundamental principle that in dictionary cataloging the "specific" subject must be our norm. We want to get exactly the caption which fits our book and no other. Especially do we wish to avoid general headings for treatises covering a limited field. A man looking for a book on trees does not want to be sent to look through all the cards on botany, nor does the inquirer for information about Nelson want to see all the cards on British naval history and biography. He wants what we have about Nelson. As I have said, everybody admits this. The smallest possible unit must be sought out and made the basis for the subject heading.

But the library has also books—many thousands of books, probably—which do not deal with one small, particular topic. It has treatises on Botany and British naval heroes. Hence there arises of necessity a set of subjects of a general nature, which are in effect identical with the large divisions of the classifications. We have general treatises on Philosophy, on Religion, on Sociology, on Philology, and so forth. And, further, we have general works on such topics as Physics, Electricity, Mathematics, Latin literature, Hydraulics, Political Science, Psychology, side by side with works of equal bulk and importance on divisions of those subjects, such as Heat, Alternating currents, Differential invariants, Latin pastoral poetry, Canal locks, Proportional representation, the Sense of touch. There must be general headings, class headings, if you please, in your dictionary catalog. The difficulty is to use them wisely. These general headings must never be used for anything but general treatises of an inclusive sort. They will be the same in a classed and in a dictionary catalog, and should be treated alike in both. Moreover, a first-rate dictionary catalog will use under these class headings—or headings common to both sorts of catalogs—a few of the simple and large subdivisions of classification, such as *History, Essays and addresses, Outlines, syllabi*, etc. In doing this it will not violate the dictionary principle.

But we should stop right here. Let us use the class headings when needed, but let everybody understand that they are strictly limited in their scope. Put it on the guide card so that all may see that "General works only are listed under this caption. For special treatises consult the cards with the heading of the particular subject wanted." An example should be given in each instance, and more than one, if necessary. In the case of the guide card for Chemistry there should be a statement that works on particular chemical products and compounds are to be sought under their own names. The illustration might perhaps take such a form as this—"for example, treatises on Chloroketodimethyltetrahydrobenzene will be found under that word."

It should be said, further, that caution is necessary at this point. Because some headings must be the same in any sort of catalog, and because some which are definitely group headings have to be used as a practical matter of common sense in a dictionary catalog, you will find catalogers continually reverting to these class headings. It's vastly easier to label a book Sociology than to pin its generally elusive contents down to one particular phase of social inquiry. We all tend to move unconsciously along the lines of least resistance. We shall never get our catalog of specific headings without constant vigilance, constant self-criticism, and drastic revision. We must have class headings so long as our libraries are not composed wholly of theses for the doctorate. And we must avoid them as much as possible.

There is a special form of class heading which bobs up serenely with exasperating frequency. I refer to the so-called "forms of literature," such as poetry, ballads, essays, orations and fiction. Shall we leave these out of our subject catalogs?

Many libraries do. Shall we say to the student looking for German ballads, "You'll find them all classified in number so and so"? But then, you know, he won't. There are dozens of volumes of them in collections of one sort and another, for one thing. Shall we let our novels go without subject cards and depend on a special finding list of fiction? Shall we lump them all under Fiction in the subject catalog? Shall we subdivide fiction and the "forms" by language, or perhaps by nationality? Or shall we classify fiction in our subject catalog, and put historical novels with the history divisions to which they supposedly belong? These are burning questions with many libraries. Probably every one of them represented here has a policy already decided on and in force in this matter. Here I will content myself with saying that it is my observation that the form divisions in a subject catalog when thoroughly made and kept up to date are a great help in reference work. (And the reference work should be in close touch with the catalog work for their mutual good.) It is, moreover, a considerable advantage to carry out the principle that every author card, generally speaking, should have a subject card matching it. Incidentally I may remark that I have found a mild form of the classification of fiction a great help. I refer to such headings as U. S. *History, Civil war, Fiction*, which have satisfied many a lazy body who wished to take his history diluted and disguised.

There are few librarians who will not follow us up to this point. We all know that we cannot wholly escape headings which are the same as the major divisions of any classification, and most libraries make some sort of subject lists of their works of so-called pure literature. But when we come to those large subjects which from their very nature suggest a geographical subdivision we leave uniformity behind. There is hardly any such thing, for example, as a treatment of Mathematics, or Logic, by countries, although we do find works on Greek Mathematics. These are, however, incidental to a certain period in the development of the science, and not a proper regional division such as may well be demanded in the case of Agriculture, or Geology, or Architecture. The pure sciences, then, do not enter very largely into this problem. But a very large proportion of the subjects about which books are written offer a double interest. They may be considered from the view-point of the region or country described, or from that of the subject treated. A work on the geology of Texas, for instance, may seem to belong to Texas, and to require the subheading *Geology*; or it may appear to have its chief interest for the geologist, in which case it goes under Geology, with the inevitable subhead *Texas*. This is all familiar enough. Mr. Cutter (Sec. 164) insisted that the only satisfactory solution of this problem was that of double subject entry. With this view I cannot agree. A consistent policy with regard to this class of subject headings which will rigorously enter under either the topic or the country is demanded in the interests alike of economy and of common sense. Whatever decision is taken, a reference must be made from the opposite form. Thus, if the library decides to enter under Geology. *Texas*, there should be a subject reference from *Texas. Geology*. Such a subject reference is much better than duplication of hundreds of subject cards.

But what shall the policy be? The practice of our leading printed catalogs is extremely varied. On the one hand we have a tendency to provide long lists of subheads under each country. This is the practice at least impliedly recommended in the American Library Association's "List of subject headings" by the printing of the long list of subheads to be used under country and state. On the other hand, to cite but a single instance, the Subject Index to the British Museum Printed Books (1881–1900) restricts vigorously the entry under the country or region, and allows but few subheads. Between the two plans there is a great gulf fixed. One assumes that a reader thinks along geographical lines when he wants a book, and looks under Greece for a book on Greek Architecture or Mythology, or for a treatise on the Geology or Agriculture or Education of that country. Perhaps he does. The other presumes that a reader considers his subject first, and then runs down its geographical ramifications later. Is there any principle on which this matter may be decided? Must we always make special decisions? There is at least one principle which favors grouping by countries rather than by topics. It is generally held that the dictionary catalog should supplement rather than copy the classification. Now the books will doubtless be classified on the shelves by subjects rather than by country in these topics which admit of double treatment. Therefore if books treating of such topics as Education, Missions, Agriculture, Slavery, Architecture, Painting, etc., from a regional or national point of view—as Central African Missions—and not covering the whole field, are entered under the country or region, the subject catalog will

show more about those regions than the classification will at any one point. This seems to me the sole argument for making use of this form of entry.

Now, on the contrary, I believe that the British Museum practice and that of the Library of Congress are more nearly in line with the habit of readers and the view-point of the makers of books. If we leave out the historical sciences, the main interest is the topic and not the region. In the pure sciences we have already eliminated the regional or national principle. In the applied sciences and the arts, both useful and fine, we may safely do the same thing. These divisions are very extensive. I advocate, then, a deliberate policy of restricting the entries under the country or region to those topics which have a strictly local interest, *i.e.*, the field of the historical sciences, and such of the social sciences as depend for their value on local conditions. To be specific, I would not put a book on the geology of Texas under Texas, but under Geology with the subheading *Texas*. I would limit the subheads under a country to those which seem absolutely necessary. For everything else which might be expected under country I would make a subject reference card. This may be begging the question. It may be abandoning the search for a guiding principle. But it seems to me that the habit of most readers and authors is a fair guide for us. After all it is for them that the catalog is made.

One word before leaving this topic. At no other point of subject catalog work is definite adherence to a fixed rule more necessary than here. A decision once taken in this matter should be rigidly executed. If this is done, the people who use the catalog will quickly learn to follow the principle adopted and will in consequence consult the catalog with ease.

If the practice of restricting the entries under subheads of countries or locality be followed, we at once encounter the difficulty of the so-called "national adjective." Having eliminated France. *Art*, are we going to cut out French Art, Greek Mythology, Roman Roads? Certainly we must. We must say Art. *France*, Mythology. *Greece*, Roads. *Rome*, or we shall soon find ourselves in a maze of confusion. It will, however, be necessary, in my opinion, to use the national or linguistic adjective with the literature or language of a country or region. We shall probably be obliged to say French language and French literature, since France. *Language* and France. *Literature* do not necessarily express the same ideas.

As in the case of France, so also in many other instances the national and linguistic areas are not identical. German language and German literature, for example, are wider in their scope than the political boundaries of the present German Empire, and the same is true of the English language. The linguistic and national areas are different in Switzerland, in India, and in many other regions. Another objection to the use of the national adjective is found in the fact that we have all sorts of corporations and institutions whose names begin with American, British, French, etc. Read the headings beginning with either "American" or "British" in the published catalogs made on the dictionary principle of any of our libraries, and see what a medley is produced by the mingling of names and topics. I hold that the national adjective should be eliminated from subject headings, save for the two linguistic usages mentioned. This will cause some trouble, for a great many people are accustomed to think of American Indians, British commerce, French porcelain, etc. But the practice will save trouble, too. It will reduce the number of places in which one must look for a topic (the chief drawback of Poole's Index), it will obviate much apparent confusion in the arrangement of headings, and it will introduce some system into alphabetical subject catalogs at a point where system is much needed. The practice of the encyclopædias is against the extensive use of the national adjective (although there are some exceptions, notably the most recent edition of Brockhaus).

It may be objected to this that we merely transfer our excessive use of subheadings from the country heading to the subject or topic heading. It may be urged that by this plan the subdivisions under topics become very unwieldy. In answer I would say that the subheads undoubtedly become more numerous under the topic, but that they belong there rationally, and there will be plenty left under the country. The person consulting the catalog is obliged, it is true, to run his eye over many guide cards, and perhaps over several trays to find his particular books. But that is far easier for him than going from one part of the catalog to another, looking now under France and now under Spain for a work on the mineralogy of the Pyrenees, for instance. Again he remains certain, after looking at the subdivisions under Mineralogy, that he will not have to look also at the cards headed Pyrenees Mts.—he has all the cards before him for Mineralogy. We can't eliminate subheadings from our alphabetical subject catalog.

At least, if we can, no one has arisen to show us how. If a separate guide card is used for each heading and subheading, we shall find the difficulty of consultation very greatly diminished. And with all the admitted difficulty of finding a small subdivision of a big topic, we still get it more quickly, I think, by this method than by the classed catalog with its alphabetical index.

It will have occurred to those who have followed this discussion thus far that a good many subheadings under both country and subject might be avoided by the use of inversion. We might say, "Roads, Roman," "Architecture, Gothic," "Psychology, Social," etc., and everybody would understand what we mean. The use of inversion has its chief defense, it seems to me, in the fact that it keeps together related topics. It is certainly convenient to have "Psychology, Animal," "Psychology, Comparative," "Psychology, Morbid," "Psychology, Social" in orderly sequence and close together. But despite this convenience, as a matter of form of heading, the practice of inversion is to be regarded as fully as pernicious in the subject catalog as in the author catalog. The objections to it are patent and well known. There is one catalog which regularly and always inverts, which enters under an adjective form only in the rarest instances. I refer, as most of you will surmise, to the magnificent Index Catalogue of the Surgeon General's Library. No one will dispute the high authority of this catalog as a scientific product. It is the most remarkable thing of the kind ever done in this country. But I imagine that despite its example we may be more truly scientific if we set our faces squarely against inversion. The worst thing about inversion is the utter lack of certainty as to which several forms may be used. If in our author catalogs we have come to the point where we can write "Michigan. University," why should we not write "Psychology. *Animals*"? There is not time to elaborate in this paper the argument against inversion. We must be content to dismiss it with the single proviso that well established phrases beginning with an adjective such as Republican Party, Political Science, etc., need not be called in question either by those who would always invert to serve their convenience, or those who are steadfastly against the practice of inversion. The larger question whether the ordinary phrase, *e.g.*, Comparative anatomy, Animal psychology, should not always be employed instead of some device whereby the noun remains in the first position is well discussed by Mr. Cutter in his Rules. My own opinion is for the regular use of the phrase in current use in the form in which it habitually occurs in titles, save in the numerous cases in which a caption with proper subhead better expresses the idea.

There is one class of subjects which gives trouble alike to classifiers and catalogers. Wherever a classification or a catalog is subdivided on a geographical basis, or wherever geographical headings are given, the fact stares us in the face that "geographical expressions," to use Prince Metternich's phrase, are by no means permanent or dependable. The map of the world has suffered startling changes since books began to be made. Certain difficulties which confront us in geographical headings deserve attention.

Even the continents give trouble. The terms America and Asia are used very loosely in popular speech, and even in indexes of subjects. Does North America include Mexico and Central America? Where does Western Asia leave off and Central Asia begin? Does the term America as a heading or subheading include both North and South America? Shall we write America, North or North America? What do we mean by Central Africa? These are questions which have but to be asked to raise sharply the point that definition and consistent adherence to definition are essential in the geographical terms to be used. I say nothing of the formidable adjective American, for I hope we may largely banish initial geographical adjectives from the catalog. But the official catalog of subjects should certainly contain very carefully planned directions as to the use of continental designations, as well as of the smaller divisions of geography.

But troublesome as ill-defined geographical concepts may be, they are nothing in the way of difficulty compared to the name of regions which have ceased to represent present political conditions. There are a number of countries which no longer exist as states, whose political life as separate entities has ceased. A region such as Poland, for example, which has been absorbed by one or more countries offers a most perplexing problem. The word Poland corresponds to nothing on the map or in official gazetteers, but it is still in everybody's mouth. Travellers still use the old national name on title pages of descriptive works; historians and others write on former or even present-day conditions. And yet in our larger libraries we have official documents and other works treating of this once independent state from the standpoint of Prussian, Austrian and Russian provinces. I do not believe that we can

get around the difficulty by bumping everything under the popular name. Neither do I believe that we can ignore it in the case of travel and descriptive works. (Of course I am not referring to books on Poland before the partition.) There are plenty of similar cases, although few with such complications. It seems to me that the common name must still be used where it is employed on title pages, and that the official regional designation of the present day must be employed where needed because of either the title or the contents of the work. This will necessitate a lengthy "See also" reference, a thing to be avoided wherever possible.

Ancient and mediæval states and countries with no continuing name or precise modern geographical equivalent give less difficulty. Their ancient names may safely be used. The trouble is, however, that both descriptive and historical works dealing wholly with present-day (or at least modern) conditions frequently employ the ancient name in titles. In such cases the modern form of name should be regularly used as a heading. Such ancient regions as Pontus, Epirus, Dacia, Africa, Gaul, Granada (Kingdom) may well receive separate subject entry, but it will instantly be seen how much confusion would arise from using these headings for modern works dealing with present conditions. Take "Africa," for example. Properly used it means in antiquity the single Roman province erected on the ruins of the Carthaginian city-state, limited in its extent to about the boundaries of modern Tunis. So used the term has a distinct value. But a modern work on Tunis, or even a discussion of archæological problems occurring in the limits of the ancient province should not receive the heading of Africa. There is, then, great need for care and a well-defined policy in these matters of ancient geographical designations which have no precise modern equivalents. Somewhere a very careful working out of the proper limits of the subject heading adopted for such countries and regions must be accessible to the cataloging staff, and perhaps to the public. It will not do, for instance, to say merely, "Tunis— See also Africa (Roman province)"; "Africa (Roman province)—See also Tunis." These loose "See also" references are the refuge of careless catalogers. In their stead must be a careful explanatory note giving the dates and boundaries within which the heading is applicable.

It may be worth while to stop at this point for a word as to these "See also" references. It was a rule at some time in the dim and distant past of cataloging to make "See also" references from each subject named on a title page to every other subject so named. All students of cataloging methods well know some of the ludicrous results of this rule. It is creditably reported that as a result of this rule rigidly applied such references as these were made and printed. "Brain, *See also* Cheek, Tumors of the;" "Cheek, Tumors of the, *See also* Brain," because forsooth both subjects got into one of the long-winded titles of earlier days. Probably these "See also" references cannot be wholly eliminated from catalogs. It is a very good thing at times to have a student reminded of allied topics and similar headings. But the tendency to their abuse is so great that it would seem a better course to make carefully worded explanations rather than to multiply these references. And I believe we should not suffer greatly were they excluded entirely from the subject catalog. They frequently give the impression—unjustly, of course—that the cataloger is either trying to show off his knowledge of subjects, or considers that the user of the catalog has none.

To return to matters geographical. Few problems are more difficult as matters of actual practice than the making of a perfectly clear arrangement in a card catalog of easily understood and intelligible headings for countries or regions which have had a continuous written history from ancient to modern days. The most conspicuous of these are Egypt, Greece, Rome, and Syria. The boundaries of Egypt have been practically the same from antiquity to the present day. Hence we are not so much troubled by the question of the physical extent of the heading. But we are directly "up against" the question whether we shall say Egypt (Ancient), Egypt (Græco-Roman), Egypt (Saracenic), Egypt (Turkish), Egypt (Modern), or something of this sort, or whether these headings should be used as second subheads following the recognized subdivisions under the country. For example, Taxation is a frequently employed subheading under country, and we happen to have a great mass of material on taxation in Egypt in many ages. Shall we write Egypt (Ancient). *Taxation*, Egypt (Græco-Roman). *Taxation*, etc., or Egypt. *Taxation*. (Ancient), Egypt. Taxation (Græco-Roman) period, etc.? The second method keeps the country as the main heading and places the period last, and is therefore preferable, in my opinion. But in neither case can we get away from three alphabets in arrangement. The method advocated, namely, of keeping the period division last and considering the topic as the more important mat-

ter, falls in with our ordinarily received method for modern states. Thus we generally find such headings as this: United States. *Taxation* (Colonial period), rather than United States (Colonial period). *Taxation*. Whichever method is adopted, whether we break up the country's history into certain well-defined periods and treat these as if they were separate wholes, or whether we regard the country in all its history as one and arrange topics under it with chronological divisions, the dates of the different periods will have to be worked out with care and recorded in the official list of headings. When this is done it will probably be found that the books seldom fit the dates previously arranged. What to do with overlapping books—books which fit into no general scheme—is a sore problem in cataloging as in classification. We must either go on forever making new and more minute subdivisions and arranging the subject cards chronologically by the first date in the heading, or else we must assign the subject by the preponderance of interest of the book itself, placing it in that division of the subject where most of the narrative or discussion falls. The majority of catalogers will doubtless prefer the latter method. The specific dates may be put in the heading as a matter of guidance to the person consulting the catalog, but in this case they will be ignored in filing.

Rome presents worse difficulties than Egypt. In the first place we have to encounter the fact that both the city and the state—originally one— have a voluminous literature. Confusion here is disastrous, and yet it is found in many catalogs. The city of the seven hills must be a subject by itself, reserved for separate treatment. Its municipal history is to be kept separate—where possible— from the march of the mighty empire, and its monuments must receive treatment distinct from that of Roman remains in general. It would seem a very good plan in arranging cards to put the country heading first, then the city heading, and finally the heading for its numerous monuments and regions. Thus I would have such classes of headings as Rome. *History. Empire*, Rome (city). *History. Middle Ages*, Rome (city). Forum Romanum. If this distinction between the city and the state is not made in this and other cases, we shall have a confusion which will make our catalogs unusable. Moreover, in treating the Roman state it will be as necessary to define dates and boundaries as in the case of Egypt. I will not go on to speak in detail of Greece and other countries having a continuous recorded history of many centuries. Enough has been said to show the need for careful planning in giving subjects to works on such countries.

Still another cause of confusion is closely allied to these we have just been considering. We have numerous cases in which ancient and modern geographical terms do not mean the same thing. I have already cited Africa as an example. The loose habit of catalogers of projecting modern geographical terms into the past is most discouraging to students. Take, for example, such designations as Germany and Austria, to cite large regions. Their boundaries are not to-day what they were even fifty years since, and books describing particular regions not formerly in their limits and referring wholly to former times should not be listed under the modern caption, if suitable ones can be found in the older names. This is merely the principle of the specific heading applied to geographical problems. Again in certain particulars the modern geographical term may represent a much smaller area than the same term at an earlier date. Venice and Genoa are instances in point, and many more might easily be cited. A book on the Venetian remains in the Greek islands hardly deserves a subject, Venice. *Description and travel*, although one on the Venetian supremacy in the Levant might well have a subject for Venice. Separate geographical entities such as islands and peninsulas are more easily treated as a rule than other regions, as confusion is less likely to arise in their cases.

Finally a word should be said in protest against subject headings of an indefinite sort for frontier or partially settled regions. "The West" in American history is one such. The phrase "Old Southwest" is another. The objection lies rather against the indefinite nature of the heading than against its use, if once it be well defined. The various regions in Central Africa offer similar difficulties.

If countries having a continuous recorded history present difficult problems to the cataloger, so also do subjects of inquiry which have given occupation to generations of scholars. Such studies as political science, economics, philosophy, mathematics, chemistry, botany, medicine, theology, rhetoric, etc., had their beginning for our Western world in Greece and are live topics today. History and description of countries show the same long line of writers. Now it is obvious that some discrimination is needed in cataloging the authors who for twenty odd centuries have discussed such important subjects as the theory of the state, the art of healing, or the science of

mathematics. The distinctions which a printed catalog can show by varieties of type and the rapid view of many pages with their headings are of course impossible in a card catalog. If it is manifestly improper to compel the student seeking the library's best treatise on agriculture to turn over numerous cards for editions of Cato and the other *Scriptores de re rustica,* so also is it unwise to neglect the fact that agriculture and all other sciences have their historical side. If we are going to give subjects to all our books, then Cato must have a subject card somewhere under agriculture. Here is where the average dictionary catalog breaks down. It furnishes under such topics as those we have mentioned a dreary array of cards, frequently many trays of them, through which the discouraged student must work to find his modern books. Every hundred thousand volumes added to the library but increases the task of consultation. The cards thus become what no one wants, an alphabetical list of all the writers who have ever treated of a given topic. The catalog must either distinguish books whose value *for the subject* is purely historical, or it must arrange its cards chronologically (by author), putting the latest works first. In other words, the alphabetical principle of sub-arrangement must be abandoned under subjects, or else we must introduce another division under these subjects having a continuous history, *i.e.*, a class of books having an historical value only.

But when does a book begin to have a merely historical value? There's the rub! It is not possible to determine this by chronolgy alone. Can we consider Aristotle of merely historical importance in the discussion of poetry or drama, of political science or ethics? Most assuredly not. But yet his works on physics and natural history are absolutely without profit to the average student of today. No one will say that Kant's writings are out of date, and yet his psychology would hardly benefit the modern student in our college classes. It is plain that discrimination of the highest order must be employed in this matter, or else we must adopt some mechanical arrangement such as the filing of cards in chronological order, which after all works a sort of rough justice in the matter of relative values. Let us be severely honest with ourselves here. Who of us can say that the trays headed Theology or Law in most of our catalogs of libraries of over one hundred thousand volumes are practically useful as they stand to-day? Who would not rather consult a good bibliography and then the author catalog for books on those topics than attack the direful array of cards in the hope by some means of at length securing an interesting and valuable set of references?

In formal political history and in economic history as well the sources should certainly be distinguished from the recent treatises. The Germania of Tacitus, for instance, is an excellent source for the early history of the German Empire, but it is positively foolish to list it side by side with the works of Von Sybel and Ranke under Germany. *History*. The subhead of "Sources" under history is a convenient and valuable limbo for bygone works and for collections of documents. There is opposition, and sensible opposition, however, to using it for merely obsolete treatises.

We might adopt some such scheme as this:

Political Science. *Modern works (since* 1850*)*
and important earlier works.
—— *Works between* 1500 *and* 1850.
—— *Medieval works.*
—— *Ancient works.*

The divisions suggested here might perhaps be the same in all cases, or they might better be made to conform to well-recognized divisions in the history of each topic. The alternative plan is the arrangement of cards by date of publication, or by first date of the author (to keep editions together). I confess I prefer the latter, although I am far from wishing to put myself in the position of assuming that the most recent work is necessarily the best. Still the chances are that it represents the most recent stage of investigation. Almost every librarian is willing to concede this in the matter of bibliographies, acknowledging that the last to appear should first meet the eye of the person consulting the catalog. Why not adopt the same principle for every topic, as is done in some of our libraries? We have, be it remembered, the author catalog at hand for every one who already knows the authors he wants. Why compel the seeker after information to wade through another author list under each topic? It may be observed that an annotated catalog would be almost forced to put first its cards for the books most highly recommended.

There are a few practical points which I wish to take up before closing this paper. First, shall we definitely limit the number of subject cards to a given book? In view of the immense size to which our card catalogs are growing is it wise to say that when the library reaches a certain size—say 500,000 volumes—it will henceforth assume that the necessity for making cards for any other than the subject of prime interest in a book has passed? Shall we take it for granted that there will always be other works which cover the topics of secondary interest? This view is maintained in some libraries whose authority we all acknowledge. I venture, however, in opposition to this idea, to call attention to the statistics of our Princeton work published in the *Library Journal* for June, 1906. It was there shown that the number of subject cards per main entry was 1.47, and per title 1.2, although no restriction was placed on the catalogers other than a rigid insistence on the specific heading in all cases. This is so nearly the result aimed at in the rule that I submit that it is a better way of attaining the desired restriction of the unduly rapid growth of the card catalog than the strict limitation to one subject per book. It permits the liberal handling of a book which treats definitely of several topics, and yet it does not too greatly burden the subject catalog. The device of using but one subject entry for the various editions of a work whose value is chiefly historical would diminish the per cent. of subject to author cards to less than one in our library.

Again, it may not be amiss to urge that the revision and co-ordination of subject headings should be definitely assigned to one person. Only thus can continuity and uniformity of the work be secured. Particularly is this provision needed in our largest libraries. I urge also as a most vital matter of practice that the chief reference librarian should be in constant touch with the cataloger who passes finally on subject headings. They will work together to great mutual advantage.

Moreover, I wish once more to set forth the imperative necessity for an official list of headings in use in the library. This should be kept up to date with the utmost care. Each cataloger should have in convenient form a list of all subheads previously authorized under each class of topics, together with definitions of all these subheads. The list without definitions and interpretative notes will be of some small value, but with them will be vastly more useful. It should be kept where every cataloger can consult it, preferably in a case of trays made to swing on a pivot so that it may be consulted without disturbing the one at whose elbow it must be placed. The American Library Association list and the Sydney list, admirable as both are in their own way, will not suffice for any large library. An up-to-date list of subjects with adequate definitions kept on cards, is an absolute necessity in a well-ordered catalog department.

Is all this worth while? Is the card catalog of subjects alphabetically arranged a real service to an institution? Most assuredly it is. When once it is made on consistent principles, when the student no longer has to fumble long trays of cards without headings or guides, filled with all the contradictory accumulations of generations of catalogers, when the specific topic stands out prominently, when each subject capable of two interpretations is sharply defined on a guide card, when consistency in geographical matters and uniformity of entry and sub-entry in topics of debatable form have been reached, there is no reason why a student should not find the card catalog of subjects self-interpreting, inclusive, useful. It has the all-important merit of definiteness and point. It tells any one who knows his topic what he can get directly on it. It lists both the obsolete book and the dead and gone state by themselves. It opens up to the reader the contents of the library. It is, in short, an alphabetical subject index to the books. If this is not worth while, what library effort is? If this be formal, dry-as-dust work, why are we working with books at all? Our aim as librarians is not merely to accumulate books. It is to help the reader to the books he wants—or ought to want. In a large library the only tool which accomplishes this result is the catalog, and of this the subject catalog is the part most difficult to make, most useful when well made.

Delights and Pitfalls of Subject Cataloging

Rudolf F. Schaeffer

Reminiscences of a subject cataloger at the Library of Congress, in which he tells of some of the challenges of subject analysis and explains methods of meeting them.

These highly personal notes are an expression of gratitude for twelve years of work which was a constant source of satisfaction and enjoyment. They will offer nothing new or startling to any experienced cataloger. My views and attitudes may occasionally have a pedagogical slant and thus offer advice or warning in the guise of reminiscences; if so, I hope an educator by profession and a teacher for a great many years will be forgiven.

SUBJECT CATALOGING AS A JOB

Subject cataloging is delightful if regarded as work worth doing, not just a job to keep one busy within prescribed hours, producing subject entries and class numbers for a certain amount of books in a given time, and a pay check every two weeks, linking one coffee break by way of lunch with another along the road to five-fifteen. If the books piled on your desk are only a chore to be disposed of as quickly and as graciously as can be managed, then my thoughts on the subject may seem to be those of a daydreamer or just wishful thinking in retrospect.

If, on the other hand, you are looking forward to each new assignment of books, entrusted to you for analysis and interpretation, with suspenseful curiosity and anticipation, then my delight at subject cataloging will become understandable. An almost personal relationship will evolve between the author speaking through his work and the subject analyst "listening" to him. In a way, this relationship begins when he takes a first look at the book.

At this point I sense a strong objection: How can there possibly be a "personal" relationship to an individual work when the overall work load is pressing, and the books have to be moved along at a fast pace. To counter that objection, let me look for a moment at subject cataloging from a psychological angle.

What happens to the subject cataloger, what goes on in his mind, when he looks at a book for the first time? While this first reaction and attitude will not and should not determine, or even affect, the subject entries he will finally assign to it, he is by human nature bound to react to a given work in a certain way. Should he feel obligated to suppress and ignore his reaction in order to do an impartial job? We are dealing here with two entirely different intellectual processes, to be kept strictly apart in subject analysis. There is, on the one hand, a personal reaction which may range all the way from fascination to indifference to repulsion. There is, on the other hand, the unbiased, objective interpretation of a work in terms of subject headings and classification. The latter is undoubtedly a desirable achievement. However, I sincerely doubt whether a cataloger is capable of entirely suppressing his personal reaction for the benefit of a completely impersonal evaluation. If he were, I should not envy him.

SUBJECT CATALOGING AS AN ART

What is it in particular that makes subject cataloging, by and large, a delightful occupation? What is its nature, its philosophy? What does it take to be a competent subject cataloger?

SOURCE: Reprinted from *Library Resources and Technical Services* XIV, 1 (Winter 1970), pp. 98–108. The author, originally a teacher of classical philology in Germany, received a Ph.D. degree from Columbia University in 1951. At the time of his retirement in 1964, he was on the staff of the Library of Congress as a subject cataloger in the humanities.

I have heard it said by men in authority that subject cataloging is an art. Verner W. Clapp in his article on David Judson Haykin probably has subject cataloging in mind, among other things, when he speaks of "the arts which are basic to library work."[1]

In what respect can subject cataloging be considered an art, unless we mean by this just a high degree of skill in the performance of a difficult task? There are, of course, a great many things which can be learned by extensive training and prolonged experience. Even advanced scholarship that may lead to a Ph. D. may be so achieved, and still we would not call it an art.

On the other hand, there are certain activities where all the schooling and practice in the world would at best lead to mediocre results. To give two illustrations, conducting an orchestra and teaching are such activities. It was Felix Mottl, I believe, who said that some men can just stand in front of an orchestra and conduct it, while others, in spite of the best training, fail miserably. The conductor is undoubtedly an artist; a teacher is not. And yet, there are similarities. All of us, I am sure, have experienced well-meaning, even scholarly teachers who face their classes in utter helplessness. Long training and experience prove to be of little help. These teachers just "did not have it in them," neither the ability to teach nor a love for teaching; and if they are wanting on either score, teaching is torment for them as well as for their victims.

With these illustrations, I believe I have already presented the case for subject cataloging as an art. For one thing, you have to love it or, with growing experience and independence, to find sustained enjoyment in it. Otherwise it will be a job just like any other you might suffer from, and the people who seek access to the books entrusted to you will suffer as well. Love alone is not enough, however. It may be an unhappy love unless, like the successful conductor and teacher, you have an innate gift, a certain mental disposition for it.

What is the intellectual endowment which seems to be the prerequisite for a competent subject cataloger? Is a resourceful scholar necessarily a good interpreter of works in his own field by other writers? When I once discussed this question with my colleagues, the case of a great scholar was mentioned, a man with an awe-inspiring list of publications, a ranking authority in his field, who, however hard he tried, just was not made to be a subject cataloger. As a scholar he was obviously too much engulfed in his own research problems to have the patience and perseverance to explore another scholar's ideas with detachment. In other words, he was not able to follow through the maze of another author's thoughts, sometimes seemingly devious or even obscure. He just could not muster the necessary empathy with the author's line of thought regardless of whether or not he shared his opinions.

In order to discover the logical structure and psychological build-up in another man's work, the subject cataloger must, first of all, be capable of clear and systematic thinking. With this mental equipment he subjects the work at hand to meticulous examination. Just as a teacher (to use this illustration again) can be successful only to the extent that he is able to follow most intimately the student's thought processes, however strange and peculiar they may appear to him, so the subject analyst has to follow closely and self-effacingly the author's mental tracks in order to determine what he is talking about. Only then can the cataloger assign the subject headings and classification which will do justice to the work and be a genuine aid for the reader to find what he is seeking. Incidentally, this psychological affinity to teaching, my life-long pursuit before becoming a librarian, may be a strong contributing factor to my personal pleasure in subject cataloging.

Moreover, the subject cataloger must project himself into the role of a potential reader and anticipate under which subject headings he might possibly—or under no circumstances—look for the work he endeavors to make accessible to him.

To summarize, love for this type of work, a specific mental readiness and disposition for it, and a clear view of the library user's needs, if put into everyday practice and developed to near-perfection, may well make subject cataloging an art in the broad sense of the word—an art which, like any true art, is more an ideal, an ultimate goal than an accomplished reality.

THE TIME ELEMENT
IN SUBJECT CATALOGING

Going into some special aspects of subject cataloging, I should like to lead off with a question that is difficult to answer. How much time should be devoted to an individual work in all its significant details? What is the average time it takes an experienced cataloger to handle a book? It is practically impossible to give a satisfactory answer. Books are individualities, and their individual treatment may take any time between half a minute and, say, three hours. While I am talking chiefly of works in the humanities, I am certain that this is also true for other disciplines. Take works of fiction, works on places whose names have been established, treatises on established periods in the history of a country—you glance at the book, and subject headings, if any, as well as class numbers, can be assigned in a matter of a few minutes. However, works like these do not offer much of a challenge. The enjoyment of subject cataloging comes from those books whose complexities and the problems they present make their analysis a real challenge.

THE AUTHOR

As it is fascinating to meet an unusual person, so it is when you encounter him as an author of a book. Your curiosity about the author, far from being merely personal and distracting, is necessary if you are to interpret the work at hand correctly. You have to find out who your author is and how the work at hand fits into the pattern of his other publications, if any, previously cataloged or listed in his bibliography.

Sometimes the works in the catalog listed under the same author cover a great variety of fields, even fields that are, or seem to be, quite unrelated. In such an instance one cannot help being skeptical. On occasion I even dared to question the descriptive cataloger's identification of a writer. I remember one author, Rolf Italiaander, whose works are classified in no less than sixteen classes; yet, the identity of the author could not be disputed. In another instance I was more successful: a teacher in a village elementary school had published a collection of local poems and folk songs of a remote Alpine valley and, so I thought, was most unlikely to be the author of several books on higher mathematics. It turned out that he was not the same man.

AIDS IN SUBJECT CATALOGING

Every experienced subject cataloger knows, of course, and every student in a course in subject cataloging certainly learns, where in a book to look for signposts in the search for proper subject headings and classifications. Therefore, there is no need to discuss such obvious sources of information, in addition to the title, as the table of contents, dedication, foreword, preface, intro-duction, acknowledgements, epilogue, summaries, conclusions, and, of course, footnotes, bibliographies, and indexes. Not so widely known is the fact that extensive listings under any one entry in the index may suggest a subject heading.

Since any scholarly work is just a link in a chain of continuous research or, to use a Platonic term, a part of the perennial dialectical process, there are bound to be in it hints or references to the author's or other writers' previous and, often, potential future research in the same or related fields. In other words, there is hardly a work that does not either continue previous research, or express appreciation of, agreement with, or opposition to, earlier works. The subject treatment already given to works referred to in a book may give a valuable clue to that of the work at hand. To hunt for these clues contributes to the enjoyment of subject cataloging, and the caution and care with which they should be pursued will not diminish it.

The dust jacket, so dear to cataloging teachers and catalogers alike, may seem to give significant clues but has primarily a commercial purpose—to arouse curiosity and to attract readers. Subject entries it might suggest sometimes mislead rather than guide the subject analyst.

Turning to what he would expect to be a more reliable clue, the table of contents, the cataloger may be in for another disappointment when, in lieu of meaningful chapter headings, he finds numbers I, II, etc., or such fanciful captions as "Hopeful Beginnings," "Disillusionment," "Trial and Error," which serve to disguise rather than to reveal the actual contents.

Even greater frustration than a meaningless table of contents may be in store for you when, before plunging into the body of the book, you hope for guidance from the title. Here again you have to be on guard. I remember one striking instance: The title of a book by Lillian Ross was *Reporting*. "This is an easy one," you think, because it is a case when the title coincides with, or comes very close to, one of our subject headings. So REPORTERS AND REPORTING and the corresponding PN class number come automatically to mind. However, *Reporting*, to quote from the book itself, turned out to present "facts in the form of fiction" or "factual short stories."

THE MEANING OF A WORK

Whatever guideposts you have already used, examining the text of the book still remains the main job. Getting at the essence of its content is like taking a picture: after first taking in the entire scene, you try to focus on what you deem the predominant and essential features, while the less important elements remain on the side or in the background. Similarly, you try to get a mental picture of a work by focusing on its main features and its crucial points. What is the author actually driving at, what are the key passages, what are the main objectives of his work? These are questions to which in many cases you may at first not find an answer. I still remember sitting in front of an open book, glancing over its pages, reading shorter or longer passages here and there, pondering over the fundamental question, "What does he mean?" and thinking "I wish I knew!" or sometimes even, "Does he himself know?"

Believe it or not, the author himself does not always know! Let me give you two illustrations, one from my early teaching days, the other from a contemporary American play.

At a time when local folklore played a significant part in the curriculum, I tried to interpret a poem by a nature-inspired lyric poet of the early twentieth century. I no longer remember the title of the poem, but I do recall a nightmarish passage in which the poet describes some gloomy events happening in deepest darkness. It was as dark, so the poem read, "as in a goat's night." Here seemed to be a very interesting piece of animal folklore, possibly still alive in the remote retreat where the poet happened to reside. What, I pondered, could the darkness of the night mean to a goat? I searched through the literature on local folklore, I consulted authorities in the field, I examined books on zoology for any peculiar behavior of goats during nights not brightened by moonlight or stars. No success. The poem was too beautiful to be passed over just because "a goat's night" defied interpretation. Facing my class, I said with all the courage and sincerity I could muster something like "It must have been an extraordinarily dark night. I wish I could tell you just what the poet's image of a goat's night really means."

A few weeks later one of my brightest students came up with a quite surprising answer. He had it from the poet in a personal letter in reply to his specific question. The writer, the letter said, was quite delighted at the student's inquisitive mind, but as to the goat's night, he had not the slightest idea how and why the image of a goat had come to his mind to characterize the utter blackness of the night.

Not long ago, Broadway was puzzled by Edward Albee's play, *Tiny Alice*. Having become interested in the author from his earlier plays, I followed the different interpretations of the play by the New York critics and out-of-town newspapers, in literary journals, and magazines on the stage. The variety of interpretations was unbelievable. Again the author was consulted, and here is his answer as reported in *Time*[2]: "There are some things in the play that are not clear to me."

Some such vagueness or self-uncertainty may well be the hallmark of an entire book. True, the foregoing illustrations concern works of the imagination, while scholarly publications or factual materials usually do not leave too much doubt as to what the author has in mind.

However, there are publications that may be referred to as crackpot literature, which do not lend themselves to being classified within known disciplines of knowledge, and which at one time at the Library of Congress were assigned to an unofficial Class X. There are books which you doubt that the author wants to be taken seriously, books which just do not make sense. A look at the imprint may disclose that the author was his own publisher, or that a close relative published the book for him. I can easily imagine an unfortunate psychopathic writer whose family will help him publish the product of his mental aberrations as a kind of psychotherapy, to let him see himself in print. Unlikely as it may sound, many such books are on deposit in the Library of Congress.

Apart from this type, let us face it: we sometimes come across books, especially doctoral dissertations, in our very own fields which we fail, at least in part, to understand. In this connection a paper comes to mind which was read at one of the University of Kentucky Foreign Language Conferences. It was a very learned paper on a minute aspect of a narrow linguistic problem. The paper's terminology, as characterized by the chairman, was so distressingly obscure that he, a well-known linguist himself, did not feel competent to make any comments. A subject cataloger may come across a work just as puzzling as this paper. Some doctoral candidates, together with their sponsoring professors, develop, in blazing new trails of research, an idiom entirely their own not to be found even in the most recent reference works in the field. Only the full text of the dissertation, not just an abstract, may perhaps throw some light on the meaning of the freshly baked terminology and on the problems discussed. Can subject cataloging of such works be called delightful, one might ask. I am afraid not. And yet, we do enjoy the never-ending challenge we face, especially in the more problematical works. Then we try desperately to get at the bottom of a study, while at the same time we realize that we may feel frustrated with the result of our endeavor.

Fortunately, there are books (yes, even dissertations) that are, or at least look, quite simple to handle, with all the signposts pointing in one direction. Even in such works surprises might be in store, and caution and skepticism should remain the order of the day. Spot-checks throughout the book sometimes reveal the fact that the actual content does not live up to what title, table of contents, chapter headings, and captions entitled you to expect. Then you feel obliged to dig further, and the final outcome may be quite different from what you had anticipated. Of course, you cannot read a book from cover to cover, although in some instances this might be the only way to get a reliable picture of a work.

As a matter of fact, I did read several books from beginning to end, not at my office desk, to be sure, but at my leisure during periods of prolonged convalescence when I had the unique opportunity for such a thorough examination of books which I had earmarked at work for that purpose. Of course, these were books of particular personal interest. Sometimes my reading of the whole book gave me quite a different opinion of its content. After finishing such a book I asked myself: would you have assigned the same subject headings if you had known the book the way you do now? In all honesty the answer was no. These are, fortunately, exceptional cases.

TEMPTATIONS

It goes without saying that you cannot help getting interested, to different degrees, in the content of the books assigned to you. Until the subject cataloging machine is invented (if this should ever happen), personal involvement cannot and, I believe, should not be discounted or discouraged; but do not let it run away with you. I must admit it sometimes calls for a sustained effort in self-control to tear oneself away from a fascinating book or a work of strong personal appeal. I still have a large file of titles of such works marked "RR" for "retirement reading."

Excessive personal interest is not the only temptation a subject cataloger is exposed to. Another temptation, closely related to the first, is that of making value judgments. Although we consider it a major crime for a subject cataloger to let his value judgment determine what kind of subject entry and class number he assigns to a work, I would, nonetheless, admire (or maybe I would not not) the superhuman detachment or indifference of the individual in whose mind criticism does not build up while he examines and interprets the content of a book.

PROBLEMS OF FICTION

Among the many puzzling factors that keep you on your toes and make your work so enjoyable, are the questions of what constitutes fiction, where is the dividing line between fiction and factual report, and when does fiction merit a subject entry.

Although there are hundreds of books for which I had to resolve these questions, two instances remain most clearly in my memory.

There is an unwritten rule, apparently handed down from one generation of subject catalogers to another: to identify fiction watch out for two elements—direct discourse and love affairs. If you find these ingredients, you may be fairly sure that you are dealing with fiction.

This is not necessarily so. These ingredients may just be the sugar-coating to attract a reader to a book, the only intent and purpose of which is to give factual, well-founded information. This is particularly true when it comes to juvenile literature.

The book I remember so well told of recent excavations in Egypt. The archaeologist in charge had his daughter visit the excavation area during her summer vacation, and one of his younger assistants promptly fell in love with her. Moreover, animated discussions, presented in direct discourse and dealing at least in part with personal matters, ran through the entire book. And yet, the purpose and subject of the book, once the ornamentation was stripped off, was a description of ancient Egypt as disclosed by recent archaeological discoveries. What other purpose could the numerous maps, charts, photographs of the excavation sites, chronologies of the Egyptian dynasties, lists of suggested readings, etc., have served? They certainly did not contribute anything to what at first glance appeared to be a love story for young readers.

The problem of another book was even more intricate and too challenging to be forgotten. A subject cataloger fell victim to its makeup, and I happened to be the one.

An old and ever-puzzling question is that of the borderline that separates biography from biographical fiction. Both are quite likely to have the ingredients of a love element and actual or at least highly believable conversations. Yet, what would you do with what appears to be the biography of a famous actress, published with the vague subtitle, "the story of . . .," whose method of presentation, to all appearances, is strictly factual? There is a detailed table of contents; events and facts are listed in chronological order; an elaborate index, an extensive bibliography, substantial footnotes, an appendix giving in exact figures the actress' financial situation at the time of her death, and the text of her will appear to document the account; in brief, the work bears all the earmarks of scholarly research. There was no question in the cataloger's mind that this particular work was a biography, and that was how I treated it.

A few weeks later, a British edition followed the American one, not only stripped of all the scholarly apparatus, but with ". . . a novel based on the life of . . ." added to the title. No doubt was left at this point that the book was a work of fiction. As such, it was assigned to another subject cataloger, who could not know that the text of of the English edition was identical with that of the American "biography." So it happened that two catalogers felt justified in treating the same work in two incompatible ways. Whoever thinks of the exciting job of subject cataloging as an easy one ("you read books to your heart's desire all day long and then get paid for it") may examine the two editions of this book and ponder over them for a while.[3]

TEAMWORK

Many books cover a variety of fields, sometimes not even closely related, or lend themselves to more than one interpretation. In such cases, the involvement of more than one cataloger in the same work is, of course, quite common and desirable.

Dan Lacy, then Assistant Director of the Processing Department, expressed this thought when he welcomed me to the Library staff. "We in the Library," he said, "are all one big family. Besides, we are a great university in our own right." It was this spirit of being one big family which I gradually came to realize in the atmosphere of the Subject Cataloging Division.

Perhaps not everybody will agree with me. Whoever does not like to be interrupted from time to time but would prefer to do his work in the quiet solitude of his study, whoever thinks little of what he may learn by discussing his problems with others cannot easily understand the pleasure of consulting with others, of seeking and giving advice, of opening up new pathways of thought through a free-flowing exchange of ideas.

My own cataloging work offered me a fine opportunity to combine theory and practice in discussion and debate, the very topic about which new books reached my desk in ever-increasing numbers. Thus, I was kept aware of the ideal situation in the fruitful give-and-take of argumentation. This calls for modesty and humility in acknowledging the possibility of differing viewpoints and, most important, for mental flexibility —all prerequisites of constructive discussion. I also became sensitive to its pitfalls when those participating in a discussion were overbearing or so rigid in their attitude that they could not believe their own opinions might possibly be modified by an exchange of ideas. Fortunately, I found very few such people in our group; in fact, I consider the predominant spirit of ideal collaboration one of the strongest factors contributing to my pleasures of subject cataloging.

What I find especially enjoyable is the research that we carry on in exploring the needs for new subject headings, investigating their nature, and searching for authoritative sources as the basis of our recommendations.

Here again, delight and pitfalls are neighbors. As we know from personal experience in research, we may easily get lost in the maze of the problems involved or be tempted to go far beyond what is needed as solid base on which to erect a new subject structure. We must be aware of the danger of being carried away by our own interest and zeal. To roam through the hunting grounds for new subject headings is no more important than to realize the limits of the chase and to recognize the point of diminishing returns.

I shall illustrate this problem by another experience. As a high school student I had a mathematics teacher who, in correcting student papers, indulged in fanciful marginal comments. One of them in my own paper read "Ulysses in Ithaca." As hard as I tried, I could not figure out what Ulysses' homecoming had to do with the solution of a mathematical problem. So I asked. Just as Ulysses, I was told, was not aware that he had already reached his homeland, I had failed to realize that I had already solved my problem and kept on figuring in the belief that the solution was still ahead.

By the same token, the subject cataloger is in danger of not recognizing that he has already reached his objective, that he has assembled material sufficient to prove the need for, and to document the proper form of, a new subject heading.

Having an ear to the ground in your special fields so that you can sense the right moment for the need of a new subject heading and help establish it is, indeed, a creative act. In this sense, too, subject cataloging may have something in common with art.

CHALLENGES, LEARNING EXPERIENCES, AND PERSONAL ASSOCIATIONS

The Library of Congress catalog would challenge the subject cataloger's creative potentials, if time permitted him to utilize them. Some extensive, unwieldy subject files have become so unserviceable that they call for new differentiations because the material in the file has through the years almost unnoticeably become so heterogeneous as to defy accommodation under a once adequate subject heading. We may come to realize such a situation while running through a file for some other purpose. Occasionally a different class number for works under the same subject entry may give a valuable clue as to where a dividing line between an existing and a potential subject heading might be drawn.

I was privileged to originate the separation of the materials dealing with the modern concept of MASS MEDIA from the all-too-inclusive and heterogeneous entries under COMMUNICATION. Other such bulky files of subject entries come to mind—or, rather, have long burdened my conscience—entries which I would have been only too glad to revise had time permitted me to do so. I realize that some such changes may have to wait until automation frees hands and minds of subject catalogers for the more creative aspects of their work.

In this context, I am not so much concerned with the pleasures of subject cataloging I missed as with those I experienced in my work. Among them I should not fail to mention the sustained personal enrichment in gaining new knowledge and remaining in the everlasting process of learning. It is in this sense also that I now understand the reference to the Library of Congress as a great university not only for the scholars who use it, but also for those who are called upon to contribute to its structure of subject headings and classification.

For example, the subject heading you help establish may concern a topic you have never heard of before. I did not have the faintest idea what a shaggy-dog story was when I handled a book tracing the history of this peculiar type of humor back to its British origin and was thus required to recommend a new subject heading, SHAGGY-DOG STORIES. I am sure most of us will have had similar experiences in the case of new concepts emerging even in our own fields of specialization.

Apart from these generally shared experiences, there are the personal ones, not always pleasant, but certainly enlightening, sometimes even moving. You simply cannot help taking a personal interest in those authors you have known as your teachers, fellow students, or friends. The number of such authors is not small for one who has been associated with two German and two American universities.

It was a fascinating experience to catalog the Festschrift compiled on the occasion of the seventieth birthday of my revered teacher of Greek literature, Konrat Ziegler, all the more appreciated when I received a letter from him in response to my congratulatory note.

It would be easy for me to add many other instances when personal acquaintance or friendship gave additional flavor to the already absorbing cataloging work. Such is, of course, not the rule, but rather the exception in a day's work. Instead of being distracting, personal associations keep subject cataloging from becoming monotonous or routine and contribute to the mental alertness so vital to subject analysis.

If someone belonging to a later generation of subject catalogers in, say, a decade or so should come across these personal notes, he might have a condescending smile for someone who put so much emphasis on the personal and human element in his cataloging work at a time when armies of computers were about to converge on the library world. It is entirely possible, and even desirable, that some technical details in the subject cataloging process one day be entered on punch-cards or magnetic tape and be turned over to computers. Subject analysis, however, will remain a task for which, I am sure, humans will not be displaced by machines.

REFERENCES

1. *Library Resources & Technical Services*, 1:147. Fall 1957.
2. January 15, 1965, p. 68.
3. Sichel, Pierre. *The Jersey Lily; the Story of the Fabulous Mrs. Langtry.* Englewood Cliffs, N. J., Prentice-Hall, 1958. *Idem. The Jersey Lily; a Novel Based on the Life of Lily Langtry.* London, W. H. Allen, 1958.

57 Ways of Keeping a Serials Librarian Happy

Clara D. Brown

A serials librarian usually takes the position because she sees in it a challenge and little does she know how well she has chosen. The famous pickle slogan "57 varieties" doesn't begin to cover the number of complications confronting her. The ramifications of publishers, dealers, mail, continual changes of personnel, claiming missing numbers, checking in of titles all combine to keep a serials librarian's life anything but a routine job. No matter how well she has established a title, such far-reaching factors as wars, revolutions, printers and dock strikes, and burning buildings throw the title out of kilter at any moment

Serials have joined the "explosion groups." The "pill" cannot be administered to serials. New titles come into being daily, and old ones split into two or three or even into twenty sections more than there were last month.

Another facet of this sheer bulk shows when a title changes name and the publisher says that if you would just read your magazine you would have found the announcement that it would change title with such and such a number (most likely right in the middle of a volume and it probably changed size too). This helps serials librarians, catalogers, the binders and patrons. We all have our share of challenge. You usually report back to the publisher that you would be happy to read his journal, but you also have 15,999 other titles to check in, and besides, are librarians supposed to be reading at work?

In fact, reading one's first and second class mail is enough to keep one's rapid reading habits in order. Aside from the usual invoices, your mail is a staggering mountain of pleas to make generous contributions to the blind, the boy's camps, the democratic party, the republican party, various religious organizations, etc. All good causes. You can aid projects by contacting a friend or a student who would benefit by this membership or that type of journal. You can fulfill your missionary urge by saving the birds, the redwoods, the races, helping needy individuals and helpless animals. Again all good causes. You are honored by being called a specialist and you receive invitations to attend institutes and work-shops for astronomy, nuclear physics, education, music, literature, social welfare. You are invited to attend dinners, hundreds of miles away in honor of historical, political, musical and scientific individuals. I have often wondered what would happen if one really appeared at these meetings.

Many things happen to the mail. Numbers go astray. Sometimes they manage this all by themselves regardless of proper addresses. Other times the numbers start out with addresses so mixed or so vague that they are apt to wind up in the President's office or perhaps in the janitor's waste basket.

One sad story of the hazardous trips of books was one package that fell into the bilge of the hold of the boat. It was brought in on the far end of a ten foot pole. We relegated it to the farthest, least frequented part of the department. We had to keep it there months before the publishers sent other copies and gave us permission to discard the water-logged copies.

Still another problem was created when the weather got so cold that all the address labels fell off the packages in transit. Another crisis when we couldn't get an invoice although the publisher insisted he had sent it. Months later it straggled in, dirty and forlorn, with a stamp on its dirty face, "Salvaged from a wreck in Shannon."

Let's turn to frequencies. There's no end of combinations to be utilized. There's the 00 number, the 1½ number. Occasionally there is more than enough material for a regular number, so we

SOURCE: Reprinted from *Stechert-Hafner Book News* XXIII, 6 (February 1969), pp. 81-84, by permission of the author and the publisher.

get 001, 002. There are the numbers that mix up sequences and pagination and sometimes dates. There is the title "published every once in a while." There is the title not published consecutively. There is the "Quarterly" that takes four years to make a volume. There is the "Quarterly" that brings forth a letter from the publisher that "it is difficult to imagine how the 'Quarterly' could be more irregular than it already is, but there is the possibility." There is the title that the publisher assures you is an annual, and that you are up-to-date, even though the last number is six years old, and that they have no idea when the next year will be published. One title calls its even numbers bulletins and its odd numbers publications. Here you have situations "well calculated to keep you in suspense."

Let us take the subject of publishers. We laugh at them, weep with them, cuss them. Sometimes, publishers can be ornery. They won't work through a dealer; you can't subscribe direct, but they will send out an announcement when it is to be published. So! among your 9,999 bits and pieces of publishers' announcements and renewals that come in the mail, your morale is kept aloft and your ingenuity is kept alert to remember which of your 16,000 titles must be ordered in this way. Of course you have your Direct renewal file but, you are left with the prospect of getting this guessing game together. "It's nice work if you can do it, and you can do it if you try." Sometimes publishers don't approve of some action taken in some other area of the campus or government. This brings down on your head such letters as the following:

"We are cancelling your subscription . . . We are not accepting trade from institutions we know to have money from the C.I.A. or the armed services for research on chemical and germ warfare . . . we know how tiny our flailing against such powers must appear . . ."

Add to this the information that you still should be getting the publication and you find the only way available is to pick up odd numbers in second hand catalogs. There you have it! This should be good for a real challenge in time, and completion of files.

If this doesn't keep you at a high pitch of interest, how about this approach?

"The accompanying stat (sic) of May 23, which indicated a subscription on an 'until forbidden' basis explains the puzzlement . . . We do not accept this sort of thing; therefore the subscription was never entered. . . .

This must be paid in advance and many great libraries from coast to coast do just this, from Harvard to Huntington, and all shades in between . . . we ask only that you accept them on faith . . . There is no other way to get the books than this from us, really . . . I am not painting anything but a frank picture of our systems . . . We cannot have different rules for any subscriber, though I well know these rules of ours are anything but business-like. But that's what they are . . ."

Another publisher announces,

"A single subscription cost is $2.00 a year. The subscription year runs from October, through the following September. It costs the same if ordered at a later date. We have no back issues. Payments must accompany the order. We do not send invoices."

There are publishers that have offices in several countries, and send pro-forma invoices that are supposed to be ignored and you must wait for another office to send the real invoice. That's a tricky one until you realize what is happening. I am wondering how many libraries who do not keep accurate financial records pay twice.

A long distance phone call resulted in the information that the main office of the publication was in Denver, the billing office was in Oklahoma City and we were supposed to claim missing numbers from Jackson, Mississippi.

We also have publishers who use the same book as a separate publication as well as numbering it perhaps volume 2 in one series and volume 10 in another, and still volume 20 in another. Either you buy three copies or you flag down all your cards. This guessing game is good for all sorts of combinations. Another variation of this is to bring out a new edition with only a few words differently edited, or better still use the same book with two different titles. A third point in case is that of a "separate" edition being reprinted with a cover containing a volume and number of a magazine.

Publishers have their troubles, too. One post card tells us.

"On Friday night . . . the printing plant . . . burned to the ground. Fortunately we have galley of the autumn issue . . . and the company will reprint in another plant. But there will be a delay and we beg your patience and understanding."

Another letter says:

"Through a combination of circumstances which even your associate editor and printers do not fully understand, several hundred copies of the November, 1965 issue . . . contain an extra page of international political science totally unrelated to any other copy appearing in the magazine.

The orphaned columns of type begin and end on page 26, sandwiched between a reprint from the September 9, 1965 issue . . .

No editor has lived who does not have somewhere hidden in his scrapbook of experiences similar goofs which have blighted his publication and embarrassed his professional pride.

Most of you, I know, will forgive this slip. Those who cannot, or will not, have my permission to take a turn at manufacturing the next issue."

Publishers can be kind. One publisher says, "I see that you have lost an issue. Here is mine . . . I must apologize for the condition it is in, my Boxer knocked it off the table and walked on it several times before I noticed it . . ."

From far away, publishers heard of our local chlorine tanks disaster, and one kind publisher wrote:

"I read in the papers about the great tragedy which has befallen your country. Please accept my deepest sympathy . . ."

Another retired publisher got busy with a book and

"therefore have no time to attend to the final publication of the remaining issues, though a great number of them are almost ready for printing. I know that other university libraries are waiting too, for the rest of the series and, feel most uncomfortable about it, I have in mind to send the issues when ready free of charge . . . So please understand my dilemma and excuse . . ."

Publishers have their troubles. One delay resulted when an editor moved from Buffalo to Texas and the result was a temporary loss of the mailing list. The list was finally found though it was not known whether it was complete for the most recent subscribers. Still another move resulted in a dilemma. "We have lost two issues in the move and these are not recoverable at this date." Another tag-end slip of paper came in: "We have had troubles!—with copy, proof, printing— everything!"

It takes from one month to eight years to get a subscription started and as long to get it cancelled. The bigger the variety of material in your file the more challenge in getting it started and keeping it coming. Congresses are held every four or five years and it takes two to three years to get them published. Supplements are as variable as the weather.

Coupled with subscriptions is the eternal claiming problem. Some publishers keep their back supply of numbers 30, 60 or 90 days, then turn them over to a second-hand dealer, for want of storage space. The cost immediately doubles or trebles. A special challenge is added to claiming, in that almost every dealer has his own claiming forms that he generously sends you. This helps a lot with an ever changing personnel with details compounded. This will keep you on your toes!

If it wasn't for people we could have a right respectable set of routines that should work. Add people and you have again new worlds to conquer. Of course, this is no different in Serials than the rest of the Library, or industry for that matter. But the eternal change of personnel multiplies the human element already allied to publishers, dealers, mail clerks and you can compound the errors to defy anyone finally getting the titles on the shelves and ready for the patrons.

Computers lend a hand (maybe two or three) in challenging the Serials approach. If you order two copies, you invariably end up with four copies. If you try to clear them up, you wind up with no copies. One computer remained stubborn for three months sending nothing; then it relented and sent two copies of the April issue in every mail that came in, until we decided the publication was multiplying like rabbits and we had better leave the department to the busy, busy title, when at last it settled down. But the January, February and March issues still remained lacking and created a special problem since they were already out-of-print. There is also the problem of returning duplicate copies, which come in for no good reason except the computer has an old and a new address plate.

Computers (or is it personnel) get so automatic that they send out annual questionnaires asking you what business you are in, when all the time it says right in the address that you are a University Library. They also fail to take into account that invoices should include the series and volume number. Instead they blithely give you an author and title of the individual book. This may be good for a couple of letters, or a search through the publisher's catalog. This is just meant to take up any slack time you may have left.

Certainly the human touch is lost in computers. We still have remaining, a touch of the human element in a few instances. One publisher has been sending a general publication to India for years, charging us for it, and in return the Indian establishment sends us the title we want. This was all due to the fact that we wanted the Indian publication very much, they wouldn't sell it and they didn't like anything we had to offer on exchange. The same obliging dealer sends typewriter ribbons to a publisher in Latin America for another title.

What we don't get is Serials! I am soon to retire with 36 slim 4 inch pencils that were meant for signing renewals; an inch high abacus, a set of tools the same size as well as a toy flashlight; two aluminum coins; a tiny hour-glass. All items were used in notifying us about expirations. The stamps and pennies went into the kitty for buying replacements. We have received paper that dissolves and ink that disappears, paper that is glass. I planted the redwood seeds, but after growing a foot high the trees died.

The renewal notices themselves tell a graphic picture of advertising and imagination. According to these renewals subscriptions get "killed," "bitten," "come to the end of the line," "challenged," are on their "final performance" and "missed the train." The challenge comes in with the publisher's policy of sending at least 4 to 6 notices blatantly announcing on the notices which one you are receiving, when all the time you had taken care of the renewal with a " 'til forbidden" subscription letter and paid the invoice when it came. But the policy is to send out six notices regardless. Try and explain in two minutes to your superiors. There you have a challenge.

Try explaining to an irate patron why you do not have a copy which he has seen on a news stand. There are several good legitimate reasons for not having it.

A point in nonreceipt is the publisher's habit of publishing regularly for years and years and then fooling everyone with a double number (just once in a while). The first time it is done is the catch and the challenge.

History plays many funny tricks on Serials. Wars, revolutions, change of a regime of government, all create an interest in serials and a lack in publications. The more war-torn the country, the less interest and time the people of the country have in cultural pursuits, and the more the clientele want the publications of that country. *La Prensa* of Buenos Aires is a good example. The original owners were exiled, Peron got the money and libraries lost out on their subscriptions.

World War II played such havoc on Serials that the challenge was endless. One kind letter told us:

"RE your kind entry of the 4th inst. we regret to inform you that most of the parts . . . wanted in your library are either out-of-print or destroyed by war actions . . ."

"The reason that you did not get any information or address from the former dealer and of our uncertainty of procuring the mentioned parts is related with the fact that all rests of the titles are hidden elsewhere in the part of Germany, occupied by the Russians. As they are not legalized by the occupiers all contact with the contactman is very difficult as this has to be done in secret and the parts have to be smuggled over the interzone frontier.

"Therefore if you want to have the offered parts, please let us know by return of mail and we shall do our utmost to get them as soon as possible."

The final outcome on this story was that the parts we got so laboriously were burned on the binder's truck. So! We started all over. How's that for a challenge.

Another World War II challenge was created when the original editor was deposed, and when he resumed publication after the war he ignored all that had been published during the war and went right on from where he left off. There you have several volumes with the numbers duplicated but, with different years. More challenge!

German Bibliography is another good point in question. After World War II both East and West Germany started up the old editions of German bibliography each claiming to be the continuation of the old bibliography. Since each edition contains different materials, it is necessary to get both. (For the long, involved variation of the story about German National Bibliographies, see Library Resources and Technical Services, volume 5, number 4, pp. 310-14. Wilhelm Moll. German National Bibliographies.)

Little Magazines! The challenges are endless here. Do you have someone with whom you can share these goodies? Pretty selfish for you to keep them all to yourself. One little magazine changed its name, format, and what-have-you after a "long and illustrious career" of 8 numbers. Most of the titles are illusive, short runs lead to them being out-of-print immediately. The contents are dull, witty, sprightly and smutty. These editors are a very individual group of people with no rhyme or reason about their business affairs. A very unusual approach woke us up, cheered us and created challenge with number 1 called Now, number 2 called Now, Now, number 3 called Now, Now, Now. This gives the Serials Librarian a continual source of challenge and joy.

For a final challenge you are told that results are wanted not excuses. Now there is something to give you all the challenge you need. Figure out how to get a volume into the library that looks like it should have been published 3 or 4 years ago, but isn't yet published, probably still waiting for funds to publish, will probably run into any one or all the previous frustrations and you should be right in your element.

Combine all these variations of possibilities and happenings and prices and dates of publications to the fact that almost everyone expects you to run along quite automatically regarding receipt of a title. You are asked if periodicals are necessary.

You are told that you are the tail that is wagging the dog (in the case of funds). Others assure you that the tail may very well become the dog. All this should give you enough challenges for any one person or department.

There is one consolation. Your name will be perpetuated for years and years on address labels long after you have ceased to be interested in serials, and people will ask who is such and such a person? Get married before you leave and you will leave two more frustrations or challenges.

Discussions on a National Serials Data Program

Donald Johnson and
Samuel Lazerow

The National Serials Pilot Project

Donald Johnson

MR. JOHNSON: Sixteen months ago today, I became director of the National Serials Pilot Project. Since then, I would like to believe, much has been accomplished; not everyone agrees with me on that point, but I will cheerfully acknowledge some small degree of prejudice.

Before proceeding, perhaps some background would be in order.

In April 1964, the Committee on Scientific and Technical Information (COSATI) created a special task force to study ways to improve the processing and utilization of journal literature. Its work prompted the National Science Foundation in April 1965 to award a study contract to the Information Dynamics Corporation whose report proposed a serials data program for science and technology.

The directors of the three national libraries subsequently agreed to undertake the National Serials Data Program. Work on the early phases of this program was performed by the Library of Congress.

In May 1969, the U.S. National Libraries' Task Force on Automation and Other Cooperative Services was authorized by the directors to seek funds for a serials pilot project. The Association of Research Libraries agreed to administer such a project on behalf of the three national libraries, under policy direction by the Task Force.

We began with funding for one year, generously provided as a grant by the National Agricultural Library. With the exhaustion of those funds, financial support is being continued through June 1971 by the Council on Library Resources, the Library of Congress, the National Agricultural Library and the National Library of Medicine. As of June 30, 1971, the National Serials Pilot Project, as such, will be terminated and direct involvement of the ARL will cease; it is expected, however, that the ARL will continue to influence the later stages of the National Serials Data Program on behalf of its members.

At the outset, there were three major questions to be resolved:

1) How to define and limit our area of activity;
2) How to record our data;
3) How to obtain the necessary machine time?

Each of these, of course, implied other questions.

It was decided that we should limit ourselves primarily to live scientific and technical serials, since these would be of interest to all three national libraries, but that we should not exclude all ceased titles. We were to build a machine-readable file containing bibliographic data on such serials and were to include the holdings of each of the three national libraries for each title entered in our files. Holdings were to be reported to us by each of the three national libraries from checklists supplied to them by us at periodic intervals.

As for the manner of recording the data, we elected to employ the MARC serials format; since we were the first to make use of it, and since we were working with the Library of Congress, we thus became an effective field test for it.

Finally, as to machine time, the National Library of Medicine offered its 360/50 for our use. Because we are using remote-access typewriter terminals (ATS), however, and because the NLM computer is not equipped to receive such input, we are also using a 360/40 at the Library of Con-

SOURCE; Reprinted from the Association of Research Libraries, "Minutes of the Seventy-Seventh Meeting 17, 1971, Los Angeles, California," pp. 11-21, by permission of the Association of Research Libraries.

gress. Our terminals are linked by telephone lines to the LC computer; each week our input data are read onto a magnetic tape, which is then processed on the NLM computer. Although we are in on-line mode with the LC computer, we are really in a one-batch-per-week mode on the NLM machine. For practical purposes, then, our entire system is batch mode.

A caveat en passant: our COBOL programs, which are still incomplete, require main-frame storage for about 160,000 characters of instruction; were we to have time to complete them, we estimate that the programs alone would equal or exceed 185,000 characters of instruction, exclusive of data. Since few 360/30's or 360/40's approach such size, the significance of this is that you may require the size and power of a 360/50 if you are to use the MARC serials format and if your programs are to be written in COBOL. Storage requirements can, of course, be reduced by programming in assembly language, or by effectively resectioning the program package.

Our hardware configuration imposes certain restraints upon us. For example, we have character set limitations. It is true that our typewriter terminals can be used to produce character codes that the terminals, themselves, do not possess; it is true that the Library of Congress computer has an expanded character set which permits printing of almost all modified letters in the Roman alphabet; but it is also true that the National Library of Medicine computer lacks such an expanded character set. So we grappled with the problem of modified letters: we could input them, with some difficulty and with increases in time and costs, but we could not output them on either our terminals or on the computer used to process our data. Moreover, were we to code for them, numerous program changes or additions would be required so that the modified letters would be output on the NLM computer as unmodified letters, i.e., the computer would have to be instructed what to do each time it encountered a special code. In view of these considerations, we decided that in our special circumstances the modifications of letters had best be ignored.

Then we had to decide whether to input in upper case only or in upper case and in lower case. It was decided that the upper/lower case combination left us more options and was, in any event, more pleasing to the eye. I do not have statistical data to support my opinion, but I would guess that this decision has come near to doubling our costs. Consider: Our bibliographers must scan

character by character and indicate for our editors which letters are to be capitalized; our MARC editors must repeat this scan; our input operators must be alert to editorial indicators for caps, and in revising we must once again study each character. In addition, only one of the two available printers has an upper- and lower-case print train. This sometimes delays the running of our jobs. Then, too, printing time is effectively doubled. Finally, far more inconsistencies result in our file, because our sources of bibliographic data are by no means internally or externally consistent in such matters as capitalization. Upper and lower case output is undeniably preferable, all other things being equal and/or cost not being a factor. Our experience indicates that upper and lower case input and output is simply too costly unless very special circumstances obtain.

The next major question we faced was whether to build our file from the holdings records of the three national libraries, base it on one or more published lists, or obtain a machine-readable file and reformat it. Since we are working with the three national libraries and would be concerned with their holdings, basing our file on their serial records had some appeal, but we were to limit ourselves to scientific and technical serials. These would first have to be identified in the various serials files: no small matter. Besides, those serials files are in constant use by many people.

Working from an established list had some merit, but why could we not select an established list available to us on magnetic tape and reformat it? Would this not spare us a lot of key input?

So we examined the possibilities for reformatting. The National Science Library of Canada, hearing of our project, had offered tapes of the *Union List of Scientific Serials in Canadian Libraries*, Third Edition. We decided to accept its kind offer.

It took us seven months to reformat this list to our ATS output format, and then the reformatting was not complete. There are, after all, significant differences in machine-readable files, and some of these differences cannot be overcome via programming. In reformat programming, one must be able to identify data elements in the file being reformatted and equate them with data elements in the file to be created. But sometimes identifiers are lacking in the input file for needed data elements. In such cases, the computer cannot be instructed so that it can find what is wanted. There is no way to tell the computer what subfields are present or where they begin and end; there is no way to program into the reformatting such things as primary and secondary indicators, necessary things if you are using MARC; there is no way that a reformat program can identify and encode fixed-field data. This is not to indicate faults in the Canadian list; in my opinion, it is simply not possible to convert from a non-MARC format to MARC via reformat programming alone. Another point: to be really useful to us in reducing key input, the reformatted file would have to be directly accessible by our terminals, and in our case this was not possible. In view of our special circumstances, I would have to say that the decision to reformat was a mistake. We would have made more progress at less cost had we simply taken the bound volume of the Canadian list and worked from there. Given other circumstances, however, my view might be different.

It should be noted parenthetically that one simply does not take liberties with a complex format; one may neither substitute nor change it, although one may add to it. This is especially true of MARC. If changes or substitutions are made in MARC by a library, its file is likely to be incompatible with other MARC files. That would hardly be the way to arrive at a standard format.

Although we have made no alterations in the basic MARC format or in the meanings of its tags, subfields, indicators, and the like, we have made some additions which might be of interest. MARC records carry a machine-provided date-entered-on-file; this is changed each time any change is made in a record. It seemed to us that in a serials file it could be important to have such dates on a field-by-field basis, and so we added a subfield to each variable field. This additional subfield contains the date that that particular data element was last entered or updated.

We also felt that we should be able to trace our data back to the authority we accepted for that data and its form; and so we created an additional subfield for each variable field. In this we enter a numeric code that tells us which of (so far) 28 sources was our authority for that data element. Lest this number startle or surprise, I hasten to add that 17 of these 28 sources are files in the three national libraries.

Since I have mentioned sources, it would be well to add that we accept LC authorities as primary (but not as sole) authority for choice of entry and form. In many ways, being able to use what must be the largest and most complete authority files in the world is to our advantage. But the LC practice known as superimposition creates problems for us.

One of the differences between the *Anglo-American Code* and previous cataloging practice relates to entry under place. The change in this respect created problems for all libraries, but especially for one as large as the Library of Congress. There was just no feasible way for LC to make all the necessary changes in authority files. So, entries for newly established corporate headings are made in accordance with the new rules, while headings previously established according to the old rules co-exist in the same files. Previously established headings for corporate bodies are not changed unless the name of the corporate body is, itself, changed. For us, the result is one of our compatibility problems.

In the recording of holdings, it occurred to us that the usual and conventional methods might not be best for our purposes. For one thing, in a large machine file the increase in file space would be prohibitive even if only a very few libraries were to be represented. For another thing, conventional methods for representation of holdings data would imply continuous updating, and, if our data were to be reliable, this means permanent formal reporting of all changes in holdings by each participating library. It would be naive to suppose that such an arrangement, even if it could be established, would last for long or would be equally well honored by all participating libraries. Therefore, we developed a very simple system for encoding holdings data for each library. In a special subfield (another of our additions to MARC) we enter a 0 if the extent of the library's holdings is not known; a 1 if its holdings are complete or substantially complete; a 2 if its holdings are substantially incomplete; a 3 if a title is held for a limited time only; or a 4 if it is received by the library but not held at all.

Staffing has been a problem for us. We are engaged simultaneously in two rather esoteric fields: electronic data processing and the serial literature. It would be too much to expect to be able to recruit people qualified in both these areas. So we have had to recruit for one field or the other and then supply the rest via training. The result is a highly skilled staff, each member of which can, in a very real sense, be thought of as an expert. We do not believe that our recruiting and training problems are unique. If you contemplate serials automation, you can also expect to encounter them and had best allow for training time in your scheduling. It is not a small factor. If not accurately calculated, it can wreck your schedules and cost estimates.

Despite all the cooperation we have had from the three national libraries, the National Libraries Task Force on Automation and Other Cooperative Services, the Council on Library Resources, and others, it must be admitted that our operation falls far short of ideal as a system. This is certainly not anyone's fault. But those of you who have automated operations where you share with others a computer facility, and perhaps supportive staff, can attest that such things as priorities (and libraries are usually low on the list), machine downtime, and the like, can become a major source of frustration. Consider, then, our set-up: typewriter terminals in our offices which can, and do, malfunction; telephone transmission in which background noise can alter the input signal; two computers, each heavily used, in two different agencies, two different locations 19 miles apart, and even within two different branches of the federal government. Add to all that the fact that we cannot directly access our master file, and you have a picture of a system wherein many components are involved and over which we have control of none. Hardly ideal. But one does not seek ideals in a pilot project: one merely tries to cope. Ideally, a library going into automation should have at least some degree of control over the men and machinery upon which it must depend. Certainly, the very minimum is guaranteed time year-round.

We have made progress. We have succeeded in demonstrating the technical and economic feasibility of a national serials data bank; we have field-tested the MARC serials format; we have created a base for standard serial numbers and, perhaps, for international standard serial numbers; in working with the National Serials Pilot Project, the three national libraries have reached higher levels of cooperation, and they have committed themselves to continuing the National Serials Data Program as a permanent operation.

By June 30, 1971, we will be delivering to each of the three national libraries copies of all our files (including our master file and both reformatted files received by us), copies of all programs used by us, detailed documentation of our automated systems, manuals of our procedures, and a final report summarizing our experiences, observations, and recommendations. These will then be used by the three national libraries in such ways as they see fit in the National Serials Data Program.

The National Serials Pilot Project was never expected to produce either immediate or direct benefits to the library community, and indeed it has not. But, as Phase Two of the National Serials Data Program, it has been a success, and the Program will, therefore, go forward. No one can predict with certainty the ways in which the National Serials Data Program will benefit all of us, but most will agree that the potential is there. As we move into Phase Three, many questions remain unresolved. Among these is the question: what do we want and/or need from it? You may be able to assist in providing the answer.

The National Serials System: Concept and Commitment

Samuel Lazerow

MR. LAZEROW: In June 1967, the national libraries set up their cooperative program. There were three major objectives announced at that time. One of these was the development of a national data bank of machine-readable information about serials.

From the beginning, therefore, the U.S. National Libraries Task Force on Automation has assigned a high priority to serials. It assisted in the development of the MARC serials format and it recommended to the directors of the three national libraries the establishment of a national serials system, the primary objective of which would be "to provide to qualified requestors in the U.S. timely access to appropriate portions of the world's serial literature." A pilot project leading to a national serials center was proposed, with the initial data base limited to scientific and technical serials, including new titles in the three national libraries, or to some segment of this universe, such as newly published scientific serials in English.

The Task Force saw a variety of potential products and services possible from a national serials system. The concept was entirely a "national" rather than a "federal" system, built from subsystems now operating more or less autonomously, and presupposing a partnership of the public and private sectors, the academic and scientific communities, the publishers and distributors, and the libraries and secondary services.

In response, the directors asked the Task Force to develop a proposal for the National Serials Pilot Project. Submitted in May 1969, this proposal was aimed at production of a union list of the live scientific and technical serials held at each of the three national libraries.

The directors approved this recommendation and arranged with the Association of Research Libraries to operate the Pilot Project through a grant from the National Agricultural Library, with policy direction from the Task Force.

The national library directors last reviewed the Pilot Project situation on November 5. They agreed to provide joint support to the project for the remainder of fiscal 1971, with some help, if necessary, from the Council on Library Resources. At that time it was agreed that:

> Toward the completion of the ARL project, the three national libraries will review the continuing work that needs to be done in further development of a National Serials Data Program, including the relationship to progress in the application of the Standard Serial Number and plans for the administration of the International Standard Serial Number. Based on approval of a program that would attempt to use the data base and essential elements of the system developed by the ARL, the National Serials Data Program will continue development at the Library of Congress during FY 1972 at a minimum level of support of $72,000 for the year and perhaps in conjunction with an SSN project and/or ISSN administration.

On July 1, therefore, when the Project's developmental work and its documentation are transferred to the Library of Congress, we expect to go forward along the following lines, to the degree that financial resources permit:

1) On the basis of our evaluation of the content of the data base and the Project's findings, we shall expand this data base to include the remainder of the live scientific and technical titles held by the three national libraries. We would also hope by this time to be applying a unique identification code (SSN) to titles in this retrospective data base.

2) We hope to be able to enlarge the data base further by adding to it all new titles (regardless of subject), to which we shall, of course, assign SSN's. Procedurally, it makes little sense to begin building a machine-readable data bank while still allowing new titles to be added to the unconverted universe. We have already requested funds for this aspect of the project and hope to have them in hand by July 1.

3) We shall further expand the data base, as resources permit, and as conversion priorities dictate, to include all serials. This expansion, however, certainly has to be regarded as long-range and as requiring large amounts of money.

Our planning is based on the concept of a centralized, integrated national serials data base. Because of the nonstandardization of bibliographic data within the library community, a centralized editorial operation is necessary. In an integrated system, one must depend upon the largest contributor, which for this enterprise is the Library of Congress. Thus, this largest block of data, i.e., the LC data, becomes the standard against which other data are adjusted. It follows logically then that entries into the system from other sources must be checked against this central LC data store, and editorial decisions made to bring about a consistent data base. Actually, this is analogous to the present *New Serial Titles* process wherein the majority of the reports come from LC and other libraries' data are searched against the LC input. I should mention that there has been considerable debate within the Task Force on this issue; LC feels that in the long run this policy will prove the most productive for the research library community.

In addition, there are certain purely bibliographic issues which have received considerable attention. These are not new issues; they have been encountered many times by those engaged in centralized processing operations or the development of union lists. They are "library" problems and have little to do with automation per se, except that a computer is a slave to consistency and file inconsistencies will show up faster and present more problems in a machine-based operation.

The first of these bibliographic issues is the problem of choice of entry. There are some who contend that in a machine-based system it makes little difference as to which entry is chosen as main entry, and in a theoretical sense perhaps they are right. However, we're going to have to live with printed products for a time, and it is this factor that makes entry important. It will be necessary to determine the order in which the master record is to be printed so that adequate referencing may be provided. Our plan is to input the LC main entry (again, because LC has the most comprehensive file of data for input), with cross-references pointing toward this entry. If there is no LC entry for a serial title, we will accept the entry given by other contributors, adjusting it if it conflicts with the data already entered into the data base. Again, this argues for continuing centralized editorial control.

A second bibliographic problem concerns the form of name used. In accordance with our concept of a centralized system, the LC form of name will be input when LC has established the name. This raises, of course, the question of how much of a name authority structure can be brought into the data base; the answer, to which studies now underway at LC will contribute substantially, seems to be the creation of a machine-readable central authority file to be used for all forms of material.

Another critical bibliographic problem, and one which is not yet resolved, concerns what, in library jargon, is known as the "successive entry" (or "split entry") vs. "single entry" issue. This is directly related to the assignment of the SSN. When a serial changes its name, is it considered as two serials, and hence should there be two records, each having its own SSN? Or is it still considered as one serial, and entered as one record under its latest name with a note as to its former name? Library practice varies. Before the *Anglo-American Rules*, most large research libraries would have cataloged the item as one record under its latest name; now libraries following the *AA Rules* would set up each name change as a separate record.

In building our data bank, several options are available:

1) Successive entry for all titles is a noble objective, perhaps, but this would mean in actuality that LC and other large research libraries would have to recatalog retrospective titles—a task that is certainly not realistic in economic or production terms.

2) Assign the SSN and input records on a successive entry basis from a designated current date on, but leave retrospective titles as they are (i.e., under latest title). This approach has much to recommend it, if libraries are willing to live with this inconsistency in SSN assignment methodology.

3) Enter every item under the latest title, and assign the SSN on basis of entity. This, however, would be inconsistent with the *AA Rules*.

4) Enter records under latest titles but assign the SSN to all former titles cited in the record and use a cross-reference structure for tracing purposes. Desirable as this alternative may seem, we must explain that this approach presents difficulties in showing relationships between several titles and SSN's within the same machine-readable record.

Another issue to be resolved is the level or amount of bibliographic information to be input. Should the content of the data base be limited only to the minimal information required for identification? We seem to have discerned the requirement for research libraries that at the very least the machine record should not carry less information than is in our present manual files. At this juncture, our view is that we should input as much of the available data as possible. This, of course, presents maintenance problems, and it may be possible to continually update on a systematic basis only those minimal elements (perhaps six) necessary for identification purposes.

We move then to the question of the feasibility of showing the location of holdings in the data base, and the degree of detail that can economically be tolerated at the national level. As to this issue, I can only tell you that we have reached no final decision. There are enormous economic constraints involved in the recording and updating of holdings in machine-readable records at the local, regional and national levels. We regard this, therefore, as a problem which we must resolve soon.

I am not going to burden you with detail about more problems except to say that they are sizeable, and that they have had and will continue to have our earnest attention. Some of them are not solvable unless we are willing to take some sharp departures from existing practices.

Ideally, in my view, a national serials system should function from one central source, with data from the three national libraries and from other sources flowing into the central facility. The data would be verified at the central source for conformity to the standard input. The SSN would be assigned at the time of input, and the tie-in with the international system would be achieved at this point also.

I must stress that the ultimate outlines of this national serials system cannot be finally determined at this juncture. While it may be unrealistic to expect the research library community to tell us in precise terms exactly what it wants from a mechanized serial file, the final designers have to know more about these expectations than is now known, and they have to be able to count on substantial financial support in order to begin a functioning system.

It is also unrealistic to expect solutions to come easily. Our experience has demonstrated that there is difficulty in constructing a consistent data base even when only three libraries (i.e., LC, NAL and NLM) are involved, a difficulty inevitably resulting from the differences in cataloging practices and policies among libraries, and this problem will be compounded, of course, when other data bases are merged eventually into the system. I believe that the goal of compatibility is more likely to be achieved if we are willing to make some compromises within our individual serials controls to achieve that compatibility.

The difficulty in which we find ourselves today comes from years of building individual files according to our individual patterns. For the first time, however, we now have a standard for a machine format. With this as a beginning, surely librarians should be able to push ahead to the goal of compatibility in serials control standards in order to achieve the service objectives all of us seek.

It is becoming plainer every day that the universe of serials has become too large and too diverse to be treated much longer by conventional patterns of control. The national libraries have taken the position that the machine-readable serials file offers an opportunity, which we must not lose, to input the data quickly, uniformly, and systematically. I believe that we can find the resources and make the decisions that will enable us to escalate this effort. We have to, because it is in the national interest to assign a high priority to the automation of serials controls.

IV

COOPERATIVE AND CENTRALIZED PROCESSING ENDEAVORS

In recent years librarians have felt the weight of a number of growing pressures—a worldwide increase in publishing, a vast expansion of area studies, a rise in manpower costs, a scarcity of staff adept in language or subject specialties and at the same time skilled in the technical processes, a clamor for early availability of a wide range of research materials, and a knowledgeable impatience with duplicative and wasteful procedures.

A foreseeable result has been the development of numerous efforts to coordinate activities ranging from the acquisition of materials from "hard-to-come by" areas to the cooperative storage and bibliographic control of lesser-used materials to a program of centralized acquisitions and cataloging on demand of current research materials. Federal and State support for education at all levels has been a considerable force for centralization of library activity also. The following selections chronicle these developments and are concluded with a description of the growing role of the Library of Congress in this area during the decade of the 1960's.

Retrospect and Prospect

Verner W. Clapp

The remark (variously traced to Victor Hugo and to Ralph Waldo Emerson[1]) that there is no stopping an idea whose time has come might well have been prompted by the subject of this issue of *Library Trends*. For the day of centralized/cooperative processing seems to be here at last, and there is no stopping it.

Yet its time might have come so often before! So many and so valiant have been the efforts that might have assisted it into being! Most of these efforts proved resounding failures; a few, great successes; but never before now (if even now) have all the needed elements been assembled in a measure adequate for success. Indeed, what most impresses the observer as he looks back over the long history of centralized/cooperative processing, is not the emergence of the idea—this has inflamed many imaginations over nearly two centuries—but the slow and arduous process by which the enabling conditions have been gradually recognized and gradually achieved. One is led to wonder whether even now we are capable of recognizing the important elements for the future development of these services, so as to enable us to seek the conditions that will assure their presence. If the survey presented in this issue of *Library Trends* should assist toward such a diagnosis and such a search, it will have justified itself.

Accordingly, let us look at the various attempts at centralized/cooperative processing with a view to seeing why some of them failed and why others succeeded.

The story of the first great attempt at cooperative cataloging in modern times, that of the French revolutionary government, still moves us both for its idealism and its naïveté.[2] By decrees of the Constituent Assembly in December 1790 and May 1791 measures were prescribed for the custody and preservation of books and other literary treasures which had been nationalized as a result of the Revolution and which were being held in local depots throughout the country. The local authorities were required to catalog—on playing cards, no less—the books in their custody, to arrange the cards alphabetically, and to forward them to Paris where they were to be merged to form the basis for a 150-volume *Bibliographie générale et raisonnée de la France* (portentous foreshadowing of the 610-volume pre-1956 National Union Catalog now commencing). By 1794, according to a report made to the National Convention by Henri Grégoire, constitutional bishop of Blois, 1.2 million cards had been assembled in Paris representing 3 million volumes in the depots; but unfortunately most of the depots had reported in notebooks rather than on cards as instructed, and it being impossible to make a single file from notebooks, the project collapsed. We can be sure that it would have collapsed in any event, for quite apart from the political and military situation which was confronting France at the time, the project was bibliographically and bibliothecally premature.

The next great effort was that of the Smithsonian Institution, described by Miss Westby[3] and John M. Dawson[4] as the plan of the Institution's first and great librarian, Charles C. Jewett. (Ironic, that a great librarian should be principally remembered for a failure. But it was a magnificent failure!) This, even by today's standards, was a very sophisticated plan, taking into account the needs and practices both of individual libraries and of the library world as a whole. At its heart, just as at the heart of the French project, was technological innovation. Like the French project it stood or fell with the success or failure of the new technique. In the Smithsonian's case, the innova-

SOURCE: Reprinted from *Library Trends* XVI, 1 (July 1967), pp. 165–175, by permission of the publisher, the University of Illinois Graduate School of Library Science.

tion was an improved stereotype which, though its initial cost was higher than type, was expected to be capable of serving, as a bibliographic unit, for an indefinite number of printings. Unfortunately, the Smithsonian was betrayed by inadequate engineering; the stereos warped, the investment and the project were lost, and centralized cataloging was delayed for another half century.

But not for want of trying! A principal preoccupation of the American Library Association from its founding in 1876 was, as Dawson reminds us, the search for central sources of bibliographic information, for both books and journals.[5] Many were the attempts made during the period to establish a source for book-cataloging information, but for one reason or another none was successful. In the field of periodical indexing greater success was initially obtained by cooperative efforts, but (as Frederick William Poole put it) as the knights left the line they were replaced by retainers and camp followers and the accomplishment that was economically feasible through unpaid cooperation became an impossibility when the services had to be bought.[6]

Miss Westby has also described the important contributions to the work of libraries made by H. W. Wilson and the company which continues his name and his bibliographic empire—invaluable contributions involving both book cataloging and periodical indexing.[7] An important element in Wilson's success was again a technical innovation—the use of the Linotype slug as a bibliographic unit. As many slugs as needed could be made from a single keyboarding of the text, and they could be sorted at will into whatever arrangement might be required. In spite of the technological revolutions that have shaken the printing industry since this innovation was introduced, it continues to serve nearly seventy years later. So far as is known to the present writer, it has never been successfully employed elsewhere. Its basic principle is that of printing itself, namely of making one typesetting or keyboarding serve multiple printings of the same text. This has now of course become a commonplace, and the effect can be achieved by photolithography as well as by tape-driven typewriters and by computers. All of these are currently used in bibliographic publication. But the H. W. Wilson Company has earned our gratitude by adhering to letterpress and to the Linotype slug.

The next great landmark noted by our chroniclers is the commencement of the Library of Congress catalog card distribution service in November 1901. Why did this effort succeed where its predecessors had failed? It is worth noting a number of the elements that favored it, while emphasizing in doing so that they were indeed a number and not just one.

The principal of these elements were: (a) the Library of Congress was acquiring for its own collections a large proportion of the books which were of interest to American libraries generally and for which they would need cataloging data; (b) it was cataloging these books for its own collections and was prepared to bear the full cost of this cataloging; (c) it was cataloging them in accordance with rules which it was at that very moment coordinating with those of the American Library Association; (d) it had adopted the recently standardized 75 × 125 mm. unit card as the building block for its own catalogs; (e) in order to expedite the printing of cards the Librarian of Congress (Herbert Putnam) had arranged for the establishment of a branch of the Government Printing Office in the Library; (f) he was securing enactment of a law authorizing the Library to sell its catalog cards at a price based on the printing of the overrun only; and (g) in charge of the work he had placed Charles Harris Hastings, a man "of remarkable vigor, initiative and intelligence in a work without precedent, full of perplexity, and requiring the utmost patience, labor and ingenuity."[8]

It is probable that there was little margin for error and that every one of these elements was essential for success. Sixty-five years later, when the card sales of the Library of Congress have climbed to fantastic millions per annum (63 millions in 1966), it is almost incredible that the service should ever have been in jeopardy. The fact is nevertheless that more than once its fate hung by hardly more than a thread in a series of cliff-hangers which still await and deserve the telling.

When the LC catalog card distribution service was announced in 1901, it seemed, as Dawson notes above, that centralized cataloging had arrived.[9] Who could forget Melvil Dewey's ringing words at the Waukesha conference?

You remember that when the Pacific railroad was built, and the ends came together to make the connection, a great celebration was held throughout the country, a thrill that the work was at last done; and I feel today, now that we hear in this able report that printed catalog cards are really to be undertaken at the National Library, that what we have waited for over 20 years and what we have been dreaming about has at last come to pass.[10]

But the success of the effort depended ultimately upon whether other libraries found the service sufficiently valuable to be willing to pay for it. They did. Although Metcalf believes that the LC card distribution system "probably cost the libraries of the United States more money than any other single event in library history,"[11] libraries generally appear to have concluded that it saved them money. William S. Dix says that it did.[12] It must be remembered that an LC card is two things: it is a source of bibliographic information which can be used quite independently of the card, and it is a piece of stationery which is useful, among other things, for maintaining a card catalog. This double usefulness has undoubtedly enhanced its money saving capability. In any case, in spite of grumblings, the libraries paid increasingly for the service.

From the beginning LC encouraged and participated in evaluations of the effectiveness of the system. The first of these was made during the very first year of operation;[13] from then through the Richardson, Ladenson, Dawson, and Skipper inquiries[14] the same principal defects were identified. These were (a) delays in service and (b) inadequacy of coverage. Both have been due to circumstances largely outside LC's control, and LC has made continuous and strenuous efforts to correct them.

It may be noted, however, that the importance attached to promptness and wide coverage has tended to absorb attention which might otherwise have been given to other aspects such as quality of cataloging, availability of analytics, etc.[15] Unfortunately, this reversed the proper scale of values, for while the effects of delay and inadequate coverage are limited and temporary, the effects of inferior quality are more likely to be both permanent and pervasive. Accordingly, it is to be hoped that the present great forward surge in the Shared Cataloging Program and the National Acquisitions and Cataloging Program may finally succeed in correcting the defects of delay and coverage, and make it possible to give deserved priority to other matters of even greater importance in the long run.

Accordingly, without exploring the other consequences—no matter how important—of the LC catalog card distribution system, such as the National Union Catalog in both card and book form, we come to the centralized processing centers of the present day. It is easy to see how they, in their turn, have been made possible by a conjunction of technical, bibliographic, legal and fiscal

elements, and of a matching of supply with demand.

All central processing rests on the principle that it is less expensive to do a job once for a number of consumers than separately for each of them. This principle is so obvious and so persuasive that one fully expects it to work in practice, and is somewhat amazed when it fails to do so. But fail it does in the absence of conditions requisite for success. When, for example, a job can be done for individual consumers by volunteer typists using aged typewriters in an ancient rent-free building, it is hardly to be expected that it can be done more cheaply by offset lithography requiring a full-time trained operator using expensive equipment in modern rented office space.

Nevertheless, by the 1950's there were a sufficient number of operations which offered savings through being done once rather than separately to encourage the establishment of numerous centers. Duchac has identified the most important of these operations when he salutes the offset press as the *raison d'être* of processing centers.[16] (Actually, the offset press shares the honors with other reproduction equipment, but the principle obtains nevertheless.[17]) There are, however, other sources of savings, e.g., in consolidation of book orders, in the larger dealers' discounts resulting therefrom, in better use of cataloging information from the central sources, and in activities such as maintaining files of LC proof slips.

If central processing does indeed rest on the reduced-cost principle, we should expect to learn something about the extent of the savings from a survey such as the present. In fact we learn nothing of the kind.

Duchac, it is true, tells us that processing centers have successfully accomplished the purposes for which they were organized, one of which was to effect savings on the cost of books, and he affirms, besides, that they have demonstrated the "economy" of cooperative operations, but he does not particularize.[18] From Miss Vann we get inconclusive evidence. We learn that cost-saving was one of the inducements to membership in a processing center but also that for those who joined and continued their membership the previous cost data is too sparse to be significant, while those who joined but dropped out give the higher cost of the center as one of the reasons for dropping.[19]

Darling, meanwhile, reports that most school library centers appear to be too small to provide "economical central processing."[20] But Hiatt, citing the Southwest Missouri example, states summarily that "the few studies that we have do not support the assumption that cooperative cataloging is necessarily cheaper"[21] and adduces an instance in which it was actually dearer. He adds the seeming paradox that while centralized cataloging may cost more it is likely to accomplish the same level of processing as the independent units.

If the existence of the processing centers is not justified by reduced costs to their users, how then is it justified? Our authors provide suggestions for an answer to this question. Duchac mentions (a) elimination of unnecessary duplication of work, (b) the release of staff from processing time for other activities, and (c) uniformity of cataloging and processing.[22] Miss Vann mentions (a) centralized ordering, (b) the availability of consultative services in cataloging and classification, (c) maintenance of the card catalog, (d) improvement of the catalog, (e) improvement of library services generally, and (f) release of staff time from cataloging to other activities.[23] Miss Westby states simply that the commercial processing centers fill a need, but reports the users of commercial services to be evenly divided between the satisfied and the dissatisfied.[24]

Darling marshals an imposing list of advantages (in addition to the now doubtful item of cost-saving) derived by school libraries from processing centers.[25] These can be summarized as (a) greater promptness and up-to-dateness in the cataloging; (b) improved cataloging, better adapted to local teaching needs; (c) better use of personnel, including release of staff time to reader service and more efficient performance of clerical operations; (d) assurance of good cataloging no matter how small (or even non-existent) the staff and cataloging experience of the library; and finally (e) enhancement of the status of school librarians.

Hiatt lists similar advantages to public libraries from cooperative processing centers (again apart from reduction of costs): (a) the better use of (processing) personnel in short supply; (b) availability of professional (processing) services to libraries not able to afford them independently; (c) release of staff time for reader service; (d) reduced duplication of effort; (e) promotion of desirable uniformity.[26]

There is undoubtedly still another advantage, not included specifically in any of the lists. That is the advantage to the library administrator of being able to get rid of the supervision of a demanding technical activity which is only a means but not an end in itself. It may be conjectured that to obtain this advantage librarians are willing to pay more to have their processing done by others than it would cost if done by themselves, given comparable promptness and quality of cataloging. In fact, 90 percent of those responding told Miss Vann that they would advise others to accept the services which they themselves were receiving, and 60 percent indicated that they would not resume their own cataloging even if the centers' prices were to rise.[27]

Furthermore, although the principal criticisms of central processing are reported to be on the very point of promptness and quality of cataloging, the evidence suggests that more often than not both promptness and quality are superior to what the individual library provided for itself.[28]

Now, into the midst of the processing center, emerges the bookform catalog, brought back to life after having been killed by the high cost and slowness of typesetting. As Weber remarks,[29] the sequential camera and chain printer have been significant factors in the development of the book catalog, assisting it to become typographically and bibliographically adequate and acceptable, freed from the crippling limitations of an exclusively upper-case alphabet. But they were able to do this only because of a previous development—the successful marriage, perfected and demonstrated during the second quarter of this century, of two century-old arts, lithography and photography. Without the successful union of these arts in photolithography it would be uneconomic to print catalogs from shingled cards, by sequential camera, or by chain printers, and the British Museum Catalog would doubtless still be in the century-long process of being printed in letterpress. Here again, however, the enabling conditions fell into place, responding magically to the needs of libraries. For the moment that a book catalog can be used simultaneously as the finding list for more than one library outlet, whether part of the same system or not, at that moment it becomes an instrument of centralized processing.

Now, too, comes library automation based on computers. This has hardly as yet penetrated libraries, let alone processing centers. However, the New England Board of Higher Education has commissioned work on the development of a computer-based regional processing center intended to serve in the first place the libraries of the six state-supported universities of New England.[30] Will conditions prove favorable for such a center? Will the techniques prove feasible? At this stage no one knows. In order to find out, an experiment must be made. The experiment may identify currently insuperable obstacles of technology or economics. In subsequent efforts it may or may not be possible to surmount the obstacles. The fact is that we are today almost as much subject to step-at-a-time progress as were Bishop Grégoire and Charles C. Jewett. Almost, but not quite, for second chances come sooner to us than to them.

Charles C. Jewett could not foresee that what he was trying to do with stereotypes in the 1850's (namely, to publish the catalogs of individual libraries making use of cataloging information from a national store) would be performed in the 1960's with the aid of a technique combining photography, lithography and catalog cards, even though all of these were within his experience. By the same token, it is not impossible that library problems of today will be solved by techniques with which we are quite familiar, but in configurations as yet unrealized and undisclosed. It is this situation among others which makes it quite bootless to attempt to read the future.

In the light of what we have learned about the progress of the centralized/cooperative processing idea up to now it is hard to doubt its ultimate triumph. The principle upon which it rests is the identical principle which Johann Gutenberg employed in the invention with which he ushered in the age of mass-production. If in its initial application to processing centers the principle fails or seems to fail to work in the sense that no clear cost-savings appear, there may be setbacks, as reported by Miss Vann.[31] (It may, nevertheless, be suspected that present doubts regarding cost-saving stem at least in part from lack of precise knowledge of the cost of processing when performed by institutions separately.) However, it may be expected on the basis of all experience hitherto, that further attempts will be made, making use of more effective techniques and of more favorable conditions of demand, until success is achieved. Indeed, as previously noted, there is already evidence that the success of the centers does not depend upon proof of cost-saving, but rather, that if their costs can be held to a reasonable figure, even though somewhat higher than the do-it-separately level, other advantages already justify their existence.[32] Meanwhile it is interesting to note that in the salutary recommendations for improvement which Miss Vann has assembled, the quality of cataloging takes first place.[33]

Nor is it necessary to look far for new techniques and changed conditions for the processing centers to test. Certainly, in the bookform catalog they are offered, as Duchac shows, an extraordinary opportunity for extending their services—an opportunity which Weber reports has already

been grasped by a number.[34] It may be expected that they will similarly attempt to make use of the techniques of automation, either by using cataloging information in machine-readable form (such as MARC tapes) in their processing (as is contemplated by the New England Board of Higher Education project previously referred to), or by the plans for central processing for public libraries in New York State[35] or in other ways.

Beyond this point it is hardly profitable to look, for there are too many unknowns. Will the processing centers, having acquired experience in automation, tend to become regional centers for purposes of reference as well as of processing? There are many possibilities and alternatives.

A final word. One lesson has been consistently taught by the experience of the last two centuries, namely, that uniformity of practice—a common standard—is basic. (In fact, if the processing centers have suffered from one handicap more than another it appears to have consisted in lack of uniformity of practice among their members.[36]) In her study of centralized cataloging in the Soviet Union Miss Buist has given us an instructive account of the accomplishment that has been achieved with the aid of widespread uniformity of practice, which is proposed to be extended still further. Specifically, Miss Buist notes the goal of "maximum similarity"[37] of methods for generating catalogs and bibliographic publications and for serving both large and small libraries.

In this connection it is important to learn that a body in the United States which Miss Shachtman describes as "one of the major forces for compatibility in the Federal establishment"[38]—the Committee on Scientific and Technical Information—is gradually bringing the cataloging practice of the great technical-report-producing agencies closer to that of the country at large. It will indeed, as Miss Shachtman says, be inexcusable if libraries fail to take advantage of the encouragement and support of the Federal government. We are at a moment when it is at last becoming genuinely possible to take a major stride toward the realization of the one world/one library ideal, when the length of the stride will be utterly dependent upon the degree to which compatibility of records will have been achieved. At such a moment one of the greatest sources of encouragement and support which the Federal government could give would be the early completion of the process by which its bibliographical records can be brought into harmony with those of the country—perhaps of the world—at large.

REFERENCES

Unless otherwise specified, all page numbers refer to *Library Trends* XVI, 1 (July 1967).

1. Stevenson, Burton E. *The Home Book of Quotations*, 9th ed., New York, Dodd Mead & Co., 1964, p. 2298.
2. Cole, George W. "An Early French 'General Catalog,' " *Library Journal*, 25:329–331, July 1900. *See also:* France, Convention nationale, 1792–1795. Comité d'instruction publique: *Rapport sur la bibliographie, présenté à la Convention nationale le 22 germinale an II (1794) par [Henri] Grégoire, évêque constitutionnel de Blois, député à la Convention.* Paris, McKean et Cie, 1873.
3. Westby, Barbara. "Commercial Services," *supra*, p. 46.
4. Dawson, John M. "The Library of Congress: Its Role in Cooperative and Centalized Cataloging," *supra*, p.85.
5. Dawson, John M. "A History of Centralized Cataloging." *Library Resources & Technical Services*, 11:28–32, Winter 1967.
6. Clapp, Verner W. "Indexing and Abstracting Services for Serial Literature," *Library Trends*, 2:514, April 1954.
7. Westby, *supra*, pp. 47–48.
8. *Report of the Librarian of Congress . . . 1902.* Washington, D.C., U.S.G.P.O., 1902, p. 33; *United States Code*, 1964 ed., Vol. 1, Title 2, p. 61.
9. Dawson, *supra*, p. 94.
10. American Library Association. "The Proceedings [of the Annual Conference] Waukesha, Wisconsin, . . . July 4– . . . July 10, 1901," *Library Journal* 26:128 August 1901.
11. Metcalf, Keyes D. "The Attitude of the Library Administrator Toward Cataloging." *In* American Library Association. Division of Cataloging and Classification. *Catalogers' and Classifiers' Yearbook*, No. 10. Chicago, ALA, 1941, p. 10.
12. Dix, William S. "Centralized Cataloging and University Libraries–Title II, Part C of the Higher Education Act of 1965," *supra*, p. 97.
13. "The Printed Catalog Cards of the Library of Congress: Comparisons of Use," Library Journal, 27:314–18, June 1902.
14. Ladenson, A. "A Study of the Performance Record of the Library of Congress Card Division," *Journal of Cataloging and Classification*, 9:51–56, June 1953. For references to the Richardson, Dawson and Skipper studies see the articles by Dix and Dawson above.
15. Skipper, James E. "The Characteristics of Cataloging in Research Libraries." *In* Association of Research Libraries. *Minutes of the Sixty-eighth* Meeting. July 9, 1966, Appendix I, p. 65.
16. Duchac, Kenneth F. "Evaluation of Processing Centers," *supra*, p. 16.
17. Vann, Sarah K. "Southeastern Pennsylvania Processing Center Feasibility Study: A Summary," *Library Resources & Technical Services*, 10:471, Fall 1966.
18. Duchac, *supra*, pp. 14, 21.
19. Vann, Sarah K. "Evaluation of Centers: The Views of Members," *supra*, pp. 31, 41–42.
20. Darling, *supra*, p. 63.
21. Hiatt, Peter. "Cooperative Processing Centers for Public Libraries," *supra*, p. 170.
22. Duchac, *supra*, p. 14.
23. Vann, *supra*, pp. 33, 39–40.
24. Westby, *supra*, p. 55.
25. Darling, Richard L. "School Library Processing Centers," *supra*, pp. 58–59.
26. Hiatt, *supra*, pp. 67, 78.
27. Vann, *supra*, p. 43.
28. Duchac, *supra*, p. 21; Westby, *supra*, p. 53.
29. Weber, David C. "Book Catalog Trends in 1966," *supra*, p. 149.
30. "Three Catalog-Related Studies Receive Grant Support from CLR," *Library Journal*, 91:4064, Sept. 15, 1966.
31. Vann, *supra*, p. 24.
32. Hiatt, *supra*, p. 78.
33. Vann, *supra*, p. 43.
34. Duchac, *supra*, p. 21; Weber, *supra*, pp. 150–151.
35. Nelson Associates, Inc. "Centralized Processing for the Public Libraries of New York State; A Summary," *The Bookmark*, 25:243–246, April 1966.
36. Duchac, *supra*, p. 21.
37. Buist, Eleanor. " Soviet Centralized Cataloging: A View from Abroad," *supra*, p. 134.
38. Shachtman, Bella E. "Other Federal Activities," *supra*, pp. 115, 122.

National Planning For Resource Development

James E. Skipper

National planning for library resource development is a relatively new concept whose evolution owes more to opportunism than to a master plan or grand design. It is true that the increased availability of published materials has always been the Polar star which has guided efforts of libraries in improving service, but, lacking the potential for realistic funding, planning has been limited to programs which were reasonably obtainable, rather than those which would afford optimum results.

Library service to scholarship and research before World War II was reasonably adequate. An examination of the titles of doctoral dissertations accepted twenty-five years ago will reveal almost total concern with Western Culture and the classical areas of science. However, within the past twenty years we have experienced the often-described "explosion" in scientific research with its consequent effect on the amount of publication. The $16 billion which the Federal government will spend on research and development this year is as much as the entire national budget before Pearl Harbor. Having become a dominant world power, the national interest of the United States requires detailed knowledge of areas of the world which were little more than geographical expressions several generations ago.

In responding to these social changes the library community has recognized that local self-sufficiency, while necessary to meet the basic information needs of teaching and research, could not possibly meet the national information needs of the future. Supplemental programs for resource availability had to be developed on the national level.

Until recently, there was little opportunity for Federal support. Foundations feared that they might be approaching a bottomless pit, and libraries knew that ultimate solutions were beyond their individual or collective financial competence. For these reasons, self-supporting programs were limited by financial realities and Federal-supported efforts resulted from amendments being added to other legislation.

However, by keeping the major objectives in focus, the library community has constructed a series of national plans which are well coordinated, but need supplemental development. Limited examples of programs for the improvement of access to resources include the Association of Research Libraries' Current Foreign Newspaper Microfilming Project, the Foreign Gazettes Microfilming Program at the New York Public Library, and the activities of the Center for Research Libraries in Chicago. The most significant national efforts, however, concern the development of the Farmington Plan, the Public Law 480 Program, and the recently enacted Title II-C of the Higher Education Act of 1965.

FARMINGTON PLAN

The Farmington Plan can be considered as the first nationally cooperative effort to improve the availability of library resources. It is a well recognized social phenomenon that institutional changes occur most rapidly under conditions of crisis. With the invasion of Poland by Germany in 1939, it became obvious to American scholars that access to the treasures of European libraries would be restricted in the foreseeable future, and that these resources were indeed threatened by wholesale destruction. Subsequent American involvement in the war placed unprecedented demands for information on our libraries. Where are the railroad tunnels in Northern Italy, or the reefs

SOURCE: Reprinted from *Library Trends* XV, 2 (October 1966), pp. 321–334, by permission of the publisher, the University of Illinois Graduate School of Library Science.

surrounding Tarawa? What is the ball-bearing production of Germany? These concurrent concerns for the needs of the scholarly community and the national defense effort resulted in a reassessment of our methods for developing library resources.

Beginning in 1939, exploratory efforts were made to design an improved mechanism for resource development by the Library of Congress, the American Council of Learned Societies, the Social Science Research Council, the Board on Resources of American Libraries, and the Association of Research Libraries. Early deliberations considered a variety of possible programs. It was suggested that library organizations and learned societies compile lists of retrospective essential material to be acquired by the Library of Congress or to be microfilmed abroad. The merits of regional development versus a national approach were discussed, as well as the necessity for completing the National Union Catalog as a national focus for bibliographic control.

On October 9, 1942, the Executive Committee of the Librarian's Council of the Library of Congress met in Farmington, Connecticut, the place from which the present plan was to take its name. The conclusions reached at this meeting established a system based on the comprehensive collection of currently published materials with individual libraries accepting cooperative responsibility based on subject divisions.

Following the basic objectives formulated at the Farmington meeting, a working paper entitled *Proposal for a Division of Responsibility among American Libraries in the Acquisition and Recording of Library Materials*[1] was produced and circulated to the library community. This draft was refined in December, 1942, limiting the scope of the program to books and pamphlets in the regular trade "which might reasonably be expected to have interest to a research worker in America." Participating libraries were expected to place direct orders or rely on dealers for blanket selection. The paper also stated that, "It may prove to be wise to arrange for centralized cataloging of some books, particularly those in minor languages." Minority arguments were made in favor of the Library of Congress doing the entire job, and suggestions were made again that the regional approach would be more manageable than a national effort. The inherent lack of selectivity in the plan was also subject to objection.

The revised *Proposal* was endorsed in principle

by the library associations in February, 1943, and funds for the operation of the Plan were solicited from the Carnegie Foundation and the Rockefeller Foundation, both of which refused support. This impasse was resolved at the Twenty-First Meeting of the Association of Research Libraries on March 1-2, 1944, in New York City, where it was voted that Messrs. Julian Bold, Keyes Metcalf, and Archibald MacLeish be appointed as members of a committee to pursue the objectives of the *Proposal*.[2] At this point the Farmington Plan became a responsibility of the Association of Research Libraries. Complete documentation of the evolution of the Farmington Plan will be found in the *Farmington Plan Handbook*.[8]

It is appropriate at this point to relate the development of a complementary program for cooperative resource development which originated from the initial discussions of the Farmington Plan. At the meeting of the Association of Research Libraries on January 31, 1943, when the *Proposal* was first discussed, Keyes Metcalf suggested the desirability for cooperative action in obtaining materials from Europe after the end of the war.[4] A committee was appointed to develop a program and, after receiving the endorsement of the State Department, the Library of Congress accepted responsibility for establishing a mission to collect materials in Europe. When the program terminated in September, 1948, 800,000 volumes had been distributed to the hundred and thirteen participating libraries.

Edwin Williams, editor of the *Farmington Plan Handbook*, has suggested several reasons why this effort to collect war-years' publications from Europe was related to the Farmington Plan. First, it was a cooperative effort for national resource development. Secondly, assignments for participating libraries were based on a modified division of the Library of Congress *Classification Schedule*, originally drawn up as the basis for participation in the Farmington Plan. In the third place, when libraries were asked to make Farmington Plan commitments in 1947, they found that "experience with the Mission had . . . demonstrated that fatal results need not follow an agreement to accept large quantities of material that had not been specifically selected and ordered."[5]

The concept of the Farmington Plan at the time of its inception contained a number of unique features. In the national interest, participating libraries agreed to accept assignments for collecting materials which were not individually selected. It was realized that some of the materials acquired would be of marginal, or of no interest to the recipient, but that the national needs of scholarship and research required that at least one copy of all currently published materials of scholarly interest should be available. Furthermore, the Plan anticipated that each participant would quickly catalog Farmington receipts and send copy to the National Union Catalog to serve as a national system of bibliographic control and location. It was also accepted that libraries would make Farmington receipts available on interlibrary loan.

Plans for implementing the Farmington Plan were developed in 1947. The Library of Congress *Classification Schedule* was divided into one hundred and eleven sections as the basis for assignments of subject responsibilities. It should be realized that although designations were based primarily on existing strengths of individual collections, it did not imply that assignments indicated the strongest collection in the country.

Recognition should also be given to the limitations of the Plan. While it is true that the earlier reports refer to emphasis on books in Latin languages, the scope of coverage quickly moved to other areas of the world. The fact that the program was to be self-funded limited its initial coverage to countries with an organized book trade where dealers could be assigned for blanket selection. Thus, the Plan was most productive in Western Europe. Certain categories of materials were eliminated because of budgetary, mechanical, or substantive reasons. The Plan was restricted to currently published books, thus eliminating all retrospective titles, as well as serials, government publications, monographs published in a numbered series, juveniles, newspapers, textbooks, reprints, sheet maps, sheet music, and translations from one modern language to another. Although dealers were encouraged to supply all books of scholarly interest, it was recognized that they would not be able to provide complete coverage for "non-trade" publications. As it was assumed that libraries were already providing sufficient coverage of current British publications, Great Britain was not included in the Plan.

In January, 1948, it was announced that the Carnegie Corporation had granted $15,000 for the developmental and operational aspects of the Plan, and the program was initiated for current publications issued in France, Sweden, and Switzerland. Representatives of the Farmington Plan Committee toured Europe to establish a network of dealers in other countries. Originally, all Farmington receipts were sent to the New York Public Library where they were distributed by subject category to participating libraries; this system was subsequently modified so that dealers sent their selections directly.

In 1949, Belgium, Denmark, Italy, Mexico, the Netherlands, and Norway were added, and the following year Bolivia, Ecuador, and Peru were included in the Plan. Australia, Austria, Germany, Portugal, and Spain were added in 1951, with Harvard accepting responsibility for the comprehensive collection of all currently published Irish materials. The German agent agreed to supply as many East Zone publications as possible. A modification of the subject basis for assignment was suggested in 1952, when it was recommended that libraries accept total responsibility for publications issued by a given country or area not presently covered by the Plan. Thus, the Caribbean area was accepted by the University of Florida, and studies were made concerning the feasibility of including such areas as Finland, Greece, Yugoslavia, and other countries. Berkeley announced that it would attempt to cover Korea, and Northwestern agreed to accept responsibility for many areas of Africa.

In 1952, fifty-seven libraries acquired 17,508 volumes from the major twelve countries involved in the Farmington Plan at a total cost of $37,914. Statistics are not available for the receipts from the additional countries and areas covered. The cost per institution ranged from $3 to $4,824. The statistics for receipts during 1965 indicate that fifty-two libraries received 22,419 volumes from fourteen countries at a total cost of $107,438, in addition to area assignment receipts.

From its inception until 1951, the Farmington Plan was managed by an office in the New York Public Library, after which it was moved to Harvard. With the establishment of a Secretariat for the Association of Research Libraries in 1963, the Farmington office was transferred from Harvard. *The Farmington Plan Letter*, first published in 1949 to establish the mechanics of the new program, has been developed into a focal source of information concerning all projects designed to improve the availability of materials published in foreign countries.[6]

Following eight years of experience, the Association of Research Libraries voted in 1957 to reexamine the Farmington Plan in an effort to assess past performance and plans for future improvement. With a grant from the Council on Library Resources, Robert Vosper and Robert Talmadge, then at the University of Kansas, made the study and reported to the Association in January, 1959.[7]

It would be impossible to consider the report in detail at this time. However, several major recommendations should be mentioned. The report deplored the popular conception of the Farmington Plan as only concerned with Western Europe. Indeed, it has continually expanded its scope to include other areas of the world. The report also strongly recommended that the Association of Research Libraries continue its support of the Plan by strengthening the organizational position of the Farmington Plan Committee, by creating effective liaison with the learned societies, and by adopting a more flexible procurement policy, rather than depending exclusively on blanket order selections from assigned dealers. Today, the Farmington Plan Committee is composed of Subcommittees on Western Europe, Africa, Eastern Europe, the Middle East, the Far East, Latin America, and South Asia.

PUBLIC LAW 480

In extending the Farmington Plan into areas of the world which had no adequate book trade or national bibliography, it was recognized that satisfactory coverage would be problematical. Libraries accepting these assignments relied on a variety of techniques including assistance from local consular staff, available bookstores, and the peripatetic efforts of roving faculty and librarians. At best, these endeavors were of marginal effectiveness in providing comprehensive coverage as the costs involved were simply too large to be undertaken by libraries collectively or individually.

Mortimer Graves of the American Council of Learned Societies had the perception to visualize a solution to the problem of collecting library materials from "developing" countries. For several years the United States had been selling surplus agricultural products to some forty countries under authorization of the Agricultural Trade Development and Assistance Act of 1954 (PL 83-480). Foreign countries were allowed to pay for these commodities with local currencies, or counterpart funds, as they lacked U.S. dollars. Thus, in a number of countries, the United States was developing considerable credits which were not needed for diplomatic or military expenditures.

Following a concerted effort on the part of ACLS and the Association of Research Libraries,

Congressman John Dingell of Michigan introduced an amendment to PL 480, which would authorize the use of counterpart funds for the purchase of library materials in countries where the U.S. Treasury had declared funds to be surplus. In 1958 the amendment was incorporated into PL 480 as Section 104n which authorized the Library of Congress, within the appropriations specified, to acquire, index, abstract, and deposit library materials from designated countries.

At the time, eight to ten countries had surplus currencies and the Library of Congress requested authorization to use funds in all of them. The Congress refused this program in fiscal year 1959 and again in 1960. In 1961, the Library of Congress reduced its request to include only India, Pakistan, and the United Arab Republic. Congress approved this approach and authorized $36,500 in U.S. currency and $363,500 in foreign currency, or a total of $400,000, to initiate the program. Table 1 illustrates the development of the program to date.

With the advice of the P.L. 480 Advisory Committee, the Library of Congress selected the libraries which would be invited to participate. As the Congress had insisted that libraries contribute a token sum for materials received, it was agreed that $500 would be paid to the U.S. Treasury annually by each participant.

It was obvious that this venture would involve libraries in unique and difficult cataloging problems. Not only would they be dealing with dozens of languages and hundreds of dialects, but there was also a serious lack of uniform authority files for authors' names and transliteration schedules for some languages. The Subcommittee on the National Union Catalog under the Chairmanship of Gordon Williams took the initiative in developing one of the first and perhaps the best example of a centralized cataloging effort to follow the card distribution service started by the Library of Congress in 1901. Each participant in the Indic program agreed to pay the Library of Congress $7,750 per year for cataloging; the Arabic cataloging cost $1,111, with Princeton paying for its "share" by providing copy for approximately 50 percent of the accessions. Total annual costs for Indic were $131,750, and for Arabic $18,887.

The definitive history of the P.L. 480 Program has yet to be written, although basic facts can be obtained from the Annual Reports of the P.L. 480 Coordinator in the Library of Congress[8] and the *P.L. 480 Newsletter.*[9] These sources give a general account of the tremendous effort and

TABLE I

DEVELOPMENT OF THE PUBLIC LAW 480 PROGRAM, 1962-66

Year (FY)	U.S.	Budget Foreign	Total	Countries	Total Items	Libraries
1962	$36,500	$363,500	$400,000	UAR	60,160	LC, UCLA, Columbia, Harvard, Hartford Seminary[A], Michigan, NYPL, Portland State[A], Princeton, Utah, Virginia, Indiana
				India/ Pakistan	338,913	LC, Cal-B, Chicago, Cornell, Duke, Hawaii, Minnesota, Penn., Texas, Washington, Wisconsin, Yale
1963	$49,900	$630,000	$679,900	UAR	184,548	[B]Boston College, Brandeis, Chicago, Hoover, Kentucky, U. of S. Cal., Syracuse, Yale
				India/ Pakistan	813,328	[B]Columbia, Illinois, Michigan, NYPL, Syracuse, Virginia
1964	$80,000	$898,000	$978,000	UAR	289,436	Same[F] and Portland State
				India/ Pakistan	846,286	Same
				Indonesia	37,135	Berkeley, Chicago, Columbia, Cornell, Hawaii, Illinois, Indiana, Michigan, NYPL, Wisconsin, Yale
				Israel	57,343	Brandeis, UCLA, Dropsie, Harvard, Hebrew Union, Indiana, College of Jewish Studies, NYPL, Texas, Yale, Yeshiva
				Burma	E–	Berkeley, Columbia, Cornell, Duke, Hawaii, Illinois, Mich., NYPL, N. Illinois, Penn., Yale
1965	$124,500	$1,417,000	$1,541,500	UAR	316,185	Same
				India/ Pakistan	840,067	Same
				Indonesia	167,068	Same
				Israel	208,425	[B]Columbia, Portland State, Princeton, Syracuse, Utah, Wayne, Virginia[C], Michigan[D]
				Burma	E–	
1966	$150,900	$1,694,000	$1,844,900	UAR		Same and Illinois
				India/ Pakistan		Same
				Indonesia		Same
				Israel		Same and Boston Public, Jewish Theological Seminary, U. of S. Cal., Yeshiva[G]
				Burma	E–	Same

[A]Shared a set.   [C]Transfer from Dropsie.   [E]Program frustrated by local political problems.
[B]Added.   [D]Transfer from Yeshiva.   [F]Brandeis switched to Israel.
   [G]Yeshiva reinstated.

imagination that were required on the part of the Library of Congress staff to establish initial programs in Cairo, Karachi, and New Delhi. Beginning in 1962, in three countries with total shipments of 820,000 items, the program grew to include operations in six countries by 1965, when 1,531,745 items were sent to American libraries.

Efforts were made in the first session of the 89th Congress to extend the program to Poland, Yugoslavia, and Brazil. As the extension was not authorized, the Library of Congress has asked the second session to consider admitting Poland and Yugoslavia, in addition to Tunisia, Ceylon, and Guinea.

Compared with the complexities of obtaining materials in the countries involved, the mechanics of the P.L. 480 Program are relatively simple. The selection teams acquire local publications and ship them to the participating libraries. Accessions lists are published and distributed to a large number of libraries in this country to provide identification and control for national access. The program is subject to continuing analysis of the quality of selection, and several changes have been made to avoid the inclusion of too much marginal material, such as Indic vernacular fiction.

In addition to direct distribution of books and periodicals, the program has started a microfilming program for newspapers. Initially, the lack of technical competence and the inability to purchase raw film with local currencies prevented the filming of Indian newspapers in New Delhi. The originals were shipped to the Library of Congress for filming until technicians could be trained and arrangements made for the Library of Congress to supply the raw film. The local newspaper microfilming program in India was scheduled to start January 1, 1966 and will include newspapers from Pakistan. Foreign gazettes from the countries involved have been incorporated into the microfilming program at the New York Public Library.

Sets of English language materials have been assembled for distribution to some three hundred American colleges, in addition to the participating libraries. Initially confined to serial publications from India, Pakistan, and the United Arab Republic, the program has subsequently provided monographic materials.

HIGHER EDUCATION ACT OF 1965

The potential of the P.L. 480 Program is obviously dependent on the continued availability of surplus counterpart currencies in the various developing countries of the world. While it has provided an invaluable extension of the Farmington Plan, the program has definite limitations. For example, with the exception of the United Arab Republic and possibly Tunisia, not one of the more than fifty countries in Africa has surplus counterpart funds. The Far East presents a similar problem. This condition left our libraries with no national support for resource development in these areas while, at the same time, African and Far Eastern area studies programs

were being developed on an increasing number of campuses. A potential solution to the problem came from the concern of the Association of Research Libraries with the lack of centrally produced cataloging copy for use in adding books to our libraries.

Without sufficient cataloging staff, and suffering from an inadequate book budget, the Library of Congress had long been able to supply catalog copy for only about 50 percent of the titles added to our larger libraries. The lack of catalog copy for foreign books was especially critical, with ARL libraries reporting that Library of Congress copy was available for only some 5 percent of Farmington Plan receipts at the time the books were processed. The Higher Education Act, introduced into the first session of the 89th Congress, contained Title II, which authorized $50 million for the development of library collections.

The Shared Cataloging Committee of the Association of Research Libraries, with William S. Dix as Chairman, testified before the House and Senate Education Committees suggesting that the potential of the $50 million authorization for resource development would be seriously eroded by the present inefficiencies in our national cataloging system. An amendment was offered which would provide funds to the Commissioner of Education for transfer to the Librarian of Congress, with authorization for the Library of Congress to collect every current publication of scholarly interest issued in all countries of the world and provide catalog copy within three to four weeks of receipt.[10] Testimony also indicated that the amendment would make a material improvement in manpower availability, especially with regard to linguistic competence, and would serve as a base for automation of bibliographic information. The amendment was accepted by both houses of the Congress will ultimately double its present rate Higher Education Act of 1965. A total of $19 million was authorized over the next three years for implementation.

While the basic orientation of Title II-C was to improve the cataloging situation, it has considerable implications in the development of resource availability. In the first place, the Library of Congress will ultimatelydouble its present rate of accessions, and this increase will take place primarily in foreign language publications. With centralized cataloging at the Library of Congress, the element of identification and location will satisfy another condition for national improvement. However, national needs require more than just the one copy at the Library of Congress, and this desideratum leads to the next phase in national planning for resource availability.

FUTURE POSSIBILITIES

The evolution of national plans for the more adequate collection of currently published materials has been noted in the development of the Farmington Plan, the Public Law 480 Program, and most recently, the authorization under Title II-C of the Higher Education Act of 1965 for the Library of Congress to develop a globally comprehensive procurement program. Bibliographic control on the national level provides the second leg of the stool. The third leg, now being fashioned, is designed to increase the availability of the material itself.

To execute its responsibilities, the Library of Congress must not only maintain its present P.L. 480 field staff, but also establish regional collecting offices in such countries as Africa and the Far East. With intelligent planning and supplemental funding, it is logical to assume that all of these procurement centers could collect multiple copies of current materials for institutions other than the Library of Congress or those designated as P.L. 480 depositories.

The Association of Research Libraries is presently organizing a Materials Development Program to complement the basic projects for acquisitions and bibliographic control noted above. This Program, of national scope, is directed to the problem of increased availability of materials, both current and retrospective. It is designed to supplement the titles obtainable from commercial sources such as reprint or microfilm editions, and is specifically oriented to those types of publications not needed in a sufficient number of copies to attract commercial action. To provide adequate national access to some types of materials from developing countries, a master microfilm negative is sufficient. Other titles may require a loan microfilm positive, or a sales positive, while a fourth category might justify offset reprinting. In addition, it is anticipated that the Materials Development Program would have sufficient capital to support the compilation and publication of ancillary bibliographical tools required for the effective use of these materials. If found to be desirable, a translation project could also be considered as part of the Program.

There is no question that each library must become self-sufficient in meeting the basic needs of the teaching and research programs which it supports. However, with the inefficiencies of our present system of interlibrary loan, individual libraries are forced to collect far beyond reasonable anticipation of need. It is probable that there are definable categories of materials which, if collected comprehensively by a national agency and made available at low cost and within acceptable time limits, could afford a material saving at the local level. Examples of these categories are microfilms of newspapers and the contents of foreign archives, trade catalogs and directories, superseded textbooks, translations, publications from developing countries, government publications, and perhaps a current periodicals lending service. The population to be served need not only be that associated with universities, but might also include faculty at smaller colleges wishing to continue their research without being subject to the constraints of a smaller library collection.

Most libraries have experienced increased difficulty in the past decade in borrowing journals from other institutions, especially science periodicals. Accelerated local demand, rather than unwillingness to share resources, has been responsible for this trend. A national facility for resource development and service for specified categories would supplement interlibrary loan and would help to relieve the inequitable costs now assumed by the large libraries in attempting to meet national information needs without reciprocal compensation.

Although the precise system for future improvement of resource availability is not known, the problems and general objectives are reasonably clear. Our largest libraries are the first to admit that they cannot hope to acquire a comprehensive collection of all types of library materials. The task for the immediate future is to design supplementary systems and programs which will complement and extend the capability of our present library structure to afford greater access to information.

REFERENCES

1. U.S. Library of Congress. Metcalf-Boyd-MacLeish Committee. *Proposal for a Division of Responsibility among American Libraries in the Acquisition and Recording of Library Materials.* (Mimeographed)

2. Association of Research Libraries. *Minutes of the Twenty-first Meeting.* New York, March 1–2, 1944, p. 3.

3. Williams, Edwin E. *Farmington Plan Handbook.* Cambridge, Mass., Association of Research Libraries, 1953, pp. 9–60.

4. Association of Research Libraries. *Minutes of the Twentieth Meeting.* Chicago, January 31, 1943, p. 2.

5. Williams, *op. cit.,* p. 20.

6. *Farmington Plan Letter,* No. 1. Cambridge, Mass., Harvard University Library, March 29, 1949.

7. Vosper, Robert. *The Farmington Plan Survey: A Summary of the Separate Studies of 1957–1961* (University of Illinois Library School Occasional Papers No. 77). Urbana, University of Illinois Graduate School of Library Science, 1965.

8. U.S. Library of Congress. Public Law 480 Office. *Annual Report.* Washington, D.C., 1962–63. (Multilithed.)

9. U.S. Library of Congress. *P.L.-480 Newsletter,* No. 1, Washington, D.C., October 16, 1961.

10. U.S. Congress. 89th Cong., 1st Sess., P.L. 89–329. *Higher Education Act of 1965,* Title II, Part C.

Centralized Cataloging for the Country—Now and in the Future

Edmond L. Applebaum

In May 1967, I stood in this building and spoke to the Ohio Valley Group of Technical Service Librarians about "Implications for the Technical Services of the National Program for Acquisitions and Cataloging." NPAC was then a vigorous one year old. I am flattered to be invited back now; for if the first invitation extended to a speaker can be considered a calculated risk, the second invitation is surely a known risk.

Tonight I am to speak to you about centralized cataloging for the country—its present and future. NPAC—The National Program for Acquisitions and Cataloging—is at the heart of the subject. For the sake of those among you who may not be intimately acquainted with the development of the program, I ask the remainder of you to bear with me for a brief recapitulation.

For years university and research libraries had been hampered by a severe shortage of trained and linguistically qualified librarians able to speedily catalog and classify all of the publications being acquired. Libraries were also hampered by lack of information about available publications and by inability to obtain needed research materials quickly because of inadequate bibliographic tools and book channels in some areas of the world. Duplication of cataloging efforts throughout the country served to further dissipate skills already in very short supply.

With the passage of Public Law 89-329, the Higher Education Act of 1965, the Librarian of Congress was charged with the following responsibilities under Title II, Part C: first, acquiring, so far as possible, all library materials currently published throughout the world which are of value to scholarship; and second, providing catalog information for these materials promptly after receipt and distributing such information by printed catalog cards and by other means. The need for a program like this had been clearly illustrated in a series of surveys showing that the college and research library community was amassing staggering quantities of uncataloged publications and that use of Library of Congress printed cards was only providing approximately half of the cataloging needed. Cooperative cataloging efforts whereby other American libraries supplied the Library of Congress with cataloging copy which was subsequently printed and distributed by LC was only providing another 2% of the cataloging needed. The complications and cost of cooperative cataloging made it further evident that if increased cataloging information was to be provided it had to come from centralized rather than cooperative efforts. The Library of Congress was the logical agency to do the job. It had the best foundation upon which to develop a central cataloging service. It had extensive reference collections and catalogs, a large staff with wide subject and language proficiency; a catalog card printing and distribution service that had been operating since 1901; it had national funding, and international prestige. A practical solution was the development of LC as a central cataloging agency, comprehensive and rapid so that libraries could depend upon it to produce the cataloging copy needed for all important American and foreign material. But in order to do the job the Library of Congress had to enter upon some new trails.

SOURCE: Reprinted from *The Changing Concept of Service in Libraries: A Centennial Lecture Series and Symposium* (Terre Haute: Indiana State University Graduate School of Library Science, 1970, pp. 42–50) by permission of the author. This paper was first presented at Indiana State University on February 18, 1970, as a part of the lecture series named above.

First, it was decided that LC could use for its descriptive cataloging work the descriptive elements appearing in the majority of national bibliographies produced in the bibliographically advanced countries; second, it was decided that LC would use a rapid acquisitions combination of blanket order dealer selection supplemented from pre-publication bibliographical information obtained from the national bibliography producers. This replaced an earlier and much slower system that awaited the arrival of the printed bibliography. Finally, by having the descriptive cataloging of these works done in centers established overseas that would forward the preliminary catalog cards and publications simultaneously by air, the Library revolutionized its own procedures and cut further weeks and months from its routines. Of course, the choice and form of author entry and secondary entries, the application of subject headings, and of Library of Congress and Dewey Decimal classification numbers continued to be done at the Library. In order to get library cataloging data quickly into the hands of the research library community and equally important, in order to learn of those publications being acquired by the research library community and not by the Library of Congress, special arrangements were consummated with over 90 of the largest research libraries, whereby full sets of newly printed catalog cards were sent out on a daily basis with the understanding that the research libraries would maintain files of these cards and report back to the Library of Congress those titles that they had ordered or received for which they did not find Library of Congress catalog copy in their depository file. In those instances, the Library of Congress placed orders for titles that had not yet been ordered or rush cataloged them if they had been received and were not yet in the cataloging stream. Also in the interest of speed a second shift at the Government Printing Office Branch of the Library of Congress was instituted, thereby doubling the GPO card printing capacity.

The Shared Cataloging Division was established specifically to handle the cataloging being done in collaboration with national bibliography producers and to maintain and service the acquisitions control file that allowed the Library of Congress to determine that publications needed to be acquired as a result of outside library reports.

Regional acquisitions officers were considered for those areas of the world where no organized book trade and no national bibliographies existed. In parts of the world where centers could not be established for political or other reasons, a variety of other arrangements were made to meet the requirements of a centralized cataloging system.

What have been the specific accomplishments to date? Where do we stand now and where do we go from here? Nine shared cataloging operations, staffed chiefly with local personnel, have been established in London, Vienna, Wiesbaden, Paris, Oslo, The Hague, Belgrade, Florence, and Tokyo. These operations cover the publications of 15 countries; the British Isles, Austria, East and West Germany, France, Sweden, Denmark, Norway, Switzerland, Belgium, the Netherlands, Yugoslavia, Italy, Finland, and Japan. Three regional acquisitions centers exist; one in Rio de Janeiro for the acquisition of Brazilian publications, one in Nairobi, Kenya, covering twelve east African countries, and one in Djakarta, Indonesia. The Library has also melded into this effort the overseas centers established under its PL 480 programs acquiring and distributing publications issued in the United Arab Republic, Israel, India, Pakistan, Ceylon, and Nepal. Accessions lists for these areas are issued as they also are for East Africa and Indonesia. In addition, arrangements have been made to use cataloging done by the All-Union Book Chamber of the USSR and to receive cataloging and publications together from the national bibliography producers of the national libraries of Bulgaria and Czechoslovakia.[1] Also coming directly to the Library of Congress is national bibliography cataloging data prepared in Canada, South Africa, Australia, and New Zealand. Altogether then, some 40 countries are more closely covered bibliographically than ever before. Cooperative arrangements also have been established with the National Library of Medicine and the National Agricultural Library whereby, in some parts of the world, materials acquired by these libraries are routed through LC overseas centers for mutually advantageous purposes. National Library of Medicine subject headings and classification numbers have been included on many LC cards as a result of these arrangements and to the benefit of other medical libraries.

The activities overseas are intriguing. They dramatize the originality and drive of the program and portend greater things to come in the areas of international cooperation. The fact of the matter is, however, that the major effort, and by far the major expenditure of funds has been and continues to be right at the Library of Congress in the concentration on an expanded and specialized cataloging staff.

The Shared Cataloging Division, which did not exist in April 1966, now numbers over 160 people. Staff has been added also to the Descriptive Cataloging Division, the Subject Cataloging Division, and the Dewey Decimal Classification Division. The growth of the LC cataloging production is significant. In 1965, before the start of the program, the Library cataloged 110,000 titles new to its collections. In 1966 it cataloged 125,000 such titles, in 1967 140,000 titles, in 1968 185,000 titles, and in the fiscal year ended June 30, 1969, over 200,000 titles were cataloged by the Library of Congress.[2] Over 390,000 reports from participating libraries have been searched during this period, and some 86,030 titles have been ordered as a result of these outside library reports. Strenuous efforts have been made to speed up the entire procedure of selection and cataloging of books and the printing and distribution of catalog cards. The first phase of an automated system for the handling of LC card orders, involving the machine reading and sorting of card orders, has been installed, and once the proposed second phase (printing of cards on demand through computer driven photo composition) can be established, a major change in card distribution service will take place.

To briefly recapitulate, we may say that since inception of the program in May 1966, the Library has greatly increased its cataloging support staff including the recruitment and training of catalogers with specialized language and subject skills. It has arranged to share the cataloging data already prepared by the producers of national bibliographies in 22 foreign countries. It has established a specialized Shared Cataloging Division. It has altered procedures to speed up selections and ordering. It has established abroad 9 shared cataloging centers and three regional acquisitions centers staffed almost entirely by local personnel in the countries where they are located. It has added an extra printing shift to hasten production of printed catalog cards. It has even established an office devoted to the training of catalogers, searchers, and filers in the Library of Congress. Under this innovative program, the Library last year distributed to more than 90 research libraries depository sets each containing over 220,000 LC cards. It has almost doubled its cataloging production from fiscal 1965 to 1969. And it has more than doubled its monographic purchases. With Library of Congress cataloging now available for 75% of the 7,600,000 volumes added to the 76 major academic libraries

comprising The Association of Research Libraries in fiscal year 1969, it is estimated that total cataloging costs were reduced for these libraries alone from an estimated $28,766,000 to about $18,449,000 representing a clear savings of over $10,000,000 to these specific institutions. If we include the libraries of other universities, college, and junior colleges we can say that over 2,500 academic libraries are saving millions of dollars and are also able to offer vastly improved services through the federal government's investment in Title II-C amounting to $5.5 million in fiscal year 1969. This greatly increased amount of cataloging information is, of course, available to all, including the more than 25,000 libraries, firms, and individuals subscribing to the Library's card distribution service and to additional thousands of users through the Library's published catalogs in book form.

I should like now to quote a few comments made by some distinguished university librarians. Dr. Jerrold Orne, University Librarian of the University of North Carolina Library, in April of 1969, "My own library . . . has been able to improve its handling of the cataloging operations by at least 100% because of this program. This experience has been duplicated in every large research library in this country. I know of no other program . . . where so important and widespread a need is satisfied with the modest sum of money assigned for the purpose. I would also point out that this is not a giveaway program and that every one of the research libraries that enjoys its benefits also contributes to it by supplying a continuous flow of bibliographic information to the Library of Congress in the interest of the service. There is consequently a coordination of effort which is unique among the many programs relating to the libraries within the Office of Education."

In April 1969, Dr. Frederick Wagman, Director of University Libraries at the University of Michigan, wrote, "Prior to the introduction of the Shared Cataloging Program . . . a library such as mine was able to use LC catalog cards for only approximately 40% of the new titles it acquired every year. Since the Shared Cataloging Program has been introduced, that percentage in my library has risen steadily until this year we can report with immense gratification that for 73% of all the titles that we acquire, we are not compelled to do the original cataloging ourselves but can use catalog cards produced by the Library of Congress. How much this saves us can be discerned from the following: The University of Michigan Library so far this year has acquired and has cataloged 39,901 new titles. Of this total it was able to use LC catalog cards for 28,946 titles, or 73% utilizing 3.87 man years of clerical staff in the process. Thus, to adapt LC catalog cards for our own use we need only one man year at the clerical level for 7,479 titles. Of the total new titles cataloged, 10,955 had to be cataloged by our own staff since LC catalog cards were not available for these. For this number we employed 11.27 man years mostly at the professional level at a much higher rate of pay and at a rate of 972 titles for each man year."

"In summary, we are currently cataloging 73% of all our intake of new titles in the library with 25% of our cataloging staff and 27% of our intake of new titles for which LC cards are not available, with 75% of our cataloging staff."

Dr. William M. Locke, Director of Libraries, Massachusetts Institute of Technology, wrote in April 1969, "The shared cataloging and foreign acquisitions program of the Library of Congress is the most important new venture on the national and international library scene since the Second World War. It points the way toward the ultimate goal where each nation would provide complete catalog information for everything being published within its borders, then exchange this information with all other nations interested."

W. Carl Jackson, Director of Libraries, Pennsylvania State University, testifying before the House Appropriations Subcommittee on Labor and H.E.W., in May 1969 said, "The benefits of this program to the libraries of the Pennsylvania State University are fairly typical and will serve to illustrate the magnitude of these savings. Before this program commenced we performed original cataloging for 50% of the materials acquired and obtained LC copy for the other 50%. This year, we have been able to obtain LC copy for 80% of these materials. Although we will add about 150,000 volumes to our libraries this year, for purposes of this illustration, I will use a lower figure of 103,000 volumes since this is the average of holdings added to the 71 ARL academic libraries during 1967–68. Thus, the difference between the amount of original cataloging before the program (50%) and the present 80% is 30,000 volumes. While the cost of cataloging varies considerably between libraries, the difference in cost of original cataloging and cataloging with LC copy is reasonably constant at $5.55 per volume. This therefore represents, as a conservative estimate, a savings to us of $170,000."

The University of Indiana Library did a control study during October, November, and December of 1968 and reported as follows: "From the study we can conclude that a high percentage indeed (80%) of all current items acquired by a large research library has an LC card available within six months of the date of placing the order. By the time current books leave the Order Department to enter the Cataloging Department, 73% have LC cards available to the Library."

The foregoing statements provide direct proof of the impact of this program.

Title II-C was amended during fiscal year 1969 to authorize some additional and significant changes. The first of these would permit the Library of Congress to acquire a second copy of those foreign publications which are difficult to obtain. It was not intended that the Library of Congress acquire second copies of books which would be easily obtained through regular trade channels. With this authority a copy would be available for use in Washington for Congressional and other government purposes and a second copy would be available elsewhere for loan purposes. The Committee report indicated that such a copy could be placed by the Library of Congress for centrally located depository use. The second amendment would enable the Library of Congress to obtain extra copies of books from those parts of the world where it had had to establish procurement centers because of an undeveloped book trade. The amendment authorized the Library of Congress to utilize our personnel at these centers to obtain extra copies as required by individual libraries for their collections. The cost of the books would be met by the libraries, only the overhead would be absorbed by the Title II-C program. The third amendment authorized the Library of Congress to prepare and distribute bibliographies, indexes, guides, union lists and the like as well as catalog card information for the research library community. To date no appropriations at all have been made available for the purpose of implementing any of these amendments.

What does the future hold in store? First, I think one would have to be quite a remarkable economic analyst to peer into his crystal ball and predict what sums of money would be available for education programs in the forthcoming years. And perhaps an economic analyst could not make this forecast either. I am reminded of Walter Heller's retort when the former Chairman of the President's Council of Economic Advisors was asked to make a forecast on stock market activity and refused on the grounds that he was only an economic analyst not a psychoanalyst. If funding becomes available, then I would say that the future is clear. We must continue to develop this program till all areas of the world are covered by a totally adequate acquisitions and cataloging program—a program that will provide American libraries and the users of these libraries with the basic wherewithall to acquire, catalog, and use research materials published throughout the world.

If funding is not made available at such a level then we must make some choices. First, coverage of the most bibliographically productive countries. Second, coverage of those areas of the world where our national interests and our research activities are foremost. I find it hard to accept the third option that sees withdrawal of support of this program, because this means at the best a return to a former unsatisfactory condition and at the worst, the entrance into a new condition where, because of increased important publishing throughout the world, we would retrogress to the point where only a fraction of the truly important materials would be acquired and cataloged promptly enough to provide the service required and merited by the American scholarly community.

A fully functioning, prompt-delivering cataloging program is one necessary part of the package if the MARC system, the system of machine readable cataloging copy developed by LC, is to become not only an American standard but an international standard. With such a standard for the communication of bibliographical information, one can foresee all countries freely exchanging such data. We are still far from the millennium at present, however. Understand that by "centralized cataloging" I really mean "shared cataloging." I don't think any one country—and this includes the United States—can marshall the money and skilled human resources necessary to catalog and classify, place under complete and accurate and prompt bibliographic control, the publishing output of the world. Even if it could, there is no economy in such an effort. There are many and obvious obstacles to achieving the desired end of finding each country promptly and comprehensively providing a fairly standardized catalog entry for each significant item published in the country. Some of these obstacles are obvious; the foremost being the inadequate financial support provided in most parts of the world for bibliographical systems. This leads to a lack of comprehensive coverage, to a lack of speed in cataloging and classification, and

frequently, because inadequate salaries result in inadequate staffing levels, to a lack of technical cataloging standards and expertise. Other hindrances that we encounter include a lack of any nationally centered responsibility and a lack of communication between countries and, frequently, within countries. Certainly we must be aware and resign ourselves to the fact that total standardization is a will-of-the-wisp. What we must strive for is compatibility and a standardization of the sequence of entry of cataloging elements and as close as possible agreement on the rules of entry and description. There will be and must always be certain cataloging differences required both by language differences and particularly by differences in how the knowledge of the world is categorized, viewed, and applied by many and widely varying societies.

An awareness of the foregoing elements should enable us to move forward in those areas where success is attainable. One of the areas is the application of a standard book number and a standard serial number system in the country of origin of each publication. This is vital as an element in the transmittal and retrieval of machine readable bibliographical information.

Another area of importance is agreement on mechanization of library services. Dr. James E. Skipper, Director of Libraries at the University of California at Berkeley, has stated this point well in speaking about NPAC and library automation. He said, "We have long dreamed of being able to communicate in an international bibliographic language . . . Experience suggests the possibility that automation itself may be the catalytic agent that will draw the international library community together under common systems of bibliographic controls which have eluded us in the past. For centuries musicians and mathematicians have been able to communicate internationally by a standard language of symbol and notation. One of the most significant future implications of the present program is the possibility of achieving greater bibliographic compatibility."

Another area that is most hopeful is that of standardization of catalog codes. Since the International Conference on Cataloging Principles held in Paris in 1961, there has been substantial progress in international cooperation in the fields of cataloging and bibliography. During this past summer further progress has been made. An international meeting of cataloging experts was held in Copenhagen under the auspices of the International Federation of Library Associations on August 22–25. There were 41 cataloging experts representing 34 countries and an additional 12 observers in attendance. Two important decisions came from this meeting. First, that a committee would prepare a definitive edition of the *Annotated Edition of the Statement of Principles* basing it on all comments received prior to, during, and after the meeting, drawing attention to the weaknesses and inconsistencies in the *Statement of Principles* and reporting on various solutions adopted in various new and revised national cataloging codes. The second decision reached by the conference was that there should be an international standard for the bibliographical descriptions of publications and that these descriptions should be comprehensive and be given in a fixed order. A working party was appointed to make detailed recommendations for the composition, form, and order of the items in the bibliographical description. The conference also agreed that efforts should be directed toward creating a system for the international exchange of information by which the standard bibliographical description of each publication would be established and distributed via cards or machine readable records by a national agency in the country of origin of the publication. All participants in this important meeting stressed the urgency of standardization of both bibliographical description and machine readable records.

You probably have noticed that what I initially started out calling "centralized cataloging" I am now referring to more and more as "shared cataloging." It is something of both. Think about the need for finding out what is being published in the developing countries—the "bibliographically underdeveloped" countries—and the need to provide information about such publications and to place them under good cataloging control. The highly technical character of the work that we now do makes it difficult for these countries to participate directly or to get the greatest use from the work being done. And yet, there are real advantages here and now that they can derive. First, in those areas where we carry out regional acquisitions programs, we encourage the dissemination of information by the publication of accessions lists. We encourage the proliferation of publications by information to the rest of the world of what is available. We encourage growth in the publishing industries by increased sales. We contribute technical know-how indirectly by the level of the cataloging work done for our accessions lists and our catalog cards and directly by whatever

technical advice our experts on the scene may be able to provide the local librarians. In certain instances the development of useful dialogues and personal as well as professional friendships have further encouraged increasingly important exchanges of information, technical library publications, and, in the end, technical proficiency. Even the example set by the scope of our efforts may beneficially affect library thinking in the lesser developed countries. Encouraging is the conclusion of a soon-to-be-published study of NPAC prepared under the auspices of UNESCO by Dr. Herman Liebaers, Director of the Royal Library of Belgium. Dr. Liebaers concludes his intensive and revealing report with the following statement: "The shared cataloging program of the Library of Congress proves that there is even now sufficient compatibility in the world to ensure effective cooperation, but, as of now the United States alone is bearing the burden of this proof at the cost of great financial effort. We cannot really continue to count on the will and the resources of a single country to supply single-handedly a supranational bibliographic effort; we must consider the shared cataloging program of the Library of Congress as an example and a spur to us to improve our national bibliographic services and to review and change our present techniques in order to be able to contribute to a common pool . . . In closing let us recall again that not enough time has gone by to permit us to make a proper evaluation of the impact of the NPAC on countries outside the United States; however the reactions which the program has aroused in all corners of the world and at all professional levels, already show the importance of what is at stake."

The foregoing is truly significant as much by what it reveals of a disposition to contribute and share (which hopefully will be fostered and will continue to grow) as by its other implications.

Before I conclude, I should like to enter certain caveats and reservations into this presentation. There are undoubted advantages to centralized cataloging. There are also certain limitations.

G. G. Firsov, of the USSR, in an article on the importance of centralized cataloging that appeared in the *UNESCO Bulletin for Libraries* in 1967 covered some of these:

"Despite its many undoubted advantages, however, centralized cataloging has certain real disadvantages which cannot take account of local conditions or the particular requirements of individual libraries. Printed cards cannot meet the needs of all libraries to the same extent. Some do not find the headings used for the entries satisfactory; others require fuller bibliographical data. For some, the quality of the class marks or the subject headings used is unsatisfactory."

To these I might add other difficulties: the complications involved in providing the type of cataloging necessary for small public and school libraries; costs of a centralized service; speed of the service. All of these elements require further attention and work on the part of any agency concerned with a centralized national service. Attention must continue to be given to the specific requirements of specialized library users. No single centralized system can provide unique entries that simultaneously meet the needs of school children, scientists, casual readers, research specialists, technicians and others. The very diversity that sees the establishment of numerous professional library associations aimed at providing different channels of communication for specialized libraries rules out any universal prescription for all bibliographic ailments. At the same time, I expect that the old saw "nothing succeeds like success" will continue to hold true for this program. I trust that success will be the reward of those much maligned virtues, patience and determination.

Since tonight's talk is a part of the University program for its centennial celebration, it seems fitting that I go back into the record almost 100 years. Here is Mr. John William Wallace, president of the Pennsylvania Historical Society, delivering the address of welcome to the first ALA conference on Wednesday, October 4, 1876, saying, "I see nothing which in coming years is to stand between the librarian and an issue upon him of books upon books so vast and so uninterrupted that, unless he brings the benefit of something like science to his aid, he will be overwhelmed and buried in their very mass." Here is the young Melvil Dewey a few days later at the same conference, saying, "People on all sides are continually urging the great desirability of doing something. About once in so long, articles appear in different countries restating the follies of the present system of doing the same thing over a thousand times as

we librarians do in cataloging books that reach so many libraries. But right here they all stop. There somehow seems to be an idea among certain leaders of our craft that such a thing is wholly visionary. At least there's failure to take any practical steps in the matter which seems to indicate such a belief. Now I believe, after giving this question considerable attention, that it is perfectly practicable . . . If we have sufficient faith to take the matter in hand I have full confidence that we shall make a success of this cooperative cataloging." And here, in a communication to the American Library Journal, Vol. I, No. 10, 1877, Mr. Bassett Cadwallader asks for a national library system with a universal catalog; an organization to be established at the Library of Congress. Not only would each publication be cataloged and classified once, but each would be given a number. In fact, Mr. Cadwallader foresees the time when publishers would issue a distinctive number in each book printed, so that "the numbers of books would become synonymous with their names all over the land," and wherever another library obtained a book that was not handled by the central library, it would make a report to headquarters. In the same communication he also urges the printing of a catalog listing all of these titles, and the form he recommends is a dictionary catalog of authors, titles, and subjects in one series with full notes and cross references; this to be published in yearly supplements and then replaced by an entirely new cumulated edition as feasible. The union catalog idea is also brought into his visionary scheme of things.

So, perhaps we can say with Chaucer that "Ther is no newe gyse that it nas old,"—there is no new thing that it is not old. Mr. Cadwallader even has an idea resembling present plans for a national serials data program.

Previously I said that we were still far from the millennium. But to the librarians and visionaries of a hundred years ago, today would most certainly appear to be the beginning of an era where the realization of dreams and the fulfillment of visions may at last take place.

Thank you.

NOTES

[1] By 1972, shared cataloging arrangements had been extended to Romania and Spain, and regional acquisitions coverage from Djakarta extended to Singapore, Malaysia and Burma.

[2] In fiscal year 1972, some 240,000 titles were cataloged.

BIBLIOGRAPHY

Applebaum, Edmond L. "Developments at the Library of Congress," *Library Resources & Technical Services*, 12: 18–22, Winter 1968.

Applebaum, Edmond L. "The National Program for Acquisitions and Cataloging," *DC Libraries*, 39: 75–78, Fall 1968. (Paper read at the seminar on "Academic Libraries in the '70's" at the U.S. Office of Education on May 2, 1968 under the auspices of its Division of Library Programs.)

Association of Research Libraries. Minutes of the Meetings. (*See* the minutes for each semi-annual meeting from the 63rd Meeting, January 1964 to the present.)

Bachman, Marie-Louise. "Svenskt Bibliografiskt Samarbete med Kongressbiblioteket i Washington," *Notiser fran Riksbibliotekarien*, Arg. 3, nr 3/4: 12–13, Okt 1970. (The article, "Swedish Bibliographical Cooperation with the Library of Congress in Washington," describes briefly the NPAC program and the relation of the Bibliographical Institute of the Royal Library in Stockholm to the Library of Congress' Scandinavian office in Oslo.)

Balnaves, John. "Shared Cataloguing," *Australian Library Journal*, 15: 196–199, October 1966.

Blean, Keith C., Jr. "Developments at Stanford," *Library Resources & Technical Services*, 12: 23–25, Winter 1968.

Bóday, Pál. "Nagyszabásu gyarapitási és közös feldolgozási program az USA-ban," *Könyvtári Figyelö*, May(?) 1967. ("National Program for Acquisitions and Cataloging: Large Scale Acquisitions and Shared Processing Program in the U.S.A." by Dr. Pál Bóday, Head of the Information Department in the Centre of Library Science and Methodology in Budapest, Hungary.)

Brock, Clifton. "Developments at North Carolina," *Library Resources & Technical Services*, 12: 25–27, Winter 1968.

"Centralized Cataloging at the National and International Level," *Library Resources & Technical Services*, 11: 27–49, Winter 1967. (Verbatim report except for Mr. Cronin's paper of a program at the New York Conference of ALA on July 11, 1966, organized by William S. Dix who served as moderator of the panel.)

Cronin, John W. "Remarks on LC Plans for Implementation of New Centralized Acquisitions and Cataloging Program Under Title II-C, Higher Education Act," *Library Resources & Technical Services*, 11 : 35–46, Winter 1967.

Cronin, John W. "The Library of Congress National Program for Acquisitions and Cataloging," *Libri*, 16 : 113–117, No. 2, 1967.

Cronin, John W. "The National Program for Acquisitions and Cataloging," *Louisiana State University Library Lectures*, Second Series, no. 5–8 (Baton Rouge 1968), p. 10–24. (Mr. Cronin's lecture on January 6, 1967 was the sixth in the second series.)

Dawson, John M. "A History of Centralized Cataloging," *Library Resources & Technical Services*, 11: 28–32, Winter 1967.

Dawson, John M. "The Acquisitions and Cataloging of Research Libraries: A Study of the Possibilities for Centralized Processing," *Library Quarterly*, 27: 1–22, January 1957.

Dawson, John M. "The Library of Congress: Its Role in Cooperative and Centralized Cataloging," *Library Trends*, 16: 85–96, July 1967. Bibliography: p. 95–96.

Dix, William S. "Centralized Cataloging and University Libraries–Title II, Part C, of the Higher Education Act of 1965," *Library Trends*, 16: 97–111, July 1967. Bibliography: p. 110–111.

Dix, William S. "John Cronin and Shared Cataloging," *Library Resources & Technical Services*, 12: 395–396, Fall 1968.

Dix, William S. "Recent Developments in Centralized Cataloging," *Library Resources & Technical Services*, 11: 32–35, Winter 1967.

Domanovszky, Akos. "A Shared Cataloging Program," *Magyar Konyvszemle*, 85: 64–70, January 1969.

Ellsworth, Ralph E. "Another Chance for Centralized Cataloging," *Library Journal*, 89: 3104–3107, September 1, 1964.

Firsov, G. G. "Centralized Cataloguing and Its Importance," *Unesco Bulletin for Libraries*, 21: 200–206, July–August 1967.

Gard, Anne V. "Library of Congress National Program for Acquisitions and Cataloging," *Bibliotheekleven*, 53: 510–513, October 1968.

Grønland, Erling. "The Role of the National Bibliography within the Library of Congress Shared Cataloguing Scheme," *Bibliotek og Forskning*, 16: 34–48 (1967). Bibliography: p. 46–48. (Paper read at the SCONUL Conference, Saltsjöbaden, Sweden, September 1967.)

Herath, Kent A. "Books from Brazil," *Américas*, 20: 36–37, September 1968. (Summary of the activities of the NPAC regional acquisitions office in Rio de Janeiro, Brazil.)

James, Jerry R. "The Establishment of an Overseas Acquisitions Center: A Personal Reminiscence," *Quarterly Journal of the Library of Congress*, 27: 206–212, July 1970.

James, Jerry. "The Library of Congress Program in Eastern Africa," *The Bibliography of Africa: Proceedings and Papers*, p. 75–82. New York, Africana Publishing Corporation, 1970. (This paper was read at the International Conference on African Bibliography held in Nairobi, Kenya, in December 1967. The papers were edited by J. D. Pearson and Ruth Jones.)

Kaltwasser, Franz Georg. "Internationaler Austausch von Kataloginformationen: Das 'Shared Cataloguing Program' der Library of Congress in europäischer Sicht," *Libri*, 18: 237–256, Nos. 3–4, 1968. (Paper entitled "International Exchange of Cataloging Information: the European View of the 'Shared Cataloging Program'" presented at the 34th Session of IFLA Frankfurt am Main, Germany, August 1968.)

Kozlov, V. *tr.* "Raspredelenniia Katalogizatsiia: Novyi Vzgliad na Staruiu Probelemu," *Teoriia i praktika nauchnoi informatsii*, no. 6: 1–7, March 19, 1969. (Translation of item 44 (A. J. Wells "A New Look at an Old Problem"), printed in the series *Theory and Practice of Scientific Information* issued by the All-Union Institute of Scientific and Technical Information (VINITI) in Moscow.)

Liebaers, Herman. "Shared Cataloguing: Part I. The National Programme for Acquisitions and Cataloguing in the United States of America," *Unesco Bulletin for Libraries*, 24: 62–72, March–April 1970.

Liebaers, Herman. "Shared Cataloguing: Part II. The National Programme for Acquisitions and Cataloguing (NPAC) Outside the United States of America," *Unesco Bulletin for Libraries*, 24: 126–138, May–June 1970. (This two-part study of NPAC was written under contract with Unesco.)

Lorenz, John G. "International Implications of the Shared Cataloging Program; Planning for Bibliographic Control," *Libri*, 17: 276–284, No. 4, 1967.

Lunn, Jean. "Shared Cataloging: The Consumer in North America," *Canadian Library Journal*, 27: 346–350, Summer 1970. (Application of the results of the NPAC program in North American libraries as reported by Dr. Lunn in Working Paper No. 5 at the International Meeting of Cataloging Experts, IFLA, Copenhagen, 1969.)

McGowan, Frank M. "The Library of Congress in Southeast Asia," *Proceedings of the Conference on Access to Southeast Asian Research Materials*, edited by Cecil Hobbs, p. 55–59. Washington, 1971.

McKinlay, J. "ANL versus LC," *Australian Library Journal*, 18: 1–5, February 1969. (This comparison between ANB and LC entries was undertaken as a result of the expansion of the *Australian National Bibliography* to include full catalogue entries and the development of the Library of Congress shared cataloging program.)

Moore, Alvin, Jr. "A Review of the Library of Congress Program in Eastern Africa," *Conference on the Acquisition of Material from Africa, University of Birmingham, 25th April 1969*, p. 1–6. Ag Zug, Inter Documentation Company, 1970. (This conference was convened in Great Britain under the auspices of the Standing Conference on Library Material on Africa. The reports and papers were compiled by Valerie Bloomfield.)

Mumford, L. Quincy. "International Breakthrough: An Account of the Operational Beginnings of the Shared Cataloging Program," *Library Journal*, 92: 79–82, January 1, 1967.

Mumford, L. Quincy. "International Co-operation in Shared Cataloguing," *Unesco Bulletin for Libraries*, 22: 9–12, January–February 1968.

Oizumi, Etsuro. "Zensekai bunken shiryō no hōkatsu shūshū to katarugu no shūchū sakusei; MARC no haikei," *Gendai no toshokan*, 8: 175–184, no. 3, 1970. ("The acquisition of materials of the world and centralized cataloging; the background of MARC," an article which appeared in *Modern Libraries* (Tokyo).)

Orne, Jerrold. "Title II-C, A Little Revolution," *Southeastern Librarian*, 16: 164–167, Fall 1966.

Piercy, Esther J. and Robert L. Talmadge, *eds*. "Cooperative and Centralized Cataloging," *Library Trends*, 16: July 1967.

Poves, María Luisa. "Un Nuevo Programa de Catalogacion Centralizada a Nivel Internacional," *Bibliotheca Hispana*, 24: 1–7, No. 2–3, 1966. ("A Program for Centralized Cataloging at an International Level," by the Chief of the Cataloging Service of the National Library of Spain in Madrid.)

Raymond, Boris and Derek Francis. "Is This Trip Really Necessary? or Should University Libraries Do Their Own Original Cataloguing?" *Canadian Library*, 25: 35–37, July 1968.

Ready, William. "Cards across the Water," *Library Review*, 21: 129–131, Autumn 1967.

Ross, Ryburn M. "Developments at Cornell," *Library Resources & Technical Services*, 12: 22–23, Winter 1968.

Schrader, Barbara, and Elaine Orsini. "British, French, and Australian Publications in the National Union Catalog: A Study of NPAC's Effectiveness," *Library Resources & Technical Services*, 15: 345–354, Summer 1971.

Sebestyén, Géza. "Nemzetközi Katalóguscédulák?" *Könyvtáros*, 16: 629–633, November 1966. ("International Catalog Cards?" by the Deputy Director of the National Library of Hungary.)

Skipper, James E. "Future Implications of Title II-C, Higher Education Act of 1965," *Library Resources and Technical Services*, 11: 46–49, Winter 1967.

Skipper, James E. "International Implications of the Shared Cataloging Program: Introductory Statement," *Libri*, 17: 270–275, No. 4, 1967.

Stevens, Norman D., *ed*. "The National Program for Acquisitions and Cataloging: A Progress Report on Developments under the Title II-C of the Higher Education Act of 1965," *Library Resources & Technical Services*, 12: 17–29, Winter 1968. (Edited version of a program at the San Francisco Conference of ALA on June 29, 1967, organized by Dr. Stevens in his capacity as Chairman of the Resources Committee.)

Sukiasjan, E. R. "Centralized Classification: Achievements and Problems in Regard to Future Development," *Unesco Bulletin for Libraries*, 22: 189–195, 198, July–August 1968.

U.S. Congress. House. Committee on Appropriations. Hearings before the Subcommittee on the Departments of Labor, and Health, Education and Welfare. (*See* the annual hearings for each fiscal year from fiscal year 1966 through fiscal year 1971.)

U.S. Congress. House. Committee on Appropriations. Hearings before the Subcommittee on Legislative Branch Appropriations. (*See* the annual hearings for each fiscal year from fiscal year 1972 to the present.)

U.S. Congress. House. Committee on Education and Labor. Higher Education Act of 1965. Hearings before the Special Subcommittee on Education, 89th Cong., 1st sess., on H.R. 3220. p. 368–384, 748–753. Edith Green, Chairman of the subcommittee.

U.S. Congress. House. Committee on Education and Labor. To amend the Higher Education Act of 1965, the National Defense Education Act of 1958, the National Vocational Student Loan Insurance Act of 1965, and the Higher Education Facilities Act of 1963. Hearings before the Special Subcommittee on Education, 90th Cong., 2nd. sess., on H.R. 6232 and H.R. 6265. p. 107–116, 155–181. Edith Green, Chairman of the subcommittee.

U.S. Congress. Senate. Committee on Appropriations. Hearings before the Subcommittee on the Departments of

Labor, and Health, Education and Welfare, and Related Agencies. (*See* the annual hearings for each fiscal year from fiscal year 1966 through fiscal year 1971.)

U.S. Congress. Senate. Committee on Appropriations. Hearings before the Subcommittee on Legislative Branch Appropriations. (*See* the annual hearings for each fiscal year from fiscal year 1972 to the present.)

U.S. Congress. Senate. Committee on Labor and Public Welfare. Higher Education Act of 1965. Hearings before the Subcommittee on Education, 89th Cong., 1st sess., on S. 600. Part 2, p. 553–631. Wayne Morse, Chairman of the subcommittee.

U.S. Congress. Senate. Committee on Labor and Public Welfare. To amend the Higher Education Act of 1965, the National Defense Education Act of 1958, the National Vocational Student Loan Insurance Act of 1965, and the Higher Educational Facilities Act of 1963, and Related Acts. Hearings before the Special Subcommittee on Education, 90th Cong., 2nd. sess., on S. 3098 and S. 3099. Part 3, p. 1157–1183. Wayne Morse, Chairman of the subcommittee.

U.S. Library of Congress. Annual Reports. (*See* the annual reports of the Librarian of Congress from the report for the fiscal year ending June 30, 1966 to the present.)

U.S. Library of Congress. Information Bulletin. (*See* various issues from 1966 to the present.)

U.S. Library of Congress. Processing Department. "Library of Congress Policy on Shared Cataloging," *Cataloging Service Bulletin*, No. 75, May 1966.

U.S. Library of Congress. Processing Department. "National Program for Acquisitions and Cataloging Progress Reports."

No. 1, September 1, 1966	No. 8, April 14, 1969
No. 2, October 26, 1966	No. 9, August 4, 1969
No. 3, February 27, 1967	No. 10, May 15, 1970
No. 4, June 14, 1967	No. 11, January 11, 1971
No. 5, December 4, 1967	No. 12, June 9, 1971
No. 6, May 1, 1968	No. 13, January, 1972
No. 7, January 2, 1969	No. 14, June, 1972

Vosper, Robert. "International Implications of the Shared Cataloging Program: Planning for Resource Development," *Libri*, 17: 285–293, No. 4, 1967.

Vosper, Robert. "The Public Interest," *Newsletter of the American Documentation Institute*, 6: 1, 14–15, January–February 1968. (Keynote Address, presented before the 29th Annual Meeting, ADI, Santa Monica, Calif., October 4, 1966.)

Vrieze, Frans de. "The Library of Congress National Program for Acquisitions and Cataloging: European Perspectives," *Libri*, 18: 257–261, Nos. 3–4, 1968. (Paper presented at the 34th Session of the International Federation of Library Associations General Council, Frankfurt am Main, Germany, August 1968.)

Wells, A. J. "Shared Cataloging A New Look At An Old Problem," *Aslib Proceedings*, 20: 534–541, December 1968. Bibliography: p. 541. (Paper presented at the 42nd Aslib Annual Conference, Canterbury, September 22–25, 1968.)

Welsh, William J. "National Program for Acquisitions and Cataloging," *Proceedings of the Conference of the Canadian Library Association*, *St. John's 1969*, p. 44–49. Ottawa, Canadian Library Association, 1970. (Address given at the Technical Services Section Meeting, 12 June 1969, Memorial University of Newfoundland. Mr. Welsh, Director, LC Processing Dept., was unable to attend and his address was delivered by C. Sumner Spalding, Assistant Director for Cataloging, Processing Department.)

Westby, Barbara M. "Library of Congress' Shared Catalogue Program and the MARC Project: Aspects of International Cooperation," *NFF-skrift*, number 1. (Oslo 1969). 9 p. Bibliography: p. 9. (The full name of this publication is *Norske Forskningsbibliotekarers Forening-skrift*.)

Westby, Barbara M. *Shared Cataloguing*. Dublin, University College Dublin, 1969. 16 p. (School of Librarianship Publications) Bibliography: p. 13–16. (This pamphlet records a lecture given by Miss Westby to the students of the School of Librarianship in December 1968.)

Williams, Lorraine. "The Shared Cataloging Program: the Importance of Being Ordered," *College and Research Libraries*, 30 : 342–343, July 1969.

State Libraries and Centralized Processing

F. William Summers

This study reviews the literature relating to processing centers which are operated or substantially funded by state library agencies to serve public libraries. The role of LSA and LSCA funds and the major problems affecting these centers are discussed. Some additional problem areas which appear to be developing are also identified.

BACKGROUND AND DEFINITION

The origins of interest in centralized cataloging and processing cannot be attributed to any single person or to any particular period. It is a subject which has long occupied the interest of librarians and about which there has been much discussion and writing.

In this country concern about the problem of duplication of efforts in cataloging began early. In 1853, in a report to the Smithsonian Institution, Charles C. Jewett outlined a plan for producing stereotype plates for printing catalog copy which could be used for all libraries. Jewett's proposal advocated cooperative cataloging by libraries with the work centered in the Smithsonian (40).

In 1893 *Library Journal* announced two plans. The Rudolph Indexer Company proposed to prepare copy for 100,000 titles in the ALA Model Library and to prepare cards for all new books after January 1, 1894. This work was to be under the direction of C. A. Cutter. The Library Bureau also proposed to begin issuing cards for new books on a semiweekly basis (12, p. 508).

These efforts were not successful on a large scale, and in 1901 the Library of Congress announced that it would begin the distribution of sets of cards prepared for its own catalogs. Apparently the initiation of the Library of Congress card service was considered a solution to the problem of cataloging in public libraries, because it was more than forty years before the literature began to pay more than scant attention to the subject.

Since 1945 a great deal has been written about centralized and cooperative cataloging. For this paper it was decided to focus on a single aspect of the subject. State library agencies have been very active in the establishment and operation of processing centers, and it was felt that an examination from this viewpoint might offer some insight into the whole topic.

As one examines the literature, it soon becomes apparent that state libraries have been involved with centralized processing in a number of ways—directly as operators of centers, indirectly as sources of funds for centers, and even more indirectly in their role as a planning agency for library services in bringing a number of libraries together to plan centralized processing activities. This paper will deal with those activities in which the state library acts either as operator of a center or provides financial resources to other libraries for the operation of centers.

Two events which occurred in 1956 appear to have provided great impetus to the development of centralized processing. These are the publication of the ALA standards for public libraries and the passage of the Library Services Act (LSA). The standards call for systems of libraries based on efficient size units and for centralized processing. The LSA and the subsequent Library Services and Construction Act (LSCA) provided funds to the states which could be used to encourage the development of systems. Prior to 1956 centralized processing activities were few: notably Georgia, Missouri, and New York.

By 1958 interest and activity had expanded to the degree that the entire Summer issue of *Library Resources & Technical Services* was devoted to centralized processing. Four of the articles in this

SOURCE: Reprinted from *Library Resources and Technical Services* XIV, 2 (Spring 1970), pp. 236–257.
Numbers in parentheses refer to the numbered items in the bibliography.

issue presented case studies of processing centers in operation. Dorothy Bendix reported a survey of existing centers and suggested that LSA would stimulate more activity (4). Evelyn Mullen suggested, in an article entitled "Guidelines for Establishing a Centralized Library Processing Center" (50), six advantages for centralized processing. Since these statements, or essentially similar ones, appear in most articles about centralized processing, they are worth noting. They are:

1. Concentration of expensive cataloging tools.
2. Concentration of able catalogers.
3. Shortened lines of communication with corresponding efficiency and administration.
4. Greater use of standardized rules and procedures.
5. Elimination of extra revising and editing.
6. Greater ease in maintaining cataloging policy (50, p. 172).

In 1959 Karl Brown reported that by the summer of 1958 twenty-one states had centralized processing programs or planned to start them (7, p. 377). Throughout the late 1950s and early 1960s the literature is filled with announcements of new services and plans for processing centers. In 1961 Mullen characterized the literature as "largely concerned with what libraries propose to do in centralized processing and how projects are starting, rather than what they have accomplished" (51, p. 35). She voiced the hope that the next eighteen to twenty-four months would produce some articles which would include well-documented information on costs—both capital outlay and operating, as well as staffing and work loads (51, p. 38).

Mullen's plea did not go unheeded. In 1962 Mary Lee Bundy published *Public Library Processing Centers*, which is the most comprehensive normative study of processing centers to appear. She found forty-five centralized processing units in twenty-five states. Bundy's findings indicated that most of the processing centers were young (only four were over ten years old); most served a small number of libraries (only eight served twenty or more libraries); most depended in some part on state or federal subsidy (only six received their total support from participating libraries); most operated at a low volume (only thirteen centers processed over 20,000 volumes) (10).

Centers continue to proliferate. In the past five years new centers have been announced in Hawaii, Kentucky, Indiana, Illinois, Texas, Connecticut, Maryland, Wyoming, and Nebraska. Planning is underway in Kansas and New Jersey. In 1964 James Hunt estimated that there were at least sixty processing centers (38).

THE ERA OF THE WIZARDS

Beginning about 1966 a new trend—the utilization of management consultants in planning and evaluating processing centers—can be discerned. New York apparently pioneered this effort with a series of studies by Nelson Associates, Incorporated. This firm has also undertaken studies of processing centers or centers as part of state libraries in Iowa, Ohio, and Colorado. The firm of Arthur D. Little, Incorporated has undertaken similar studies in Florida, North Carolina, Texas, and Kentucky. It is interesting to note that all of these states had initiated centralized processing activities well prior to the studies undertaken by these firms.

It is generally not possible (and is always dangerous) to assign causes of behavior based solely on a literature search, but one cannot help but wonder whether or not the utilization of management consultants represents an awareness on the part of these states that centralized processing is an extremely complex business enterprise requiring highly specialized skills and administrative ability.

THE PRESENT SITUATION

The evolution of the literature presents an interesting picture of change. While the writing about this subject has not been unduly optimistic, a pattern of high expectation certainly characterized the early announcements of a centralized processing activity. For most of these activities, the few announcements in state library association journals and the state library newsletter plus a news item in one or more national library publications is the extent of the literature coverage. The literature would also support a belief that all of the announced centers flourished and are still in existence because there are no reports of centers which failed or even reports of centers which are having operating difficulties, except the Oak Park (Illinois) Center, whose backlog and financial deficit received coverage, but whose more recent successful recovery has largely gone unnoticed (58).

At the moment there would appear to be from sixty to eighty processing centers operated, or substantially funded, by state libraries. These centers are for the most part still plagued by the problems noted by Bundy: small centers, serving small libraries with limited volume for processing and heavily dependent upon state and federal funds. The fact that thirteen years after the standards and LSA these centers, which were born with such high expectations for growth and development, still exhibit infantile characteristics is a problem with which the profession will need to grapple in the very near future.

RESEARCH

To categorize one group of writings as research and thereby exclude other writings on the same subject is to tread on very thin ice. It is a supportable statement, however, that centralized processing activities have not been supported by significant research studies. In 1960 Maurice Tauber characterized the literature of centralized cataloging as "largely philosophical, historical, polemical and descriptive" (66, p. 182). Relatively little has occurred in the last decade to make that statement untrue. Most of the research has occurred after the establishment of the centers.

Normative Studies—As processing centers began in the post-LSA period, it was necessary to provide information about these relatively new activities. The Bendix study cited earlier described the methods of operation of several centers and discussed the various administrative arrangements in use (4). The Bundy study (also cited earlier) is the most comprehensive of these studies and provided the first clear picture of what was taking place across the country (10). In 1966 Sarah Vann reported on a study of thirty state library operated centers (sixteen of these in New York) and five state library funded centers. Of twenty-three respondents, eighteen were still receiving state and/or federal aid for continuance of the operation. The range in volumes processed was from a low of 20,000 volumes to a high of 200,000 volumes but only five of the centers has passed the 100,000 volume mark. The range in members of these centers was from ten or less to sixty. She reports that the centers still have difficulty with local idiosyncracies of cataloging, that

ordering is still a serious problem and that many member libraries still tinker to some extent with the cataloging done at the center (70).

Theses and Dissertations—Only a few theses or dissertations have been devoted to centralized processing. One of the most significant is Donald D. Hendricks' *Comparative Costs of Book Processing in a Processing Center and in Five Individual Libraries*. The study dealt with the Oak Park, Illinois, center and five of its clients. The study found that the costs at the Center (when all costs were included) were significantly higher than at the individual libraries, although he suggests that there were reasons for the differences (33). Other researchers have found difficulty in getting accurate cost data.

Studies of Individual Centers—It was very interesting to the author that one of the earliest studies of centralized processing was also one of the best. In 1959 Mrs. Brigitte L. Kenney studied the Southwest Missouri Library Service, Incorporated. This nonprofit corporation organized by a group of libraries attracted much interest and is the subject of a number of articles in the bibliography. Mrs. Kenney's study is notable because it did not focus upon the techniques of operating the center but dealt with how well the center had accomplished its objectives (42). Of particular interest is the fact that she attempted to measure what impact the center had on the services of the member libraries. While this was not always possible, she was able to establish that in several cases the center has saved both time and money for the members and that this time and money has been diverted to new activities (42). This was the only study which could be found which attempted to measure whether the claimed advantages for processing centers actually exist and whether these advantages do, in fact, accrue to the member libraries.

Clayton Highum followed Hendricks' studies of Oak Park with a study for the Illinois State Library on the feasibility of a statewide center. He recommended that such a center be established and that the Oak Park center become its nucleus (36).

Bibliographies—There are two bibliographies in the field which are very valuable to the researcher: Mary Hanley's *Centralized Processing, Recent Trends and Current Status* (31), and Lawrence E. Leonard's *Cooperative and Centralized Cataloging and Processing: A Bibliography, 1850-1967* (43). The Leonard work is the more useful because it is later and has a much broader scope.

Standards—A set of performance standards which could guide policy decisions about centralized processing has not been developed by the profession. In 1958 Mullen suggested some guidelines (51), and in 1966 the ALA Regional Processing Committee issued a broader and more detailed statement entitled "Guidelines for Centralized Technical Services" (3). These statements represent the experience and judgment of practitioners in operating and using centers. The literature does not permit any judgment of the effectiveness of these statements in shaping policy decisions.

IMPLICATIONS

One frequently turns to the literature in search of answers and finds only more questions. Such is the case with this study. As the bibliography indicates, a great deal has been written about state libraries and their activities in centralized processing, but a great many more questions are not answered in the literature. The literature reveals a great many problems which remain to be solved. Among these are the following:

1. *Is centralized processing an economically feasible activity for the states in the long run?*

The fact that many centers are dependent upon state and/or federal subsidy long past the establishment period should be a cause for concern. At the moment this paper is being written, Congress is debating a budget proposal which would cut federal funds for state libraries by 50 percent. It is also important to note that 1970–71 is the year in which the Library Services and Construction Act will expire unless renewed by Congress. Should there be a curtailment of federal funds, the states will certainly have to reassess the priority given to centralized processing. To the extent that the availability of federal funds has permitted the states to engage in economically unsound activities, centralized processing may face substaitial reverses.

Related to this is the growing importance of commercial processing centers. There are now many of these, and they are competing for business. In earlier years these centers existed primarily as a means for book jobbers to obtain book business. Now commercial centers exist whose sole business is book cataloging and processing. If this sector of business continues to grow, the state libraries may find it difficult to justify the operation of activities which compete with private business in the state.

2. *What are the parameters for a centralized processing operation?*

In their study of New York State, Nelson Associates suggested a single statewide cataloging operation for all of the libraries in the state excluding the New York City libraries and, additionally, suggested three centers to process books (52).

The libraries which would be served in this system add well over a million volumes per year. At the other end of the size scale, the data in the Vann study (71) indicates that the average per processing center is well below 100,000 volumes. The low-volume center still predominates. Related to this is the fact that centers seem to have some difficulty in attracting new clients after the initial establishment period. In Bundy's study (10), twenty-five out of thirty-seven centers reported that their future plans included obtaining more clients.

The low-volume statistics would also intimate that the centers may not have attracted large public libraries as clients. One study which this literature search calls for is the need to draw a composite picture of processing center clients. The literature points to a hypothesis that the new "larger unit," i.e., a county or regional library or a municipal library extending its service by contract, which has been created by state agencies with state and/or federal funds, are the primary clients and that older libraries not part of these new systems would be under-represented among the clients. In some instances state library agencies have created and used processing centers as an incentive to encourage libraries to affiliate with systems. This use of centralized processing as a glue in the sticking together of library systems may in part explain the persistence of state and federal subsidy as a basic element of processing center support.

3. *What kinds of management skills do processing centers need?*

The studies by management consultants, reports of flourishing centers, and the few reports of failures suggest that the mastery of business management principles may be more essential to success than the knowledge which the professional librarian brings to the operation. A processing center is more like a commercial enterprise than it is like a library. Yet, often it is governed and operated solely by individuals who are accustomed only to the operations of libraries. The use of management consultants may well indicate that state libraries are aware of this fact and that they use these firms to obtain needed management inputs into policy decisions.

4. What is the future of centralized processing?

During the last decade or so in which state library operated processing centers have proliferated, these same agencies have been giving increasing attention to interlibrary cooperation. Thus far the literature indicates that centralized processing will not be a vehicle for initiating cooperation among types of libraries. Very few instances of centers serving more than one type of library can be found and the Bundy study (10) reported that public librarians did not feel that a center which met their needs could also serve other types of libraries.

The ALA guidelines (3) state that it is possible for a single center to serve both school and public libraries. The experience at the Oak Park Center (35) and the Nelson Associates study in New York (54) point to the fact that there may be serious problems in so doing and that only strong, well-established centers should attempt it. College and university librarians have traditionally been unenthusiastic about centralized operations even among institutions of the same type.

Commercial services and partial cataloging services like the *Library Journal* kits will make it increasingly easier for libraries to achieve economical cataloging without centralization. If centralized processing is to survive as a major service of state libraries, it will need to provide a specialized service beyond the cataloging and processing of books and other library materials. The Arthur D. Little study of Florida (45) and the Nelson Associates study of New York (52) suggest the added role of serving as a statewide bibliographic center for libraries of all types. Without this or some similar enlargement of function, state libraries may find it increasingly difficult to justify the continued subsidization of centralized processing.

BIBLIOGRAPHY

1. Adcock, Elizabeth. "A Comparison of the Operation of Various Processing Centers," *Library Resources & Technical Services*, vol. 8, no. 1 (Winter 1964), 63–70.

2. Ake, Robert S. "Central Processing Unit," *LRTS*, vol. 2, no. 3 (Summer 1958), 183–84.

3. American Library Association. Resources and Technical Services Division. Regional Processing Committee. "Guidelines for Centralized Technical Services," *LRTS*, vol. 10, no. 2 (Spring 1966), 233–40.

4. Bendix, Dorothy. "Regional Processing for Public Libraries, a Survey," *LRTS*, vol. 2, no. 3 (Summer 1958), 155–70.

5. Bishop, Mary. "Wanted: Books to Process," *Library Occurrent*, vol. 21 (March 1964), 103–04.

6. Blease, W. "Cooperative Cataloging," *Library Association Record*, vol. 16 (December 15, 1914), 513–24.

7. Brown, Karl. "What's Happening Under L.S.A.," *Library Journal*, vol. 84 (February 1, 1959), 373–78.

8. Bundy, Mary Lee. *Attitudes of Non-members of Missouri Cataloging Cooperatives Toward Centralized Processing*. Urbana, Illinois: The Author, 1961.

9. Bundy, Mary Lee. *Missouri Processing Cooperatives*. Troy, New York: The Author, 1962.

10. Bundy, Mary Lee. *Public Library Processing Centers*. Troy, New York: The Author, 1962.

11. Cavender, Thera P. "Regional Processing," *Journal of Cataloging and Classification*, vol. 2, no. 4 (October 1955), 208–11.

12. "Central Card Cataloging," *Library Journal*, vol. 18 (December 1893), 508–10.

13. "Central Processing Studied," *Kansas Library Bulletin*, vol. 36, no. 1 (Winter 1967), 15.

14. "Connecticut State Library Moves Toward Centralized Processing," *Law Library Journal*, vol. 61 (May 1968), 161.

15. Connor, John M. and Mrs. D. W. "Proposed: A Processing Center for Public Libraries in Southern California," *California Librarian*, vol. 14 (March 1953), 155–57.

16. "Cooperative Processing in Kansas," *Kansas Library Bulletin*, vol. 37 (Spring 1968), 31.

17. Corbin, John B. "Centralized Processing Center of the Texas State Library," *Texas Libraries*, vol. 27 (Fall 1965), 118–25.

18. Corbin, John B. "Cooperative Processing Centralized in Texas," *Texas Library Journal*, vol. 41 (Winter 1965), 144–45.

19. Cors, Paul B. "Centralized Processing Theory into Practice," *Wyoming Library Roundup*, vol. 23 (December 1968), 10–17.

20. "C.L.R. Grant to N.E.L.I.N.E.T.," *Wilson Library Bulletin*, vol. 43 (May 1969), 825.

21. Dennis, Willard K. "Central Processing in Southwest Missouri," *Library Journal*, vol. 84 (November 1, 1959), 3378–80.

22. Dennis, Willard K. "Too Soon Oldt and Too Late Schmardt," *Oklahoma Librarian*, vol. 9 (January 1959), 4–5.

23. Drennan, Henry T. "Centralized Technical Services in Idaho," *Pacific Northwest Library Association Quarterly*, vol. 26 (April 1962), 150–58.

24. Drewry, E. Virginia. "Central Cataloging on the State Level in Georgia," *Public Library Division Reporter*, No. 5 (November 1956), pp. 42–44.

25. Drewry, E. Virginia, "Centralized Cataloging Frees Georgia Librarians," *Library Journal*, vol. 73 (March 1, 1948), 382-83.

26. Drewry, E. Virginia. "Georgia State Catalog Card Service," *LRTS*, vol. 2, no. 3 (Summer 1958), 176-80.

27. Eckford, Mary L. "The Library Service Center of Eastern Ohio, *LRTS*, vol. 5, no. 1 (Winter 1961), 5-33.

28. Georgia. Education Department Textbook and Library Service Division. "Centralized Cataloging Being Tried," *Library Journal*, vol. 70 (April 1, 1945), 310.

29. Gould, Charles H. "Regional Libraries," *Library Journal*, vol. 13 (1908), 218.

30. Griffith, David. "Eastern Ohio Regional Purchasing and Processing Center," *Focus*, vol. 13 (August 1959), 8-9.

31. Hanley, Mary. *Centralized Processing: Recent Trends and Current Status*. University of Illinois Graduate School of Library Science Occasional Paper, no. 71, 1964.

32. Harshe, Florence E. "Processing Procedures at the Watertown Regional Library Service," *Journal of Cataloging and Classification*, vol. 11 (October 1955), 217-20.

33. Hendricks, Donald D. *Comparative Costs of Book Processing in a Processing Center and in Five Individual Libraries*. Springfield, Illinois: Illinois State Library. 1966. (Abridgment of Ph.D. dissertation, University of Illinois).

34. Hendricks, Donald D. "Cooperative Growing Pains," *Library Journal*, vol. 90 (November 1, 1965), 4699-4703.

35. Hendricks, Donald D. "Organization for Processing at the BPC Oak Park, Illinois," *LRTS*, vol. 10, no. 4 (Fall 1966), 479-89.

36. Highum, Clayton D. *Centralized Processing for Public Libraries in Illinois*. Springfield, Illinois: Illinois State Library, 1967.

37. Holmgren, Edward S. "ANYLTS Reports Progress," *Bookmark*, vol. 27 (February 1968), 193-97.

38. Hunt, James R. "Historical Development of Processing Centers in the U. S., " *LRTS*, vol. 8, no. 1 (Winter 1964), 54-62.

39. Jast, L. Stanley. "Simple and Economical Plan for Founding a Cataloging Bureau for Public Libraries," *Library*, New Series, vol. 5 (1904), 146-57.

40. Jewett, Charles Coffin. *On the Construction of Catalogues of Libraries, and of a General Catalogue; and Their Publication by Means of Separate Stereotyped Titles*. Washington, Smithsonian Institution, 1852.

41. Kenney, Brigitte L. "Centralized Processing–Missouri Style," *LRTS*, vol. 2, no. 3 (Summer 1958), 185-90.

42. Kenney, Brigitte L. *Cooperative Centralized Processing*. Chicago: American Library Association, 1959.

43. Leonard, Lawrence. *Cooperative and Centralized Cataloging and Processing: A Bibliography, 1850-1967*. Urbana, Illinois: University of Illinois Graduate School of Library Service Occasional Paper, no. 93, 1968.

44. Little, Arthur D., Inc. *A Plan of Library Service for the Commonwealth of Kentucky*. A Report Prepared for the Kentucky State Library, 1969.

45. Little, Arthur D., Inc. *Centralized Processing for the State of Florida*. A Report Prepared for the Florida State Library, 1968.

46. Mahoney, Orcena. "Centralized Cataloging Developments and Problems," *Oklahoma Librarian*, vol. 6 (October 1956), 80-81.

47. Mahoney, Orcena. "Centralized Processing Centers," *LRTS*, vol. 5, no. 1 (Winter 1961), 40-47.

48. "Maryland Four-County Study Recommends Service Center," *Library Journal*, vol. 93 (October 15, 1968), 3738.

49. Morsch, Lucille M. "Cooperation and Centralization," *Library Trends, vol. 2 (October 1953), 345-55*.

50. Mullen, Evelyn Day. "Guidelines for Establishing a Centralized Library Processing Center," *LRTS*, vol. 2, no. 3 (Summer 1958), 171-75.

51. Mullen, Evelyn Day. "Regional Processing for Public Libraries," *LRTS*, vol. 5, no. 1 (Winter 1961), 34-40.

52. Nelson Associates, Inc. "Centralized Processing for the Libraries of New York State," *Bookmark*, vol. 25 (April 1966), 243-46.

53. Nelson Associates, Inc. "Feasibility of Further Centralizing the Technical Processing Operations of the Public Libraries of New York," *Bookmark*, vol. 25 (May 1966), 295-96.

54. Nelson Associates, Inc. *Feasibility of School and College Library Processing Through Public Library Systems in New York State*. A Report Prepared for the New York State Library, 1966.

55. Nelson Associates, Inc. *Implementing Centralized Processing for the Public Libraries of New York State*. A Report Prepared for the New York State Library, 1967.

56. "Nelson Associates Survey Recommends One Catalog Center for the State of New York," *Library Journal*, vol. 91 (June 15, 1966), 3132.

57. "New Centralized Processing Center in Honolulu," *Wilson Library Bulletin*, vol. 38 (October 1963), 129.

58. "New Illinois Processing Center is $31,000 in Debt Has Backlog," *Library Journal*, vol. 89 (December 15, 1964), 4876.

59. "New Jersey Library Group Debates Central Processing," *Library Journal*, vol. 93 (February 1, 1968), 501.

60. Price, Paxton P. "CCC in Missouri," *Missouri Library Association Quarterly*, vol. 17 (June 1956), 66-70.

61. Price, Paxton P. "Missouri State Library, a Cataloging Center for Local Libraries," *Public Library Division Reporter*, No. 5 (November 1956), p. 44.

62. Putnam, Herbert. "Relation of State Libraries and Library of Congress," *Library Journal*, December 1900, pp. 729-33.

63. Renfro, K. R. "Nebraska Centralized Processing." *Mountain Plains Library Quarterly*, vol. 13 (Winter 1969), 4-6.

64. "Space to be Provided for Extra Service to Kentucky Libraries," *Kentucky Library Association Bulletin*, vol. 27 (October 1963), 18-19.

65. Stoffel, Lester. "Equal Time for Smaller Debt," *Library Journal*, vol. 90 (February 1, 1965), 414.

66. Tauber, Maurice F. "Cataloging and Classification," vol. 1, Part 1, *State of the Library Art*, edited by Ralph R. Shaw. New Brunswick, New Jersey: Rutgers University, Graduate School of Library Service, 1960.

67. "Texas State Library Will Begin Centralized Processing Center as Pilot Project Under LSCA," *Library Journal*, vol. 90 (May 1, 1965), 2113.

68. Thompson, M. W. "California State Library Processing Center Under L.S.A.," *LRTS*, vol. 2, no. 3 (Summer 1958), 184–85.

69. Vann, Sarah K. "Centralized Processing Technologically Feasible but . . . ," *Pennsylvania Library Association Bulletin*, vol. 23 (May 1968), 228–31.

70. Vann, Sarah K., *et al.* "Processing Centers for Public Libraries," *LRTS*, vol. 10, no. 4 (Fall 1966), 489–92.

71. Vann, Sarah K. "Southeastern Pennsylvania Processing Center Feasibility Study," *LRTS*, vol. 10, no. 4 (Fall 1966), 461–78.

72. Wendel, Clara E. "Book Processing Center, Orlando, Florida," *LRTS*, vol. 8, no. 1 (Winter 1964), 71–76.

The Processing Department of the Library of Congress in 1969

William J. Welsh

INTRODUCTION

As the sixties drew to a close, it seemed an appropriate time to reflect on and evaluate the Processing Department's myriad activities of the past decade. Processing activities have steadily expanded over the years—an inevitable reflection of the publishing explosion, the increase in libraries and their demands on the Library of Congress, and the refinement and extension of bibliographic controls. The past ten years have marked a significant expansion in the Processing Department's operations and have brought it to the threshold of important new opportunities for the future. Acquisitions, cataloging, card production, publication of book catalogs and technical publications have all reached new highs, as shown in Tables 1-3.

Highlights of the Processing Department's activities in the sixties read like a text in technical services:

Publication in 1961 of the *National Union Catalog, 1952-55 Imprints* in thirty volumes, pushing coverage of the *National Union Catalog* back from January 1, 1956, to January 1, 1952, also believed to be the first large-scale bibliographical tool published on permanent-durable paper.

Publication in 1962 of the *Guide to Use of Dewey Decimal Classification*, interpreting the practices of the Decimal Classification Office and supplementing the basic general rules included in the introduction to each edition of the *Dewey Decimal Classification*.

Initiation of the Public Law 480 Program in 1962 for the acquisition of multiple copies of foreign publications for American research institutions through the use of U.S.-owned foreign currencies as authorized by section 104(n) of the Agricultural Trade Development and Assistance Act of 1954 (Public Law 83-480), as amended on Sept. 6, 1958.

Establishment of the Cataloging Instruction Office in 1964 to provide intensive in-service training and instruction in theoretical and practical cataloging for cataloger-trainees since the language skills, subject specialization, and professional library education necessary to catalog the wide range of materials received by LC cannot always be found in one person.

Publication in June 1965 of the seventeenth edition of the *Dewey Decimal Classification*.

Successful introduction in 1965 of the new publication, the *National Union Catalog—Register of Additional Locations*, recording additional locations for titles which have appeared in an annual or quinquennial edition of the *National Union Catalog*.

Development of a continuing publication to identify and list preservation copies of microforms in the *National Register of Microform Masters*, inaugurated in 1965 with the cooperation of scholars, librarians, and the producers of microforms.

Completion and publication on February 1, 1966, of the third and final edition of the monumental *Union List of Serials*, comprising five volumes, 4,649 pages, listing 156,499 serial titles in 956 North American libraries.

Application of automated techniques in the 1966 production of the seventh edition of the *Subject Headings Used in the Dictionary Catalogs of the Library of Congress*, the biggest book produced at that time by the Government Printing Office through the use of photocomposing machines and computers.

Approval and acceptance of the revolutionary concept of "shared cataloging" in 1966.

SOURCE: Reprinted from *Library Resources and Technical Services* XIV, 2 (Spring 1970), pp. 236-257.

FIGURE 1 Library of Congress, Processing Department*

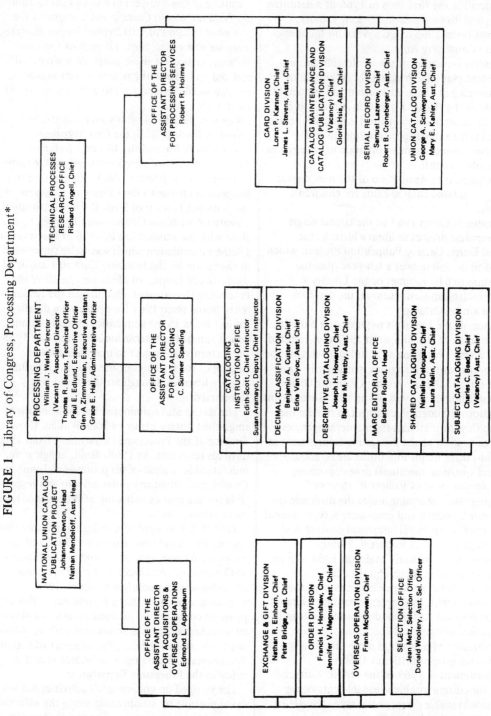

TECHNICAL PROCESSES
RESEARCH OFFICE
Richard Angell, Chief

PROCESSING DEPARTMENT
William J. Welsh, Director
(Vacant) Associate Director
Thomas R. Barcus, Technical Officer
Paul E. Edlund, Executive Officer
Glen A. Zimmerman, Executive Assistant
Grace E. Hall, Administrative Officer

NATIONAL UNION CATALOG
PUBLICATION PROJECT
Johannes Dewton, Head
Nathan Mendeloff, Asst. Head

OFFICE OF THE
ASSISTANT DIRECTOR
FOR PROCESSING SERVICES
Robert R. Holmes

CARD DIVISION
Loran P. Karsner, Chief
James L. Stevens, Asst. Chief

CATALOG MAINTENANCE AND
CATALOG PUBLICATION DIVISION
(Vacancy) Chief
Gloria Hsia, Asst. Chief

SERIAL RECORD DIVISION
Samuel Lazerow, Chief
Robert B. Croneberger, Asst. Chief

UNION CATALOG DIVISION
George A. Schwegmann, Chief
Mary E. Kahler, Asst. Chief

OFFICE OF THE
ASSISTANT DIRECTOR
FOR CATALOGING
C. Sumner Spalding

CATALOGING
INSTRUCTION OFFICE
Edith Scott, Chief Instructor
Susan Aramayo, Deputy Chief Instructor

DECIMAL CLASSIFICATION DIVISION
Benjamin A. Custer, Chief
Edna Van Syoc, Asst. Chief

DESCRIPTIVE CATALOGING DIVISION
Joseph H. Howard, Chief
Barbara M. Westby, Asst. Chief

MARC EDITORIAL OFFICE
Barbara Roland, Head

SHARED CATALOGING DIVISION
Nathalie Delougaz, Chief
Laura Malin, Asst. Chief

SUBJECT CATALOGING DIVISION
Charles C. Bead, Chief
(Vacancy) Asst. Chief

OFFICE OF THE
ASSISTANT DIRECTOR
FOR ACQUISITIONS &
OVERSEAS OPERATIONS
Edmond L. Applebaum

EXCHANGE & GIFT DIVISION
Nathan R. Einhorn, Chief
Peter Bridge, Asst. Chief

ORDER DIVISION
Francis H. Henshaw, Chief
Jennifer V. Magnus, Asst. Chief

OVERSEAS OPERATION DIVISION
Frank McGowan, Chief

SELECTION OFFICE
Jean Metz, Selection Officer
Donald Woolery, Asst. Sel. Officer

Completion of Schedule KF for U.S. federal, state, and local law in 1967 and beginning of application for the first time in 1966 of a definitive classification to materials in the Law Library.

Completion in 1966 of LC's work on the *Anglo-American Cataloging Rules.*

Successful launching of the worldwide and unprecedented National Program for Acquisitions and Cataloging in 1966, authorized and funded by Title II-C of the Higher Education Act of 1965.

Establishment in 1966 of the Technical Processes Research Office to develop, coordinate and administer a comprehensive program of research in bibliographical control.

Establishment in April 1966 of the new service offering annotated catalog cards for children's literature.

Commencement in 1967 of the largest single bibliographical project in library history, the National Union Catalog Publication Project, which is slated to complete over a ten-year span the publication in 610 volumes of the Library's greatest bibliographical resource, the pre-1956 National Union Catalog.

Issuance, at the Library's request, of a bulletin by the Bureau of the Budget in 1967 that resulted in the Library's receiving a far broader selection of U.S. Government publications, particularly those printed outside the Government Printing Office, and establishment in 1968 of the U.S. Government Publications Bibliographic Project to handle the growing flow of materials from federal agencies.

Reorganization of the Processing Department in 1968 into three major functional areas: acquisitions and overseas operations now continuing under the direction of Robert R. Holmes. cataloging also continuing under the direction of C. Sumner Spalding; and processing services including production and bibliographical control now under the direction of Robert R. Homes.

Division of the Official Catalog in 1968 into an Author-Title and a Topical Subject file.

Beginning of full scale mechanization of the Card Division with the implementation of Phase I of CARDS (Card Automated Reproduction and Distribution System) in 1968.

Inauguration of a new and more effective system of cataloging priorities in 1969.

Establishment in 1969 of the MARC Editorial Office for editing machine-readable cataloging copy now available on magnetic tapes for sale to libraries through the Card Division.

Completion in 1969 of a basic study for mechanized control of the Library's book purchasing activities.

Editing of the five-year (1963-67) cumulation of the *National Union Catalog* and delivery to the publisher in 1969 of 1,012 cubic feet of mounted copy weighing 10.5 tons. (If each of the three columns of text on those pages were separated and laid end-to-end the resulting continuous column would extend for more than thirty-eight miles.)

The past decade has also seen the demise of certain activities. Both the *East European Accessions Index* and the *Monthly Index of Russian Accessions* ceased publication, the former in 1961 and the latter in 1969. Eighteen years of cooperation between the Library of Congress and the National Library of Medicine in the *National Library of Medicine Catalog* were brought to a close with the publication in 1966 of the sexennial 1960-65 cumulation which was to be superseded in the future by the biweekly *Current Catalog* of the National Library of Medicine. In 1969 the Processing Department relinquished the responsibility borne since 1961 for preparing a detailed subject index to the summaries of dissertations which appear in *Dissertation Abstracts.* In 1968 the sixteen-year project to maintain a union catalog of the holdings of the U.S. Information Agency libraries throughout the world was terminated.

The sixties also culminated the long and distinguished library career of John William Cronin, director of the Processing Department from 1952 until his retirement in 1968. Bold, imaginative, indefatigable, a giant of his profession, John Cronin, more than any other person, was responsible for the past decade's log of Processing Department achievements.

Talk of the concept of Cataloging-in-Source both opened the decade and closed it. *The Cataloging-in-Source Experiment: A Report to the Librarian of Congress by the Director of the Processing Department* was published in March 1960, announcing regretfully that a permanent, full-scale program could not be justified in terms of financing, technical considerations, and utility. Almost ten years later to the day, the prospect of a modified program of Cataloging-in-Source is under study in the Processing Department.

The stepped-up volume in all activities has been made possible by steadily improving the effectiveness of LC's organization. The ten divisions in 1960 have become sixteen divisions employing

TABLE I
PROCESSING DEPARTMENT ACTIVITIES COMPARATIVE TABLE

	1960	1969
Additions to the collections (pieces)	868,980	1,488,876
Acquisitions (pieces)		
Purchased	570,454	1,105,299
Exchange	655,089	533,492
Gifts	839,824	910,536
Book for the Blind	16,821	417,319
Federal documents	600,395	872,754
State and local documents	104,027	217,298
Copyright	387,172	486,010
Donation from official sources	1,688,180	2,607,994
Cataloging		
Titles cataloged for printed cards	87,863	212,466
Manuscript collections cataloged	2,750	23,150
Dewey decimal numbers assigned	28,643	74,366
Other Processing Activities		
Cards prepared and distributed to LC's Catalogs	1,872,828	3,640,187
Catalog cards sold	32,057,488	63,404,123
Card subscribers	10,000	25,000
All-the-Books Program cooperating publishers	2,300	7,516
Titles received through the All-the-Books Program	12,476	37,958
Titles listed in *New Serial Titles*	75,000	210,000
Documents Expediting Project recipient libraries	54	139

TABLE 2
CUMULATIVE TABLE

	1960	1969
Total Collections of the Library	38,995,221	59,890,533
Cards in the Main Catalog	10,685,826	14,428,450
Cards in the Official Catalog	11,608,621	16,490,109

TABLE 3
GROWTH OF THE *National Union Catalog*

	1958–62 edition	1963–67 edition
Volumes	54	72
Pages	35,000	49,304
Titles listed	830,000	1,320,798
Location symbols listed	3,200,000	6,509,387

more than 1,700 people in 1969, as shown on the organization chart (Figure 1). LC's ability as the nation's bibliographical center to respond to the legitimate needs of libraries will be measured primarily by the blueprint for the future which can be unfolded over the next decade. The Processing Department feels a strong sense of opportunity and of mission in this field. Its goals must keep pace with changing conditions to match the aspirations of the research and library community. We see the product of the future not only as cards and catalogs but as a vastly improved information network, characterized by its vastness of scope and ease of access and creating values far in excess of cost. Each step in the growth of the Department has strengthened its capacity to understand the ingredients of such a network and, hopefully, to plan for it comprehensively, and to produce it successfully.

1969 REPORT OF THE PROCESSING DEPARTMENT

Acquisitions and Overseas Operations

National Program for Acquisitions and Cataloging

In fulfillment of the Library's responsibility under Title II-C of the Higher Education Act of 1965 and to meet the urgent needs of the library and information community through a centralized national cataloging effort, the Library of Congress initiated the National Program for Acquisitions and Cataloging (NPAC) late in fiscal year 1966. With appropriations totaling $13,800,000 for the three and one-half years of operation, the Library has increased its cataloging and support staff, arranged to "share" the cataloging data already prepared by the national bibliographies of twenty-two foreign countries, established a specialized Shared Cataloging Division, altered procedures to speed up book selection and ordering, established abroad nine shared cataloging centers and three regional acquisitions centers staffed chiefly by local personnel in the countries where they are located, added an extra printing shift to hasten production of printed catalog cards in the Library Branch of the Government Printing Office in Washington, distributed daily to more than ninety research libraries depository sets of LC printed cards numbering more than 200,000 titles in fiscal year 1969, searched 382,302 reports from libraries for titles not found in the depository sets which resulted in orders for 83,758 titles, increased cataloging production from 110,000 titles in fiscal year 1965 to more than 200,000 titles in fiscal year 1969, and produced accessions lists based on the regional acquisitions efforts in Eastern Africa and Indonesia. This greatly increased amount of cataloging information is available to all libraries in the form of printed catalog cards or in the proof-sheet service as well as in the Library's printed book catalogs.

On May 15, 1969, the Librarian of Congress appeared before the subcommittee on Labor, Health, Education and Welfare Appropriations of the House Committee on Appropriations to urge additional funding for fiscal year 1970 for Title II-C as amended. The revised Administration budget request for NPAC, which is funded by Title II-C, was for $4,500,000—$1,000,000 below the amount appropriated for fiscal year 1969, and $2,856,000 below the original 1970 Administration budget request.

As a result of the proposed reduction in funding, it became necessary in early May to consider several NPAC program changes and to initiate a reduction-in-force. The proposed changes were discussed with members of the Shared Cataloging Committee of the Association of Research Libraries on May 13 and their advice was sought on these and other methods of adjusting to the fund reduction. All plans for the expansion of the program to other countries such as Spain and Portugal were necessarily postponed. The *Monthly Index of Russian Accessions* was discontinued. This publication was previously funded separately by HEW and was attached to the Title II-C appropriation last year by an amendment. In all, 131 positions on Title II-C funds were eliminated—71 in the Processing Department, 7 in the Administrative

Department, and 53 in *MIRA*. The 71 positions eliminated in the Processing Department were primarily in the Shared Cataloging and Descriptive Cataloging Divisions. Implementation of the amendments to Title II-C was necessarily deferred.

The shared cataloging program for Brazilian publications was terminated and the NPAC office in Rio de Janeiro reverted to its original function as an acquisitions office for Brazilian publications. Publications continue to receive LACAP (Latin American Cooperative Acquisitions Program) numbers assigned in Brazil and all LACAP selections continue to receive high priority cataloging at LC. The American Field Directors in Scandinavia and France have been recalled to Washington, bringing the number of European shared cataloging centers operating under the direction of local staff to a total of four: London, The Hague, Paris, and Oslo.

The lack of excess currencies has brought to an end the PL-480 program in Indonesia. Until such time as funding is available for implementation of the Higher Education Amendments of 1968 which would permit the Librarian of Congress "to pay administrative costs of cooperative arrangements for acquiring library materials published outside of the States and not readily obtainable outside the country of origin," an interim arrangement has been developed which will permit operations to continue in Djakarta under a system of joint support. Participation was opened to interested libraries beginning July 1, 1969, and the following ten libraries have agreed to participate in this jointly-supported acquisitions program for current Indonesian publications: the University of California at Berkeley, the Center for Research Libraries, Columbia University, Cornell University, the East-West Center, Indiana University, the University of Michigan, New York Public Library, Northern Illinois University, and Yale University. Uniform sets of monographic publications are being provided to all participants. Serial publications are distributed on a selective basis depending on the needs of the individual recipients. Each participant contributes $4,000 covering the costs of a set of publications with shipping and related charges, plus a share of the administrative overhead costs. This support charge will be modified as necessary in fiscal year 1971. Publication of the *Accessions List: Indonesia* is being continued.

The Library's NPAC office in Nairobi recently concluded a cooperative arrangement with J. D. Pearson, Librarian of the School of Oriental and African Studies (SOAS), University of London.

Since the SOAS has one of the greatest single concentrations of talent and knowledge of the Bantu languages extant, LC has made provisional arrangements for the preparation of data sheets for books in African vernacular languages for which language competence is not available in the Nairobi office. According to estimates, 132 such vernacular titles were received by the Nairobi office in 1967 and 124 in 1968, covering an identification to date of 83 vernacular languages in which some printing is done in Eastern Africa. The SOAS will prepare a data sheet for each title sent and will return a copy to Nairobi for inclusion in the *Accessions List: Eastern Africa*. Another copy will be sent with the publications to Washington where processing of the books will be completed if the project proves feasible.

On December 20, 1969, the House and Senate Conference Committee on the Appropriations for the Departments of Labor, and Health, Education, and Welfare submitted their Conference Report to accompany H.R. 13111, recommending $6,737,000 for transfer to the Librarian of Congress for Title II-C of the Higher Education Act for fiscal year 1970 instead of the $5,500,000 provided by the House in its report issued on July 24, 1969, and $7,356,000 passed by the Senate on December 17, 1969.

Public Law 480 Program

In addition to purchases for its own collections, the Library administers a program authorized by Public Law 83-480, as amended, the Agricultural Trade Development and Assistance Act of 1954, to buy publications abroad with United States-owned foreign currencies. Multiple copies of these publications are purchased and distributed to a selection of scholarly institutions throughout America. From this program's inception in 1962 through June 1969, the Library acquired over eleven million items from eight countries for some 350 American libraries. During fiscal year 1969 PL 480 programs were administered in the following countries: India, Ceylon, Nepal, Pakistan, Indonesia, Israel, Yugoslavia, and the United Arab Republic. The English-language Program, which distributes a limited number of English-language periodicals and books to approximately 300 American libraries in fifty states, is now limited to India, Pakistan, Nepal, and Ceylon.

The South Asia Program, covering India, Ceylon,

Nepal, and Pakistan provided a total of 1,047,317 serial and monographic pieces to American libraries during the fiscal year ending June 30, 1969. This represents an increase of more than 18 percent over the previous year's figure. To some extent this is accounted for by the fact that an additional set of publications is now being shared by the Center for Research Libraries, the National Library of Medicine, and the National Agricultural Library. Although total receipts last year from Nepal remained higher than receipts from Ceylon, the number of monographs received from Ceylon was considerably higher. The number of monographic titles received from Ceylon also increased in comparison with last year's figure by approximately four to one. This may be attributed at least in part to the establishment of a separate office in Colombo and to the presence of a local agent working for the Library under contract. The Bureau of the Budget has informed the Library that excess currencies are being exhausted in Ceylon. It is expected, however, that the balance on hand from previous years will permit the acquisition of publications from Ceylon for some time to come.

In addition to civil disturbances during 1969, shipment of publications from Pakistan was affected by a strike of postal workers in March. According to the National Book Centre of Pakistan, the level of educational publishing was greatly reduced during a period of approximately five months when colleges and universities in Pakistan were closed. Nonetheless, PL-480 acquisitions remained fairly constant, thanks to the efforts of the local staff in Karachi and Dacca.

During the past year the joint PL-480/NPAC office in Belgrade continued to improve its coverage of Yugoslav publications, particularly with respect to titles not included in the national bibliography nor provided routinely by its regular dealers. As a result, the number of monographs acquired in fiscal 1969 increased by approximately 6,000 pieces over the previous year's figure.

In spite of paper shortages and signs of reduced publishing activity in Indonesia, the Djakarta office acquired an estimated 190,710 pieces (books, periodicals, and newspapers) during the fiscal year ending June 30, 1969. This is an increase of approximately 10 percent over receipts during the previous fiscal year, which amounted to 170,913 pieces. Excess currencies with which the PL-480 Program in Indonesia had been administered since its inception in 1963 were no longer available after June 30, 1969, forcing termination of that program. The multiple acquisitions activities of the office in Djakarta have continued under NPAC, however, and participation was opened at that time to all interested libraries who were willing to underwrite the cost of participation in the program (see NPAC statement above for details).

Beginning in August the Field Director of the Library's NPAC office in Nairobi in addition to his regular coverage of Eastern Africa assumed responsibility for the PL-480 program in the United Arab Republic (UAR), including supervision of the Cairo office by means of monthly visits. The contribution of the local staff in Cairo to the successful operation of the program during the absence of the Field Director was given official recognition by the Librarian of Congress in the form of a Meritorious Service Award in July, 1969. Acquisitions are restricted to Middle Eastern publications available in the UAR, and as a result about 84 percent of all materials currently acquired are of Egyptian imprint. During the past year the regular program was maintained at approximately the same level as in fiscal 1968. There was a sharp drop in the number of newspapers distributed, but this was largely due to the suspension of the English-language Program at the beginning of fiscal year 1969 because of the necessity to limit the activities of the Cairo office. The number of monographs acquired more than doubled and a change in contractual arrangements, as of July 1, 1969, resulted in improved coverage of noncommercial publications during the first half of fiscal 1970.

Funding of the program in Israel in fiscal year 1970 was reduced because of the limitation of available excess currencies. To conserve funds as long as possible, five libraries agreed to withdraw from the program, effective June 30, 1969. Serial subscriptions for participants ceased as of December, 1969. In late November, lists of serials were distributed providing complete ordering information for each title. Inclusion of Israel in the English-language Program was canceled in December, 1968, because of budgetary restrictions. In spite of cutbacks, the Tel Aviv office provided a total of 268,550 pieces to American libraries during the fiscal year ending June 30, 1969.

Recent developments indicate that the limited Israeli pounds which support the present reduced PL-480 program in fiscal 1970 will probably be renewed in fiscal 1971, thus extending the programs in Israel for at least one more year. The amount to be made available is unknown but,

hopefully, it will suffice to provide copies of current monographs for the present twenty participants.

The Library's request for funds to expand the PL-480 program to Morocco and Tunisia in 1969/70 was disallowed.

Acquisition and Distribution of Federal Documents

The establishment of a Federal Documents Section in the Exchange and Gift Division has been approved. One of the division's primary responsibilities is to acquire U. S. Government publications for the Library's own collections as well as for use in the Library's exchange program. The new section will centralize all activities concerned with acquiring and distributing federal documents which were previously carried on independently by several of the sections of the division, with unavoidable duplications of effort and a division of responsibilities that now appears outmoded. Under the proposed reorganization, the present U. S. Government Publications Bibliographic Project and the Document Expediting Project will be brought together into one Section. Both projects will continue to perform their previously assigned duties but will coordinate their activities to achieve a better distribution of work load and avoid needless overlapping of specific tasks. Additional division staff members whose work is exclusively concerned with the handling of federal documents will also be transferred to the new section. The preliminary phase of this consolidation is already underway, and early results indicate that many of the complications formerly encountered in procuring and distributing federal documents will be eliminated, with important economies in time and manpower.

Disposition of Surplus Materials

During 1968–1969 the Exchange and Gift Division conducted a thorough analysis of all procedures relating to the disposition of surplus materials, one of the key functions of the division. Recommendations were made to regularize and clarify these procedures, in accordance with the laws governing the disposition of surplus government property, and to assure equitable arrangements for interested and properly qualified individuals to examine and select from these materials. These recommendations were put into effect immediately after approval by the Librarian.

The storage area adjoining the Exchange and Gift Division, in which the surplus materials are located, is divided into three broad priorities, as follows:

Priority I: materials of more than ordinary reference or research value. Available only to Federal Agencies *by transfer*, and to other libraries *on exchange*.

Priority II: general duplicates, available to Federal Agencies *by transfer* and to libraries and book dealers *on exchange*.

Donation (Priority III): available *free* to *libraries and educational institutions located in the United States*.

The surplus materials are open for examination Monday through Friday, excluding holidays, from 8:30 A.M. to 4:30 P.M. All selections must be made by representatives of the interested institutions, and members of the Library of Congress staff are prohibited from selecting these materials on behalf of other organizations.

Non-GPO Imprints

The Exchange and Gift Division's U. S. Government Publications Bibliographic Project (commonly referred to as the Non-GPO Project) reports significant advances in its effort to obtain U. S. Government publications issued outside of the Government Printing Office and to assure some form of bibliographic control over them. Compliance by federal agencies with Bureau of the Budget *Bulletin* 67–10 appears now to be very satisfactory and virtually all agencies which did not respond to the *Bulletin* during the year following its issuance have been contacted. The *Bulletin* requested all Executive Branch agencies to supply the Library with four copies of each publication produced by authorized departmental and field printing plants or procured commercially under contract.

Throughout the past year receipts of Non-GPO imprints have averaged 5,200 pieces per month, with the Department of Transportation continuing to be the largest supplier. The Project staff has also noted an increase in receipts under this program from the Department of Agriculture,

especially publications of the Soil Conservation Service.

Since its inception, the Non-GPO Project has regularly sent to the Superintendent of Documents sample copies of the publications it receives that are within the scope of the *Monthly Catalog of U. S. Government Publications*. Although it originally appeared that only a few of the titles submitted would be selected for inclusion in the *Catalog*, the trend since April 1969 has been toward inclusion of virtually all titles submitted. Between April and the end of October in 1969 the Project sent 1,596 publications for consideration by the editors of the *Monthly Catalog* of which 1,490 (or approximately 93.3 percent) were included in the *Catalog*. As a result of this continuing trend it no longer appears necessary for the Library to issue a monthly list of Non-GPO imprints. A Non-GPO Imprints List issued once yearly to provide a bibliographic record of the items excluded from the *Monthly Catalog* is now under consideration.

Sixtieth Anniversary of Monthly Checklist of State Publications

With its December 1969 issue, the *Monthly Checklist of State Publications* marked the completion of sixty years of continuous publication. Compiled by the Exchange and Gift Division, the *Checklist* is the Library's oldest serial publication with the exception of the *Annual Report of the Librarian of Congress* and issuances of the Copyright Office. The *Checklist* covers the publications of all fifty states and the territories and insular possessions of the United States, as well as associations of state officials and interstate organizations. Besides documents issued by the various departments, bureaus and other administrative agencies of state governments, the *Checklist* includes publications of state-supported societies and institutions. During its six decades the *Checklist* has grown from an initial listing of 3,500 titles to over 21,000 entries in Volume 60. The publication has not only provided bibliographic control for the documents listed, but also through the acquisition of the publications themselves has made it possible for the Library to assemble a broadly comprehensive collection of state documents. In connection with its interest in this field the Library has encouraged state governments to establish central documents depositories to collect and distribute the publications of their respective states. At present forty states have such central depositories, almost all of which furnish documents to the Library of Congress, and twenty-one states have enacted laws requiring distribution of specified types of publications to the Library. Nine states—Iowa, Kentucky, Maryland, Minnesota, New Hampshire, North Carolina, Ohio, South Dakota, and Utah—require by law that at least one copy of each state publication be sent to the Library.

Automation of the Order Division

The decision to consider applying automated techniques to technical processing beginning in the Order Division was made because the logical point of attack seemed to be at the input to the central bibliographic system, and a machine record for subscriptions has long been in operation.

This year brought to completion plans for the first phase of the mechanization with the approval of the formal systems design for machine-assisted book ordering and recording. Programming modules were organized to permit input of individual orders as well as complete fiscal and statistical controls early in calendar year 1970. Programs to handle blanket order input and fiscal and statistical controls will be completed during the remainder of calendar year 1970.

Studies were made of the expansion of the data base to include elements compatible with systems planned by NAL and NLM. Further studies of the uses of the machine record beyond the Order Division were made in the areas of the Process Information File, the cataloging work-sheet, and the machine-readable catalog (MARC).

Cataloging

The cataloging output for printed cards in fiscal 1969 was over 212,000 new titles, an increase of 18 percent over the previous year, continuing the rate of growth shown in the preceding year. In the latter half of calendar 1969, descriptive cataloging production was still running ahead of the corresponding period in 1968, despite the severe reductions in staff of the cataloging divisions in July as a result of the cutback in the request for funds for Title II-C of the Higher Education Act.

Fortunately, these reductions fell heaviest on the nonprofessional staff, and catalogers who had been in training began to produce at an accelerated rate. Subject cataloging production increased sharply as a result of the discontinuation of the subject cataloging of American dissertations for *Dissertation Abstracts*. The tight fiscal situation, however, has had its effect in the shelflisting operation with the result that some of the increase in cataloging production has become backlogged at the shelflisting stage.

If the evidence cited above illustrates the truism that there is no silver lining without its dark cloud, further evidence may be found in our experience with the radically revised priority system that was instituted early in the year. The primary result was the bringing of order into a situation that had been bordering on the chaotic so far as a rationally regulated grouping of the materials to be processed was concerned. On the other hand, our fond hopes that top priority materials could be made to move through the system with much greater rapidity so that cards for them could be issued more promptly have so far not been realized. Severe shortages in top cataloging staff that clear completed work for forwarding to the next stage combined with accumulations of severe backlogs in the card printing operation continue to plague us and to make the accomplishment of our objective elusive. We are not disheartened, however, because we have better controls to monitor the situation than we had before and have made good progress in some areas. There is reason to hope that persistence will eventually bring success.

New ground was broken by the beginnings of cataloging in African languages. At least some material in nineteen different African vernaculars was descriptively cataloged during the year. Titles in Armenian and Sinhalese, also, were cataloged for the first time.

Cataloging Rules and Romanization Tables

Some fifteen additions and changes in the *Anglo-American Cataloging Rules* were proposed by the Library of Congress and approved by the ALA Committee on Descriptive Cataloging. They will be published in *Cataloging Service*, Bulletin 88, now in the hands of the printer. In addition, this issue contains the approved romanization table for the Sinhalese language, an explanation of the Library's use of form subject headings for translations of particular versions of the Bible, an explanation of the Library's subject heading practice regarding corporate bodies and political jurisdictions whose names have changed, and revised rules for capitalization in certain Slavic languages.

The Library's draft revision of Chapter 12 of the *Anglo-American Cataloging Rules* relating to motion pictures, filmstrips, and similar audio-visual works is still under study, and work continues on the revision of the rules for Thai and Indonesian names. A meeting of Thai experts was held at the Library in August to prepare a revised draft of the Thai rule.

The Tibetan romanization table has been approved by the Descriptive Cataloging Committee together with some changes in the tables for languages using the Arabic alphabet and slight changes in the table for Armenian. These will be published early in 1970. An Amharic romanization table has been completed and is ready for consideration by the Library's Orientalia Processing Committee.

Classification Schedules

In September the classification schedule KF for the law of the United States, the first chapter of Class K (Law) to reach the stage of completion, was published. The schedule begins with provisions for the common law of the United States and federal statutory and regulatory law (KF), followed by the classification scheme for the states. It consists of separate schedules for the law of California (KFC1-1199) and that of New York (KFN5001-6199) and a uniform 600-number table for the law of the other states and territories, as well as a schedule (KFX) for the law of the U. S. cities. Schedule KF, which is for sale by the Card Division for $5.00, has been applied to newly cataloged law material and to reclassified holdings of LC's Law Library in the field of United States law since March, 1967.

The preliminary groundwork necessary for the preparation of the notation for Subclass KE (English law), consisting in the identification of classes and topics represented in LC's collections and the relative number of titles in the various classes, has been completed. High priority has been given to the preparation of an outline of the notation for the various subclasses of Class K as a whole and to the preliminary ground-work for developing Subclass K (Philosophy of law and jurisprudence, comparative law, international legislation, and other general topics).

A further segment of the Library's KF shelflist in 3 X 5″ electrostatic print form became available from the Photoduplication Service during the year, work on a revised edition of Class N (Fine arts) and on new editions of classes T (Technology) and Q (Science) proceeded towards expected publication in 1970, and a new cardboard display chart outlining the LC classification system was published.

Subject Headings for Children's Literature

This publication, available from the Card Division for seventy-five cents, was published in October after more than a year of planning and development. It details principles of application, provides a list of headings that vary from those for adult literature, and is designed as an aid to users of LC annotated cards for children's literature and for librarians involved in cataloging children's material and maintaining children's catalogs. Additions to and changes in the list will be incorporated in revised editions which will be published at irregular intervals.

MARC Editorial Office

The MARC experimental project, designed, created, and nursed by the Information Systems Office, became a production unit of the Library in March with the launching of a weekly distribution of cataloging data on computer tapes as a service to subscribers. In April this operation was taken over by the Processing Department and designated as the MARC Editorial Office. During the spring of 1969 its coverage of English language titles steadily increased, and by July its capacity had expanded to include all current cataloging in this language. By the end of the year it was not uncommon for the weekly tapes to contain between 1,300 and 1,400 cataloging records.

Decimal Classification Activities

The continuing work on Dewey 18, publication of which is anticipated for 1971, focused attention on the new relative index, which, like the traditional Dewey indexes to Editions 14, 16, and revised 17, will give precise leads to all significant terms in the schedules, but, in addition, will provide a broad guide to the hidden resources of the system. Plans were also developed for the 10th abridged edition, based on a new premise: the 8th and 9th abridged editions were developed with the idea that libraries using them could expand into the full 16th and 17th editions merely by lengthening classification numbers on existing materials; but the 10th abridged edition will be prepared for public and school libraries that are small and expect to remain small. By this simple change of objective, most of the features of the 9th abridged that were found to be objectionable can be easily eliminated. It is expected that the 10th abridged will be substantially briefer than its two most recent predecessors.

Liaison was developed with British users of Dewey, which should result in increased attention in future editions to the needs of British libraries, and in close correlation in Dewey numbers assigned to individual titles by the Library of Congress and by the *British National Bibliography*. Assignment of Dewey numbers continued at last year's high level and included, for the first time, works of fiction in English.

Cataloging Instruction

The Cataloging Instruction Office, originally set up to provide the training required to develop promising subprofessional employees into full-fledged catalogers, continued to expand the scope of its activities into new fields of training while supplying thirty-three newly trained catalogers for the descriptive cataloging divisions and seven trained editors for the Catalog Maintenance and Catalog Publication Division and the MARC Editorial Office. The new courses that were offered were developed around the needs of subprofessional staff members for systematic training in the use of catalogs for the effective performance of their duties. One such course was offered to those who search with the book in hand. This course proved to be most helpful to supporting staff sent from the Order, Descriptive Cataloging, and Serial Record Divisions. Two other such courses have been given for persons having only a catalog entry or a citation instead of the material. One of these was offered exclusively for searchers in the Catalog Publications Section of the Catalog Maintenance and Catalog Publication Division; the other to assistants from the Exchange and Gift and Order Divisions and the Photoduplication Service. Still another course was developed for assistants who prepare preliminary copy according to the *Anglo-American Cataloging Rules*.

Processing Services

Card Division Automation Program

Perhaps the most significant development of 1969, both for the Library of Congress and the library world at large, was the approval given in May, 1969, by the Congressional Joint Committee on Printing, for the acquisition of the equipment needed to implement Phase II of "CARDS," the Card Automated Reproduction and Distribution System. As described in last year's report (*LRTS*, vol. 13, no. 2, Spring 1969), Phase II will greatly change the present method of distributing printed cards. Instead of the process of matching card orders against cards in stock, the card order will itself generate the printing of the catalog cards. The equipment for Phase II is scheduled for installation during 1970, and the Library hopes to have the system operational on a limited basis late in 1970. MARC records will form the basic input of the system, and it is expected that some 100,000 catalog entries will be available in machine-readable form by the time Phase II becomes operational. Conversion of retrospective titles for which cards are presently stocked will take several more years, during which time it will be necessary to fill some orders from inventory, but the proportion of such orders will decrease as time goes on. Phase II of "CARDS" calls for storing 6,000,000 catalog entries, accepting 100,000 orders per day, and printing 600,000 cards per day in response to those orders. At present the Card Division receives about 50,000 orders per day.

The automation of card distribution was prompted by the increasing difficulties encountered by the Card Division as its inventory of titles expanded beyond the 5,000,000 mark. The operation of the service already requires nearly an acre of space and the services of almost 500 people. During 1968 some 180,000 new items were added to stock and in 1969 the figure jumped to 212,466 cards representing titles cataloged and added to the Library's collections. As these massive quantities were added to the inventory of printed cards, sheer lack of physical space demanded that smaller quantities of each card be added to stock, with the result that individual titles were more easily exhausted. The Card Division is now undertaking a large-scale reprinting program to replenish its inventory, but the ultimate solution of its problem lies in Phase II of "CARDS."

New Card Prices

New prices for printed cards became effective August 1, 1969. The price of the first card supplied on an order by card number has been increased from 10 cents to 15 cents, but the minimum charge of 22 cents has been dropped. Second and following cards supplied on an order by card number have been cut from 6 cents to 4 cents, but an additional 40 cents is charged to each order which must be searched to locate the card number. Under the new pricing structure the average 6-card set costs 35 cents instead of 40 cents when ordered by card number, but 75 cents instead of 35 cents when ordered by author and title. Libraries that submit fewer than 22 percent of their orders by author and title will normally receive cards at less cost than before, while other libraries will find the cost of cards proportionately increased.

Machine-Readable Order Forms

By the fall of 1969 some 75 percent of all card orders were being received on the new machine-readable order forms; but so long as 25 percent still came on the older yellow slips, it was necessary for the Card Division to maintain dual processing procedures. In December 1969, it was announced that yellow slips would no longer be accepted by the Card Division after March 1, 1970.

To assist libraries whose internal procedures are not satisfied by the single-part order form provided by the Card Division, the division encouraged as many library supply houses as possible to create multiple-part order forms which could be used to order LC cards in a machine-readable format. At present it is known that such multiple-part forms are available from DEMCO, Gaylord, and Fordham Equipment Company.

"7 Series" Card Numbers

On December 1, 1968, a new series of catalog card numbers was initiated—the "7 series" with which most libraries are now familiar. The new series simplifies the numbering system and the arrangement of stock in the inventory of printed cards, reduces the amount of space that must be allowed for expansion of the present inventory, and will also reduce the amount of machine processing required in the new automated system. The first digit after the initial seven is a check digit which provides automatic detection of errors in transcribing the number. (For full details on how this digit is derived, see *Cataloging Service*, Bulletin 85, October 1968.) [This series was discontinued in 1972. See *Cataloging Service*, Bulletin 102, January 1972—Ed.]

Standard Book Numbers

LC printed cards have also begun to include the Standard Book Number for those titles to which such numbers have been assigned. Following the example of the British Standard Book Numbering plan, the American Book Publishers Council and the American Textbook Publishers Institute appointed the R. R. Bowker Company to administer a similar book numbering scheme in the United States. Bowker's Standard Book Numbering Department has already assigned blocks of numbers to most American publishers and has published a manual explaining various aspects of the SBN scheme. The Standard Book Number (SBN) is now printed on LC catalog cards, flush left below the call number, whenever the number is provided by the publisher. The nine-digit system is so large that it is capable of handling both British and American publishers in the same series, and the final digit in each number is also a check digit.

The implications of this development are significant. If the card distribution program of the Library of Congress is based on a number system (at present the "7 series"), it is evident that the Standard Book Number could easily become the number by which LC catalog cards could also be ordered. A librarian would need to know only the Standard Book Number in order to order the book from the publisher or dealer and to order catalog cards from the Library of Congress; and the Standard Book Number, in many instances, would be more readily available than the LC card number. At the present time, however, the Library of Congress has gone ahead with its new "7 series" of card numbers, for two reasons: (1) a large proportion of current publications still appear without the Standard Book Number; and (2) the SBN will not be assigned retrospectively.

In the long view, the Library of Congress is preparing to accept the Standard Book Number as a possible ordering device for its catalog cards. In its automation plans the Library envisions the use of both SBN and LC card numbers as valid order data, the two systems being used together because of the absence of Standard Book Numbers for earlier publications.

Symbols of American Libraries

During the year, *Symbols of American Libraries*, a directory of identification symbols for libraries in the United States and Canada, was prepared in the Union Catalog Division and published. This title supersedes the ninth edition of *Symbols Used in the National Union Catalog of the Library of Congress*, and includes more than 1,400 newly established and revised symbols that did not appear in the ninth edition. It records all of the symbols that are to be found in the *National Union Catalog, a Cumulative Author List*, in *New Serial Titles*, in *Newspapers on Microfilm*, in the second and third editions of the *Union List of Serials*, and in the *National Union Catalog, Pre-1956 Imprints*, currently being published by Mansell Information/ Publishing Ltd., London. A certain number of symbols that had been assigned for use in various state and local lists of serials and in regional union catalogs will also be found in the new directory. The volume is arranged both by symbol and by the name of the library.

Division of the Official Catalog

Last year's report mentioned the division of the Official Catalog into a Name-Title Catalog and a Subject Catalog. This task was completed during 1969. The Name-Title Catalog occupies 14,355 card trays, the Subject Catalog 4,875 trays, or a ratio of 3 to 1. Since the Official Catalog is used almost exclusively by processing department personnel and is not open to the public, the Name-Title Catalog is, of course, more heavily used than

the subject part of the Official Catalog. The new arrangement seems to be working satisfactorily, and both parts of the catalog contain room for expansion within their present limits for some time to come.

Closing of the Annex Catalog

For a variety of reasons it became necessary to close off the public catalog in the Annex Building during 1969. Since July, 1969, no additional cards have been filed into this catalog, which was established in 1939 when the Annex Building opened, nor are changes in bibliographic information reflected in its entries. However, this card catalog will continue to be housed in its present location and will be available for public use. Sets of the various book catalogs covering the whole range of Library of Congress printed cards are available in the Annex Catalog Room for reference purposes and as supplements to the incomplete card catalog.

National Union Catalog, 1963–67

Completion of the 1963–67 cumulation of *The National Union Catalog* was a major achievement of 1969. This five-year catalog consists of seventy-two volumes containing 49,304 pages and includes cumulations of the *Register of Additional Locations* and the *Library of Congress Catalog–Music and Phonorecords* and *Motion Pictures and Filmstrips*.

The quinquennial issue of *The National Union Catalog–Author List* is itself complete in fifty-nine volumes containing 38,747 pages. It includes a total of 1,320,798 catalog entries and references for 930,593 publications.

The *Register of Additional Locations, 1963–67*, supplements both the 1958–62 and 1963–67 cumulations of *The National Union Catalog*. It contains a total of 5,221,326 locations for 812,249 of the post-1955 publications represented by catalog entries in *The National Union Catalog* since it began publication in 1956. This cumulative issue comprises 6,587 pages and is published as volumes 60–67 of the quinquennial set. It replaces the 1965 and 1966 annual cumulations of the *Register*.

The *Library of Congress Catalog–Music and Phonorecords, 1963–67* consists of 2,567 pages in three volumes. Volumes 1 and 2 comprise an author and added entry catalog of music in the broadest sense, i.e., literature on music and other related materials, as well as music scores. It also includes entries for musical and non-musical phonorecords. Volume 3 consists of a *Subject Index* to the catalog.

The *Library of Congress Catalog–Motion Pictures and Filmstrips, 1963–67* is published in two volumes, a total of 1,403 pages. Volume 1, *Titles*, contains the full catalog entries, together with appropriate added entry references; volume 2 is its *Subject Index*. The complete sets were distributed by J. W. Edwards Publisher, Inc., to subscribers early in the fall of 1969.

Books: Subjects, 1965–1969

On June 19, 1969, the contract for the publication of the 1965–69 issue of *The Library of Congress Catalog–Books: Subjects* was awarded to J. W. Edwards Publisher. This issue will include approximately 27,000 pages in forty-two volumes. It will be for sale by J. W. Edwards at $445.00 per set. To date, over 800,000 cards, of an estimated 1.7 million, have been filed. Filing is already completed in some earlier letters of the alphabet (A-D). Editorial revision of the trays began on December 9, 1969. Editing and preparation of camera copy will be completed before the end of 1970, with delivery of copies to subscribers expected early in the calendar year 1971.

Other Publications

In addition to the quinquennial issue of *The National Union Catalog*, a total of 44,217 pages of camera-ready page copy was prepared during calendar year 1969. This included editing and preparing 27,464 pages for *The National Union Catalog* (1968 annual issues and 1969 monthly and quarterly issues), 929 pages for the *Register of Additional Locations* (1968 annual issue), 11,194 pages for *Books: Subjects* (quarterly and 1968 annual issues), 941 pages for *Music and Phonorecords*, 1,023 pages for *Motion Pictures and Filmstrips*, 839 pages for *The National Union Catalog of Manuscript Collections* (1968 annual), 1,428 pages for subject and author indexes to *Dissertation Abstracts* (January to June monthly and 1968/69 annual) and preparing mounted

page copy only for *Books for Junior College Libraries* (345 pages).

Publication of the Pre-1956 National Union Catalog

The work of editorial conversion of the card files of the National Union Catalog into a bibliography in book form continued during 1969. Despite the difficulties in recruiting additional qualified personnel, by November 1, 1969, shipments 26 through 50 had been sent to London, adding a total of 722,740 edited cards to the previous total of 711,052 for a grand total of 1,433,792. This represents material for more than seventy volumes, forty-five of which have been distributed.

The cordial reception accorded the appearance of the first volumes of the *National Union Catalog, Pre-1956 Imprints* was greater than had been anticipated. Reviews in various library journals were gratifying; for example, the review in the *Australian Library Journal*, June, 1969, "words such as monumental and invaluable cannot be used lightly, but if any publication merits their use, this undoubtedly does."

RQ, Summer 1969, granted the *Catalog* the following accolade: "The National Union Catalog invites superlatives. Its 610 volumes will be the largest constellation in the Gutenberg galaxy." *The Library Association Record*, May 1969, hailed the *Catalog* as "the greatest instrument of bibliographical control in existence."

The *Canadian Library Journal* stated: "To estimate the amount of planning and preparation which this undertaking has required staggers the imagination. Nor is it possible to calculate the number of hours which will be saved by catalogers and bibliographers. . . . The standards set by the Library of Congress in their publication will be difficult to meet and virtually impossible to surpass. The Library of Congress and the staff involved in the editorial work of the *Catalog* are to be congratulated, the librarians and bibliographers all over the world owe them a debt which it is impossible to assess or to repay."

These comments were typical of the reviews received and they were a welcome spur to the editors and other members of the staff to continue their painstaking work of editing and reconciling diversities of entries in order to prepare this massive file for publication in book form by Mansell Information/Publishing Ltd.

Technical Processes Research Office

During 1969 the Technical Processes Research Office (TPR) pursued investigations of the characteristics and performance of the Library's devices for bibliographical control with particular reference to their suitability for a computer-based system.

The statistical design of a study of LC name authority records was completed and a sample of 2,700 records was drawn. These records were analyzed and edited for machine input using a provisional MARC format for name authority records. Keying the data began toward the end of the year. When the data are in machine-readable form, they will be processed by GENESIS (Generalized Statistical Program), a MARC program that can tabulate the occurrence of any element. Preliminary results of the subsequent statistical analysis will indicate whether additional subsamples will be needed to determine particular characteristics of this type of record. The findings of the study will provide basic information about the file requirements, use, and potential of name authority records in a computer environment.

The basic sampling method for the above investigation was found to be applicable to the study of other types of catalog records. Therefore, a master sample of the Official Catalog was drawn. This sample provides a statistically reliable means of analyzing various facets of the organization of name and title entries in this key instrument of bibliographical control. Data from studies of this type are fundamental to many efforts to improve its quality.

A detailed study of the relationship among LC classification numbers, Dewey decimal numbers, and LC subject headings for the same bibliographic items was well under way by the end of the year. Two major purposes of the study are to determine the relative specificity of each means of subject control and the extent to which classification numbers and subject headings complement each other. Much of the data from the study is being taken from a sample of LC catalog records covering all languages, but additional data will be obtained from machine analyses of the MARC data base which, at present, is confined to English-language publications.

TPR and the Information Systems Office continued their joint efforts to enlarge computer filing capability by studying the requirements of the LC subject heading list. SKED (Sort-key Edit Program), the generalized program for building sort keys for records in the MARC format, is being used as the framework for further refinements in file arrangement based on the type of heading. It is expected that techniques developed for this task will be applicable to other computer filing situations. TPR also assisted in the effort to create a workable machine file of subject headings by studying the requirements for editing the list with respect to accuracy of the data and content designation (addition of indicators and subfield codes).

The Specialist in Technical Processes Research was heavily involved as a member of the RECON Working Task Force studying the feasibility of conversion of retrospective records to machine-readable form. He edited the final report and TPR staff members aided the project materially by providing technical and editorial support. The Office continues to be associated with RECON (Retrospective Conversion Program) in its pilot project phase.

TPR continued its advisory role in the development of an indexing vocabulary for the Legislative Reference Service. The aim has been to develop a vocabulary that satisfies the requirements of the LRS information system while still maintaining a high degree of compatibility with LC subject headings. Achievement of this goal will have an important bearing on the Library's ability to create a central bibliographical store in machine-readable form.

National Libraries Task Force

Since the chief of the Serial Record Division is also the chairman of the U. S. National Libraries Task Force, a brief account of the accomplishments of the Task Force in 1969 is in order here to complete this annual review of Processing Department activities.

Standards: During 1969 the U. S. National Libraries Task Force on Automation and Other Cooperative Services (an association of the Library of Congress with the National Library of Medicine and the National Agricultural Library) continued work toward the development of standards for the inputting, transmission, and dissemination of bibliographic information in machine-readable form. On recommendation of the Task Force, which reviewed detailed studies by special working groups, the three national libraries jointly adopted three new standards: a standard calendar date code, a standardized character set for roman alphabets and romanized non-roman alphabets, and a standard language code. These followed earlier agreement on a standard communications format for machine-readable cataloging and standards for descriptive cataloging.

National Serials System: The Task Force concentrated a high proportion of its attention on the national serials problem. In April, 1969, following the submission of the Library of Congress Phase I report on data elements for serials, it proposed detailed recommendations to the directors of the three national libraries concerning the establishment of a national serials system. The Task Force then developed plans for a National Serials Pilot Project as a first step toward a National Serials Data System. On September 3, 1969, the National Agricultural Library, on behalf of the Task Force, announced a grant to the Association of Research Libraries to launch the pilot project. The pilot project envisions the production of a union list of live scientific and technical serials held by the three national libraries and a capacity to provide data about certain of the multiple characteristics of serials.

National Libraries System: The Task Force also submitted to the three directors a comprehensive report on studies concerning a possible "National Libraries System," both short-range and long-range. Proceeding from the premise that the three national libraries will eventually automate their respective library processes, the Task Force focused attention on designating points in the three separate systems where connecting links exist or can be developed, to assure compatibility, provide the opportunity for exchange of data, and eliminate nonessential duplication. Studies are also under way relating to standardized controls over technical report literature, compatibility in subject headings, and the complex problem of filing rules. A mechanism for cooperation in the use of photocopies, in lieu of loans, of original library materials among the three national libraries has already been established.

V

THE FUTURE

Developments in the technical services foreshadow the future condition of libraries. Automation of the technical services, if successful, should eventually provide a relatively economical way to store, search, and recall vast amounts of well-indexed, machine-readable bibliographic data recorded once centrally at the national level for decentralized future use. Benefits should include broader and earlier cataloging control, more efficient exploitation of published materials, and increased pressure toward international bibliographic standardization. Computer constraints may require each country to place its publishing output under the control of a machine-readable cataloging format that may be utilized internationally, thus further reducing current problems of time lag and duplication of effort. The variety of ways that different societies see the world around them will initially militate against the automated control of subject data similar to what we now may expect for descriptive cataloging data, but eventually, perhaps, we may see a useful confluence of thought in this area that might even contribute toward clearer communications and better understanding between peoples.

There is an urgent need to question current library concepts, to develop sound cost-benefit analyses, and, most important, to turn ever again to the users for whom the library exists in determining those things that are really needed. It is an irony that up to now library uses such as the elimination of multiple searching or the computer production of catalog cards or book catalogs continue to be among the stronger arguments for automation while specifically research oriented use—for example, extensive and sophisticated subject searching—lags well behind except in marginal areas such as the computer production of the classed shelf list.

Research and testing programs are exploring the new technologies such as the marriage of the computer and the micro-image. Many and diverse groups are contributing to the development of useful standards at both the national and international levels. Coordination of efforts and the sharing of resources in a number of bibliographic fields is proceeding with appropriate emphasis on compatibility rather than conformity.

The following selections describe a few advanced operational activities, ask and answer some serious questions about library automation, discuss on-going research and development programs, and provide a look at those requirements, constraints, and tentative solutions that comprise a framework around which the future of the technical services may evolve.

MARC International

Richard E. Coward

The cooperative development of the Library of Congress MARC II Project and the British National Bibliography MARC II Project is described and presented as the forerunner of an international MARC network. Emphasis is placed on the necessity for a standard MARC record for international exchange and for acceptance of international standards of cataloging.

This paper is an examination of two major operational automation projects. These projects, the Library of Congress MARC II Project and the British National Bibliography (BNB) MARC II Project, are the result of sustained and successful Anglo-American cooperation over a period of three years during which there has been continuous evaluation and change. In 1969, for a brief period, the systems developed have been stabilised, partly to give time for library systems to examine ways and means of exploiting a new type of centralised service, and partly to give the Library of Congress and the British National Bibliography the opportunity to look outwards at other systems being developed in other countries. There has, of course, already been extensive contact and exchange of views between the agencies involved in the planning and developing of automated bibliographic systems and the possibilities of cooperation and exchange have been informally discussed at many levels. The time has now come for the national libraries and cataloguing agencies concerned to look at what has been achieved and to lay the foundation for effective cooperation in the future.

The history of the Anglo-American MARC Project began at the Library of Congress with an experiment in a new way of distributing catalogue data. The traditional method of distributing Library of Congress bibliographic information is to provide catalogue cards or proof sheets. These techniques will undoubtedly continue indefinitely into the future, but the rapid spread of automation in libraries has created a new demand for bibliographic information in machine readable form.

The original MARC project (1) was "an experiment to test the feasability of distributing Library of Congress cataloguing in machine readable form". The use of the word "cataloguing" underlines the essential nature of the MARC I project; its end product was a catalogue record on magnetic tape. There is a very significant difference between a catalogue record on magnetic tape and a bibliographic file in machine form. The latter does not necessarily hold anything resembling a catalogue entry, although MARC II still reflects, both in the LC implementation (2,3) and in the BNB implementation (4,5), a preoccupation with the visual organisation of a catalogue entry. Fortunately retention of the cataloguing "framework" does not hinder the utilisation of LC or BNB MARC data in systems designed to hold and exploit bibliographic information, as the whole project is designed as a method for communication between systems. The essence of the MARC II project is that it is a communications system, or a common exchange language between systems wishing to exchange bibliographic information. It is highly undesirable, in fact quite impossible, to plan in terms of direct compatability between systems. Machines are different, programs are different, and local objectives are different.

The exchange of bibliographic information in any medium implies some level of agreement on the best way to organise and present the data being exchanged. The need to use a fairly standard type of bibliographic structure on a catalogue card is obvious enough, and over the years a form of presentation, as best exemplified by a Library of Congress catalogue card, has been developed

SOURCE: Reprinted from the *Journal of Library Automation* II, 4 (December 1969), pp. 181–186, by permission of the American Library Association.

which holds all the essential data and also, by means of typographical distinctions and layout, conveys the information in a visually attractive style. When bibliographic information is transmitted in a machine readable form the question of visual layout does not arise but the question of structure is vitally important. This structure is called the machine format and the machine format holds the data. It literally does not matter in what order the various bits and pieces that make up a catalogue record appear on a magnetic tape. What does matter very much is that the machine should be able to recognise each data element: author, title, series, subject heading, etc. In practice, either each data element must be given an identifying tag that the machine can recognise, or each data element must occupy a predetermined place in the record. In view of the unpredictable nature of bibliographic information, the former method—that of tag identification—is now widely used and is the technique adopted in the MARC system.

The LC and BNB MARC systems are two very closely related implementations of a communications format which in its generalised form has been carefully designed to hold any type of bibliographic information. The generalised format description is now being circulated by British Standards Institute and United States of America Standards Institute. It can be very briefly described as follows:

bibliographic record. Once such a level of compatability is established it is possible to prepare general file handling systems (6) which will convert any bibliographic record to a local file format. There is certainly much scope for agreement on local file formats as well, but such formats will necessarily be conditioned by the type of machine available and the use to be made of the file.

The establishment of a generalised file structure is a great step forward but by itself means very little unless a wide measure of agreement can be reached on the data content of the record to be exchanged. Here the responsibility for cooperation and standardisation shifts from the automation specialist to the librarian, and particularly to those national libraries and cataloguing agencies who can by their practical actions assist libraries to implement the standards prepared for the profession.

In order to appreciate the real importance of standardisation, particularly in the context of the MARC Project, it is necessary to look a few years into the future. It is inevitable that the rapid spread of automated systems in libraries will create a demand for machine readable bibliographic records and that in turn will lead to the setting up of bibliographic data banks in machine readable form in national and local centres. These data banks will be international in scope and will contain many millions of items. In the long run the only feasible way to maintain them is for each

LEADER	DIRECTORY	CONTROL FIELD(S)	DATA FIELDS

The leader is a fixed field of 24 characters, giving the record length, the file status and details of the particular implementation. The directory is a series of entries each containing a tag (which identifies a data field), the length of the data field in the record, and its starting character position. This directory is a variable field depending on the number of data elements in the record. The control fields consist of a special group of fields for holding the main control number and any subsidiary control data. The data fields are designated for holding bibliographic data. Each field may be of any length and may be divided into any number of subfields. A data field may begin with special characters, called indicators, which can be used to supply additional information about the field as a whole.

It can be seen that the basis of MARC II is a very flexible file structure designed to hold any type of

country or group of countries to develop automated centralised cataloguing systems for handling their own national outputs and to receive from all other countries involved in the network machine readable records of the latter's national outputs. Countries cooperating on this basis must agree on standards of cataloguing (and ultimately on standards of classification and subject indexing), so that the general data bank presents a consistently compiled set of bibliographic data. There is no doubt that national data banks will be set up. Libraries today are faced simultaneously with a rapid increase in book prices, a need to maintain ever-increasing book stocks to meet the basic requirements of their readers, and a persistent shortage of trained personnel to catalogue their purchases. These trends are already well established and in the United States, where they are most advanced, the result has been the massive and highly successful Shared Cataloguing Program. Historically the Shared Cataloguing Program will probably be seen as the first and last attempt to provide a comprehensive bibliographic service by unilateral action. A large number of countries have cooperated in this attempt but the Shared Cataloguing Program does not rest on the principle of exchange. It is doubtful if even the United States will be able to maintain and extend this programme in its present form. The Shared Cataloguing Program must ultimately be replaced with an international exchange system.

National machine readable bibliographic systems will be established, but there is a grave danger that those agencies responsible will be primarily concerned only with the immediate problem of producing records suitable for use in their own national context or for their own national bibliography, regardless of the fact that the libraries and information centres they need to serve are acquiring ever-increasing quantities of foreign material. The exchange principle will be downgraded to an afterthought, a by-product of the fact that an automated system is being used.

If this outcome is to be avoided, international standards must be prepared and national agencies must accept them instead of only paying lip service to them. In the past librarians have tended to be more concerned with codification than standardisation, but in the field of cataloguing at least a great breakthrough was made sixteen years ago when Seymour Lubetzky produced his "Cataloguing Rules and Principles; a Critique of the A.L.A. Rules for Entry and a Proposed Design for Their Revision" (7). The work of Lubetsky led to the "Paris Principles" (8) published by IFLA in 1963 and in due course to the preparation of the "Anglo-American Cataloguing Rules" 1967 (9). These rules, though unfortunately departing from Lubetzky's principles in one or two areas provide a solid basis for standardisation. We are fortunate to have them available at such a critical moment in the history of librarianship. They must form the basis of an international MARC project.

Of all the great libraries of the world, the Library of Congress has done more than any other to promote international cataloguing standards. It is now in a uniquely favourable position to promote these standards through its own MARC II Project. The LC MARC II project, together with the BNB MARC II project, can provide the foundation of the international MARC network. These projects alone cover the total field of English language material and yet already the basic requirement of standardisation is absent.

The Library of Congress finds itself unable, for administrative reasons, to adopt fully the code of rules it worked so hard to produce and which British librarians virtually accepted as it stood in the interests of international standardisation. That a great library should be in this position is understandable. What is less understandable is that the Library of Congress should transfer the non-standard cataloguing rules established by an internal administrative decision to prescription of cataloguing data in the machine readable record that it is now issuing on an international basis. One of the great advantages of machine readable records is that they can simultaneously be both standard and non-standard. There is no reason that the Library of Congress, or any national agency, should not provide for international exchange a standard MARC record together with any local information the Library might want. If as a result other national agencies are encouraged to do the same, it will not be long before the absurdity and expense of examining each record received via the international network in order to change a standard heading to a local variant, will become apparent. The British National Bibliography has already accepted the Anglo-American code and by this action has now done much to promote its acceptance in Great Britain. Incomplete acceptance of the code is really the only significant difference between the two MARC projects.

At a detailed level there are differences in some of the subfield codes. These are chiefly due to the fact that the British MARC Committee was particularly concerned with the problems of filing bibliographic entries, and as no generally accepted filing code exists it was decided to provide a complete analysis of the fields in headings. This analysis will enable the BNB MARC data base to be arranged in different sequences to test the rules now being prepared. The other difference, or extension, in the British MARC format is the provision of cross references with each entry, on the assumption that in a MARC system a total pack of cataloguing data should be provided. However these differences reflect the experimental nature of the British project, not the fundamental differences in opinion.

In this paper an attempt has been made to look at the British and American MARC Projects not as systems for distributing bibliographic information but as the forerunners of an international bibliographic network. Intensive efforts have been made to lay a foundation for this international network. The Anglo-American code provides a sound cataloguing base, the generalised communications format provides a machine base, and the Standard Book Numbering System provides an international identification system. These developments are all part of a general move towards real cooperation in the provision of bibliographic services. They must now be brought together in an international MARC network.

REFERENCES

1. Avram, Henriette D.: *The MARC Pilot Project* (Washington, Library of Congress: 1968).

2. U.S. Library of Congress. Information Systems Office. *The MARC II Format: A Communications Format for Bibliographic Data.* Prepared by Henriette D. Avram, John F. Knapp and Lucia J. Rather. (Washington, D.C.: 1968).

3. "Preliminary Guidelines for the Library of Congress, National Library of Medicine, and National Agricultural Library Implementation of the Proposed American Standard for a Format for Bibliographic Information Interchange on Magnetic Tape as Applied to Records Representing Monographic Materials in Textual Printed Form (Books)," *Journal of Library Automation,* 2 (June 1969). 68–83

4. BNB MARC Documentation Service Publications, Nos. 1 and 2 (London, Council of the British National Bibliography, Ltd., 1968).

5. Coward, R. E.: "The United Kingdom MARC Record Service," In Cox Nigel S. J.; Grose, Michael W.: *Organization and Handling of Bibliographic Records by Computer* (Hamden, Conn., Archon Books, 1967).

6. Cox, Nigel S. M.; Dews, J. D.: "The Newcastle File Handling System," In op. cit. (note 4).

7. Lubetzky, Seymour: *Code of Cataloging Rules . . . Prepared for the Catalog Code Revision Committee . . . With an Explanatory Commentary* by Paul Dunkin. (Chicago: American Library Association, 1960).

8. International Federation of Library Associations. *International Conference on Cataloguing Principles, Paris, 9th–18th October, 1961:* Report; Edited by A. H. Chaplin.

9. *Anglo-American Cataloging Rules.* British Text (London: Library Association, 1967).

Some Questions about the MARC Project

A. T. Hall

With comment by J. E. Linford

An analysis of the statistics of books purchased by Aberdeen University Library suggests that more than one-third of them will not be covered by the MARC project and that almost a half of those which are will be bought when the entry has already appeared on the tape. In these circumstances to use MARC tapes to produce catalogue entries will be administratively confusing and wasteful of computer time. The possible effects of MARC on classification and cataloguing are considered, and it is concluded that the advantages of such projects for centralized cataloguing need to be clearer than they are if such schemes are to be worth while.

The MARC project, as a means of centrally producing catalogue entries, has by now received a good deal of publicity and even those librarians who do not move easily in the world of computers are more or less aware of what is going on. The extensive literature has not, however, answered the questions which are worrying some of those who will soon have to make the decision whether or not to take part.

Each library will have its own problems and some will be common to all. Here we are considering the library of an old, medium-sized university, with a stock of about half a million volumes.

The MARC tape is in effect a machine readable form of BNB to which purely American publications may in time be added. Any library which is considering the use of MARC needs therefore to answer two questions. What proportion of its intake appears in BNB? What proportion of the books appearing in BNB are added to the library?

To answer the first question the library of Aberdeen University analysed its purchases over a period of eight months. They were grouped into three categories: items appearing in BNB or which could be expected to appear there, purely American books, and others. The latter were primarily European, but a number of African, Oriental, and older British publications appeared also. The respective percentages were as follows:

	BNB	American	Others
	50 · 2	13	36 · 8

Thus a MARC project which had the same coverage as BNB would supply catalogue entries for half the library's purchases. If purely American books were to be added, this proportion would rise to 63 per cent. That is a fairly large proportion, but from another point of view the 37 per cent which would not be covered at all is large also. The library would need to maintain, in continuous operation, two separate ordering and cataloguing systems, and one may wonder whether the MARC project offers enough to make the duplication worth while.

It is possible that the European, African and Oriental books may in time appear on the MARC tapes. We have been reminded that "The Library of Congress is now under an obligation imposed by the United States Congress to supply catalogue data for any book required by their university and research libraries regardless of its country of origin".[1] Presumably this means that any book can be made to appear on a tape if needed. By the time that it does, however, cataloguer and

SOURCE: Reprinted from the *Library Association Record*, XXI, 9 (September 1969), pp. 275–278, by permission of The Library Association.

This paper has been read by Miss M. A. Cuthell, Mr. H. J. H. Drummond and Mr. W. N. Menzies, who have made a number of useful suggestions but are not responsible for the contents.

reader will probably have lost patience as so often has happened in libraries using BNB cards and slips, and the book will have been catalogued by old-fashioned methods. How is one to know if a given book will ever appear on a tape or not?

The percentages given above are not as straight-forward as they seem for not every book is bought as soon as it is published. It seems to be assumed in some of the literature on MARC that books will be ordered before publication or immediately after it, with the aid of the Standard Book Number. To investigate this assumption these figures were broken down to show the proportion of books ordered in the year of publication, this number appearing first under each heading:

BNB	*American*	*Others*
33·6 16·6	4·1 8·9	15·2 21·6

Obviously these figures cannot be applied precisely to any weekly MARC tape but the general picture appears to be clear. Whatever the scope of the project, little more than half of the library's purchases will be made at such a point in the life history of the book that a tape can be used to produce the catalogue entries as soon as it is issued. Even this is probably an overestimate, for a book may be bought in the year of publication and still be ordered when it has already appeared on the tape. For the rest conventional methods will have to be used or old tapes run through again. To do this for a handful of books on each would be wasteful of computer time, and it is not clear how the cataloguer will know which tape contains the entry that he wants. It has already been announced that "It is not proposed in this project to offer libraries a cumulated tape".[2]

Even if a high proportion of a library's accessions appears on the MARC tape, it may still not be economic to use it. This raises the second of our two questions: what proportion of the books appearing in BNB does the library buy?

It is scarcely feasible to establish a precise answer to this as it no doubt varies considerably from time to time, but an approximation may be arrived at. An examination of three successive numbers of BNB from November 1967 has shown that, of the 1,766 items which appeared, 310 were added to the library, that is about 17 per cent. This includes a number which have not been individually catalogued but might have been if the MARC record had been available. It may be suggested that this figure is too low, that the library ought to be buying a much larger percentage of the books in BNB. Two comments may be made

on this. Firstly, the university teaches a wide range of subjects including medicine and law, and during the period in question the library suffered from no lack of money. If books were not bought it was because they were not thought to be worth buying rather than because they could not be afforded or were outside the university's scope. Secondly, the significant fact for this enquiry is surely what one buys in practice rather than what would be bought in a perfect world.

If these figures are anything typical, it seems likely to be a wasteful business to produce one's catalogue entries from a MARC tape, especially as the proportion of books purchased would fall still further if all purely American publications were covered by the project.

Some thought needs to be given to the effect of MARC on classification. If full advantage is to be taken of the project, one must use Congress or Dewey. Few libraries use Dewey in its pure form, but that is not the only difficulty. Does the use of MARC mean that hope of revising its more obviously inadequate sections must be given up, at least until an edition is produced differing drastically from all previous ones? Mr. Coward has commented that the need to contain five sets of subject information on the tape is "a frightful price" to pay for failure to reach agreement on these matters.[3] To be permanently saddled with the Dewey schedules for literature, mathematics and engineering would be a frightful price indeed for whatever MARC has to offer.

Even if the Dewey and Congress schemes were better than they are, libraries would still wish to classify books to meet their peculiar needs. Thus the library of a university which did not teach metallurgy might buy books on the subject for their relevance to solid state physics, but it could not classify them there without spoiling the smooth flow which MARC is supposed to create. Special collections and the libraries of research institutes seem to be particularly vulnerable here.

As MARC is to use the new AA code, one's attitude to the one will clearly go a long way to deciding one's approach to the other. By adopting the code without modification, this library and others would commit themselves to recataloguing perhaps many thousands of volumes, and probably to maintaining two separate catalogues until the work were completed. The readers' reaction to this may be imagined, but the inconvenience might be acceptable if the recataloguing were to be satisfactory for all time. This is improbable. The new code is not perfect, and some libraries may very properly be unwilling to drop, for the sake of uniformity, rules which they consider satisfactory. *Catalogue and index* has already carried the headline "Danger—code erosion," and it is not surprising that suggestions for improvements are being made.[4] Cataloguing is not a static art and we probably will never have the perfect code.

Two further points may be made here. The Library of Congress is evidently not to use the code, at least not without considerable modification.[5] Will not this remove as potential customers many of those who use Congress cards, and thus jeopardize the whole future of MARC? If this does not happen and American publications are added to British ones on the tapes, which variants of the code are to be used?

No doubt there are other problems; not enough thought, for example, seems to have been given to costs. However, the possibility which seems most urgently to need investigation is that the general adoption of MARC may inhibit experiments and progress in cataloguing. The experts have been of little help here. One representative of BNB has said that "A universal movement towards standardization is demanded by mechanization," while another has asked, "why should we be pushed around by computers?"[6] To be obliged to commit oneself irrevocably to an imperfect cataloguing code and to classification numbers which one may not want *is* to be pushed around, and if this is what centralized cataloguing entails its advantages will need to be more clearly brought out before the MARC project can justify itself.

REFERENCES

1. Coward, R. E., BNB and computers. *Libr. Ass. Rec.*, 70 (8) August 1968, 199. [The information cited is not precisely accurate.—Ed.]
2. *MARC record service proposals*, BNB MARC documentation service publications, No. 1, 1968. Section 1.9.
3. Coward, R. E., op. cit. 200.
4. *Catalogue and index*, **14,** 1969, 1.
5. Downing, J. C. A national cataloguing policy. *Libr. Ass. Rec.,* **71** (3) March 1969, 64.
6. Downing, J. C. op. cit. 61. Coward, R. E., op. cit. 199.

Comment on Mr. Hall's Paper

J. E. Linford

The questions raised in the preceding article are fairly typical of those that librarians will necessarily ask about the MARC Project. They are indeed typical of those that are already being asked at the centre of the MARC Project and by its network libraries. The literature published on MARC has been largely descriptive of the project. In this context Mr. Hall's article is a welcome indication of external thought on the use of information available through the MARC Project.

It is important to stress that the MARC Project is a research project into the feasibility of organizing bibliographic data in such a way that it can be manipulated by a computer. If this is possible, the attendant gains are potentially vast. The speed and accuracy with which a computer can perform such operations as sorting and cumulating are themselves of such a magnitude that it must be the concern of libraries and bibliographic organizations to utilize these advantages. It seems short-sighted to look at the MARC Project simply in terms of an existing library system with its present structure. Computers are here to stay and librarians should be thinking today of the implications of computer technology for the future. The MARC Project should not be considered in the limited light of a means of centrally producing catalogue entries. The decision to take part in the MARC Project should be looked at in the wider context of developing an automated system designed to improve the overall efficiency of library services.

The elements of data which comprise a bibliographic record are essential to many library activities. They are required to alert library users to the existence of a work (current awareness services); they are used in ordering; they are used in cataloguing; they are used to control circulation; they are used in selective dissemination of information;

they are used in the compilation of reading lists and bibliographies. Not all data fields are required for each of these purposes, but the essential data fields are present in the MARC record, identified in a precise manner. The computer has the flexibility, through well designed implementation programmes, to select and present relevant data to meet all of these needs.

It is certainly true that each library will have its own problems and that some will be common to all. It is equally true that the "extensive literature" on the MARC Project cannot answer questions which the librarian must answer himself. Certainly studies are needed which will determine what proportion of currently ordered material is available from the MARC data base. By the time this article appears, both BNB material and English language material catalogued at the Library of Congress will be available on the UK/MARC tape distributed to network libraries. The Library of Congress intends to include material in the Romance languages by 1971.

The future seems to offer two possibilities. The first is that the Library of Congress will continue its role as a central cataloguing agency for the world's output of literature, making a progressively wider data base available in machine-readable form. The second is that the national bibliographic agencies of individual countries will produce their own machine-readable records on a current basis in a format compatible with the MARC format. BNB has already been involved in informal discussions revolving around this possibility with representatives of overseas bibliographic agencies.

The relevant question which needs to be asked now seems to change significantly. Instead of asking "what proportion of material currently acquired by a library is represented in the machine-readable data base?", we should perhaps ask "what are the economics of using a large data base for the relatively small number of records required by a medium-sized library?".

A weekly UK/MARC tape—containing both BNB and Library of Congress generated entries—will contain approximately 1,300 records. A five-yearly file (1970-1974) would contain 325,000 records. A medium-sized university library may acquire up to 20,000 items a year. Is it reasonable to assume that a high proportion of works acquired by a library fall within a five-year "currency range." Nevertheless a data base of 325,000 records would have to be searched on something

like a weekly schedule for those items. This would require searching the store of 325,000 records for approximately 400 records per week.

Certain conclusions seem inevitable. One of these is that a new pattern of national and regional organization of centralized services must emerge. It is possible to envisage a national bibliographic centre to which a library will feed a list of standard book numbers and in return receive a magnetic tape containing records relevant to that library, together with a list of numbers not on file. Thus a library's own use of the computer would be directed towards a file of records acquired by it. Certain library systems acquiring a high proportion of current British material could base their systems on the weekly receipt of the UK/MARC tape. Regional computing centres may well produce total service requirements for small libraries in the future.

All librarians are aware of the "residual" cataloguing problem that exists in any centralized cataloguing situation. The answer to this in a computer orientated library situation is to have a back-up system of machine input which is converted to magnetic tape and added to the local master file. Such an input system compares well in input terms with conventional catalogue record creation in that, from a single input typing, all bibliographic records can be created.

The MARC Project is at present only concerned with the input of current material. There is an awareness of the need to widen the data base to give both retrospective and pre-publication coverage. If this were achieved, it would certainly be possible to ensure that the computer generated whatever entry was required at the time it was required. For example, at the time a work was ordered prior to publication it would be possible to generate temporary catalogue records which would be automatically upgraded to a full catalogue entry when the full bibliographic entry appeared on the weekly tape. There is a misconception in the article that old tapes will have to be used or run through again. Weekly tapes will be used to build up a master file which would contain either all the data, or such a proportion of the data that a library decides is relevant to store. Few university libraries will wish to acquire works published and signalled in the machine-readable record as suitable for children. A library centred on the humanities would not build up a master file with records relating to science and technology.

The later part of Mr. Hall's article questions the

implications of MARC in both classification and cataloguing. It is difficult to see the trend of thought clearly here. There is nothing in the MARC Project which should inhibit the development of more adequate classification schemes. Indeed the inexorable logic of the computer will demand much more rigorously constructed systems if libraries are to reap the benefit of the computer in information retrieval systems. In the conventional situation, when a revised edition of a classification is published with amended schedules, a decision is made by the library or bibliographic organization to use the new edition in whole or part, to revise past practice, or to run two not entirely compatible systems side by side. This fundamental situation is not changed in a computer-based system. BNB may well decide to use an 18th edition DC number when this edition is published, and earlier published records will bear different classification numbers. The computer does offer a major advantage here, however. It would be possible to produce a table of conversions between variant numbers in the different editions and, via an implementation programme, change the classification number of every record on the master file and out-print a catalogue bearing 18th edition numbers. The computer offers a very real avenue of escape from some of the more intractable problems of the past. Local variations in classification could be taken care of in local systems by the input of the variant field into the system. The variant class number for the metallurgical work which a library wished to class with solid state physics would be input into the local system as a correction to a single field keyboarded with the standard book number for the work.

Mr. Hall's comments on cataloguing seem curiously ambivalent. One wonders what the link with MARC really is. By adopting the AACR rules without modification, a library may well commit itself to recataloguing many thousands of volumes. It would be theoretically possible to construct an alternative strategy which linked old and new form of headings. But again this is true whether a MARC-orientated cataloguing policy is adopted or not. It is just as possible to alter the headings on a MARC record as it is to make a typed alteration to a catalogue card. Only the method differs. Once again the advantages tend to lie in the computer-based system. Let us assume that we wish to retain the "London University" type of heading rather than the "University of London" type. Since the latter is defined in a MARC Record as a

corporate body in the direct form and identified by field tag 110020, it would be possible to print out all headings in this field with their standard book numbers, apply a correction by the input of the desired heading and the machine-readable record would conform to the local style. The allusion to "dangerous erosion" seems to have been included in Mr. Hall's article rather more for its dramatic impact than for its contribution to the discussion of factors which would influence a library's decision to use MARC records or not. Once again one can state that there is nothing in the MARC project which should inhibit the development of new cataloguing practices. Agreed changes can be made to take effect in machine-stored records in an existing data base with an ease impossible in manually created catalogues. It is unfortunate for the combined US/UK Projects that the Library of Congress did not decide to follow AACR practice for its MARC input. It is certainly fully aware of the implications of its variation from the standard code and is sympathetic in its viewpoint. There are signs that its decision in this matter is not irrevocable. However, even if its present policy is continued, it is not necessary to assume that the UK/MARC tape (including Library of Congress generated records) will bear records which do not conform to AACR practice. It would be possible to input both the standard form of heading *and* the national variant by making some amendment to the present format. Alternatively, a print-out of the American records could be made and AACR headings applied as corrections to records prior to the creation of the UK/MARC tape.

Mr. Hall gives two brief, and seemingly contradictory, quotations from articles by J. C. Downing and R. E. Coward. Read in fuller context there is nothing contradictory about them at all. Mr. Downing was speaking of a renaissance in librarianship which led *inter alia* to the production of a new cataloguing code. He then spoke of a "universal movement towards standardization" as a pressure influencing bibliographic organization and library practice before concluding that "a national cataloguing policy, and even an international one is the inevitable extension of our own local activity—bringing order out of disorder . . . ". Does this imply inhibition of experiment and progress in cataloguing? Mr. Coward offered the view that "the new AA code is a sound basis for the next generation of our catalogues" and mentioned that it has been criticized for totally failing to take the computer into account. He then went on to say "thank goodness it did not. Why should we be pushed around by computers? I cannot see the slightest reason why the transient limitations of a new branch of technology should be taken into account when we are engaged in a serious business of preparing catalogue codes." Does this imply inhibition of experiment and progress in cataloguing?

The opportunity offered by Mr. Hall and the editor of the *Record* to comment on Mr. Hall's paper is appreciated.

The Utilization of the MARC Project in Libraries Outside the United States and Canada

K. W. Humphreys

In writing this paper many months after the Frankfurt meetings where it was agreed that this subject should be discussed in Copenhagen, I realize that this should have been complementary to a paper on the use of MARC in American libraries. Unfortunately it was then too late to ask someone to write such a paper. It may be helpful, however, to point out that a valuable account of the uses made of the original MARC Pilot project is to be found in Miss Avram's final report.[1]

Perhaps the first point I should make is that I have not dealt here with the National Program for Acquisition and Cataloguing of the Library of Congress although reference is made to shared cataloguing in some of the reports which follow.

I must confess that this report almost wrote itself as I received material from many colleagues which I have put together with very little intellectual effort on my part. I have included reports on automation generally which are not specifically relevant to MARC but which often indicate the intentions of the country concerned to make use of the MARC record in the future.

In assessing the activities of a number of countries in this field it must be remembered that the MARC II tapes have only very recently been available from the Library of Congress and that although the British National Bibliography tapes preceded the Library of Congress ones most libraries are still in the early stages of experimental use of the tapes even if they have progressed that far. The methods adopted in each country for the forward planning of this operation will, however, I think be of value to those at present only considering the initial steps.

I start with the Federal Republic of Germany which reports as follows:—

"Dr. Kaltwasser in his report during the IFLA Session 1968 in Frankfurt has already given an idea of the problems which arise when German libraries plan to take over LC cataloguing information. Two steps must be distinguished clearly when an attempt is made to use LC cataloguing information for German libraries and, I think, the same problems arise for all European libraries except perhaps those of Great Britain. The first step is to analyse in what way and to what extent American title entries can be adapted to national requirements. Can LC title cards be used and to what extent must they be transformed? This is a question of cataloguing rules. Only when it is possible to settle these problems in a satisfactory way can the second step be taken, that means the transposition into machine readable form. When the problems of the first step are solved, the second step should offer no insurmountable difficulties.

Stimulated by the German Committee on Central Cataloguing the German Research Association (Deutsche Forschungsgemeinschaft) has made a grant in order to initiate some tests with the LC title-prints.

Two test series are aimed at. One is to be widely dispersed and to test the value of the title information for acquisition purposes. The other, a concentrated study, is to investigate the use of the title entries for both cataloguing and acquisition purposes. The two test series can be run at the same time.

The first test will find out whether LC cards are suitable for acquisitions control, that is, if gaps in the libraries' acquisition activities can be found by the aid of these titles. This experiment is to be carried out where acquisition is very comprehensive in certain fields. In the Federal Republic of Germany such concentrated purchasing is in spe-

SOURCE: Reprinted from *Libri XX*, 1–2 (1970), pp. 133–143, by permission of the author and the publisher.

cial fields of acquisition (Sondersammelgebiete), which are assigned to the larger research libraries and supported by the German Research Association (Deutsche Forschungsgemeinschaft). It is therefore planned to distribute one set of LC title cards among those libraries according to their special fields, so that they can check which of the titles not in their collections are worth acquiring. The distribution of the cards will be organised by the Bavarian State Library at Munich.

The second, more exhaustive experiment will be carried out only at four libraries (probably, the University Libraries at Göttingen and Saarbrücken, the Library of the Institute of World Economics at Kiel and the University Library at Konstanz). The investigations will be restricted to the fields of Physics (Göttingen and Saarbrüken) and Economics (Kiel and Konstanz). Three sets of problems are involved:

(a) time study;
(b) revision of title entries;
(c) completeness of the titles submitted.

(a) The speed with which LC cards are available will be tested. This can be done by comparing the receipt dates of LC cards with various dates of normal library activities. The receipt date of a LC card will be compared with the dates of ordering by the library and delivery by the bookseller, and the date at which the bibliographic description of the library is entered in the catalogue. From a careful comparison of these dates a knowledge of the speed of delivery of printed cards from Washington may be derived.

(b) Furthermore we want to know how much work the revision of printed cards requires. These are the formal questions. We are interested in knowing how many titles or what percentage of them will have to be revised, and this within the various complexes of problems. The investigation is to reveal how many entries of corporate names and how many names of persons have to be altered (this applies to all the names, for which main or added entries or references are made). Finally, the number of differing transcriptions will be ascertained in two series, one in comparison with the old German rules ("Preussische Instruktionen"), the other one in comparison with the new German rules.

(c) Finally, it is worth knowing how many titles of the whole production of a country are supplied by LC and which of them. To a certain extent this can be learned already from the first of the tests described. Yet it seems desirable to have precise figures. Therefore we think of collecting LC printed cards of one full year of publication, and to compare these with the same year of the national bibliographies.

The investigation will be started in the course of 1969, as soon as the technical details are fixed, and these are being discussed at the moment.

If the investigations come to a positive conclusion, that is, if the problems of time and form can be overcome, the setting up of an editing office would be possible in order to supply revised LC titles to those libraries which order them.

That the Deutsche Bibliothek in Frankfurt is contributing to the shared cataloguing of the Library of Congress by delivering in advance catalogue entries of German publications through the Library of Congress office in Wiesbaden, may be assumed as a generally known fact."[2]

I received from Dr. Karl Kammel of Vienna a valuable account of work in progress in connection with the application of electronics data-processing in Austrian libraries. No specific reference is made to the MARC project but the following indicates the intentions of Austrian librarians in the automation field. As a result of discussions held at the investigation of the ÖIBF "it was agreed that the right moment had come to avoid expensive individual experiments, such as had been conducted in other countries and from the beginning to aim at co-operation amongst Austrian libraries in this field. Just as the cataloguing rules in Austrian libraries are uniform, so now a non-commercial integrated information system should be designed, in which all the information, wherever stored, is compatible, i.e., can be called on by all other centres. This information system would at the same time also be applicable to documentation.

No library is in any way to be compelled to introduce electronic data-processing. The decision lies with the library itself, or with the immediate library authority. If, however, a library wishes to introduce it, it should find a framework, into which it can adapt very well and at the same time through the possibility of the exchange of data— the processing of which is always a most time consuming task—can gain for itself and offer others the the greatest benefit.

Parallel with this administrative and technical co-operation there should also be co-ordination on the official level, as only in this way can the sparing use of the public resources available for electronic data-processing be assured."

Mr. Grønland of Oslo University Library reports

that "in April/May 1969 three librarians from the National and University Library in Oslo (the group consisted of one data specialist and two catalogue heads) went to England to study the progress made by the British National Bibliography in experimenting with the conversion of catalogue information to magnetic tape using the MARC format. Some offset printing houses were also visited to have a look at their phototype setting.

Drawing on this know-how, the Library authorities will then evaluate the possibilities of producing the Norwegian National Bibliography in the MARC format, preferably from 1st January 1971. Only at this stage will it be possible to judge whether the result is satisfactory enough for the Library of Congress to base its Shared Cataloguing on our tapes. Much still remains to be done, however, such as the introduction of a book numbering system in co-operation with the publishers' and booksellers' associations."

The Italian report from Professor Casamassima is one of hope rather than of immediate achievement so far as MARC is concerned but indicates the interest shown by the National Library in the project: "The National Library of Florence has collaborated in the shared cataloguing program at the invitation of the Library of Congress for more than a year. The agreement signed on 26th January 1968 commits the Italian National Bibliography to preparing currently bibliographical printed entries for Italian publications and to furnish a copy to the Bibliographical Office in Florence of the Library of Congress. The National Bibliography also prepares an entry for those publications not received by copyright of which copies have been reported by the Library of Congress.

The National Library of Florence is at present considering a plan for the mechanisation of certain services and in the first place of the National Bibliography, and is now examining the possibility of using MARC II. The problem was studied at a recent meeting on automation and mechanisation at the National Library, Florence, held from 29–31 October 1968, and a definite decision [on future work] is expected in the next few months."

Similarly, the very useful contribution received from Mr. Kondakov expresses a strong desire to be associated with the international development of shared cataloguing and automation. "In principle we take a positive attitude to the questions of the unification of bibliographical description and international co-operation in cataloguing. We are interested in studying the experience of the national libraries of all other countries and we con-

sider that the Section of National and University libraries should actively support the mutual exchange of information and experience in the field of the application of the newest technology and the organisation of library work.

The high degree of centralisation of cataloguing in our country and the large number of libraries using the printed cards issued by our central bibliographical institute—the All-Union Book Chamber, do not permit us to change the existing system in the near future. Soviet book-production constitutes the basis of the acquisitions of all Soviet libraries, and it is indisputable that the printed cards issued by the All-Union Book Chamber are the best means of satisfying the requirements of these libraries in the matter of cataloguing.

Nonetheless the Lenin State Library of the U.S.S.R. is in constant contact with the Library of Congress and gives it considerable help in the implementation of its Shared Cataloguing Program.

The Lenin State Library has since January 1968 systematically, on receipt from the All-Union Book Chamber, sent by air-mail three sets of cards, which are used by the Library of Congress for the centralised cataloguing of Soviet books in the Russian language.

This work has also led to a considerable expansion of the exchange of literature between our libraries. In the course of 1968 the Lenin Library sent the Library of Congress almost three times more books and microfilms than in 1967.

As regards machine-produced catalogues I can inform you with satisfaction that in the leading libraries of our country, amongst them the Lenin Library, the All-Union State Library of Foreign Literature and the State Public Scientific and Technical Library work is being intensively carried out on the processing of bibliographical information with the help of a Soviet-produced electronic computer. At the basis of this work lie projects for for the creation of information retrieval systems and of systems for printed catalogues in book form.

Besides this the Lenin Library is beginning to develop a project for an information retrieval system of the descriptor type for library science and bibliography, also on the basis of an electronic computer.

Unfortunately, progress in these projects has as yet been inadequate for me to give you more detailed material.

In our work we try as far as possible to take into account the experience gained by the Library of Congress in the projects MARC and MARC II.

However, the functional difference between the Library of Congress and the Lenin Library, the inadequacy of our information on these projects, and also difficulties connected with the acquisition of electronic computers of the type used in the American project do not make it possible for us as yet to assess the degree of acceptability of the MARC project for Soviet libraries."

Dr. Rojnić has no information for me on automation plans in Yugoslavia although, of course, his country is committed to the Library of Congress Shared Cataloguing Program.

I understand from Mr. Vinarek that project SOKRATUS, a computerized acquisition, cataloguing, bibliographical and statistical centre for scientific, university and technical libraries, is to be established at the State Library of CSR; this project will be MARC compatible.

The Librarian of the Australian National University Library, Mr. Graneek, says: "We are interested in MARC tapes but have not yet made any decision about the use we are likely to make of the set of tapes which is being acquired by the National Library and on which all libraries in Australia will be able to draw for bibliographical information. Details of the service provided by the National Library have not yet been worked out. They are the concern of a subcommittee of the Australian Advisory Council on Bibliographical Services."

Various universities in South Africa are investigating the possibility of using MARC for internal purposes, and in the near future a committee of interested librarians will begin a comprehensive study of the project.

At national level, the State Library asked the National Library Advisory Board in 1968 to initiate an investigation into the project and also to send a small committee overseas to do an on-the-spot study. There has been no reaction to this request to date.

Mr. Reedijk and Mr. Van Wesemael sent the following interesting report on the position in the Netherlands. "Since the MARC II report was published, it has received a wide interest from Dutch librarians. The possibilities for application of the MARC format in the Netherlands were systematically studied in several contexts. The State Advisory Committee on Library Affairs has concrete information concerning the following projects and studies:

1. The Dutch publishing firm Sijthoff (Leiden), which produces the Dutch bibliography (Brinkman's Cumulatieve Catalogus van Boeken . . .), is completing now with Infonet (the data-processing division of the Excerpta Medica Foundation) a computer program for the editing and printing of this bibliography. In a fairly advanced stage of development of software package two facts enlarged the impact and perhaps even the scope of this project:
   (a) the publication of the MARC II format;
   (b) the increasing probability that in the years to come legislation for a legal deposit in the Netherlands will be passed by Parliament. It became clear that, once this law was accepted, a national bibliography which will be more extensive and more complete by its nature of a national bibliography than Brinkman, will have to be published.

The Royal librarian and the Director of Sijthoff decided to set up a committee to discuss this new Dutch national bibliography and its technical and bibliographical problems. The MARC II format was very intensely discussed in this committee. It was generally felt that for the sake of international co-operation in the future great stress should be laid on interchangeability of bibliographical data. It was decided that the the format already prepared for the computer editing of Brinkman's should be made more compatible with the MARC format and that the same format, perhaps somewhat extended, should be used in a larger stage for the Dutch national bibliography.

2. A committee of Dutch cartographers and librarians is preparing plans for a union catalogue of maps. Although the MARC II format for maps is until now not known in its details, it seems highly probable that this union catalogue will use the MARC II format. One of the points that offer some difficulties is the absence of a tag in the fixed fields for the co-ordinates of maps. The general feeling of the committee is that in an on-line computer system these co-ordinates are extremely helpful, if not necessary, for quick on-line retrieval of maps. The setting up of such on-line facilities for this union catalogue of maps is very seriously considered. Informal discussions with the Library of Congress about the adding in the fixed fields of the co-ordinates for each map catalogued have taken place.

3. An informal group of cataloguing experts of

the Royal Library and the University Libraries is, in close collaboration with the Director of Infonet (see above), developing the systems analysis for automated libraries. The first point to be considered was, as a matter of fact, the creating of an automated catalogue system in which all Dutch scientific and research libraries could participate. In view of the very important percentage of Anglo-American library material in Dutch libraries and in view of future developments where interchange of bibliographical data in machine-readable form will be the general practice, it was self-evident that the format for this on-line system should be completely compatible with the MARC II format. The tagging system of the MARC II format was abandoned in favour of the tagging system of the format of the Dutch bibliography, because it was felt that the latter was more apt to be used in on-line retrieval systems, the difference between the two formats consisting almost exclusively in the numbering of the tagging.

4. The MARC activities of the individual Dutch libraries have until now been of a restricted nature. Some libraries, however, have undertaken experiments with the MARC II proof tape; one of those libraries, the Library of the Delft Technological University is trying out the MARC II format for the cataloguing of its acquisitions."

I have relied for my information on Belgian applications of MARC on the paper prepared by Frans de Vrieze for the International Meeting of Cataloguing Experts held here prior to the IFLA session. In this paper Mr. de Vrieze is concerned with the mechanisation of the Bibliothèque Royale Albert Ier mainly from a cataloguing point of view. He does, however, say that "the system at the Bibliothèque Royale aims to record information which will be as comprehensive as possible and which can be used for a wide range of purposes . . . In order to avoid repeating bibliographical descriptions which reach us from abroad we look forward to conversion from other automated systems into one single format which will be characteristic of the Bibliothèque Royale." Mr. de Vrieze ends his paper with an important statement: "Once automation is really within the grasp of all libraries . . . a flexible machine system will be needed which will be adaptable in every case within the framework of national and international interdisciplinary networks."

In Britain the developments in connection with MARC may be described on two levels, firstly, the work undertaken by the British National Bibliography, and secondly the practical experiments in train in a number of different libraries. The British National Bibliography is already producing its BNB/MARC tapes and distributing them to libraries. The format of the tapes is not identical with that of the Library of Congress but after considerable discussion a wide measure of agreement has been possible with the Library of Congress. Disagreement lies mainly in the application of the Anglo-American Cataloguing Code, the details of which are not relevant here.

The immediate development plan of the British National Bibliography involves the exchange of tapes with the Library of Congress, a study of the problems of producing the Bibliography by computer type-setting and the possibilities of utilizing other MARC-type records from abroad by exchange. In addition, it is intended to develop a suitable scheme for assigning a new series of subject descriptors. This will allow the tapes to be used for deeper subject retrieval than is possible through the Dewey decimal classification which BN has refined for its current bibliography.

One important British contribution to the international utilisation of common records is the insertion of the Standard Book Number which is a unique identifying descriptor for each book as it is published and which can even be assigned to it before publication. The data bank for the store of Standard Book Numbers will, it is hoped, be available through the British National Bibliography, enabling libraries to use pre-MARC tape information of books to be published, for book-selection and ordering purposes. The British National Bibliography is also interested in issuing lists of all books in print with a Standard Book Number.

It should be pointed out that investigations on the editing of MARC records from abroad will have important implications for a body like IFLA not only from the cataloguing point of view but from the general applications to each country's libraries.

The cost of implementing much of this research has been borne by the Office of Scientific and Technical Information in the Department of Education and Science. It has also provided funds for testing the use of MARC records in a number of libraries. The Bodleian Library plans to begin in January 1970 the construction with the aid of MARC of a name catalogue of seven Oxford libraries of books in the English language: later it will provide a subject catalogue based on LC sub-ject descriptors (or possibly the new BNB subject descriptors referred to above). The University of Southampton is investigating the use of MARC records for an ordering system. The proposed developments of the Standard Book Numbering scheme will obviously have a bearing on this research.

Although strictly not within the British organisation and not therefore in receipt of a grant from OSTI, the work in progress at Trinity College, Dublin, is relevant here. The College is a legal deposit library for British books and therefore can make effective use of the BNB/MARC tapes. The library is engaged not only in testing cataloguing input but also in the issuing of subject lists of books received to academic staff and to scholars outside the College.

It is envisaged that a number of other libraries, including public and county libraries will make up a network of MARC users throughout the country. One of the projects which is concerned with the co-operative use of MARC tapes is that for certain Birmingham libraries, of which I will give a brief description. I hesitated about discussing the project with which I am personally concerned, but decided that there were a few advantages in such treatment:

1. It may help libraries in other countries which have no considerable financial resources to realise the implications of experimenting with automation.
2. It is the only project referred to in this paper from which I am not once or even twice removed from active research.
3. As MARC tapes have only recently become available an up-to-date report may be of more use than descriptions of experiments which have advanced very rapidly in the past few months.
4. An account of one project may offer more useful information on the problems involved than the general state of the art in a number of countries. With no more excuses therefore I describe the Birmingham Libraries Co-operative Mechanisation Project and its work so far.

The Universities of Aston and Birmingham and Birmingham Public Libraries are co-operating in an investigation of ways in which the information on the weekly tapes can be used to meet the vary-ing needs of the three library systems. Methods of adding local catalogue information to that included in the national tapes will also be examined. It is expected that the study may lead to a common form of catalogue in all three libraries, which will make information about their total resources more easily available to readers in the area and will stimulate mutual co-operation on other activities as well as cataloguing. It is hoped that a further stage of the project will examine the feasibility of establishing a regional data bank of MARC records available to all libraries and even, possibly, the book trade generally, in the area.

The OSTI grant pays for a Systems Analyst and a Programmer to be employed full-time on the project and in addition 19 members of the staffs of the three libraries are engaged part-time on it through a number of Working Groups. The Products and Services Group has prepared a specification for a New Books list by subject for book-selection purposes. It is also concerned with cataloguing input from MARC tapes. The Machine Group is mainly responsible for designing the Birmingham local MARC file and for gathering or writing programs and sub routines which may be used with this file format. The Compatibility Group has examined the Anglo-American Cataloguing Rules 1967 (British text) and reached a very large measure of agreement in acceptance of the rules. Filing rules will now occupy the attention of this Group. The first task of the Statistics Group was to design and carry out an analysis of the intake of the three libraries: a preliminary pilot exercise prepared us for the major scheme now in operation. Lastly, the Serials Group has established the basic requirements for all the libraries in preparing catalogues and lists of periodicals.

This session today is being held jointly with the Automation Committee and undoubtedly many of the members of that Committee will be able to correct statements in my report and, I hope, supplement it. It seems to me that it was very important that this Committee should have the opportunity of considering the work already undertaken in this field from a different point of view from that of the Automation Committee. In many ways it may be expected that the Committee will be concerned with the experimental and the technical aspects of automation whereas we must look at the implications of automation as an integral part of our management functions.

We need to know exactly what it can do and what it will cost, but above all, perhaps, we must be clear about what we want it to do. Unless we are prepared to give a great deal of thought to our own requirements and to be definite about the direction in which automation research should go we may find ourselves accepting methods and forms which do not improve our library services and may even reduce their effectiveness.

NOTES

1. Avram (Henriette D.). *The MARC Pilot project. Final report on a project sponsored by the Council on Library Resources, Inc.* Washington, Library of Congress 1968.

2. See also Wieder (Joachim). 'Computer techniques in libraries of the Federal Republic of Germany', *Unesco Bull. Libr.*, XXIII (1969), 245–252.

IFLA Communications: Report of the International Meeting of Cataloguing Experts, Copenhagen, 1969

A. H. Chaplin and Dorothy Anderson

INTRODUCTION

I. Origins of the Meeting

The decision to organize an International Meeting of Cataloguing Experts was taken by the General Council of IFLA in a resolution adopted at its 34th Session at Frankfurt-am-Main in August 1968. The resolution was proposed by the Committee on Uniform Cataloguing Rules after consideration of developments in its work and in cataloguing activity generally following the International Conference on Cataloguing Principles, Paris, 1961 (ICCP).

The *Statement of Principles* adopted by that Conference had been used as the basis of a number of new codes and as a guide in the revision of existing codes, and its influence upon cataloguing theory and practice in the seven years since 1961 had thus been considerable.[1] But some of its sections had been found in their application to be ambiguous, unsatisfactory or too general to be incorporated in a code. An annotated edition of the *Statement,* with examples, had been compiled in provisional form, in response to a request from the delegates at the ICCP, by the then Secretary and Assistant Secretary of the Committee, and had been circulated for comment.[2] In this edition the difficulties arising in the application of the Principles had been recognized and some remedies had been suggested. Comments received had shown, however, that consideration by a group representative of the different cataloguing traditions was needed if a generally acceptable definitive edition was to be produced.

Several projects relating to the standardization of catalogue headings, proposed in resolutions of the ICCP, had been undertaken and had resulted

in one publication[3] and two provisional texts circulated for comment.[4,5] The Committee had also initiated in 1966 a project outside the scope of the ICCP and the Statement of Principles—the establishment of an international standard for the descriptive content of catalogue entries. With this in view a comparative study of the practices of a number of national bibliographies had been undertaken, under a UNESCO contract, by Michael Gorman. At the time of the Frankfurt meeting this study had not been finished but it was considered important that on completion it should be examined by a representative body of cataloguers.

The Committee had also taken into consideration two recent developments which had begun to influence radically the prospects for international co-operation in cataloguing. First, the Shared Cataloging Program of the Library of Congress had aroused great interest in IFLA, and had been discussed, under the auspices of the Section of National and University Libraries, at the General Council sessions at The Hague (1966)[6] and Toronto (1967)[7]. Secondly, the growing importance of electronic data processing in libraries had led to the creation by IFLA of a Committee on Mechanization. That there was a close relation between these two developments was shown by the fact that resolutions on the possibility of an international extension of the Shared Cataloging Program had been adopted jointly, both at Toronto and at Frankfurt, by the Section of National and University Libraries and the Committee on Mechanization. It now seemed opportune that the implications of these new developments for the form and content of catalogues and catalogue entries should be studied by a body representing professional cataloguers.

SOURCE: Reprinted from *Libri* XX, 1-2 (1970), pp. 105-118, 124, by permission of the publisher.

It was with all these considerations in mind that the Committee on Uniform Cataloguing Rules put forward its resolution, proposing "That a meeting of cataloguing specialists be organized . . . to review progress in cataloguing since the Paris Conference of 1961, to consider the text of the Annotated Edition of the *Statement of Principles* in the light of wider representation, and the problems raised at this meeting in Frankfurt in relation to the Shared Cataloguing Programme of the Library of Congress" and that "the officers of the Committee . . . should investigate the possibility of financial support so that the meeting can be representative of all important cataloguing interests."

II. Preparation of the Meeting

The necessary financial support was sought by means of an application to the Council on Library Resources, of Washington, D.C., whose assistance had earlier made the 1961 Paris conference possible. The application outlined the purposes and general character of the proposed meeting and suggested as an immediate step the formation of a small Organizing Committee composed of members who would be broadly representative of the different interests involved. In March 1969 the Council approved a grant to cover the cost of the Meeting of Cataloguing Experts and of the necessary preparatory work by the Organizing Committee.

The Organizing Committee was constituted as follows: A. H. Chaplin (Chairman), J. C. Downing (Secretary), Dorothy Anderson (Organizing Secretary), F. G. Kaltwasser, R. Pierrot, Eva Verona, Barbara M. Westby.[8] It met for two days, 21-22 March 1969 to plan the Meeting and outline the programme. It was decided that the Meeting should take place at Copenhagen in the three days immediately before the IFLA General Council, i.e. 22-24 August 1969, so providing an opportunity for participants to attend the General Council session also without making a separate journey. The number of participants would be restricted to 40, partly to give the Meeting the character of a working conference which could be expected to deal with a complicated agenda and arrive at conclusions in a short space of time, partly to limit the cost. The participants should include the members of the Organizing Committee, persons commissioned to write Working Papers, representatives from national associations or cataloguing committees of countries where important work had been done arising out of the ICCP, representatives of national bibliographies interested in shared cataloguing activity, and certain other persons known for their individual contributions to the subjects under discussion or able to represent regions of the world not otherwide included. Organizations sponsoring representatives were asked to pay at least part of the cost of attendance at the Meeting: the expenses of the other participants would be wholly paid from the Council on Library Resources grant.

It was decided that the agenda of the Meeting should include a review of progress in the application of the *Statement of Principles* and approval of a definitive text for the annotated edition, establishment of principles for the descriptive content of catalogue entries, an examination of the Shared Cataloguing Program and the possibility of extending it internationally, and consideration of the use of the computer in the recording and exchange of bibliographical information and the impact of mechanization on catalogues and cataloguing codes.

The Organizing Committee drew up a list of documents for consideration and Working Papers to be commissioned, and drafted a programme of sessions to cover 22nd and 23rd August and the morning of the 24th.

Immediately after the meeting of the Committee, two Documents for Examination, providing a basis for discussion on the first two themes, were circulated to participants in French and English texts. These were:

DE 1: Statement of Principles: annotated edition with examples. Provisional text.
DE 2: Bibliographical data in national bibliography entries: a report on descriptive cataloguing. By Michael Gorman.

Comments on these documents were collected from participants and were then analysed and collated in digests which formed Working Papers 1 and 2. These and eleven other Working Papers[9] providing a background for discussion on the remaining themes of the Meeting were circulated— also in English and French—during the months April to July 1969. Working Paper 13: *The future implications of automation for cataloguing*, by Suzanne Honoré, is considered a useful summary of the prospects offered to cataloguers by the application of computers in their sphere of activity.

Arrangements were made to accommodate all

the participants at a new hotel, the Bel Air, on the outskirts of Copenhagen, where it was orginally intended that the sessions would also be held. Unfortunately the hotel was unable to fulful its promise to have conference rooms in operation by the Summer, and it therefore proved necessary to make other arrangements. The hotel was retained as a residential centre but the sessions were at the Royal School of Librarianship, where meeting rooms and other facilities were made available through the courtesty of its Director, Mr. Preben Kirkegaard.

III. Participants

The Meeting was attended by thirty-eight participants from thirty-two countries. Among them were chief cataloguers and heads of cataloguing departments, directors of national bibliographies and others with a specialized knowledge of cataloguing or the production of national bibliographies. Two who were expected were unable to attend: Mrs. A. Budach, Deutsche Bibliothek, Frankfurt am Main, and Mr. Luís Silveira, Inspector General of Libraries, Lisbon. Mrs. Henriette D. Avram, Director, MARC Project, Library of Congress, was able to take part, as a specialist consultant, through the courtesy of the Council on Library Resources. There were also twelve observers, including representatives from Unesco, from the IFLA Section of National and University Libraries, and from Danish libraries and the Danish cataloguing committee.

The administration of the Meeting was in the hands of the Chairman, the Secretary and the Organizing Secretary with two assistants; in the course of the first session, Dr. Eva Verona, Chairman of the Yugoslav Cataloguing Committee, was appointed Vice-Chairman. Three interpreters were in attendance.

THE SESSIONS

Day 1. Friday 22 August 1969. Sessions 1–3

Statement of Principles

The first three sessions of Day 1 were devoted to discussion of the Paris *Statement of Principles* and of the provisional text of the Annotated Edi-

tion. The discussion, which was mainly directed toward approving changes in the provisional text to be made in a definitive edition, was led by Dr. Eva Verona, who had prepared the digest of comments (WPI).

Many of the participants were able to make valuable conbributions based on experience in their own libraries or committees of the interpretation and application of the Principles. It was agreed that, although the Meeting was not authorised to make any alteration to the Statement, which had been approved and voted by a representative gathering of national delegates at the Paris Conference, it could draw attention to weaknesses and inconsistencies in the text of the Statement, and could make recommendations for revisions of the text and for solutions of problems not adequately dealt with by the Principles. Decisions on points which relate to particular sections of the Statement and of the commentary in the annotated edition are set out below:

Section 1. The commentary should be revised to remove any impression that the Principles were intended only for large libraries and to emphasize that they should be used also in small and special libraries as far as possible.

Section 4.1. In order to avoid any inconsistency with Footnote 2, the text should be interpreted to read that added entries given information not "under other headings" but *"in other places in the catalogue"*.

Section 6.2. The commentary should not recommend that an author who writes under different names for different types of material be entered under the various names: rather, that there be a uniform heading with added entries, not references, under the other names.

Section 7.1 & 8.2. The Principles do not provide satisfactory guidance for dealing with a change of name by a living author. The treatment of these in catalogues may vary according to circumstances. In certain cases it may be more useful to adopt the most recent name immediately.

Section 7.1. In order to advance international uniformity, the commentary should encourage the use wherever possible of the orginal forms of names and titles, rather than the forms used in the language of the country in which the library is located. In catalogues using the roman script, names in non-roman alphabets should be transliterated according to a standard international system. As an exception ancient Greek names may be written in the Latin form. In catalogues using other scripts a uniform phonetic transcription should be used for each name.

Section 9.11 and 9.12. Footnote 7. The Meeting recognized the unsatisfactory nature of sections 9.11, 9.12 and Footnote 7 and noted that no codes evolved since the Paris Conference had found it possible to formulate rules consistent with both these sections. It was agreed that the commentary should include a survey of the various solutions adopted or under discussion. The Meeting discussed the problem of works issued by dignitaries, such as Popes and Presidents of the U.S.A., which, although appearing under their personal names, carried a collective authority. Opinions were expressed both for personal and for corporate entry for such works and it was decided that the commentary should draw attention to these opposing views.

Section 9.41. The Meeting agreed that, although the proposal in the commentary was not in accordance with the text of the section, it would provide a more satisfactory basis for a consistent rule.

Section 9.44. The commentary should encourage the tendency which already exists to adopt the original forms of the names of cities and states.

Section 9.5. It was recognized that the commentary was not consistent with the text of this section. Any revised commentary should consider more fully the nature of entries under states for laws, constitutions, etc., and of the terminology involved in grouping the entries for such works. The various points of view on these questions should be set out and examined.

Section 10.2. The suggestion in the commentary (p. 50, English ed.) that a work with more than three authors might sometimes be entered under the first author should be omitted.

Section 10.3. While sections 10.1 and 10.3 provide clear guidance for the entry of works produced by several authors which are intended to constitute an entity and section 10.3 provides clear guidance for collections of previously existing material, the Principles do not provide for the intermediate cases in which a publication consists of separate contributions which are written for the occasion but not intended to form an entity, or in which previously existing and new material are combined in one publication. The commen-

tary should deal with this defect in the Principles by recommending the application of section 10.3 to these intermediate cases—the editor to be treated in the same way as a compiler.

It was pointed out that the *Statement* gave no guidance on the precise form of the entry, that is, on its layout and typography. A note to this effect should be introduced into the commentary so that the layout of the examples would not be regarded as fixed and binding. It was also agreed that the definitive text of the Annotated Edition should take into account, in addition to the points discussed and agreed upon at the Meeting, the comments received before the Meeting but not discussed and any comments received as a result of the Meeting. The commentary should report as far as possible the various solutions adopted in the different codes and revisions of codes compiled since 1961. It was decided that a small working party should be set up to prepare a definitive text and to arrange for its publication at the earliest possible date.

Day 1. Sessions 4 & 5. Day 2. 23 August 1969. Session 1

International Standard for Descriptive Content of Catalogue Entries

The last two sessions of Day 1 and the first session of Day 2 were devoted to consideration of an international standard for the descriptive content of catalogue entries, using as the basis for the discussion DE 2 and Dr. Domanovszky's digest of comments, WP 2. The first problem to be settled was the purpose of such a standard, as there was some feeling that the requirements of the catalogue and of the national bibliography were different and that the usage of national bibliographies was therefore not a valid guide for cataloguing. It was pointed out that a number of national bibliographies were used as cataloguing services, or were closely associated with such services, and that one of the publications examined in the document, the U.S. *National Union Catalog*, was a compilation of catalogue entries serving some of the purposes of a national bibliography. It was agreed that the creation of a framework for bibliographical description that would serve the needs of both catalogues and bibliographies should be possible.

This agreement led to two further important decisions. The first of these was that the framework should be designed to accommodate all the descriptive data commonly required not only in catalogues and bibliographies but also in other records used in libraries and elsewhere in the control and handling of books. This would mean that not all parts of the standard description would be used in all circumstances: those elements required for each particular purpose would be extracted from it. The second decision was that a fixed order for the main elements of the description was desirable and was more important than exact transcription of the title page. After some doubts, based on the special need for accuracy of transcription in the cataloguing of older books, had been expressed, it was agreed that only the title itself need be transcribed exactly, other elements being in general more usefully given in a standardized form.

The scope of the standard bibliographical description was further defined by excluding from it the catalogue heading as such—this might vary according to the particular use being made of the description, but would normally be determined in a catalogue by reference to the *Statement of Principles*. The following provisional order for the main elements of the description was agreed:

  title
  subtitle
  author statement
  subsidiary author statement relating to the work
  edition statement
  subsidiary author statement relating to the edition
  imprint statement
  collation
  series statement
  notes (including any other title for the same work which it is useful to mention)

There was some discussion of the proper position to be given to variant titles for the same work. It was decided that the original title—i.e. the first title under which a work had been published in its original language—should always be included in the standard description, even if it did not appear in the book; but that, although this title might sometimes appear in a catalogue or bibliography as a "uniform title" at the beginning of an entry, it would not occupy this position in the standard description but would be given in a note.

The Meeting resolved unanimously that one element not mentioned in DE 2—the Standard Book Number—should, when available, always be included in the standard bibliographical description.

It became apparent as the discussion progressed that, while decisions on questions of principle might be taken, it was not possible in the time available to draw up a full standard. It was therefore decided that a working group should be set up to make detailed recommendations for the composition of the standard bibliographical description and the form and order of its component parts.

Day 2. Session 2

Shared Cataloguing

The subject of the second session of Day 2 was the Shared Cataloging Program. The operation of the Program had been described by Mr. Sumner Spalding in Working Paper 4 and the application of its results in North American Libraries had been described by Dr. Jean Lunn in Working Paper 5; Dr. F. G. Kaltwasser in Working Paper 6 had discussed the problems involved in extending shared cataloguing activity internationally, and particularly in European libraries. Each of these authors also contributed to the discussion. Mr. Spalding spoke of the possibility that the Library of Congress might close its catalogues at the end of 1970, so that the new Anglo-American Cataloguing Rules could then be applied in their entirety: this would be a great step towards international standardization. In giving some account of the operation of the Shared Cataloguing Program, he emphasized the great saving in time and money that had already been made in American libraries; but he drew attention to the dependence of the Program on the co-operation of national bibliographies, which imposed a limit on its scope. Dr. Kaltwasser reported on the experiments being undertaken by German libraries in the use of Library of Congress cards, and on the problems arising from differing rules for headings. He thought that the additional problem of matching books with cards would be effectively solved by the use of the International Standard Book Number. The participants agreed that the Shared Cataloging Program had shown that variations in descriptive detail could be accepted and so had encouraged a more flexible attitude among cataloguers towards changes in their own systems, but that greater uniformity was nevertheless desirable, as variations could lead to uncertainty in identification. The Shared Cataloging Program, in making cataloguers more aware of existing variations, had also increased their willingness to work towards uniformity. It became clear in the course of the discussions that the Shared Cataloging Program and the progress of mechanization were both strong influences favouring the creation of an international standard bibliographical description. All the subjects under consideration by the Meeting were therefore aspects of a single problem: the objective in view was the establishment of an international system of bibliographical communication. In such a system the national bibliographies would have the fundamental role of providing standard descriptions of new publications which could be used both for cataloguing in the libraries of their own countries and for international communication.

Day 2. Sessions 3 & 4

Standard Book Numbers; Machine Format

The discussion on the Shared Cataloging Program and on the associated problem of matching books with cards led naturally to the third session in which Mr. A. J. Wells enlarged on his paper (Working Paper 8) on the International Standard Book Number (ISBN). He gave a full explanation of the purpose of the ISBN and the way in which numbers for particular books were constructed, and stressed the particular usefulness of standard book numbers in a machine context.

Mrs. H. D. Avram then gave a brief account of the principles of the MARC format for bibliographical records. She spoke of the requirements and limitations of the machine in relation to catalogue entries and emphasized that, while it was technically possible for the machine to retrieve items of information in whatever order they were stored, economy in machine time dictated a fixed order of items within each record. It was also important to remember that the most expensive item in the mechanization of bibliographical records was the human factor, the cost of the skilled work of editors who had to be cataloguers with training in computer work. Machine recognition of elements in the bibliographical description, which could be made possible by the use of standard symbols and standard punctuation in the printed or typewritten records which were to be con-

verted to machine-readable form, would be important as a means of saving labour and cost. These were powerful arguments in favour of international uniformity in the structure of bibliographical descriptions.

In the discussion attention was also drawn to the urgency of solving certain other problems—notably that of transliteration. A number of participants reported on progress in their own countries in the development of mechanical systems for handling bibliographical information. The Meeting heard with particular interest an account of the problems encountered by the University of Bochum in adopting for use in its own mechanized system tapes provided by both the Deutsche Bibliographie and the British National Bibliography, which emphasized the need for compatibility both in record-formats and in machines. It was pointed out that as a number of national bibliographies were now in the course of introducing computer-aided methods of production, agreement on the format of machine records was urgent.

It was agreed on the suggestion of Dr. K. W. Humphreys, Chairman of the IFLA Section of National and University Libraries, that there should be consultation with the Advisory Committee of that Section with a view to co-operation within IFLA to further the objectives which the Meeting had defined.

Day 3. Sunday 24 August 1969. Session 1

Contributions From Africa And Asia

During this session there was an opportunity for the participants from Africa, Ceylon and Japan to give some account of the particular cataloguing problems arising in their own countries. A paper on the treatment of African names, which had been prepared by Mr. J. Fontvieille as a contribution to the completion of one of the projects sponsored by the ICCP, was distributed to the Meeting. Mr. Fontvieille gave a brief and illuminating account of the difficulties presented by these names. It was agreed that he and Mr. A. Nitecki, with authority to co-opt other specialists, should form a working group to prepare a survey of African names which would follow the pattern adopted in the IFLA Manual *Names of persons* and could be published as a supplement to that work. With reference to Ceylon, Mr.

Goonetileke pointed out that as the majority of books published there and in other Asian countries were in non-roman alphabets it was important that guidance should be given on cataloguing in these scripts. He also suggested the formation of a working group on Asian names, and expressed the hope that it might be possible to organize a meeting of Asian cataloguing experts which could consider their special problems and establish liaison with their western colleagues. Mr. Oda spoke of the peculiar problems presented by Japanese names, which are written in non-alphabetic Chinese characters. Because of this it had been traditional in Japan to enter books under their titles. In the last thirty years, however, the use of entry under author had become widespread, although difficulties still persisted.

Day 3. Session 2

Resolutions

The final session approved the minutes of earlier sessions, including the following statement of policy:

"Efforts should be directed towards creating a system for the international exchange of information by which the standard bibliographical description of each publication would be established and distributed by a national agency in the country of origin of the publication. The means of distribution in such a system would be through the medium of cards or machine readable records. The effectiveness of the system will be dependent upon the maximum standardization of the form and content of the bibliographical description."

Two Working Groups to continue the work of the meeting were constituted as follows:

1. *Working group to complete the Annotated Edition of the Paris Statement of Principles:* Dr. Eva Verona (Chairman); Dr. F. G. Kaltwasser; Mr. Peter Lewis; Mr. Roger Pierrot.
2. *Working group on an International Standard Bibliographical Description:* Mr. A. J. Wells (Chairman); Mrs. H. D. Avram; Dr. A. Domanovszky; Mr. M. Gorman; Madame S. Honoré; Mr. K. Nowak; Mr. A. L. van Wesemael.

The Meeting concluded with the adoption of resolutions of thanks, to the Council on Library Resources for its grant which had made the Meet-

ing possible, and to Mr. Preben Kirkegaard, Director of the Royal School of Librarianship, and other Danish colleagues, whose help and co-operation had contributed notably to its success.

LATER DEVELOPMENTS

I. Secretariat

The IFLA Committee on Uniform Cataloguing Rules at its meeting at Copenhagen on 28 August 1969 received a report of the Meeting and adopted the following resolution:

1. That it is desirable to establish a continuing secretariat to assist and co-ordinate future work arising from the resolutions of the International Meeting of Cataloguing Experts and directed at creating an international system for the exchange of bibliographical information and promoting the necessary uniformity in headings and description.
2. That the officers of the Committee on Uniform Cataloguing Rules, in consultation with the IFLA Executive Board, seek financial means to maintain this secretariat.
3. That the various sections and committees of IFLA interested in these problems be invited to co-operate with the secretariat, which should also make contact with the appropriate organs of other interested bodies, e.g. IFD, ISO, Unesco.

This resolution was approved by the General Council of IFLA and is under consideration by the Executive Board.

The Council on Library Resources has since agreed that the remainder of its grant may be used for furthering the work of the Meeting. This has permitted the organizing bureau to continue to function in London for a short period (in accordance with the above Resolution), and funds have been available to advance the activities of the working groups.

II. Working groups

The Working Group on a Standard Bibliographical Description, under the Chairmanship of Mr. A. J. Wells, met in London at the end of October. Provisional decisions were reached on a fixed order of elements for the standard bibliographical description and on the content of the elements. The document prepared as a result of this meeting has been circulated for comment to interested bodies and people, and it is hoped that another meeting in May 1970 will finalize the text of the standard.

Dr. Eva Verona, Chairman of the Working Group on the Revised Annotated Edition of the Statement of Principles, has prepared draft texts of sections 1–9 and of the introductory notes, which have been circulated to the members of the Group for comment. It is planned that the text of the revised edition will be in the press by August 1970.

III. Contacts in Asia

The Organizing Secretary made a tour of countries in south east Asia, Ceylon, India and Iran early in 1970, visiting libraries and talking to groups of librarians and cataloguers about the IMCE and the work of the IFLA Cataloguing Committee. She was also able to meet the IMCE participants Mr. Goonetileke, in Ceylon, and Mr. Sengupta, in India.

New projects concerned with aspects of Asian cataloguing are now being planned to which, it is hoped, Asian librarians will contribute.

IV. Short accounts of the IMCE have appeared in:

Newsletter, No. 4, October 1969. (IFLA Committee on Uniform Cataloguing Rules) *Catalogue and Index*, No. 16, October 1969. (Library Association Cataloguing and Indexing Group)

Nouvelles, No. 5, 1969 (Association des bibliothécaires suisses).
Biblos. Jg. 18, 1969, H. 4.
Zeitschrift für Bibliothekswesen und Bibliographie, V. 17, No. 1, 1970.

It is with great regret that we record here that the participant from the Lebanon, Mr. F. R. Abu-Haidar, died in London as he was returning from the IFLA Conference.

A. H. Chaplin, Chairman.
Dorothy Anderson, Organizing Secretary.

NOTES

[1] "Principles of cataloguing: the situation five years after the Paris Conference", *Unesco Bulletin for Libraries*, **21** (3), May–June 1967.
[2] Statement of Principles: annotated edition with examples, by A. H. Chaplin assisted by Dorothy Anderson. Sevenoaks: IFLA Secretariat, 1966.
[3] Names of Persons: national usages for entry in catalogues, by A. H. Chaplin. Definitive edition edited by A. H. Chaplin and Dorothy Anderson. Sevenoaks: IFLA, 1967.
[4] International list of uniform headings for anonymous classics, by Roger Pierrot. Provisional edition. Paris, 1964.
[5] International list of approved forms for catalogue entries for the names of states, by Suzanne Honoré. Provisional edition. Paris, 1964.
[6] IFLA. Proceedings of the General Council. Session 32. The Hague, 1967.
[7] IFLA. Proceedings of the General Council. Session 33. Toronto, 1967.
[8] See Appendix 1 for further particulars.
[9] For complete list see Appendix 2.
[10] In the original French. Appendix 3.

LIST OF DOCUMENTS AND WORKING PAPERS

DE1   Statement of Principles; annotated edition, with commentary and examples, by A. H. Chaplin, assisted by Dorothy Anderson. 1966.
DE2   Bibliographical data in national bibliography entries. A report on descriptive cataloguing, by Michael Gorman. Provisional abridged text.
WP1   Digest of the comments received on the Annotated edition of the Statement of Principles (DE 1), by Eva Verona.
WP2   Digest of the comments received on Bibliographical data in national bibliography entries (DE 2), by Ákos Domanovszky.

WP3   Cataloguing principles formulated by the International Conference, Paris, 1961: an evaluation, based on the Annotated Edition of the Statement of Principles (DE 1), by S. R. Ranganathan.

WP4   The American Shared Cataloging Program: its origins, characteristics, problems, and effect, by C. Sumner Spalding.

WP5   Shared cataloguing: the consumer in North America, by Jean Lunn.

WP6   The international exchange of cataloguing information: the Library of Congress 'Shared Cataloging Program' in European eyes, by F. G. Kaltwasser. Abridged and revised text of paper read at IFLA Conference, Frankfurt, 1968.

WP7   The matching of books with centrally produced catalogue cards, by A. L. van Wesemael.

WP8   International Standard Book Numbers, by A. J. Wells.

WP9   Some implications for the automation of bibliographic services of the MARC I pilot project, by C. D. Batty.

WP10   MARC international, by Richard Coward.

WP11   Mechanization of the Bibliothèque Royale Albert I in Belgium: applied cataloguing principles, by Frans de Vrieze and Roger de Backer.

WP12   The German Bibliography and electronic data processing: experience since 1966 and aims for the future, by Kurt Nowak.

WP13   The future implications of automation for cataloguing, by Suzanne Honoré.

MARC Program Research and Development:
A Progress Report

Henriette D. Avram, Alan S. Crosby, Jerry G. Pennington,
John C. Rather, Lucia J. Rather, and Arlene Whitmer

A description of some of the research and development activities at the Library of Congress to expand the capabilities of the MARC System. Gives details of the MARC processing format used by the Library and then describes programming work in three areas: 1) automatic tagging of data elements by format recognition programs; 2) file analysis by a statistical program called GENESIS; and 3) information retrieval using the MARC Retriever.

The MARC System was designed as a generalized data management system that provides flexibility in converting bibliographic descriptions of all forms of material to machine readable form and ease in processing them. The foundation of the system is the MARC II format (hereinafter simply called MARC), which reached its present form after many months of planning, consultation, and testing. Implementation of the system itself has required development of a battery of programs to perform the input, storage, retrieval, and output functions necessary to create the data base for the MARC Distribution Service.

These programs are essentially like those of the MARC interim system described in the report of the MARC pilot project (1). Briefly, they perform the following tasks:

1. A pre-edit program converts records prepared on an MT/ST to a magnetic tape file of EBCDIC encoded record segments.
2. A format edit program converts the pre-edited tape file to a modified form of the MARC processing format.
3. A content edit program generates records in the final processing format. At this stage, mnemonic tags are converted to numeric form, subfield codes may be supplied, implicit fixed fields are set, etc.
4. IBM SORT program arranges validated content-edit output records by LC card number.

This program is also used later in the processing cycle.

5. A generalized file maintenance program (Update 1) allows addition, deletion, replacement, or modification of data at the record, field, or subfield levels before the record is posted to the master file. A slightly different version (Update 2) is used to update the master file.
6. A print index program generates a list of control numbers for a given file. The list may also include status, date of entry, or date of last transaction for each record.
7. A general purpose print program produces a hardcopy to be used to proofread the machine data against the original input worksheet. Since the program is table controlled, it can be modified easily to yield a great variety of other formats and it can be extended routinely to handle other data bases in the MARC processing format.
8. Two additional programs select new records from the MARC master file and convert them from the processing format to the communications format on both seven- and nine-track tapes for general distribution.

As the basic programs become operational, it was possible to investigate other aspects of the MARC System that would benefit from elaboration and refinement. Reports of some of this ac-

SOURCE: Reprinted from the *Journal of Library Automation* II, 4 (December 1969), pp. 242–265, by permission of the American Library Association.

tivity have found their way into print, notably a description of the MARC Sort Program and preliminary findings on format recognition (2, 3), but much of the Library's research and development effort in programming is not well known. The purpose of this article is to give a progress report on work in three significant areas: 1) automatic tagging of data elements by format recognition programs; 2) file analysis by a statistical program called GENESIS; and 3) information retrieval using the MARC Retriever.

In the following descriptions, the reader should bear in mind that all of the programs are written to accommodate records in the MARC processing format. A full description of the format is given to point up differences between it and the communications format. All of the programs are written in assembly language for the IBM S360/40 functioning under the disk operating system (DOS). The machine file is stored on magnetic tape and the system is operated in the batch mode.

At present, the programs described here are not available for general distribution, but it is expected that documentation for some of them may be filed with the IBM Program Information Department in the near future. Meanwhile, the Library of Congress regrets that it will be unable to supply more detailed information. It is hoped that the information in this article will answer most of the questions that might be asked.

MARC PROCESSING FORMAT

The MARC data base at the Library of Congress is stored on a nine-channel magnetic tape at a density of 800 bpi. The file contains records in the undefined format; each record is recorded in the MARC processing format (sometimes called the internal format). Data in the processing format are recorded in binary, packed decimal, or EBCDIC notation depending on the characteristics of the data and the processing required. The maximum length of a MARC processing record is 2,048 bytes. The magnetic tape labels follow the proposed standard developed by Subcommittee X3.2 of the United States of America Standards Institute.

A MARC record in the processing format is composed of six parts: record leader (12 bytes), communications field (12 bytes), record control field (14 bytes), fixed fields (54 bytes), record directory (variable in length, with each directory entry containing 12 bytes) and variable data fields (variable length). All records are terminated by an end-of-record (EOR) character.

Record Leader

0	1	2		4	5	6	7	8	9	11
Record length		Date			Status	Not used	Record type	Bibliographic level	Not used	
	YY	MM	DD							

Element Number	Name	Number of Characters	Character Position in Record	Definition
1	Record length	2	0-1	Total number of bytes in the logical record including the number of bytes in the record length itself. It is given in binary notation.
2	Date	3	2-4	Date of last transaction (i.e., the date the last action was taken upon the whole record or some part of the record). The date is recorded in the form of YYMMDD, with each digit being represented by a four-bit binary-coded decimal digit packed two to a byte.

		Number of Characters	Character Position in Record	
3	Status	1	5	A code in binary notation to indicate a new, deleted, changed, or replaced record.
4	Not used	1	6	Contains binary zeros.
5	Record type	1	7	An EBCDIC character to identify the type of record that follows (e.g., printed language material).
6	Bibliographic levels	1	8	An EBCDIC character used in conjunction with the record type character to describe the components of the bibliographic record (e.g., monograph).
7	Not used	3	9-11	Contains binary zeros.

Communications Field

12 13	14 15	16	17	18	19	20 23
Record directory location	Directory entry count	Record source	Record destination	In-process type	In-process status	Not used

Element Number	Name	Number of Characters	Character Position in Record	Definition
1	Record directory location	2	12-13	The binary address of the record directory relative to the first byte in the record (address zero).
2	Directory entry count	2	14-15	The number of directory entries in the record, in binary notation. There is one directory entry for every variable field in the record.
3	Record source	1	16	An EBCDIC character to show the cataloging source of the record.
4	Record destination	1	17	An EBCDIC character to show the data bank to which the record is to be routed.
5	In-process type	1	18	A binary code to indicate the action to be performed on the data base. The in-process type may signify that a new record is to be merged into the existing file; a record currently in the file is to be replaced, deleted, modified in some form; or that it is verified as being free of all error.
6	In-process status	1	19	A binary code to show whether the data content of the record has been verified.
7	Not used	4	20-23	Contains binary zeros.

Record Control Field

| 24 | 26 | 27 | 28 | 29 | 34 | 35 | 36 | 37 |

Library of Congress catalog card number	Supplement number	Not used	Segment number

Element Number	Name	Number of Characters	Character Position in Record	Definition
1	Library of Congress	12	24-35	On December 1, 1968, the Library of Congress initiated a new card numbering system. Numbers assigned prior to this date are in the "old" system; those assigned after that date are in the "new" system (4). The Library of Congress catalog card number is always represented by 12 bytes in EBCDIC notation but the data elements depend upon the system.

OLD NUMBERING
SYSTEM

	Prefix	3	24-26	An alphabetic prefix is left justified with blank fill; if no prefix is present, the three bytes are blanks.
	Year	2	27-28	
	Number	6	29-34	
	Supplement number	1	35	A single byte in binary notation to identify supplements with the same LC card number as the original work.

NEW NUMBERING
SYSTEM

	Not used	3	24-26	Contains three blanks.
	Initial digit	1	27	Initial digit of the number.
	Check digit	1	28	"Modulus 11" check digit.
	Number	6	29-34	
	Supplement number	1	35	See above.
2	Not used	1	36	Contains binary zeros.
3	Segment number	1	37	Used to sequentially number the physical records contained in one logical record. The number is in binary notation.

Fixed Fields

The fixed field area is always 54 bytes in length. Fixed fields that do not contain data are set to binary zeros. Data in the fixed fields may be recorded in binary or EBCDIC notation, but the notation remains constant for any given field.

Record Directory

92 94	95	96 98	99	100 101	102 103
Tag	Site number	Not used	Action code	Data length	Relative address

Element Number	Name	Number of Characters	Character Position in Record	Definition
1	Tag	3	92-94	An EBCDIC number that identifies a variable field. The tags in the directory are in ascending order.
2	Site number	1	95	A binary number used to distinguish variable fields that have identical tags.
3	Not used	3	96-98	Contains binary zeros.
4	Action code	1	99	A binary code used in file maintenance to specify the field level action to be performed on a record (i.e., added, deleted, corrected, or modified).
5	Data length	2	100-101	Length (in binary notation) of the variable data field indicated by a given entry.
6	Relative address	2	102-103	The binary address of the first byte of the variable data field relative to the first byte of the record (address zero).
7	Directory end of field sentinel	1	n	Since the number of entries in the directory varies, the character position of the end-of-field terminator (EOF) also varies.

Variable Data Fields

Indicator(s)	Delimiter	Subfield code(s)	Delimiter	Data	Terminator code

Element Number	Name	Number of Characters	Character Position in Record	Definition
1	Indicator	Variable	n	A variable data field may be preceded by a variable number of EBCDIC characters which provide descriptive information about the associated field.
2	Delimiter	1	n	A one-byte binary code used to separate the indicator(s) from the subfield code(s). When there are no indicators for a variable field, the first character will be a delimiter.
3	Subfield code	Variable	n	Variable fields are made up of one or more data elements (5). Each data element is preceded by a delimiter; a lower-case alphabetic character is associated with each delimiter to identify the data element. These alpha characters are grouped. All variable fields will have at least one subfield code.
4	Delimiter	1	n	Each data element in a variable field is preceded by a delimiter.
5	Data	Variable	n	
6	Terminator code	1	n	All variable fields except the last in the record end with an end-of-field terminator (EOF); the last variable field ends with an end-of-record terminator (EOR).

FORMAT RECOGNITION

The preparation of bibliographic data in machine readable form involves the labeling of each data element so that it can be identified by the machine. The labels (called content designators) used in the MARC format are tags, indicators, and subfield codes; they are supplied by the MARC editors before the data are inscribed on a magnetic tape typewriter. In the current MARC System, this tape is then run through a computer program and a proofsheet is printed. In a proofing process, the editor compares the original edited data against the proofsheet, checking for errors in editing and keyboarding. Errors are marked and corrections are reinscribed. A new proofsheet is produced by the computer and again checked for errors. When a record has been declared error-free by an editor, it receives a final check by a high-level editor called a verifier. Verified records are then removed from the work tape and stored on the master tape.

The editing process in which the tags, indicators, subfield codes, and fixed field information are assigned is a detailed and somewhat tedious process. It seems obvious that a method that would shift some of this editing to the machine would in the long run be of great advantage. This is especially true in any consideration of retrospective conversion of the 4.1 million Library of Congress catalog records. For this reason, the Library is now developing a technique called "format recognition." This technique will allow the computer to process unedited bibliographic data by examining the data string for certain keywords, significant punctuation, and other clues to determine the proper tags and other machine labels. It should be noted that this concept is not unique to the Library of Congress. Somewhat similar techniques are being developed at the University of California Institute of Library Research (6) and by the Bodleian Library at Oxford. A technique using typographic cues has been described by Jolliffe (7).

The format recognition technique is not entirely new at the Library of Congress. The need was recognized during the development of the MARC II format, but pressure to implement the MARC Distribution Service prevented more than minimal development of format recognition procedures. In the current MARC System a few of the fields are identified by machine. For example, the machine scans the collation statement for keywords and sets the appropriate codes in the illustration fixed field. In general, however, machine identification has been limited to those places where the algorithm produces a correct result 100 percent of the time.

The new format recognition concept assumes that, after the unedited record has been machine processed, a proofsheet will be examined by a MARC editor for errors in the same way as is done in the current MARC System. Since each machine processed record will be subject to human review, it will be possible to include algorithms in the format recognition program that do not produce correct tagging all of the time.

The format recognition algorithms are exceedingly complex, but a few examples will be given to indicate the nature of the logic. In all the examples, it is assumed that the record is typed from an untagged manuscript card (the work record used as a basis for the Library of Congress catalog card) on an input device such as a paper tape or a magnetic tape typewriter. The data will be typed from left to right on the card and from top to bottom. The data are input as fields, which are detectable by a program because each field ends with a double carriage return. Each field comprises a logical portion of a manuscript card; thus the call number would be input as a single field, as would the main entry, title paragraph, collation, each note, each added entry, etc. It is important to note that the title paragraph includes everything through the imprint.

Identification of Variable Fields

Call Number.

This field is present in almost every case and it is the first field input. The call number usually con-

sists of 1–3 capital letters followed by 1–4 numbers, followed by a period, a capital letter, and more numbers. There are several easily identifiable variations such as a date before the period or a brief string of numbers without capital letters following the period.

The delimiter separating the class number from the book number is inserted according to the following five-step algorithm:

1) If the call number is LAW, do not delimit.
2) If the call number consists simply of letters followed by numbers (possibly including a period), do not delimit. Example: HF5415.13
   If this type of number is followed by a date, it is delimited before the blank preceding the date. Example: HA12‡ 1967
3) If the call number begins with 'KF' followed by numbers, followed by a period, then:
   a) If there are one or two numbers before the period, do not delimit. Example: KF26.L354 1966a
   b) If there are three or more numbers before the period, delimit before the last period in the call number. Example: KFN5225‡.Z9F3
4) If the call number begins with 'CS71' do not delimit unless it contains a date. In this case, it is delimited before the blank preceding the date. Example: CS71.S889‡ 1968
5) In all other cases, delimit before the last capital letter except when the last capital letter is immediately preceded by a period. In this latter case, delimit before this preceding period.
   Examples: PS3553.E73‡W6
   PZ10.3.U36‡Sp
   E595.F6‡K4 1968
   TX652.5‡.G63 1968

Name Main Entry.

The collation statement is the first field after the call number that can be easily identified by analyzing its contents. The field immediately preceding the collation statement must be the title paragraph. If there is only one field between the call number and the collation, the work is entered under title (tagged as 245) and there is no name main entry. If there are two or three fields, the first field after the call number is a name main entry (tagged in the 100 block). When three fields occur between the call number and collation, the second field is a uniform title (tagged as 240).

Further analysis into the type of name main entry and the subfield code depends on such clues as location of open dates (1921–0000), date ranges covering 20 years or more (1921–1967), identification of phrases used only as personal name relators (ed., tr., comp.), etc. The above clues strongly indicate a personal name. Identification of an ordinal number preceded by punctuation and a blank followed by punctuation is strongly indicative of a conference heading.

In the course of processing, delimiters and the appropriate subfield codes are inserted. Subfield code "d" is used with dates in personal names; subfield code "e" with relators.

Example: MEPS‡de Smith, John,‡1902–1967, ‡ed.

Analysis for Fixed Fields

Publisher is Main Entry Indicator.

This indicator is set when the publisher is omitted from the imprint because it appears as the main entry. The program will set this indicator whenever the main entry is a corporate or conference name and there is no publisher in the imprint statement. This test will fail in the case where there is more than one publisher, one of which is the main entry, but occurrences of this are fairly rare (less than 0.2 percent).
Biography Indicator.

Four different codes are used with this indicator as follows: A = individual autobiography; B = individual biography; C = collected biography or autobiography; and D = partial collected biography. The "A" code is set when 1) "autobiographical", "autobiography", "memoirs", or "diaries" occurs in the title statement or notes, or 2) the surname portion of a personal name main entry occurs in the short title or the remainder of the title subfields. The "B" code is set when 1) "biography" occurs in the title statement, 2) the surname portion of a personal name subject entry occurs in the short title or the remainder of the title subfields, or 3) the Dewey number contains a "B" or a 920. The "C" code is set when 1) "biographies" occurs in the title statement or 2) a subject entry contains the subdivision "biography." There appears to be no way to identify a "D" code situation. Despite this fact, the biography indi-

cator can be set correctly about 83 percent of the time.

Implementation Schedule

Work on the format recognition project was begun early in 1969. The first two phases were feasibility studies based on English-language records with a certain amount of pretagging assumed. Since the results of these studies were quite encouraging, a full-scale project was begun in July 1969. This project is divided into five tasks. Task 1 consisted of a new examination of the data fields to see if the technique would work without any pretagging. New algorithms were designed and desk-checked against a sample of records. It now seems likely that format recognition programs might produce correctly tagged records 70 percent of the time under these conditions. It is possible that one or two fixed fields may have to be supplied in a pre-editing process.

Tasks 2 through 5 remain to be done. Task 2 will provide overall format recognition design including 1) development of definitive keyword lists, 2) typing specifications, 3) determination of the order of processing of fields within a record, and 4) description of the overall processing of a record. When the design is completed, a number of records will go through a manual simulation process to determine the general efficiency of the system design.

Task 3 will investigate the extension of format recognition design to foreign-language titles in roman alphabets. Task 4 will provide the design for a format recognition program based on the results of Tasks 2 and 3 with detailed flowcharts at the coding level. The actual coding, checkout, and documentation will be performed as Task 5. According to current plans, the first four tasks are scheduled for completion early in 1970 and the programming will be finished later in the year.

Outlook

It is apparent that a great deal of intellectual work must be done to develop format recognition algorithms even for English-language records and still greater ingenuity will be required to apply these techniques to foreign-language records. Nevertheless, on the basis of encouraging results of early studies, there is evidence that the human effort in converting bibliographic records to machine readable form can be materially reduced. Since reduction of human effort would in turn reduce costs, the success of these studies will have an important bearing on the rate at which current conversion activities can be expanded as well as on the economic feasibility of converting large files of retrospective cataloging data.

GENESIS

Early in the planning and implementation of automation at the Library of Congress it became apparent that many tasks require information about the frequency of data elements. For example, it was helpful to know about the frequency of individual data elements, their length in characters, and the occurrence of marks of punctuation, diacritics, and specified character strings in particular data elements. In the past, most of the counting has been done manually. Once a sizable amount of data was available in machine readable form, it was worthwhile to have much of this counting done by computer. Therefore, the Generalized Statistical Program (GENESIS) was done as a general purpose program to make such counts on all forms of material in the MARC Processing Format on magnetic tape files.

Any of a variety of counts can be chosen at the time of program execution. There are three types of specifications required for a particular run of the program: selection criteria; statistical function specifications; and output specifications.

Selection Criteria

Record selection criteria are specified by statements about the various data fields that must be present in the records to be processed. Field selection criteria specify the data elements that will actually be analyzed. Processing by these techniques operates logically in two distinct stages: 1) the record is selected from the input file; i.e., the program must determine if a particular record is to be included in the analysis; and 2) if the record is eligible, the specified function is performed on selected data fields. It should be noted that records may be selected for negative as well as positive reasons. The absence of a particular field may determine the eligibility of a record and

statistical processing can be performed on other fields in the record. Record selection is optional; if no criteria are specified, all records on the input file will be considered for processing.

Since both record selection and field selection reference the same elements, specifications are input in the same way. Selection of populations can be designated by tagging structure (numeric tags, indicators, subfield codes or any combination of these three), specified character strings, and specified characters in the bibliographic data. The following queries are typical of those that can be processed by GENESIS. How many records with an indicator set to show that the volume contains biographic information also have an indicator set to show that the subject is the main entry? How many records with a field tagged to show that the main entry is the name of a meeting or conference actually have the words "meeting" or "conference" in the data itself? Table 1 shows the operators that can be used with record and field select statements.

Statistical Function Specification

The desired statistical function is specified via a function statement. Four functions have been implemented to date. They involve counts of occurrences of specified fields, unique data within specified fields given a range of data values, data within a specified range, and particular data characters. In addition to counting the frequency of the specified element, GENESIS calculates its percentage in the total population.

The first function counts occurrences per record of specified field selection criteria. This answers queries concerning the presence of given conditions within the selected records; for example, a frequency distribution of personal name added entries (tag 700). This type of count results in a distribution table of the number of records with 0 occurrences, 1 occurrence, 2 occurrences, and so forth.

The second function, which counts occurrences of unique data values within a specified range, answers queries when the user does not know the unique values occurring in a given field, but can state an upper and lower value. For example, the specific occurrences of publishing dates between 1900 and 1960 might be requested. The output in response to this type of query consists of each unique value, lying within the range specified,

TABLE 1

OPERATORS OF GENESIS

EQUALS	Count all occurrences where data represented by tag 530 EQUALS "Bound with"
NOT EQUAL	Count all occurrences where the publication language code is NOT EQUAL to "eng"
GREATER THAN OR EQUAL TO	Count all occurrences and output records that are GREATER THAN OR EQUAL TO 1,000 characters
LESS THAN OR EQUAL TO	Count all occurrences of records entered on the MARC data base before June 1, 1968 (LESS THAN OR EQUAL TO 680601)
AND	Count all occurrences where the publication equals "s" AND the publication date is greater than or equal to 1960
OR	Count all occurrences of personal name main entry (tag 100) a relator (subfield code "e") that equals "ed." OR "comp."

with its frequency count. In addition, separate counts are given for values less than the lower bound and of values greater than the upper bound.

The function is performed by maintaining in computer memory an ordered list of unique values encountered, together with their respective counts. As selected fields are processed, each new value is compared against the entries in the list. If the new value already appears in the list, its corresponding count is incremented. Otherwise, the new value is inserted in the list in its proper place and the remainder of the list is pushed down by one entry. The amount of core storage used during a particular run is directly related to the number of unique occurrences appearing within the specified range. Since the length of each entry is determined by the length of the bounds specified, the number of entries which can be held in free storage can vary from run to run. Thus it is possible that the number of unique entries may fill memory before a run has been completed. When this happens, the value of the last entry in the list will be discarded and its count added to the "greater than upper bound" count. In this way, while the user may not obtain every unique value in the specified range, he will obtain all

unique values from the lower bound which can be contained in memory. He is then in a position to make subsequent runs using, as a beginning lower bound value, the highest unique value obtained from the preceding run.

The third function processes queries concerning counts within specified ranges. When this function is used, unique values are not displayed. Instead, the occurrences are counted by specified ranges of values. More than one range can be processed during a single run. On output, the program provides a cumulative count of values encountered within each range as well as the counts of those less than and those greater than the ranges.

Function four counts occurrences of particular data characters. An individual character may be specified explicitly or implicitly as a member of a group of characters. This allows the counting of occurrences of various alphabetic characters within specified fields. The current list of character classes that can be counted are: alpha characters, upper-case letters, lower-case letters, numbers, punctuation, diacritics, blanks, full (all characters included in above classes), nonstandard special characters, and any particular character hex notation. It should be noted that there are various ways of specifying particular characters. For example, an "A" might be designated causing totals to accumulate for all alphabetics; or, a "U" and an "L" might be specified causing separate totals to be accumulated for upper- and lower-case characters. In addition to the total counts for each class, individual counts of characters occurring within any class can be obtained for display along with the total count.

Output Specifications

Formatted statistical information is output to the line printer. Optionally, the selected records can be output on magnetic tape for later processing.

Limitations

For the purpose of defining a query, more than one field may be specified for record and field selection, using as many statements as necessary. At present, however, the statistical processing for a particular run is performed on all of the run-criteria collectively. For example, separate runs of the program are required to obtain each frequency distribution.

It is important to note that GENESIS is essentially a means of making counts. The statistical analysis of data is a complex task that requires sophisticated techniques. GENESIS does not have the capability to analyze data in terms of standard deviation, correlation, etc. but the output does constitute raw data for those kinds of analyses. Although the four functions of GENESIS implemented to date do not, in themselves, provide a complete statistical analysis, they greatly lessen the burden of counting; and techniques for designating data elements to be counted suffice to describe extremely complex patterns. Continued use of the program will no doubt provide guidelines for expansion of its functions.

Use of the Program

GENESIS has already provided analyses that are helpful in the design of automated procedures at the Library of Congress, as is indicated by the following instances. A frequency distribution of characters was made to aid in specifying a print train. An analysis of certain data characteristics has determined some of the specifications for the format recognition program described in an earlier section. GENESIS is providing many of the basic counts for a thorough analysis of the material currently being converted for the MARC Distribution Service to determine frequency patterns of data elements. The findings should be valuable for determining questions about storage capacity, file organization, and retrieval strategy. Although GENESIS is a new program in the MARC System, there is little doubt that it is a powerful tool that will have many uses.

MARC RETRIEVER

Since the MARC Distribution Service has been given the highest priority during the past two years, the emphasis in the implementation of the MARC System has been on input, file maintenance, and output with only minimum work performed in the retrieval area. It was recognized, moreover, that as long as MARC is tape oriented, any retrieval system put into effect at the Library

of Congress would be essentially a research tool that should be implemented as inexpensively as possible. It did seem worthwhile, however, to build retrieval capability into the MARC System to enable the LC staff to query the growing MARC data base. Query capability would answer basic questions about the characteristics of the data that arise during the design phases of automation efforts. In addition, it seemed desirable to use the data base in an operational mode to provide some needed experience in file usage to assist in the file organization design of a large bibliographic data base.

The specifications of the system desired were: 1) the ability to process the MARC processing format with modification; 2) the ability to query every element in the MARC record, alone or in combination (fixed fields, variable fields, the directory, subfield codes, indicators); 3) the ability to count the number of times a particular element was queried, to accumulate this count, print it or make it available in punched card form for subsequent processing; and 4) the ability to format and output the results of a query on magnetic tape or printer hardcopy. To satisfy these requirements it was decided to adapt an operational generalized information system to the specifications of the Library of Congress. The system chosen was AEGIS, designed and implemented by Programmatics, Inc. The modification is known as the MARC Retriever.

General Description

The MARC Retriever comprises four parts: a control program, a parser, a retrieval program, and a utility program. Queries are input in the form of punched cards, stacked in the core of the IBM S/360, and operated on as though all queries were in fact one query. Thus a MARC record will be searched for the conditions described by all queries, not by handling each query individually and rewinding the input tape before the next query is processed.

The control program is the executive module of the system. It loads the parser and reads the first query statement. The parser is then activated to process the query statement. On return from the parser, the control program either outputs a diagnostic message for an erroneous query or assigns an identification number to a valid query. After the last query statement has been parsed, the control program loads the retrieval program and the

MARC input tape is opened. As each record on the MARC tape is processed, the control program checks for a valid input query. If the query is valid, the control program branches to the retrieval program. On return from the retrieval program, the control program writes the record on an output tape if the record meets the specifications of the query. After the last MARC record has been read from the input tape, the control program branches to the retrieval program for final processing of any requested statistical function (HITS, RATIO, SUM, AVG) that might be a part of the query. The output tapes are closed and the job is ended.

The parser examines each query to insure that it conforms to the rules for query construction. If the query is not valid, an error message is returned to the control program giving an indication as to the nature of the error. Valid query statements are parsed and converted to query strings in Polish notation, which permits mathematical expressions without parentheses. The absence of embedded parentheses allows simpler compiler interpretation, translations, and execution of results.

The retrieval program processes the query strings by comparing them with the MARC record data elements and the results of the comparison are placed in a true/false stack table. If the comparison result is true, output is generated for further processing. If the result is false, no action takes place. If query expressions are linked together with "OR" or "AND" connectors, the results in the true/false stack table are ORed and ANDed together resulting in a single true or false condition.

The utility program counts every data element (fixed field, tag, indicator, subfield code, data in a variable field) that is used in a query statement. The elements in the search argument are counted separately from those in the output specifications. After each run of the MARC Retriever, the counts can be printed or punched for immediate use, or they can be accumulated over a longer period and processed on demand.

Query Language

General.

Query statements for the MARC Retriever must be constructed according to a precisely defined set of rules, called the syntax of the language. The language permits the formation of queries that can address any portion of the MARC record (fixed fields, record directory, variable fields and associated indicators and subfields). Queries are constructed by combining a number of elements: MARC Retriever terms, operators, fixed field names, and strings of characters (hereafter called constants). The following sections describe the rules for constructing a query and the query elements with examples of their use.

Query Formation.

A query is made up of two basic parts or modes: the if mode which specifies the criteria for selecting a record; and the list mode which specifies which data elements in the record that satisfy the search criteria are to be selected for printing or further processing. In general, the rules that apply to constructing if-mode expressions apply to constructing list-mode expressions except that the elements in the list mode must be separated by a comma. A generalized query has the following form:

IF if-mode expression LIST list-mode expression;

Where:

IF	Signals the beginning of the if mode.
if-mode expression	Specifies the search argument.
LIST	Signals the beginning of the list mode.
list-mode expression	Specifies the MARC record data element(s) that are to be listed when the search argument specified in the if-mode expression is satisfied.

The format of the query card is flexible. Columns 1 through 72 contain the query which may be continued on subsequent cards. No continuation indicator is required. Columns 73 through 80 may be used to identify the query if desired. The punctuation rules are relatively simple. One or more blanks must be used to separate the elements of a query and a query must be terminated by a semicolon.

Queries that involve fixed fields take the following form:

> IF fixed-field-name1 = constant LIST fixed-field-name2

Where:

fixed-field-name1	The name of fixed field.
=	Any operator appropriate for this query.
constant	The search argument
fixed-field-name2	The fixed field to be output if a match occurs.

To query or specify the output of a variable field, the following general expression is used.

> IF SCAN (tag = nnn) = Constant LIST SCAN (tag = nnn);

Where:

SCAN	Indicates that a variable field is to be referenced.
tag	Indicates that the tag of a variable field is to follow.
=	The only valid operator.
nnn	Specifies the tag of the variable field that is to be searched or output.
constant	Specifies the character string of data that is the search argument.

The MARC Retriever processes each query in the following manner. Each record in the data base is read from tape into core and the data elements in the MARC Record specified in the if-mode expression are compared against the constant(s) in the if-mode expression. If there is a match, the data element(s) specified in the list-mode expression are output.

Key Terms.

The terms used in a query statement fall into two classes. The first group instructs the program to perform specified functions: SCAN, HITS, AVG, RATIO, SUM. The second group relates to elements of the record structure. The most important key terms in this class are: INDIC (indicator), NTC (subfield code), RECORD (the entire bibliographic record), and TAG (variable field tag). These terms are used to define a constant; e.g., TAG = 100.

Operators

Operators are characters that have a specific meaning in the query language. They fall into two classes. The first contains relational operators, such as equal to and greater than, indicating that a numeric relationship must exist between the data element in the MARC record and the search argument. The second class comprises the logical operators "and" and "or". The operators of the MARC Retriever are shown in Table 2. In the definitions, C is the query constant and D is the contents of a MARC record data element.

TABLE 2

OPERATORS OF THE MARC RETRIEVER

Operator	Meaning
=	C equals D
>	C is greater than D
≥	C is greater than or equal to D
<	C is less than D
≤	C is less than or equal to D
≠	C is not equal to D
&	"and" (both conditions must be true)
		"or" (at least one condition must be true)

Constants

A constant is either a string of characters representing data itself (e.g., Poe, Edgar Allan) or a specific variable field tag, indicator(s), and subfield code(s). Constants may take the following form:

CC	Where CC is an alphabetic or numeric character or the pound sign "#". When this form is used, the MARC Retriever will convert all lower-case alphabetic characters in the data element of the MARC record being searched to upper-case before a comparison is made with search argument. This conversion feature permits the use of a standard keypunch that has no lower-case capability for preparation of queries.
'CC'	Where CC can be any one of the 256 characters represented by the hexadecimal numbers 00 to FF. This form allows nonalphabetic or nonnumeric characters not represented on the standard keyboard to be part of the search argument. When

this form is used, the MARC Retriever will also convert all lower-case alphabetic characters in the data elements in the MARC record being searched to upper-case before a comparison is made.

@CC@   Where CC can be any one of the 256 characters represented by the hexadecimal numbers 00 to FF. When this form is used, characters in the data element of the MARC record being searched will be left intact and the search argument must contain identical characters before a match can occur.

The pound sign indicates that the character in the position it occupies in the constant is not to take part in the comparison. For example, if the constant were #ANK, TANK, RANK, BANK would be considered matches. More than one pound sign can be used in a constant and in any position.

SPECIMEN QUERIES

The following examples illustrate simple query statements involving fixed and variable fields.

IF MCPDATE1 = 1967 LIST MCRCNUMB;

The entire MARC data base would be searched a record at a time for records that contained 1967 in the first publication date field (MCP-DATE1). The LC card number (MCRCNUMB) of the records that satisfied the search argument would be output.

IF SCAN(TAG = 100) = DESTOUCHES
LIST SCAN (TAG = 245);

The personal name main entry field (tag 100) of each MARC record would be searched for the surname Destouches. If the record meets this search argument, the title statement (tag 245) would be output.

In addition to specifying that a variable field is to be searched, the SCAN function also indicates that all characters of the variable field are to be compared and a match will result at any point in the variable field where the search argument matches the variable field contents. For example, if the if-mode expression is SCAN(TAG = 100) = SMITH a match would occur on the following

examples of personal name main entries (tag 100): SMITH, JOHN; SMITHFIELD, JEROME; JONES-SMITH, ANTHONY.

It is possible to include the indicators associated with a variable field in the search by augmenting the constant of the SCAN function as follows:

IF SCAN(TAG = 100&INDIC = 10) =
DESTOUCHES LIST SCAN (TAG = 245);

Where:

INDIC   Specifies that indicators are to be included.

1   Specifies that the first indicator must be set to 1 (the name in the personal name main entry [tag 100] is a single surname,

0   Specifies that the second indicator must be set to zero (main entry is not the subject).

The personal name main entry field (tag 100) of each record would be searched and a hit would occur if the indicators associated with the field were 1 and 0 and the contents of the field contained the characters "Destouches." If the record met these search criteria, the title statement (tag 245) would be output. It is also possible to restrict the search to the contents of one or more subfields of a variable field.

For example:

IF SCAN(TAG = 100&INDIC = 10&NTC
= A) = DESTOUCHES LIST SCAN(TAG = 245);

Where:

NTC   Indicates that a subfield code follows.

A   Specifies that only the contents of subfield A are to be included in the search. Note that in this form the actual subfield code "a" is converted to "A" by the program (see section on Constants).

Special Rules.

So far the discussion has concerned rules of the query language that apply to either the if mode or the list mode. This section and the remaining sections will discuss those rules and functions that are unique to either the if mode or the list mode.

In the if mode, fixed and variable field expressions can be ANDed or ORed together using the logical operators & and |. For example:

IF MCPDATE1 = 1967&SCAN(TAG = 100)
= DESTOUCHES LIST SCAN(TAG = 245);

This query would search for records with a publication date field (MCPDATE1) containing 1967 and a personal name main entry field (tag 100) containing Destouches. If both search criteria are met, the title statement field (tag 245) would be printed.

In the list mode more than one fixed or variable field can be listed by a query as long as the fixed field names or scan expressions are separated by commas. For example:

IF SCAN(TAG = 100) = DESTOUCHES
LIST SCAN(TAG = 245), MCRCNUMB;

The list mode offers two options, LIST and LISTM, which result in different actions. LIST indicates that the data elements in the expressions are to be printed, and LISTM indicates that the data elements in the expression are to be written on magnetic tape in the MARC processing format.

It is often desirable to list a complete record either in the MARC processing format using LISTM or in printed form using LIST. In either case, the listing of a complete record is activated by the MARC Retriever key term RECORD. For example:

IF SCAN(TAG = 100) = DESTOUCHES LIST
RECORD;

The complete record would be written on magnetic tape in the MARC processing format instead of being printed out if LISTM were substituted for LIST in the above query.

Four functions can be specified by the LIST mode. HITS signals the MARC Retriever to count and print the number of records that meet the search criteria. For example:

IF SCAN(TAG = 650) = AUTOMATION
LIST HITS;

RATIO signals the MARC Retriever to count both the number of records that meet the search criteria and the number of records in the data base and print both counts.

The remaining two LIST functions permit the summing of the contents of fixed fields containing binary numbers. SUM causes the contents of all specified fields in the records meeting the search criteria to be summed and printed. For example:

IF MCRCNUMB = 'ƀƀƀ68 ######'
LIST SUM (MCRLGTH);

The data base would be searched for records with LC card number field (MCRCNUMB) containing three blanks and 68 in positions one through five. The remaining positions would not take part in the query process and could have any value. If a record satisfied this search argument, the contents of the record length field (MCRLGTH) would be added to a counter. When the complete data base had been searched, the count would be printed. AVG performs the same function as SUM and also accumulates and prints a count of the number of records meeting the search criteria.

Use of the Program

The MARC Retriever has been operational at the Library of Congress since May 1969 and selected staff members representing a cross-section of LC activities have been trained in the rules of query construction. The applications of the program to the MARC master file include: identification of records with unusual characteristics for the format recognition study; selection of titles for special reference collections; and verification of the consistency of the MARC editorial process. As the file grows, it is expected that the MARC Retriever will be useful in compiling various kinds of bibliographic listings, such as translations into English, topical bibliographies, etc., as well as in making complex subject searches.

The MARC Retriever is not limited to use with the MARC master file; it can query any data base that contains records in the MARC processing format. Thus, the Legislative Reference Service is able to query its own data base of bibliographic citations to produce various outputs of use to its staff and members of Congress.

Because the MARC Retriever is designed to conduct searches from magnetic tape, it will eventually become too costly in terms of machine processing time to operate. It is difficult to predict when the system will be outgrown, however, because its life span will be determined by the growth of the file and the complexity of the queries. Meanwhile, the MARC Retriever should provide the means for testing the flexibility of the MARC format for machine searching of a bibliographic file.

REFERENCES

1. U.S. Library of Congress. Information Systems Office: *The MARC Pilot Project*. (Washington, D.C.: 1968), pp. 40-51.

2. Rather, John C.; Pennington, Jerry G.: "The MARC Sort Program," *Journal of Library Automation*, 2 (September 1969), 125-138.

3. RECON Working Task Force. *Conversion of Retrospective Catalog Records to Machine-Readable Form*. (Washington, D.C.: Library of Congress, 1969.

4. U.S. Library of Congress. Information Systems Office: *Subscribers Guide to the MARC Distribution Service*, 3d ed. (Washington, D.C.: 1969), pp. 31-31b.

5. Ibid., p. 40.

6. Cunningham, Jay L.: Schieber, William D.; Shoffner, Ralph M.: *A Study of the Organization and Search of Bibliographic Holdings Records in On-Line Computer Systems: Phase I*. (Berkeley, Calif.: Institute of Library Research, University of California, 1969), pp. 85-94.

7. Jolliffe, John: "The Tactics of Converting a Catalogue to Machine-Readable Form," *Journal of Documentation*, 24 (September 1968), 149-158.

Scholarly Needs for Bibliographical Control and Physical Dissemination

Edwin E. Williams

Research can be defined as studious investigation directed toward the extension of knowledge. Obviously it must build on what is already known. It may require expeditions to unexplored regions of the earth or beyond, laboratory experimentation, or study of the collections in galleries and museums; the sources of knowledge are as varied as knowledge itself. Almost always, however, research depends in part (and often it depends almost wholly) on libraries. Almost always, likewise, the results of research are reported in written, printed, or other records that libraries collect, organize, and make available to scholars.

Research libraries have helped to create modern civilization; their strength and vigor directly affect the health of scholarship and hence of society as a whole. The rapidly growing abundance of knowledge, which would have been impossible without research libraries, now confronts them with far more difficult tasks than ever before.

This abundance is reflected by striking quantitative increases in publishing; the output in many fields is now doubling every seven to ten years. There are new forms of publication, many of them difficult to obtain and to organize, and they are now produced by every inhabited area of the earth. Traditional boundaries between subject fields are breaking down, so fewer scholars now find that highly specialized collections are adequate to meet most of their needs. Moreover, traditional methods of collecting and organizing research materials are too slow to satisfy these needs.

The demands upon research libraries are made by a rapidly growing clientele. In 1870, less than a century ago, there were 5,553 faculty members in American institutions of higher education; by 1964 there were 494,514. One Ph.D. was earned in 1870; there were 382 in 1900, 2,299 in 1930, 3,290 in 1940, 6,633 in 1950, 9,829 in 1960, 11,622 in 1962, 14,490 in 1964, and 16,467 in 1965. Scholars engaged in formal postdoctoral work are now more numerous than graduate students working for the doctorate were until a few years ago. A study made during 1960 indicated that there were then some 10,000 postdoctoral scholars (most of them in the sciences and in medicine, and most of them supported by Federal funds) in addition to perhaps 15,000 medical interns and residents, college teachers, and visiting faculty. It can be anticipated that the National Research Council's Study of Postdoctoral Education, which is now under way, will reveal a substantial increase in numbers during the past seven years, and the rate of increase should accelerate for years to come.

This is yet another result of the speed at which knowledge is growing; postdoctoral study is becoming essential for professional scholars and those in more and more callings that demand constant upgrading and updating of knowledge. Those who teach in colleges and universities are by no means the only scholars whose research is producing the new knowledge that will shape the future; research materials are as essential to the industrial as to the academic community, and research libraries are essential to economic as well as to cultural development.

Fortunately the increased demands of scholars

SOURCE: Reprinted from E. Shepley Nourse and Douglas M. Knight, eds., *Libraries at Large* (New York: Bowker, 1969), pp. 126–142, by permission of Dr. Douglas M. Knight and the publisher. The paper was originally from *On Research Libraries* by the Committee on Research Libraries of the American Council of Learned Societies, submitted to the National Advisory Commission on Libraries November 1967. This paper was written for the Committee, and the author is indebted to its members for valuable suggestions that have been incorporated in the text. The complete study, On Research Libraries, was published by the M.I.T. Press in 1969.

come at a time when the opportunities are also unprecedented—most notably those opportunities that arise from automation and other technological advances and those that stem from increasing recognition of scholarship, and the libraries essential to it, as national resources that must be nationally supported. Needs must be assessed and plans must be made.

BIBLIOGRAPHY IN GENERAL

Collecting by libraries is essential, but it is equally essential that there be bibliographical apparatus by means of which the scholar can learn of the existence and location of materials that may be useful to him. The catalogs and classification systems of libraries, important as they are, meet only a fraction of scholarship's needs; research depends also upon periodical indexes and abstracting services, national and subject bibliographies, and a multitude of other records of what has been written.

The latest edition of Besterman's *World Bibliography of Bibliographies*, though it excludes general library catalogs and all bibliographies that are not separate publications, lists 117,187 volumes of bibliography under 15,829 headings. Four years ago the Library of Congress prepared a *Guide to the World's Abstracting and Indexing Services in Science and Technology* listing 1,855 works that were then currently appearing at regular intervals. It is not easy to enumerate even all the major kinds of bibliography. Some bibliographies, like the 1,855 just mentioned, are current serials that attempt to provide information as promptly as possible on recent publications; others are restricted to works prior to a given date. Some attempt to include everything in their field; others are selective and critical. Some list titles only; others include annotations or extensive abstracts. Some list works only under the names of their authors; others list them under subject headings or in classified arrangements. Some confine themselves to books; others are restricted to articles in periodicals. Despite the international character of scholarship, national bibliographies are among the most ambitious and most useful achievements in recording what has been published; it is unfortunate that such bibliographies are still lacking for many countries.

Many bibliographies give no indication of where the scholar may obtain copies of the works they list; but library catalogs are among the major species of bibliography, and some of the outstanding subject bibliographies are catalogs of single great collections. Union catalogs and lists also include some of the greatest achievements of bibliography. The *National Union Catalog* at the Library of Congress has demonstrated that a great unpublished bibliography existing in a single copy can be highly useful, but its contribution to research will be greatly increased when its publication in book form, which is now under way, has been completed and it can be consulted in libraries throughout the world. Finally, it should be observed that not all published bibliographies appear as books or periodicals; alternative forms include cards, microfilms, and now magnetic tapes and other machine-readable media.

No one nation is going to do all the world's bibliographical work; no one agency or type of agency is going to do all the bibliographical work of the United States. Government departments, libraries, professional societies, and commercial publishers will continue to produce bibliographies, and this diversity ought to serve the constantly changing needs of scholarship better than any monolithic system. Yet coordination is an obvious need; the field of bibliography has become so vast that it is difficult to obtain the information on which decisions and plans ought to be based. At present the Federal Government has no bibliographical policy, and no one is responsible even for a continuing survey of the growing bibliographical output of the Government itself, much of which fails to meet recognized bibliographical standards.

There is no comprehensive and systematic effort to collect, appraise, and disseminate information on current developments in the application of computers to bibliographical work, yet these developments seem to offer the best grounds that scholarship has for hopes that bibliography can after all succeed in keeping track of the rising output of recorded knowledge. As library catalogs, bibliographies, indexes, and abstracting services are automated, it is vital that their machine-readable stores of information be compatible. Lack of uniformity in present book-form bibliographies may do relatively little harm, but a great advantage of converting bibliographical information to machine-readable form is that it can be mechanically consolidated, manipulated, and rearranged to meet specific local needs. Only a vigorous and extremely well-informed effort can hope to assist and persuade the host of organizations that produce bibliographies to cooperate for the benefit of scholarship as a whole.

Consequently, a National Bibliographical Office should be created.[1] This, it should be emphasized, is not envisaged as a regulatory agency in any sense, but as a central source of information on which voluntary coordination can be based, an advisory body identifying needs and formulating bibliographical standards, a referral center for bibliographical inquiries, and possibly, under contract, an agency for making special searches and compiling bibliographies.

This office would have international as well as domestic responsibilities; it should work closely with UNESCO and other international agencies as well as with bibliographical centers in other countries. Here it should be kept in mind that assistance to foreign bibliographical undertakings directly aids American research and American libraries; when any other nation establishes a good national bibliography, for example, it benefits scholarship everywhere.

Domestically the office should supplement rather than supplant effective existing agencies such as the Office of Science Information Service of the National Science Foundation, which "is responsible for providing leadership among non-Federal science information services, and in developing appropriate relationships between Federal and non-Federal activities," its objective being "to supplement internal Federal information activities, and insure that scientists and other users have ready availability to the world's current and past output of significant scientific and technical literature."[2]

In medicine, with the National Library of Medicine, and in other scientific fields a great bibliographical advance is now under way. MEDLARS, the National Library of Medicine's Medical Literature Analysis and Retrieval System, stores citations to a portion of the world's biomedical literature on magnetic tapes and retrieves information electronically, making individual demand searches, producing bibliographies, and printing the *Index Medicus* by means of a computer-driven phototypesetter. Decentralization has now begun with the establishment of regional search centers to which tapes are supplied. The National Science Foundation reported in 1965 that national science information systems now appear to be within reach, and the same report announced that the American Chemical Society had contracted for a two-year program for mechanized informational services; under this $2,043,600

contract, 800,000 chemical references are to be fed into the system. The Foundation suggested that this arrangement might well be a prototype for future Government-scientific society relationships. It has been observed that bibliographies are produced and supported by a wide variety of agencies, but it should be emphasized that the scholars in each field cannot expect to be well served bibliographically unless they determine and make known their needs; hence their own organizations, the professional and learned societies, have a clear responsibility for leadership here.

Bibliographically, the nonscientific fields of learning, with their different kind of literature, have lagged behind. However, the United States Office of Education has now inaugurated ERIC (Educational Research Information Center) with a center in Washington and twelve clearinghouses in universities and other institutions throughout the country, each with responsibility for covering a specific subdivision of research in problems of education, such as junior colleges, counseling and guidance, exceptional children, and educational administration. These clearinghouses acquire, select, abstract, and index relevant documents; the center stores full texts of documents on microfilm, announces all new acquisitions, and makes copies available at nominal cost. Important data-archive projects such as the Inter-University Consortium for Political Research at Michigan and the Roper Public Opinion Research Center at Williams College should also be noted.

The sciences, where pressure is greatest and where financial support has been relatively easier to obtain than in other fields, can be expected to lead the way in comprehensive and automated bibliography. Other areas of scholarship must be assisted to follow.

LIBRARY CATALOGING

Subject bibliography and informational systems involve analysis in depth of the content of publications, and it is evident that urgently needed improvements in present services will require continued efforts by learned societies and other organizations as well as by libraries. Library catalogs, since they deal for the most part with whole volumes, may seem less complex, but the listing and classification of millions of books in a great library—or in the libraries of the nation—is not a simple matter. Cataloging at present is often too slow to serve the needs of scholarship, and libraries can ill afford to waste their inadequate supply of trained manpower on the duplication of work that far too often is still required.

A great step forward in library cataloging should result from the Higher Education Act of 1965, which authorized a proposal by the Association of Research Libraries for expanding the foreign acquisition and shared cataloging programs of the Library of Congress. This legislation authorized sums of $5,000,000 for 1965-66, $6,315,000 for 1966-67, and $7,770,000 for 1967-68, but fully adequate appropriations were not or have not yet been voted. Under this legislation the Library of Congress is to acquire, as far as possible, all library materials of value to scholarship that are currently published throughout the world, and it is promptly to provide catalog information for these materials. This is by no means an easy task, but the efforts made thus far are already enabling American research libraries substantially to reduce their duplication of work, and hence to save money as well as to give better service to scholars by speeding up their cataloging.

Later in this section there is some discussion of developments that may grow out of the acquisitions part of this program; here it should be noted that the new program promises to contribute to bibliographical progress internationally and to library automation. The Library of Congress has been collaborating with foreign national libraries and national bibliographies in setting up its machinery for acquisition and cataloging. American libraries are beginning to use cataloging done abroad, and the result is to reduce duplication of effort internationally as well as within the United States.

In addition to the efforts in acquisition and cataloging that it is making under the Higher Education Act of 1965, the Library of Congress, in cooperation with a few research libraries, is experimenting in the dissemination and use of cataloging data in machine-readable form. Research library records, for acquisition and circulation functions as well as for cataloging, have long been based on cards; now, as the transformation to a computer-based record system gets under way, it is essential that compatible methods be adopted. In other words, computers in each research library must soon be prepared to incorporate into the local system information received from computers at the Library of Congress and elsewhere, just as in the past it has been possible to incorporate printed cards of standard format into card catalogs. It is

to be hoped also that the new computer age will lead to more standardization internationally than has been achieved in library cataloging up to now.

Whatever else research libraries do in the immediate future, they can afford to let nothing take precedence over the effort to move ahead with the shared cataloging program that has been launched under the Higher Education Act of 1965. This is not to suggest, however, that all major problems of research library cataloging can be solved by this program or that other efforts are not required. It deals with current publications and hence must emphasize the speedy transmission of data, which makes it all the more desirable to automate procedures as soon as possible. But research library catalogs contain millions of cards listing publications of past years, and research libraries must continue to acquire and catalog such publications by the thousands. The largest libraries do this as they strengthen their great collections by filling in the gaps, but the multitude of new or relatively weak libraries must attempt to build up research collections adequate to meet the growing needs of their scholarly communities.

A major advance in the vast field of retrospective cataloging was assured recently when the American Library Association was able to announce the completion of arrangements for publication in more than six hundred volumes of the *National Union Catalog's* record of books published prior to 1956. (The record for publications since that date has already been published, and is kept up to date by monthly supplements with annual and quinquennial cumulations.)

This colossal publishing project, the largest ever undertaken anywhere, has been planned and contracted for without Governmental or foundation subvention. It will disseminate a store of bibliographical data accumulated since 1901, when the Library of Congress began to print catalog cards and to exchange them for those printed by other libraries. A Rockefeller grant enabled the *Catalog* to add more than 6.3 million cards from the period between 1927 and 1932. Major American research libraries have been reporting their acquisitions for many years, and there are now some 16.5 million cards recording locations of books in eight hundred libraries of the United States and Canada.

Hitherto, this information has been available only in the single card file at the Library of Congress; its publication will enable scholars to locate books without directing inquiries there and will give catalogers in each subscribing library access to catalog information for more than 10 million publications. In selection and acquisition it will be of great value in identification of books, and more importantly, it will enable libraries to avoid needless duplication of books already held by other American collections. Costs of editing and publication will be paid by subscribing libraries.

The *National Union Catalog's* record of American research library holdings is far from complete and far from impeccable. It has not yet been automated. Something better will be possible a few years from now, but postponement of publication would have meant that for some years to come scholarship and research libraries would have had to do without the incomplete and imperfect but highly useful catalog that can now be made available. It should be added that provision has been made for changing the "printer's copy" during the course of publication from the present cards to machine-produced output at any time when this becomes practicable; thus the present undertaking will not entail any delay in future automation. Eventually the American *National Union Catalog* should be consolidated with similar records of research library holdings in other countries.

Clearly it is now reasonable to expect that research library catalogs will eventually move from card files into computerized form, but it is unrealistic to suppose that this will come as a single step; the beginning, presumably, will be made with data for current publications. This might well be followed by putting the Library of Congress catalog on computer tapes (or their successors) and enabling other research libraries to draw from the tapes, for their own automated catalogs, data for those books of which they have copies. At the same time, they would add to the tapes data for those of their holdings that were not represented at the Library of Congress. This procedure would minimize duplication of effort in putting catalog data into machine-readable form; eventually it would also produce a completed, revised, and greatly improved *National Union Catalog*. This catalog, since it presumably could be consulted electronically from a distance or through duplicate local stores of machine-readable data, might never need to be reproduced and disseminated in book form.

Completion of the *National Union Catalog* would deserve a very high priority even if it could not be done with the help of computers, and even if it could not be regarded in part as a by-product of research on library automation; its value to the scholar who works with noncurrent publications can hardly be overestimated. The effort to complete it should not be confined to the incorporation of a record of holdings of large research libraries; many other collections, particularly those of historical societies, possess books of great value for the study of America's past that are to be found nowhere else.

An attempt to set up a timetable for this mechanization of research library catalogs would seem premature until present experiments in the transmission of data for current publications have led to an effective program for supplying machine-readable data in conjunction with the shared cataloging project. Valuable experience is also being accumulated as work continues on projects such as Harvard's shelflist automation, the University of Chicago's "integrated, computer-based, bibliographical data system," and Project INTREX at the Massachusetts Institute of Technology (M.I.T.).

Harvard is transferring its handwritten loose-leaf shelflist to machine-readable punched cards and publishing print-outs produced by the computer in three sequences: a classified arrangement, alphabetically by author, and chronologically by date of publication. The University of Chicago, with the help of a National Science Foundation grant, is attempting to combine into a computer-accessible permanent record all elements of information about each book or other bibliographical item added to the library; the stored information will be used for many purposes: to determine holdings, prepare orders, maintain acquisition files, generate acquisition lists, prepare charge cards and labels, and produce full sets of catalog cards. M.I.T. is experimenting with its 125,000-volume Engineering Library in providing scholars with remote access to a computer-controlled magnetic memory store of bibliographical information on books and other library materials; consultation is to be through consoles linked to a central computer by ordinary telephone lines.

Costs of installing automated systems may seem high, but costs of operating these systems compare favorably with those of operating the present manual systems, and the scholar can be expected to benefit greatly from the improvements and innovations in service that automation can produce. The 1963 study *Automation and the Library of Congress* estimated the costs of conversion to an automated system at $50 million to $70 million, but operating costs of the system in 1972 were forecast at $4.5 million, compared with $5 million for the present system and its substantially less satisfactory services.[3] Other libraries, incorporating into their systems machine-readable bibliographical data produced by the Library of Congress, should have relatively lower costs of conversion and operation, and the scholars who use them should benefit enormously from access to an automated national system as well as from the increased accessibility of local holdings.

Despite its magnitude, the *National Union Catalog* is by no means the only important source of information on the location of research library materials, and it must continue to be supplemented by publications such as the *Union List of Serials*, which contains more than 225,000 entries describing periodical and other serial holdings of 680 libraries in the United States and Canada. Its current supplement is *New Serial Titles*, and the Library of Congress, having completed publication of the *Union List's* third edition, is now planning a *World Inventory of Serials in Machine-Readable Form*, as recommended by the Association of Research Libraries. When completed, such an inventory can be a tool of inestimable scope and utility. The next step would be a union list of serials in machine-readable form, the additional information being, of course, locations.

Further improvements in the system for reporting and disseminating the record of serial holdings are needed. Other important aids to the scholar in finding specialized types of material include *Newspapers on Microfilm*, the *Union List of Microfilms*, the *Guide to Archives and Manuscripts in the United States* (now seriously out of date), the *National Union Catalog of Manuscript Collections*, and services like the new Center for the Coordination of Foreign Manuscript Copying. The Library of Congress is also maintaining a National Register of Microcopy Masters and is disseminating lists based on this, but there is as yet only rudimentary machinery for the coordination of copying or for support of the massive program of copying both books and manuscripts that would be highly desirable.

Guides to the location of materials in American libraries such as those that have been mentioned have numerous foreign counterparts, and the development of microfilming facilities abroad is making it increasingly easy for American scholars to obtain copies of library holdings wherever they may be. The demand for copying rises sharply as information regarding manuscripts becomes more readily available.

It should not be forgotten that manuscripts are by no means the only important type of material omitted from both the *National Union Catalog* and the *Union List of Serials*. Union lists of African, Russian, and Latin American newspapers have appeared during the past fifteen years, but there is no source of information on holdings of most foreign newspapers, and Winifred Gregory's *American Newspapers, 1821-1936*, now thirty years old, has not been brought up to date. Neither has her *List of the Serial Publications of Foreign Governments, 1815-1931*. Publications of great importance in special fields—sheet music and art exhibition catalogs, for example—have largely escaped the bibliographical net, to say nothing of maps and nonwritten materials such as sound recordings and photographs of all kinds.

COLLECTING AND COLLECTIONS

It may seem illogical to have considered bibliography and library cataloging before dealing with library collections, on which many bibliographies and all catalogs must be based. The scholar, however, normally approaches research materials through bibliographies and catalogs. Moreover, the work of selection and acquisition that builds any research collection must depend in large measure on bibliographies and on catalogs of other research collections. This was the case even when libraries were more self-sufficient than they are today; as it is, the sharing of information and of physical materials is so fundamental to research library operation that one cannot intelligently discuss collections and collection-building without constantly keeping in mind the bibliographical apparatus that makes each individual research library part of a much larger—though as yet very imperfectly articulated—library organism that extends beyond local and even national boundaries.

The members that make up this organism have been called research libraries, but it needs to be kept in mind that this term covers a multitude of diverse institutions, many of which are not exclusively engaged in supporting research. The small college library serves research needs of its faculty to the extent that it can; the large university library is heavily used by undergraduate students as well as by graduate students and faculty. Some state and municipal public libraries have important research materials; there are still proprietary libraries like the Boston Athenaeum with outstanding collections, and a number of major libraries, including the American Antiquarian Society, Folger Shakespeare, Huntington, Library

Company of Philadelphia, Linda Hall, Morgan, and Newberry, that depend largely if not wholly on endowments and gifts for their support but continue to make their resources available to an increasing number of scholars under increasing difficulties.

The Reference Department of the New York Public Library is among the largest and most significant institutions in the country. Its holdings (i.e., those of the Reference Department alone, which is not supported by taxation, as is the Circulation Department of the New York Public Library) are surpassed in extent only by those of the Library of Congress, Harvard, and Yale, and they are unequaled in many subjects. Yet funds available for services, current acquisitions, and preservation of the collections are becoming more and more inadequate; endowment is being used up in order to keep the library going.

The current *American Library Directory* lists more than 7,700 specialized libraries in the United States, some 2,000 of which form part of university or other library systems. The total includes 1,231 medical, 569 law, and 246 religious libraries, and collections on scores of other subjects, maintained by government agencies, private industry, and associations of all kinds. There are special libraries with more than one million volumes—the National Library of Medicine, National Agricultural Library, and Harvard Law School Library— but it should be emphasized that a relatively small, highly specialized collection may also contain important research materials. Notable examples, as previously suggested, are many historical society libraries possessing manuscripts and other unique documents of inestimable value for the study of history.

Research libraries, then, are of many kinds, and research materials are more varied still. Much has been written during the past few years about how difficult it is to collect and organize the rapidly growing abundance of scientific publications. The difficulties are indeed great, and they will not easily be overcome, but the difficulties of collecting and controlling research materials for history and other social and humanistic subjects are far greater.

At the risk of oversimplification, chemists may be contrasted with historians. The record of research done by other chemists and by scientists in related fields is what the chemist normally needs to consult. There are far more research chemists than there used to be, yet they form a relatively limited and identifiable group. Their writings are issued by publishers who intend to disseminate them to scientists and to the libraries used by scientists. These writings now appear in "near print" and in technical reports as well as in the books and journals published by academic institutions, laboratories, learned societies, governments, industrial corporations, and commercial publishers. As has been said, collection and control of this literature is no longer easy, yet the chemist's needs are of a strikingly different order from those of the historian.

Like the chemist, the historian needs access to all the relevant writings of his scholarly colleagues. But his method of adding to this body of knowledge is not laboratory experimentation like the chemist's; it is to search and sift materials of all kinds that were not produced by historians or, for the most part, issued for the use of historians. The latest and most up-to-date compilation of information in his field cannot provide all that he needs, for historical literature is noncumulative and older writings never become completely obsolete. He may find useful data in a newspaper or pamphlet, an advertising leaflet or a schoolbook, a dime novel or a sermon, a photograph, tape recording, correspondence file, or personal account-book. The memoranda or working papers prepared for use within a government department may be much more illuminating than its published reports. Perhaps it should be noted also that if the report of a chemical experiment is lost, it is possible to duplicate the experiment; but when the last copy of a printed book or the unique copy of a manuscript diary is destroyed, some portion of the record is erased forever.

Selection and acquisition of materials to serve research of this kind can never have been a simple matter, and the difficulties have multiplied as the interests of American scholarship have extended to all areas of the earth. When American research in the humanities and social sciences was largely focused on the United States and Western Europe (and when these areas also produced nearly all the world's scientific and scholarly literature), American libraries could identify much of what they needed in good bibliographies and obtain much of it from an established publishing industry and from dealers who specialized in supplying libraries. In many of the countries that are now of particular interest to American scholars, it is almost impossible to discover what has been printed or to obtain copies unless a library can send its representative to scan the shelves of bookshops and deal personally with officials of the government departments that issue useful publications.

The world's publishing output has not been listed nor, indeed, has it been counted; there are no reliable statistics even for books and journals. The Library of Congress was adding more than 300,000 volumes and pamphlets per year *before* expanded foreign acquisitions began under the Higher Education Act of 1965, and the largest university libraries, though some of them acquire 200,000 books per year at a cost of more than $1 million, find their collections less and less adequate to meet the current demands of teaching and research.

Hence American research libraries have sought Federal assistance. In 1962 appropriations authorized by an amendment (Section 104-n of 1958) to Public Law 480 (of 1954) enabled the Library of Congress to begin to use foreign currencies from the sale of surplus agricultural commodities for buying and distributing to American libraries current books, periodicals, and related materials. Though few countries have as yet been included in this program, it has clearly demonstrated the desirability of establishing acquisitions agencies in countries lacking a well-organized publishing industry and book trade. Now, as the Library of Congress augments its foreign acquisitions program under the Higher Education Act of 1965, it evidently should be enabled to make its acquisitions facilities available to other libraries. (Appropriate legislation is now before the Congress.)

Regardless of the assistance that it may be possible for them to obtain from the Library of Congress, research libraries will need to continue cooperative efforts in foreign purchasing. Publications that are unobtainable commercially can often be acquired by exchange, which also provides useful American books and periodicals for many foreign institutions that cannot get dollars for buying in the United States. It has often been recommended that each country establish a national exchange center, and the UNESCO *Bulletin for Libraries* already lists thirty-nine such national centers.

Though the Smithsonian Institution has long functioned as a shipping agency for international exchanges, the United States has no national center; and funds should be provided to enable the United States Book Exchange (USBE), a nonprofit clearinghouse sponsored by major American library associations, to serve as the American national center. As such, it would maintain up-to-date information on current American and foreign serial publications available for exchange from the libraries of universities and other institutions,

assist in arranging direct exchanges between institutions, and extend its duplicate clearinghouse activities to foreign libraries, which cannot for the most part afford the service charges that are necessary since USBE is self-supporting. It is unfortunate that the Agency for International Development (AID) terminated, in 1963, the program under which USBE had supplied more than 2.5 million books and journals to 1,800 foreign libraries during the preceding nine years at a cost to AID of some $1.5 million for service charges. A revived and expanded program of this kind should be supported; in addition, the program for information and service as an exchange intermediary that has been recommended could be financed for some $150,000 per year.

It should be emphasized that the acquisition of new publications is not enough to build the research collections required by American scholarship. The largest and oldest libraries constantly discover gaps in their collections—even the best of their collections—that ought to be filled in, and as new programs develop in their institutions, they are frequently called upon to support research in fields that hitherto had been neglected. There are more new and rapidly developing universities than ever before, and all of these, if they are not to be seriously handicapped by inadequate libraries, must build up extensive retrospective collections in many subjects.

There are great differences here between the needs of one scholar and the next; many a scientist and many a specialist in such contemporary problems as economic development may rarely need to consult a publication that is more than five or ten years old. For such scholars, a library with a good program of current acquisitions may soon become adequate. In the case of many other scholars, regardless of all that can be obtained by borrowing or photocopying, no equally useful substitute is now in sight for the great retrospective collections that traditionally have required decades and even generations for libraries to assemble.

The oldest and largest American university library is at Harvard, where a recent planning study estimated that the University's library collection (7,791,538 volumes in 1967) would grow to more than 10 million volumes in 1976, and that annual expenditures for the library (7,543,791 for 1966–67) would increase to $14,655,000 in 1975–76. These estimates were based upon surveys of student and faculty needs, and took account of substantial savings anticipated from automation and increasingly effective library cooperation; the actual rate of increase in expenditures for the past eleven years has been greater than was predicted for the next eleven. It has also recently been estimated that within ten to fifteen years there will be 60 to 70 universities in the United States with graduate programs of real quality. Each, presumably, will need to acquire current publications on a scale comparable to Harvard's, and some of them at least, in an effort to increase the relative strength of their retrospective collections, can be expected to spend more than Harvard does on the acquisition and organization of noncurrent publications.

It has been emphasized that research libraries are diverse and numerous, but it would be a mistake to overlook the particular significance of the libraries of major universities, both those now in existence and those that can be expected to reach maturity during the coming decade. It is these libraries in which most of the nation's scholars— most of those who teach the teachers and most of those who add to the store of human knowledge— receive their advanced training.

Even when funds are provided very generously, the new institutions find that it takes enormous effort and considerable time to build great collections. Some desirable books rarely come on the market, and the competition for all useful out-of-print books is increasing, which has its natural effect on their prices. This competition, incidentally, is both domestic and foreign, since new universities are by no means an exclusively American phenomenon. Theoretically it would be possible to argue that the new institutions have been born too late, should specialize in research that normally requires only recent publications, and ought to leave old books to their elders. However, if this theory had been adopted a century ago, all the great research libraries would be in Europe; if it had been adopted a generation later, it would have restricted American research libraries to the eastern seaboard.

The reasonable assumption, therefore, is that traditional library-collecting ought to continue and will continue. The problem is how best to supplement it: how to reduce as much as possible the disadvantage under which scholars in new institutions would labor for years to come if they had to depend entirely upon the slow traditional processes of collection-building. Plans for coordination and sharing of resources are discussed later in this section. First, however, substitutes for original books ought to be considered.

These substitutes are provided by photographic reproduction in all its forms. The market provided by hundreds of new colleges and universities has stimulated a vigorous republication industry, which is bringing back into print many important books. Obviously the works that are reprinted are those of which the most copies can be sold, so needs of the college library and of undergraduate instruction are more likely to be met in this way than the specialized needs of advanced research.

For small editions, particularly for small editions of voluminous sets or collections, microphotographic reproduction is evidently more likely to be practicable than full-size republication. Recognizing the fact that scholarship can no longer afford to depend almost wholly on commercial sources for reprints or for microform projects, the Association of Research Libraries has recently established a program to improve access to materials that currently can be obtained from mainland China only in unique copies or very small quantities. Supported by a grant of $500,000 from the Ford Foundation, this program will identify texts that are of interest to the scholarly community and make them available in a variety of formats, ranging from microforms available on loan to offset reprints. The Association is now investigating the possibility of extending its Scholarly Resources Development Program to other areas of the world, such as Africa and the Slavic nations.

With modern reader-printer machines that will immediately produce a full-size copy of pages selected by the scholar, the disadvantages of having to work with microreproductions can be considerably reduced. The lack of an integrated system of library copying has delayed and seriously limited the exploitation by scholarship of the potentialities of microreproduction. Essential features of such an integrated system include quick and automatic conversion apparatus for all forms of copying, microforms readily manipulable by hand and by machine, automatic conversion to microform of machine-readable information, and microforms that facilitate immediate access to each page of text as well as rapid scanning of many pages.

It should not be forgotten, however, that some scholars—notably those engaged in bibliographical investigations of how texts were printed and of their vicissitudes in successive editions—must examine originals, and that many others may be seriously impeded by the inconvenience of having to depend on microfilm reading machines and the impossibility of browsing through the shelves of a collection arranged according to a systematic subject classification. On the other hand, it should be observed also that the largest and strongest libraries are relying to an increasing degree on microreproduction, both to supplement their collections and to replace publications that have physically disintegrated.

No problem confronting major research libraries is more alarming than the deterioration of paper, and nothing short of a comprehensive national effort will suffice to deal with it. The oldest books, on the whole, are surviving much better than most recent publications; the paper that was used for more than four hundred years after the invention of printing was remarkably durable. About a century ago, however, there was a great change with the adoption of certain acid-sizing processes in the manufacture of paper and with the increasing use of wood pulp; as a result, a very large proportion of the books printed during the past hundred years are rapidly becoming too brittle to use and many are already crumbling into dust. In 1965 the Association of Research Libraries adopted in principle a plan based on investigations financed by the Council on Library Resources. This calls for a national center that would preserve, insofar as possible, the best example of each deteriorating book deposited with it, would maintain a collection of master microfilm negatives, and would disseminate photographic copies (both microphotographic and full size) to libraries. The total cost of the program during its first ten years was estimated at slightly less than $10 million.

A preliminary study of procedures for identification of materials is now under way at the Library of Congress. Establishment of the National Register of Microcopy Masters there was also an important development because it provides information that is essential if libraries are to minimize needless duplication of filming for preservation as well as for other purposes, but nothing has yet been done to insure the preservation of master negatives, which ought to be in the custody of a national center or of research libraries. These negatives must conform to high standards and must not be exposed to the hazards of use except for making positive microcopies; likewise it is essential that they be permanently available for this whenever a scholar may need such a copy.

An effective national center for preservation and dissemination of research library materials would seem to be the appropriate agency to coordinate copying projects of all kinds. The need for coordination and for support of such projects has been mentioned apropos of the National Register of Microcopy Masters and other bibliographical services, and it has been noted that the Association of Research Libraries has now launched a Scholarly Resources Development Program in order to supplement commercial copying. A national center, with the full cooperation of research libraries, could in effect bring back into print all books held by these libraries, and the benefit to scholarship throughout the nation—to scholars based in the old and large libraries as well as to those in new institutions—would be hard to overestimate.

Further steps should be taken as soon as possible to put the 1965 plan of the Association of Research Libraries into effect, and continued research is needed on several questions, including optimum storage conditions for the books that are to be preserved, practicable methods of deacidification that will retard the disintegration of books now on research library shelves, the durability of film copies, and the chemistry and thermodynamics of paper. Very preliminary reports of current research at the University of Chicago suggest that deacidification may soon be practicable on a large scale, which would be an enormous boon to individual libraries and would help to make the national program more effective.

Every effort should also be made to induce publishers to use permanent/durable paper for the books that libraries will be acquiring during the coming century, and organizations representing the scholarly community ought to launch a vigorous campaign.

COORDINATION AND SHARING OF RESOURCES

From bibliography to the proposed center for preservation and dissemination of research materials originally printed on disintegrating paper, repeated reference has been made to cooperative or centralized activities. In a sense all the research collections of the world form a single great library; certainly the holdings of American research libraries constitute a national collection that is more a functioning entity than an abstraction. Scholars depend on many of the same bibliographies regardless of which unit of the national collection they may be using. Each unit has on its shelves the catalogs of many others and can refer to union catalogs giving the locations of millions of volumes that are not in its own stacks. Each uses—and hopes in the future to use far more effectively—cataloging done elsewhere. There are joint acquisition projects, copies of whole collections in other library units are acquired on film, and there must be a joint attack on the menace of disintegrating paper. In addition, each major library lends thousands of volumes annually to others and borrows thousands for its own community. Microfilms and other photocopies are being produced in rapidly growing numbers as a substitute for loans. Finally, each major library attracts hundreds of visiting scholars each year.

There are many flaws in the present organization. It is expensive to obtain copies of books, photographic and interlibrary loan services are far too slow, and there are too many uncertainties. Even so, the scholar who knows that a book he needs is in a distant research library can usually obtain a copy, and the sources of information through which he can learn it is there are being improved. Most of the suggestions that have been made here for strengthening American research libraries would do so by improving the national system and taking advantage of the opportunities now offered by automation.

When resources are shared to the extent that they have been for many years, each research library benefits directly as their total increases. It does not gain much from those books in other libraries that duplicate its own holdings, but it can and does draw upon collections that supplement its own. This inevitably suggests the possibility of specialization in collecting, and some sixty American research libraries have now been participating for twenty years in the Farmington Plan, under which each has agreed to collect current foreign books intensively in certain fields. Each, in other words, has undertaken to acquire more in the areas for which it has accepted responsibility than would be selected if only the needs of its own institution were taken into account; in return, each has the assurance that a similarly inclusive collection in every other subject is being built up by one of the other participants, from whom it can borrow.

The time now seems to have come for considering changes in this plan in the light of another major cooperative achievement, the Center for Research Libraries in Chicago. This began as the Midwest Inter-Library Center, a regional organization for acquiring and housing infrequently used publications, but modern communications make collections of books and microfilms in Chicago almost as accessible to new members of the Center in Vancouver, Cambridge, and Los Angeles as to its original participants in Minneapolis and Columbus.

Now, as has been noted, it is hoped that the Library of Congress, under provisions of the Higher Education Act of 1965, will acquire current foreign publications comprehensively—more comprehensively, it is reasonable to expect, than individual Farmington Plan participants have been successful in doing. If the Library of Congress could acquire two copies of each new publication and forward one of these to the Center for Research Libraries, the Center might function as a national lending library, and individual responsibilities under the Farmington Plan could then be discontinued.

Would a centralized national collection be preferable to the decentralized one that is now being created by Farmington Plan specialization? An affirmative answer seems to be justified by the fact that it would no longer be necessary to guess how a book had been classified for purposes of Farmington Plan allocation or to consult the *National Union Catalog* to determine the location of recent foreign publications. Furthermore, centralization of responsibility should make possible better service (in cataloging, in interlibrary lending, and in filming) than can be expected from sixty individual libraries, each of which has primary obligations to its own community. (Indeed, a few of the participating libraries cannot lend publications and can only provide photocopies.) If centralization is desirable, should it be at the Center for Research Libraries rather than at the Library of Congress? Here it may be observed that the Center is an instrument of American research libraries and is responsible to them, but the Library of Congress naturally must continue to give priority to service to the Congress and to agencies of the Federal Government.

A certain measure of insurance would also be provided by having two collections rather than one. The United Kingdom, it may be noted, has supplemented the British Museum, its great noncirculating national research library, by establishing two separate institutions specifically for circulation and dissemination: the National Central Library and the National Lending Library for Science and Technology. The former has a relatively small collection (less than 400,000 volumes) of its own but maintains a large union catalog and is the center of the national interlibrary loan system. The latter, dealing primarily with periodicals, currently receives 30,000 serials; it undertakes to handle loan requests the day they are received and to send out photocopies the day after orders reach it.

The Farmington Plan has been the major national effort in specialization by American research libraries. Hence it might appear that disillusionment with specialization is implied by the proposal discussed here to include Farmington Plan collecting among the national services that the Center for Research Libraries should be assisted to develop. In fact, however, as has been indicated, this proposal for centralization is prompted by the desire to make the nation's comprehensive collection of current foreign publications as accessible as possible. It should be emphasized that even when maximum accessibility has been achieved, the existence of this national collection will not relieve each research library of the need to build a strong collection of its own to serve its own community.

There is evidence that specialization and cooperative effort are becoming increasingly desirable at the local and regional levels. One reason for this is that there are more universities. Few metropolitan areas have had more than a single genuine university or a single major research library. Soon, however, there will be few such areas without a number of institutions conducting substantial research programs. This suggests the possibility of local agreements to specialize in collecting as well as the development of central research collections to supplement the other academic libraries in a metropolitan area. Here, as in other programs for sharing and increasing resources, the special problem of the college (as distinguished from university) professor should be kept in mind; the undergraduate college cannot build up research collections, yet many members of college faculties need access to such collections for their own scholarly research.

Locally as well as nationally there are limits, of course, to the extent to which any institution can depend on central collections and on those of libraries with which it may share responsibility under agreements for specialization in collecting. Each university library must support the changing research programs of its own university, and no university can or should undertake to forgo certain specified subjects for all time and to continue forever to emphasize certain others; indeed, the individual scholar sometimes finds that his investigations have led him to areas in which he had not

expected to require strong library resources. Each institution must plan but must also be prepared to modify decisions regarding what must be collected on its own shelves and what can properly be left to other collections, either national or local.

It seems evident that scholars will depend more and more upon microtexts and other photographic copies. The many new institutions must acquire photocopies of millions of volumes that are no longer available in any other form, and older research libraries have millions of volumes on their shelves that will soon—if they have not already—become too brittle for normal use. An increasing number of scholars will live at a distance from major research collections. The largest libraries can acquire only a constantly decreasing percentage of the total output of the world's presses, and consequently will rely to a growing degree upon other collections such as the national lending library that has been proposed. If much of the increased use of microcopies is inevitable, there are also many instances in which choices can be made between lending and filming, between storing immense collections of books and substituting microcopies plus, of course, the reading machines required for their use.

Investigation of both research needs and of economic factors must provide information on the basis of which intelligent choices can be made. Thus the Center for Research Libraries, under a grant from the National Science Foundation, is now studying the costs and service characteristics of alternative methods of making journal literature available to scientists. There must be further studies of this kind, and there must be periodic reexaminations of the problem in the light of technological developments, particularly in the area of high-reduction techniques, which promise to make it possible to reproduce multiple copies of large collections at relatively very low cost. Difficult copyright questions are involved. So are questions relating to fees for use and their effect on scholarship; libraries traditionally have absorbed the costs of interlibrary loan, but with a few exceptions—notably the National Library of Medicine—have charged for photographic copies supplied in lieu of loan.

Something has been said of the limitations of microphotographic reproductions as substitutes for original books, and it should be added that although everything practicable ought to be done to aid scholars in institutions that do not have great library collections, there is little prospect that any substitutes can serve the scholar in many fields quite as well as a great collection on his subject located where he is working. It is one thing to search bibliographies and catalogs and to request that books be supplied on loan or in film or other copies; it is another to live with a great collection, freely able to look into scores of books shelved next to the ones that have been identified through bibliographies and catalogs. We must not fail to support such collections. As barriers to access are reduced and a national network is perfected, it must be emphasized that the strength of the network depends on the strength of the outstanding collections that it links.

GENERAL OBSERVATIONS

As the problems of access to recorded knowledge are considered and as efforts are made to facilitate the scholar's access, it may be well to keep in mind certain general principles.

First, balance should be maintained, and progress is needed along more than a single line. New institutions must be assisted to build collections of their own and to draw readily upon the resources of older and larger libraries. Important as this is, however, it would be a mistake to concentrate all efforts upon helping the new and the weak; we must build upon strength and maintain the quality of existing great collections while creating the new ones that are now urgently needed. All libraries benefit from further strengthening of the outstanding research collections on which all depend to supplement their own holdings, just as all benefit from improvement of bibliographical apparatus, research in the application of automation to library operations, and cooperative projects in cataloging and acquisition.

It should be kept in mind that most research libraries are now hard pressed to maintain the collections and services required by their own particular constituencies; they cannot be expected to provide greatly increased regional or national services unless means can be found to reimburse them for the additional costs of these services. The nation's first great universities and great libraries were built by private benefactions; a few state governments have had the vision and the resources to emulate this example. Now, as the time has come when Federal funds must supplement private donations and state appropriations in supporting research and research libraries, the gravest mistake that could be made—yet, unfortunately, perhaps

the most natural—would be to neglect the institutions that are strongest and seem relatively affluent.

Second, existing services and procedures must not be abandoned until better services and procedures are in operation. Scholars must be supplied with research materials today and tomorrow; service cannot be suspended while systems are installed that will provide much better service the year after next. Present libraries are sometimes described as obsolete; perhaps this is really praise, for there is a saying in technological circles, "If it works, it's obsolete." One can almost always assert that with the technology that may become available a project might be done better next year than it can be done now, but to wait for this reason means never to do anything. Publication of the *National Union Catalog* is an example; rather than wait, it seemed preferable to do the imperfect job that can be done with present machinery, particularly since embarking on the project now did not preclude a change to better machinery during the course of publication.

Finally, without losing sight of the diversity of scholarship and of the materials it requires, all research libraries should be alert to opportunities for profiting from the advances that are being made by specialized scientific libraries. The National Library of Medicine is collecting comprehensively, producing the great bibliography in its field, sharing its resources with medical libraries throughout the nation, and pioneering in the development of automated procedures. The Medical Library Assistance Act of 1965 has made provision for a comprehensive program including assistance in library-building, instruction, special projects, research and development, improvement of basic library resources, publication, development of a national system, and establishment of regional search centers and possibly a branch of the National Library of Medicine. The authorization was for $23 million per year, and the budget of the National Library of Medicine is now approximately $6 million per year. These are not extravagant sums, it would seem, in view of the contributions that this program should make to teaching and research in the medical sciences.

National library service and national programs for development should be practicable in other subjects. It has been noted that the National Science Foundation has contracted with the American Chemical Society for mechanized informational services, and this suggests that services like those of the National Library of Medi-

TABLE 1

POSSIBLE APPROACHES TOWARD THE OBJECTIVES OF SCHOLARLY ACCESS FOR THE FURTHERANCE OF RESEARCH*

(With particular reference to university and other research libraries)

Continuing, innovative, and experimental approaches

1. *Much that is now being done must continue with increased support and at an accelerated rate:*
   a. Support of numerous useful current bibliographies, indexes, and abstracting services.
   b. Maintenance of the strength of existing strong libraries and rapid development of the additional strong collections that will be needed for a total of 60 to 70 universities with graduate programs of real quality.
   c. Strong emphasis on Library of Congress programs for shared cataloging, increased foreign acquisitions, and sharing of acquisition facilities with research libraries.
   d. A variety of experiments in library automation.
   e. Publication of the present *National Union Catalog* and improvement of supplementary guides to the location of research materials; there must be no delay in making information on serial holdings readily available through a machine-readable *Union List of Serials*.

2. *Several innovations are essential*:
   a. Creation of a National Bibliographical Office to promote coordination of effort in this vast area.
   b. Provision, for a number of other subjects, of bibliographical services and informational systems like those now being developed for a few scientific fields.
   c. Study of needs and bibliographical planning in all fields, with leadership from the professional and learned societies.
   d. Completion of the *National Union Catalog* by the incorporation in it of a record of all significant American research collections.
   e. Dissemination to research libraries in machine-readable form of the bibliographical information contained in the *National Union Catalog*.
   f. Automation of bibliographical systems and research library operations as rapidly as proves feasible.
   g. Extension of responsibilities of the Center for the Coordination of Foreign Manuscript Copying to include American as well as foreign materials.
   h. Development of a National Exchange Center at the United States Book Exchange.
   i. A program for preservation and dissemination of materials on deteriorating paper along the lines proposed by the Association of Research Libraries.
   j. Use of durable paper by publishers.
   k. Creation of a National Lending Library, supplemented by regional centers.

3. *Continuing study and experimentation is required throughout; two areas need particular attention:*
   a. Periodic reexamination of the bibliographical needs of each research field in the light of changes in the field and new developments in technology.
   b. The economics of microphotography and the use of microcopies, taking into account both the changing needs of scholarship and the changing state of the art.

This recapitulation from the paper by Edwin E. Williams is consistent with the spirit of the conclusions and recommendations of the National Advisory Commission on Libraries but should not be interpreted as a set of formal Commission recommendations.

cine might sometimes be provided by contract between a Federal agency and an existing non-Federal library.

The President's Science Advisory Committee found in 1963 that "Since strong science and technology is a national necessity, and adequate communication is a prerequisite for strong science and technology, the health of the technical communication system must be a concern of Government."[4] It was good that science and technology led the way in 1963; recent establishment of the National Foundation on the Arts and the Humani-ties, modest as its resources are thus far, seems to demonstrate that the nation now realizes that scholarship and research as a whole are national necessities. It must likewise be recognized that research libraries are the indispensable basis for an adequate communication system in all fields of scholarship.

The increasing concern of Government is inevitable and it is welcome, but this must be accompanied by increasing concern also on the part of private organizations and individuals. The natural sciences and, to a lesser extent, the social sciences have been fortunate in having an industrial constituency to demand that bibliographical and library resources be provided and to help in financing these resources. The humanities must enlist private support on a comparable scale; equal opportunity for research in all fields of knowledge is essential for the healthy growth of scholarship and for the civilization that scholarship builds.

NOTES

[1] The National Advisory Commission on Libraries does recommend that one of the functions of the Library of Congress as the formalized National Library of the United States would be to provide basic national bibliographical services (see chapter 12, also chapter 10). Consideration of the future establishment of another agency for overall bibliographical coordination would presumably be one of the many functions of the recommended permanent National Commission on Libraries and Information Science.

[2] *Annual Report* (Washington: National Science Foundation, 1965), p. xviii.

[3] *Automation and the Library of Congress* (Washington: Library of Congress, 1963), pp. 2, 32.

[4] *Science, Government, and Information: A Report of the President's Science Advisory Committee* (Washington: U.S. Government Printing Office, 1963), p. 1.

"Books in English":
A Microform Bibliography Goes on Trial

From *The Bookseller*

This report stems from a seminar held jointly by the British National Bibliography (BNB) and the National Cash Register Company (NCR) at the London headquarters of the Library Association on 12th October. At the seminar, representatives of some 60 university, public and specialist libraries received copies of the new bibliography "Books In English" produced by the new ultramicroform system known by the initials PCMI. In the joint project described below, BNB created all stages of the system up to the final PCMI process, which is a patent of NCR. The trial microforms which were handed out at the meeting were produced at the expense of NCR (as will be the others produced during the period of testing) and the "readers", which cost £300 each, one of which has been installed in every library taking part in the trials, are all on free loan from NCR.

Two weeks ago at the headquarters of the Library Association the British National Bibliography and the National Cash Register Company introduced the first issue of a new bibliography, *Books in English,* to representatives of selected British libraries who are to put it through its field trials.

In his introductory speech, Mr. A. J. Wells, managing editor of the British National Bibliography, said that the BNB would be 21 years old in a few months' time, and that they were happy to have the opportunity of offering to librarians during their coming-of-age year a whole series of birthday presents.

The experiment in which librarians were now being invited to take part was the result of a combination of three new techniques. One was the computer handling of bibliographic data; another was the ability to transfer computer-generated images to microfilm; and the third was the high reduction technique developed by the National Cash Register Company, the colleagues of the BNB in this venture. "We are confident that you will find, as the year goes on, that you have in your hands one of the most significant bibliographical tools of the century," Mr. Wells said.

The book records are those contained on Library of Congress and British National Bibliography MARC tapes which have been merged together. The microform is about 4 × 6 in. (105 × 148 mm.). It contains 2,380 pages at a reduction of normal page size by 150 times. The three microforms that make up the first issue of *Books in English* contain roughly 150,000 bibliographic entries relating to some 40,000 English language works published anywhere in the world and catalogued by BNB and the American Library of Congress between January and June of this year.

It claims to be the most complete English language current bibliography every produced, and it will also be the shortest-lived, since in about six weeks' time another set of microforms will go out—through the 5d. post—which will include 15,000 new entries cumulated with those that went before. The production cycle is 15 days from the merging of the Library of Congress and BNB information to the posting of the bibliography itself.

As for the process itself, the book records on the merged Library of Congress and BNB tapes pass in magnetic tape form to a computer output microfilming device (usually referred to by the initials COM) which produces 35 mm. microfilm; this in turn goes to National Cash Register machinery for further reduction to ultra-microfilm level; and

SOURCE: Reprinted from *The Bookseller,* 3384 (October 31, 1970), pp 2222–2228, by permission of the publisher, J. Whitaker & Sons, Ltd.

from the product of this last machine are produced PCMI microforms (these initials stand for photo chromic micro image).

There are thus two entirely new developments: the most massive current bibliography ever produced; and the novel production methods that it employs.

BOOKS IN ENGLISH

Mr. Richard Coward, head of Research and Development at the British National Bibliography, described *Books in English* and what it contains. The main sequence, which is in classified order, contains a full bibliographic record. All American books carry Library of Congress and Dewey classification numbers, Library of Congress sub-headings and card numbers, and an increasing percentage of these American books also carry SBNs. All British books carry the Dewey classification numbers and Library of Congress subject headings. The great majority of main entries have SBNs, more carry Library of Congress classification numbers and by next year they all will.

"This cataloguing and classification package is well in excess of anything that is economically possible in a printed bibliography," Mr. Coward said. The classified sequence was in Dewey order. All British main entries and the great majority of Library of Congress ones were catalogued according to Standard Anglo-American Code Cataloguing practice. A quick location index was provided at the beginning of each transparency.

MARC

Turning to the technical side, the first of the confusing array of initials that need elaboration is MARC. This is a mnemonic for Machine Readable Catalogue. For over a year now catalogues of all books bought or received by the Library of Congress or by BNB have been stored in a computer, and the files created in this way have been made available in magnetic tape form to those libraries both here and in America large enough to be using a computer with substantial storage capacity. The information about each book is held on the tape in standard format and computer programmes are created for user libraries that enable them to draw off from the tape cataloguing and other details that they require.

For the BNB itself a further and important use for the MARC files that they are creating is that their weekly, monthly and quarterly printed bibliographies can be drawn off from them in magnetic tape form and passed to a computer controlled phototypesetter which creates page negatives for litho printing. The first issue of the BNB to come off the computer will be that for the first week of January of next year.

But valuable as these uses are—the provision of cataloguing data for large computer-using library systems, and the supply of basic data for the printed BNB—they do not represent full exploitation of the massive files being built up. The printed BNB, which has been produced every week for 21 years, will go on being produced and while the production methods have radically altered, from the user's point of view there will be little change; and useful as the weekly MARC tapes are, only a handful of librarians can take advantage of them. As time passes and the files grow larger, particularly those that result from merging Library of Congress and BNB data, the possibility of exploiting them in traditional printed form grows increasingly remote. Traditional printing methods could not meet the demands of the situation, neither from the point of view of time or of cost.

Mr. Coward put the situation in these words: "The COM technique linked to PCMI has provided us with the possibility of breaking out of a bibliographic bottleneck which is already reaching rather nightmare proportions. We have learnt over the last few years how to transfer bibliographic data to machine stores and for several years librarians have been pushing bibliographic data into machines with unrestrained enthusiasm. The BNB is making a fairly modest contribution by adding material to its own MARC file at the rate of about 700 main entries a week and the combined Library of Congress and BNB output—or perhaps I should say input—is of the order of 1,800 main entries per week.

"BNB has for the last three years been deeply involved in this type of activity. But from the very beginning we have been aware that the provision of a weekly tape full of catalogue records to a handful of libraries was too limited an objective in itself to justify the creation of such a massive data base. Perhaps it is because we are a publishing organisation that we think in terms of an end product, of a bibliography."

COM

The COM technique that Mr. Coward described as breaking the bottleneck was developed because one of the troubles with computers is that they produce too much paper. Anyone who has seen one working will have had explained to him the operation of the associated line printer, and, doubtless the pedagogue will have added, in tones in which both awe and pride are mingled, that it prints at one thousand lines per minute.

Sadly few continue by saying that the 12-pt. monospace capitals in which it prints, besides being ugly, are excessively wasteful of space, and that the standard paper size employed means that for the majority of jobs there is more area blank than printed. Storage of print-out has become a major problem. The COM helps by taking magnetic tape that would otherwise drive a line printer and producing instead 35 mm. or 16 mm. microfilm which can be stored economically and both filed and viewed when necessary with relative ease, certainly when compared to paper print-out.

Normal microfilm uses as its original copy book, magazine or manuscript pages. A machine like a Photon, Digiset or Linotron takes computer tape and produces full-size page negatives of the information on the tape for litho printing processes or, if necessary, the making of line blocks (the information in the book list in this issue of *The Bookseller* is drawn from a computer-held file and passed through a Photon 713 which set and formatted the pages in the rear portion of the paper). A COM goes in one sense one step further (although its typography is adequate rather than elegant) and produces microfilm page negatives. The significant feature of the process is that microfilm pages are reproduced without an intervening printed page.

One of the two COM devices used for *Books in English,* called the Datagraphix, was not invented for the use to which it has been put by BNB and the National Cash Register Company, and there was only one recently installed machine in this country that was suitable for the work.

"In the event the technical problems were pretty severe," Mr. Coward said. "So NCR decided on a belt and braces operation and at the same time flew tapes out to Dayton, Ohio, where a new installation was being tested. The computer there is quite different, so the technicians in charge had to persuade it that it really was a Datagraphix before it would read our tapes. This is a process technically known as simulation. To achieve a nearly faultless production run in these circumstances is no mean achievement. As it happens, both the European and American operations were successful.

PCMI

Both the novelty and the advance represented by the ultra-microform PCMI process can be most easily illustrated by figures. Normal microfilm reduction is by 15 to 20 times. PCMI is by 150. Traditional microfilm requires several microforms to accommodate one book, or even periodical. PCMI can accommodate 3,000 A4 pages on one 4 × 5 in. transparency, so that not only can most books be contained on one card—few books go beyond 3,000 pages—but frequently several books can be held on one card if this is wanted.

The power of reduction by 150 was illustrated by Mr. J. P. H. Cunningham of NCR, using the now invaluable Post Office Tower for comparison. It has been worked out that 1,250 London telephone directories (old style) piled on top of each other would be as high as the tower. The same number of directories held on PCMI would make a pile 5 in. high. Mr. Cunningham has also calculated that 36,000 book pages could be sent by first-class mail for 6d. (the extra penny is for a stout envelope).

The PCMI process involves taking 35 mm. film from a COM device and putting it through an NCR camera recorder (of which there are at present only six in the world—two in Germany and four in Dayton) which reduces by 10 times the images on the 35 mm. film and makes a master plate with the pages positioned in rows and columns. The production of one master takes two hours, and the master has a short life so that it is used immediately to make a number—usually six—high resolution negatives from which any required number of transparencies are then taken, in roll form. The roll is cut into individual transparencies and these are protected on both sides by a mylar laminate of great strength. The laminate is scratch resistant, but the optics of the NCR microform "reader" are such that scratches anyway do not appear on the screen. The microforms have a long life and need no special storage conditions.

The "reader" for PCMI microforms takes up much the same desk space as a standard electric typewriter. The viewing screen is 11 in. square. There is a focusing dial at the bottom centre of the screen.

One of the most rigorous requirements of a microform carrying up to 3,000 pages is that finding the right page should be as simple as possible and a great deal of work has been done on indexing methods. Each card carries its own index using row and column co-ordinates to take the "reader" to the required page. The power for moving the microform through its rows and columns is provided by simple fingertip pressure. The images are clear and stable, but would not be suitable for continuous reading of many pages.

There is also a "reader-printer." This works to a maximum page size of 10 X 11 in. The copies that it makes are usable but not beautiful, and it would probably have trouble with small type, but no doubt it will be developed further. There are 20,000 "readers" either installed or on order throughout the world—mainly by car manufacturers who use the PCMI process for their spare parts catalogues—but only a handful of "reader-copiers." When the quality improves and as the material that can be copied increases, they may well add considerably to the dimensions of the illegal photocopying problem.

PCMI AND PUBLISHERS

Books in English does not represent the first venture of the British end of the National Cash Register Company into the book world. Their problem was the old chicken and egg one. Without a product to view, libraries and others would not be interested in taking NCR "readers," and if they had no "readers" there was little point in producing anything for them to read.

Accordingly, in 1969, NCR sought a way out of the impasse and suggested to the Other Media Committee of the Publishers Association that a company should be formed by NCR and a consortium of publishers to exploit the process jointly. The idea had many attractions. PCMI, with its 3,000-page microform capacity, can accommodate almost any book produced with only one transparency, which reduces filing problems considerably. Alternatively, one transparency can hold several books. The present microfilm or microfiche market has never reached its full potential, because as much as for any other reasons, previous reductions have simply not been enough—there is little appeal, except in specialist circumstances, in a mass of loose cards or a long reel of film for each book.

PCMI looked like changing all that, and it was felt that libraries with storage problems would look kindly on a means whereby necessary but/infrequently used works could be kept available. Many librarians, particularly those in the educational field, or with new libraries, would welcome a space-saving and inexpensive way of building up

collections of source documents which could not otherwise be assembled except at prodigious expense. PCMI is very much cheaper than traditional reprinting methods. Big reprint interests might look askance at the new method, but scarcely the buyers.

The company proposed by NCR was to have had a capital of £250,000, half from NCR and half from the publishing side. The money was guaranteed within a matter of weeks, and work began on a publishing policy, a company structure, costings and a vast amount of other necessary planning and research.

But within three months there came a collision. The NCR head office at Dayton, Ohio, would not agree to certain safeguards—very reasonable ones, it was considered—which British publishers asked for themselves. Also, it struck the British, the American NCR seemed to be unaware of the great potentialities of a scheme into which some of the largest and most distinguished publishing houses in the world were putting themselves and their vast and valuable back lists. Subsequently the American NCR decided to go it alone and its publishing programme—acknowledged to be excellent in many parts—is becoming involved in copyright problems and loss of goodwill, presumably through ignorance of international copyright laws.

But the consortium is past history, the copyright problems are in the capable hands of the Publishers Association, and the British end of the NCR was never more than an impotent bystander throughout the disagreement. If *Books in English*, their second attempt to break the circle, satisfactorily passes its "field trials" and proves to be as important an addition to the bibliographical field as both they and the BNB hope, then the way for other PCMI publications will be open. The very substantial investment in research, effort and material that NCR have put into the new bibliography will have paid off.

TRIALS AND COSTS

Mr. Coward enumerated the main points that the trials are designed to clarify. Was it possible to combine successfully, with the minimum of editorial interference, records that had been produced by the Library of Congress and BNB? How would the system, with all that it was theoretically capable of, fare in a "real life" situation in which production processes that were started in one continent were finished in another? How would *Books in English* be used in practice? and—a critical question—what was the "optimum service" pattern? The cost of the service depended on the number of transparencies produced. A monthly service was more or less twice the cost of a two-monthly service. On the other hand such an extensive service might well replace even more expensive bibliographies, and might also significantly reduce labour costs.

"To get the answers to these questions we are distributing what must be looked on as test data," Mr. Coward said. "It is not the end product of a long series of experiments. Rough edges are still showing."

The costs of the service, as only to be expected at this trial stage, are uncertain. Final costs, obviously, will depend upon the answers to the questions posed above. But as a very rough guess, if the two-monthly cycle is found satisfactory, then would-be subscribers might expect to pay £300 for the "reader," or, alternatively, a rental of something like £70 a year. For *Books in English* itself they would pay not less than £50 a year, but certainly not as much as £100.

COMPUTERS

Mr. Coward concluded by saying "I should perhaps point out that *Books in English* is a natural development of what is happening in the provision of bibliographic services. Librarianship is not generally regarded as an area of technological innovation, or for that matter of technological involvement and yet when we look at the facts it would seem that almost every outside service you will use in 1971 will depend on the sophisticated use of computers. An order file is checked against say *The Bookseller* or *Books of the Month*—both computer produced.[1]"

"You check BNB or, hopefully, *Books in English*, for cataloguing information—both computer produced. Your bookseller may process your order through a computer system and if the order goes back to the publisher it may be handled by a computerised invoicing and dispatch system. If you order cards from BNB or the Library of Congress the order will be relentlessly processed by computer. When you receive a stream of requests from a regional bureau it will, if it has come from the London and South East Region, have been checked against a computer listing of the stock of your library. *Books in English* has been produced because it fits this new pattern. I am sure that its success will lead to a rapid development of other microform services."

Mr. Coward might have added, and with pride, that although the larger part of the materials in *Books in English* is derived from the Library of Congress, the development work and the systems arrived at to use both Library of Congress and BNB data in this new form are, right up to the PCMI stage, the work of, and of course the property of, the BNB alone.

NOTE

[1] *The Bookseller, Books of the Month and Books to Come* and *Whitaker's Cumulative Book List* have been produced from computer held data files, and computer controlled phototypesetting since the beginning of this year. The 1971 edition of *British Books in Print* will be produced by similar methods. The information is held on file in a stripped-down version of the MARC format which is fully MARC compatible. The systems analysis was done by Mr. Coward and the programming by the BNB under contract to Whitakers. The BNB receives reciprocal services from Whitakers, at present mainly associated with Standard Book Numbering.

Books in English

An announcement issued by the British National Bibliography, Autumn, 1970

INTRODUCTION

The first issue of the BNB "Books in English" Bibliography is a landmark in the development of bibliographic services designed to meet the requirements of libraries and information systems of the seventies. It is a product of three new technologies. First, the bibliographic data base technology which is the background to the massive Anglo-American MARC project. Second the COM technology which is a new base of modern microfilm systems. Third the PCMI technology, which on current standards offers a reduction ratio of one hundred and fifty to one compared with the normal microfilm reduction of twenty-four to one. In this project COM and PCMI techniques are, for the first time being combined to produce a 'print-out' of the tremendous quantities of information already held in the British and American MARC data banks. COM stands for Computer Output Microfilming. Using this technique it is possible to transfer data directly from magnetic tape to microfilm at a very high speed. The transparency distributed today was prepared by this direct transfer technique. Each frame which can hold about 8,000 characters was printed in less than one second. The microfilm produced by this technique was then transferred onto a transparency using the NCR PCMI (Photo Chromic Micro Image) system. The reduction is now of the order of one hundred and fifty to one. This is made possible by the use of special grain-free photochromic film.

BOOKS IN ENGLISH

The technological development on which Books in English is based is significant because COM is likely to cause a quiet revolution in bibliographic data processing systems. The amount of data being transferred to computer data banks is already so enormous that it can hardly be estimated. BNB for example is adding material to MARC at the rate of 350,000 characters per week. The combined British and American output is of the order of 1,000,000 characters per week. Behind these figures is a very real crisis in the provision of bibliographic services.

The cost of printing combined with the steady increase in the amount of material to be listed is pushing costs upwards at an alarming rate. The COM revolution and the PCMI system provides a means of breaking this cost spiral.

With two years of the MARC Project development behind it the British National Bibliography is now in a unique position to carry out a major bibliographic experiment in this area. A small but heterogeneous group of British libraries has been invited to take part in the experiment by evaluating, not the finished product, but the first trial transparency that has been prepared. Many technical and bibliographic problems have been overcome in the last few months but many remain. It is unlikely that field testing of a bibliographic service on this scale has ever before been attempted.

"Books in English" lists all adult books in the English language which are recorded by the British

---

SOURCE: This promotional announcement was issued by the Council of the British National Bibliography in the autumn of 1970.

National Bibliography and the Library of Congress on the U.K. and U.S. MARC Tapes. It is the most complete English language bibliography ever produced and will list in an annual transparency upward of 70,000 items with a total of some 300,000 entries. The main listing is classified order arranged by the latest edition of the Dewey Decimal Classification (D.C.). The main entry gives a full bibliographic description and the great majority of entries carry Library of Congress card numbers, Standard Book Numbers, Library of Congress class numbers, and Library of Congress subject headings. Although not yet complete, the data package given with each entry is exceptional and well in excess of anything that is possible in a printed bibliography.

Each title is indexed in a separate alphabetical sequence under author, added authors and titles. The index entries do not contain the full bibliographic data but each entry is a complete record and the same information appears under each entry point. This kind of index which is designed for the convenience of the user should be extremely easy to consult. The index entries are linked back to the main classified listing through the DC number.

CUMULATION

"Books in English" has been planned as a throw away bibliography. During the field trials an updated and revised publication will be produced every two months. This cumulation cycle completely cuts out the tedious bibliographic searches that take up so much time of highly paid professional staff. There is only one place to consult—or to be more accurate there will only be two places to consult in 1971. The user will not throw away the "Annual Volume" which will be produced at the end of this year, but he will be able to discard each issue of the 1971 publication as soon as the next snowball cumulation arrives. It is too early yet to predict the final cumulation cycle either within the year or across the years but the immense flexibility and almost non-existent storage charges associated with machine-held data suggests that the practical limits will be defined by the user and not, as in traditional printing, by the economics of production.

SPECIAL BIBLIOGRAPHIC FEATURES

The techniques of production, interesting though they are, must be of secondary concern to the librarian. The final product, whether it appears on a scrap of film or on a printed page, is his research tool and his main concern is to establish the limits of its accuracy and authority. Each item in "Books in English" has been prepared by trained cataloguers at BNB and at the Library of Congress with the book in hand. The British records are catalogued to Anglo-American Code Standards. The great majority of the Library of Congress records also follow the Anglo-American Code but the policy of "superimposition" which forms the present basis of Library of Congress cataloguing practice will introduce certain variants. It is also inevitable that in a small percentage of cases different code interpretations by the two organizations will result in variant headings being chosen. However the close informal contact between BNB and the Library of Congress and the detailed and continuous work of the Anglo-American Committee concerned with catalogue code interpretation and changes will hold this down to a minimum. Nevertheless conflict will occur and detailed consideration has been given to this point in the design of the bibliography. The possibilities of reconciling the two files as a separate editorial operation has been rejected. The task would be enormous and would take weeks to carry through. If this were attempted a vital factor of the service—speed of production—would be completely lost. Also the editors would be forced to make difficult decisions without the books in hand. It has been decided to let the records stand with the authority of either the British National Bibliography or the Library of Congress behind them.

This summarises the position in 1970. In 1971 BNB is carrying out in the MARC project a separate investigation which will significantly effect this "incompatibility factor." There are certain small formal differences in the British and American versions of the Anglo-American Code. Entries likely to be affected can be detected by computer algorithm. These will be extracted from the Library of Congress MARC tape as it is received and the British heading will be substituted. This operation is relatively small, it does not involve any delay, and does not call for editorial judgment.

The presence of any incompatibility factor, however small, makes it impossible to use sophisticated programmes to merge multiple entries. Each entry is separate and complete. On the whole this matches the librarians requirements rather more closely than the normal compound record presentation adopted to save space in printed bibliographies.

With a full bibliographic entry the effect of the incompatibility factor in the classified sector is probably of very little significance. Searches are made by specific subjects and the main objective is to identify material which is available on that subject. The full bibliographic entry given provides a complete description of each item and contains enough information to allow a cataloguer to assess the suitability for use in his own catalogue of the heading given.

In the index, where the search factor is a heading, this incompatibility could be more serious. To overcome this a special indexing policy has been adopted. Each entry in the British and American MARC records has associated with it a complete set of added entry headings. Programmes have been written to provide a full index entry under each of these alternative headings. If the user looks up the name of an editor of a conference he will find exactly the same entry whether the work was formally catalogued under the editor or conference name or title. In short the concept of main-entry has been abandoned in the index. All index entries are 'main entries'.

HOW TO FIND INFORMATION

To assist users, a frame index is provided at the beginning of the transparency. This index is machine generated as frames are produced and locates the position of material by reference to the transparency number, the row number and the column number. For example the entry 635 1-10-36 indicates that works classified at 635 will be found on the first transparency and the sequence will begin at row 10 frame 36. In the classified section the frame index locates material down to the third digit of the D.C. number. To reach a specific number the frames are scanned from this point onwards. The index will not always list every three figure D.C. number that appears in the classified list. If the first entry on a frame is classified at 636 only these numbers are picked up for the frame index. So in practice if the specific number wanted is missing the nearest lower number represents the search entry point. The same principle is followed in the alphabetical frame index. Here a two character location is given.

ERRORS AND OMISSIONS

A very important part of the field trials will be to identify the nature of the errors which arise for purely mechanical or program-failure reasons. Very complex programs have been prepared to convert the Library of Congress records, which represent about 60% to 70% of the file, to the tag, field, and sub-field structure of the British records. As most of these programmes attempt to interpret unstructured bibliographic data fields the slightest variations can produce unexpected results. However, since it is physically impossible to proof read such an enormous file, absolutely no provision is made for any human intervention in the process. This is a very important point of principle. None of the Library of Congress entries had been seen at any stage by BNB. None of the entries had been organized into this form before. The success of the project will finally depend on our ability to "read" an entry in the computer core and detect the presence of 'conversion' error.

As well as these 'conversion' failures there is also the more devastating and unpredictable impact of mechanical error to be taken into consideration. The Library of Congress records that finally reach the master file held by BNB were created in Washington, copied at the Argonne National Laboratory and despatched to London. Each weekly file reaching BNB carries about 3 million magnetic signals. These are not entirely proof against dirty tapes, rough handling or climatic hazards. Degredation can and does occur. Usually it can be detected by the computer but sometimes a bad record is accepted. When conversion programs are applied to such a record almost anything can happen. Evidence is needed as a basis for preparing refined validation programs to test the structural features of records so that mechanical errors can be detected and put right before microfilms are prepared.

SUBJECT INDEX

An omission which will immediately strike all librarians is the lack of a subject index for the classified section. Various alternatives, all unsatisfactory, were considered. It has finally been decided that for the trial period, at least, the best available index will be the separate printed index to the DC schedules. It is hoped however that this is a very temporary situation. The problems of providing subject data on a MARC file are being vigorously tackled by BNB and from 1971 onwards index data will be added to the British records. It will take at least a year to evaluate the results but if the techniques prove satisfactory a solution appears to be in sight.

CONCLUSION

BNB has chosen to run an extensive series of field trials with 'Books in English' so that detailed and informed comments can be made by potential users before either the final design or the publication programme is fixed. Users will be able to make recommendations and possibly see the effect of changes made as a result during the trial period. It will be necessary however to assess the trend of comment and reaction at a fairly early stage so that firm decisions can be announced on the general form of the continuation service and its cost to subscribers. These decisions must be made fairly early in 1971. Participants in these trials are particularly asked to bear in mind that the value of a bibliographic tool increases with age. In a few years time a file of transparencies an inch or so thick will contain more information in a more accessible form than a whole shelf of bibliographies. A book case can be held in a single card tray. Another factor which should be borne in mind is the close relationship between 'Books in English' and the MARC data base at present being built up. The trend towards computer catalogues is now well established and through the MARC project BNB is ready to provide catalogue data in machine readable form. 'Books in English' will form a constantly updated visual index to the international data base.

'Books in English'

An announcement issued by the British National Bibliography, Summer 1971

JANUARY–JUNE ISSUE

The Jan–Jun issue of 'Books in English' is the first to be published since the evaluation meeting. Special efforts were made to ensure that publication deadlines were met. The National Cash Resigter Co. have set up special arrangements to eliminate delays in transit of magnetic tape to the United States, and of the transparencies between the States and the U.K.

This half-yearly issue contains 46,814 entries in the classified section and 121,662 entries in the alphabetical index. The fact that it is available to you within three weeks of the file cut-off date amply demonstrates the power of the system in its extensive coverage, continuous cumulation and speed of production.

Two desirable improvements which were noted by many librarians on their returned questionnaires have been incorporated in this issue:—

(i) The BNB number is now carried in the author/title index, as are other national bibliography identifiers. The national bibliography identifiers are largely mnemonic and will usually serve to identify country of of publication, e.g.,

    C*** - Canada
    USSR* - USSR
    F*** - France
    N70-4 - Norway

(ii) An external location index is enclosed with the transparencies.

1972 SERVICE

Promotion literature and order forms for the subscription service are at press. These will be circulated in July issues of the BNB weekly list.

The subscription for the 1972 annual service has been set at £100. The 1970 and 1971 transparencies will be available at £50 per set.

PCMI readers will be available on both a rental and purchase basis. Details are as follows:—

    Rental terms @ £60
    Reconditioned purchase @ £173
    New purchase @ £274

    (These prices are at educational discount)

Readers installed in libraries taking part in the experiment will be available to those libraries on the same terms as reconditioned readers.

OTHER DEVELOPMENTS

Following the analysis of returned questionnaires and the comments of the evaluation meeting the specification for 'Books in English' has been re-written. This specification defines an author/title bibliography. The main entry will carry a full bibliographic description together with all available subject information, L.C. card no., BNB no. etc. Added entries have been upgraded to carry rather more information than before.

When the new program has been written and tested it will be used immediately, thus giving an early opportunity to evaluate the new presentation of information.

The problem of identifying the currency of the price statement is being investigated. This is quite a complex one since it involves incompatibilities between input codes and output codes on COM device.

PCMI READER SERVICING

Comments have filtered back to us from some libraries suggesting that the quality of images on transparencies varies considerably and thus requires constant refocusing. It is almost certain that this is simply a matter of adjustment to the reader. A fractional looseness of the transparency cover will cause a distortion of the image at a magnification of 150 X 1.

Free servicing is available to you through your NCR technical service depot, and you are urged to take advantage of this fact to ensure the optimum performance of the reader.